IN THE BEGINN
WAS THE STATE

IDIOM INVENTING WRITING THEORY

Jacques Lezra and Paul North, series editors

IN THE BEGINNING WAS THE STATE

DIVINE VIOLENCE IN THE HEBREW BIBLE

ADI M. OPHIR

Fordham University Press *New York*   *2023*

Funding for this book was provided in part by the Helen Tartar Memorial Fund.

Fordham University Press has no responsibility for the persistence or accuracy of URLs for external or third-party Internet websites referred to in this publication and does not guarantee that any content on such websites is, or will remain, accurate or appropriate.

Fordham University Press also publishes its books in a variety of electronic formats. Some content that appears in print may not be available in electronic books.

Visit us online at www.fordhampress.com.

Library of Congress Cataloging-in-Publication Data

Names: Ophir, Adi, author. | Ophir, Adi. Alimut Elohit.
Title: In the beginning was the state : divine violence in the Hebrew Bible
  / Adi M. Ophir.
Description: First edition. | New York : Fordham University Press, 2023. |
  Series: Idiom: inventing writing theory | Originally intended as
  revision of author's Alimut Elohit. Greatly revised with new focus. |
  Includes bibliographical references and index.
Identifiers: LCCN 2022013132 | ISBN 9781531501419 (paperback) | ISBN
  9781531501402 (hardback) | ISBN 9781531501426 (epub)
Subjects: LCSH: Bible. Pentateuch—Criticism, interpretation, etc. |
  Violence in the Bible.
Classification: LCC BS1225.6.V56 O6413 2023 | DDC 222/.1—dc23/eng/20220909
LC record available at https://lccn.loc.gov/2022013132

Printed in the United States of America

25 24 23 5 4 3 2 1

First edition

CONTENTS

ACKNOWLEDGMENTS

This book began as a translation of a Hebrew book—*Divine Violence: Two Essays on God and Disaster*—which I completed in 2012 (Ophir 2013). It consists of two essays. A rather long essay focuses on the ways the God of the Hebrew Bible generated catastrophes and used them to rule over mankind and govern his people; a much shorter essay presents a sketch for a European history of divine catastrophes, from the late Middle Ages to the contemporary global order. Even before submitting the manuscript for consideration at Fordham University Press I had planned to revise it. The book's length and things I had learned in the time that had passed placed my initial interest in biblical catastrophes in a more straightforward political context, made this plan necessary, and changed the terrain of my work.

The work on the revised manuscript was protracted. I could finally immerse myself again in the translated manuscript only after I committed to two major decisions that changed the nature of the entire project. My first was to limit myself to a political reading of divine catastrophes in the Hebrew Bible and limit my systematic reading of the Bible to the Five Books of Moses. As I have not been trained as a Bible scholar, this decision allowed me to expand my acquaintance with the field, appreciating its major debates and distinct directions, and to enlarge the corpus of Bible studies on which I could rely as I was trying to integrate questions and guiding concepts coming from political theory with the hermeneutic requirements peculiar to the biblical texts. The second, closely related decision was not to isolate the use of disaster from other aspects of divine rule and the political figure of God, that is, to read violence as one among several modes of exercising divine power. I paid more attention to methodological questions and to some historical questions concerning the composition of the texts and the first phases of their reception.

At the same time, a question kept at the background before now surfaced as unavoidable. I started asking myself why I could find so little interest in divine violence among contemporary political, theoretically oriented readers of the

Bible. I came to realize that this lack of interest is in fact a symptomatic blind spot that hampers the ability to grasp the full scope to which the political imagination has invested in the writings concerning divine rule. I realized that this blind spot is related to the postbiblical hiatus separating God from the human world, which many modern and contemporary readers replace—and repress—by splitting the biblical worlds into a realm of politics and a realm of religion. It then became clear that this same blind spot has its counterpoint in the way political thinkers tend to miss the theological imagination invested in theorizing the modern state.

The result of these decisions and the work they allowed and required was a new framing of some of the main insights of my previous work and their development in new directions. Although the present book's point of departure is still divine violence, this violence is now studied in the context of other aspects of divine rule—the quest of recognition and legitimacy, the law, and the persistence of dissent and disobedience. The distinct modes of using divine violence according to various Pentateuchal sources now appear as a key for reconstructing three distinct theocratic formations, three distinct political regimes in which God reigned as a political sovereign. The political figure of God reconstructed in each formation slowly gave way to a theopolitical imagination of the formation itself, in which God played a certain role, just like the people he ruled or the human leaders he appointed. The revised manuscript has become a wholly new book, a study of Pentateuchal theocracy, and the latter has gradually appeared as a strange forerunner of the modern state. Accounting for this unexpected isomorphism is the question to which I come last in this book and that I am leaving lingering, waiting for further research.

However convoluted was the path that led to this book, the many people who supported the earlier stages of my work and contributed to my long learning process deserve my wholehearted thanks: my colleagues at the Kogod Research Center for Contemporary Jewish Thought at the Shalom Hartman Institute, where I spent a few formative years, including Menachem Fisch, Menachem Lorberbaum, Yair Lorberbaum, Ilana Pardes, Ishai Rosen Zvi, and Dror Yinon; Michal ben Naftali, Ronald Hendel, and Judith Butler, who, many years ago, commented on my first attempt to come to terms with divine violence; Ed Greenstein and Menachem Lorberbaum, who read the manuscript's first version as two wise, patient teachers, not only as (then) anonymous readers for the publisher; Liron Mor, Moria Barak, and Dikla Bytner, who as research assistants in different phases of writing the Hebrew book helped me with unrivaled wittiness, rigor, kindness, and efficiency; Efrat Weiss and Merav Zonshein, who translated the Hebrew text, most of which I later abandoned or heavily revised, and provided me with an excellent basis for my later work; Hannan Hever and Yehuda Shenhav, who responded to the book's first draft and encouraged me to complete it; and Yehuda Shenhav, again, the series editor, who accompanied the book with professional care and friendship throughout the production process. This new book still bears the imprint of all these people's wisdom, scholarship, and intellectual generosity.

Ever since I started working on the English manuscript, I had at my side a dear friend and colleague, Ishay Rosen Zvi, my indefatigable guide, gentle teacher, and stern critic. Traces of his generosity, close acquaintance with almost any field I dared to enter, the depth and scope of his scholarship, the astuteness of his reading, and his uncompromising questioning are spread throughout this book, far beyond what multiple footnotes could have acknowledged. Work on the English book took place at the Cogut Institute for the Humanities, at Brown University, my academic home over the last decade. A chapter I presented at the institute's fellows seminar generated productive comments and questions from the participants, which helped me in the last stage of writing, and an ongoing, fascinating conversation with Tanvir Ahmad, for which I am particularly grateful. My dear friends Tim Bewes, Thangam Ravindranathan, and Raphael Sassower were keen, generously patient, and inquisitive listeners throughout the last long stage of writing. Rachel Kalisher, a research assistant who turned out to be a most talented copyeditor, lent me a helping hand whenever my writing was too cumbersome or not English enough. Many constructive, critical comments from my anonymous readers at Fordham, along with questions and suggestions from my always trustful editors, Tom Lay, Jacques Lezra, and Paul North helped me improve my reading, better frame the entire project, and, no less importantly, reconcile myself with its inevitable limitations.

Ariella Aïsha Azoulay accompanied me throughout this long journey. Our ongoing dialogue provided me with numerous insights and the courage to begin anew whenever necessary. Without her attentive ear, astute criticism, and rare ability to restore and weave, time and again, a common sense and a shared world in which our conversation could unfold, I would not have been able to bring this writing to completion.

IN THE BEGINNING WAS THE STATE

INTRODUCTION

Why does the God of the Hebrew Bible use lethal force so excessively, harm the people he created, and destroy their lands, cities, and worlds? Since antiquity, the question has been asked mainly to exonerate God from the alleged injustice of his excessive violence or, less often, to blame him for the cruelty of his acts. This book asks the question not to pass judgment on God but rather to understand the logic of his rule. To do so, it poses this question anew, seeking to study divine rule as a political system. I read the biblical narratives, the codes of law and prophetic proclamations, and the threats and the blessings the way political thinkers read documents from ancient royal or state archives, and I examine divine violence in relation to law, modes of ruling, and governmental practices in an effort to determine its place within the general economy of God's rule. When the text is read through this conceptual prism, it becomes a surface for the appearance of several distinct, recurring formations of divine rule.

Clearly, God is not only a supreme political figure in the Hebrew Bible, and the nature of his lordship cannot be exhausted within the realm of political relations, however conceived. His power to create and destroy exceeded his claims to rule and govern, and the personal relationships he established with a few privileged individuals often preceded and overshadowed his public relations to peoples and lands. But across the biblical corpus, there are numerous moments in which God is depicted as a sovereign engaged in domination, subjection, ruling, and judgment, reigning over lands and peoples. In such contexts, his violence can best be explained as a matter of politics and not merely of judgment or moods, as biblical stories of extreme violence have often been read.

One hardly needs justification for studying the God of the Hebrew Bible as the supreme ruler, a founding force, and an organizing principle of a sui generis political system. Readers of the Hebrew Bible know well that God appears there as an authority with unsurpassable power—commanding, directing, leading, prohibiting, giving laws, bestowing aid, passing judgment, rescuing, redeeming, and meting out punishment. God makes pacts with many individuals and with one nation, sends troops to war, sows calamity and destruction, and represses rebellions. He crowns kings who reign in his name and is directly involved in toppling others. In all these he certainly exercises a political power of a sort. He does not always appear in all these powers and capacities, but when he is the organizing principle of a political system he himself founds, the formations of power at stake are properly called theocracy. This book proposes to study divine violence in the Hebrew Bible as a study of theocracy.

And yet, despite the great influence and recurring presence of the Hebrew Bible in the history of political thinking in Jewish, Christian, and Muslim cultures, the question of *which kind of theocracy* has not been properly posed. Questions about the way God uses force have been persistently displaced from a political context to a moral or religious framework, which asks "why" without asking "how." A typical reading of an eruption of divine violence focuses on its justification and interprets this justification in terms of the ideology the putative authors supposedly promoted and the interests they served. As the reading passes from justification to its ideological or instrumental motivation, the violence is transformed from a divine act into a human projection and displaced from the divine realm in which it took place in the world depicted by the text to the realm of human affairs in which the text was composed. A textual and relatively indisputable phenomenon, a description of some violent acts of God, becomes intelligible only through its association with extratextual, more or less speculative human factors, and the meaning of the violence in the world(s) depicted by the text is blurred if not lost altogether. This book insists on asking *how* divine violence was exercised and what its rationality was *within* that world. The book also insists on opening these questions and at least starting to answer them mostly *before* shifting attention to the text's positivist, speculative, or critical history. The point is not to censure this shift of attention but to resist its tendency to displace God or leave him out of the picture and to offer key questions for guiding this attention when necessary.

The Hebrew Bible, however, is an assemblage of multiple texts, composed, edited, and revised across many centuries. For reasons that will become clear later, this study is limited to the figures of divine rule in the first part of the Hebrew Bible: the Five Books of Moses, or the Pentateuch. One chapter from Joshua (24) is read closely to highlight parallel sections in Deuteronomy, and many scattered passages throughout the Hebrew Bible are visited as well, but the claims made are mainly about divine power in the Pentateuch, which, I will later show, should be read as theocratic formations. Three such formations are distinguished and examined here, three models of a regime in which God is both the *archē* and the *kratos*, the first principle and the ruling power. All three formations are found embedded in the Pentateuch and can be extracted from its multiple layers. The reconstruction of the three formations is based on the articulation and analysis of distinct notions of power and authority, law and justice, the subjection and education of the ruled subjects, internal limits on the governability of the political body, political participation, and dissent. In each case, the divine violence invested in the formation's originary institution and ongoing reproduction is foregrounded, only to be integrated in the reconstruction of the other aspects of divine rule. The configuration of violence, divine or otherwise, I assume, must be understood in the context of the formation of rule in which it is integrated, and any attempt to make sense of that violence depends on a holistic understanding of the formation of rule in which it took part.

My reconstruction of Pentateuchal theocracies was motivated by my interest in divine violence but eventually yielded an unexpected discovery: The three theocratic formations share some features, which, once abstracted from the details of the narratives and laws where they are embedded, seem as if emerging from an ancient, blurry blueprint of the modern state. Besides the figure of the sovereign, these include a shared realm to which both the ruler and the ruled belong, a governing apparatus irreducible to the sovereign's interventions, investment in the closure of the governed space and in ruling one and all within it, and, most importantly, obedience to an invisible power to which the origin of violence is attributed and in the name of which killing and destruction are permitted.

The study of these features suggests that as far as the Pentateuch is concerned, the theological concepts, which Schmitt saw as surviving in a secularized form in the modern theory of the state, were always *political* concepts, because the Pentateuchal God was—or was made to be—a political figure. Furthermore, the secularization of these concepts had already started in the Hebrew Bible. The accumulated evidence extracted from this reading shows that the true relation between ancient theocracy imagined in the (Hebrew) Bible and the modern

(European) state is not one of migration and transfiguration of concepts to a secular domain. It is rather a case of inverted mirroring and repressed isomorphism: Against the modern state's repressed theological dimension there stands the repressed or neglected political dimension of God's rule in the Hebrew Bible. The biblical models of theocratic regimes reconstructed here will be shown as having a pronounced statelike configuration, which the modern concept of sovereignty alone does not capture. The repression of this configuration and of the figure of God associated with it in postbiblical theological thinking is still at work today, thwarting the force of contemporary critiques of the state. Thus, beyond its intervention in Bible studies and its new perspective on the early history of political thinking, this book offers the political analysis of divine rule as a guide for uncovering and systematically studying the unacknowledged, persistent theological dimension of the modern state.

A direct and crucial consequence of the reluctance of Bible scholars, from antiquity to the present, to study God's rule politically has been the failure to examine God's use of force in relation to law and justice, planning and policy, authority, obedience and disobedience, stability and change, and other key elements of the political configuration. The analytic gaze of ancient and contemporary readers alike turned away from divine violence even when it was supposedly contemplating it. The earliest case of this blind spot is shown to appear together with the first use of the term "theocracy," in the first century CE, in a work by the Jewish historian Josephus. A close reading of three, quite different contemporary political studies of the Hebrew Bible that *do* question divine rule and its violence shows that the reluctance to study God's violence in a political context is still persistent and symptomatic. Facing such reluctance, this book presents a systematic tracing of divine violence across the Pentateuch. Guided by a contemporary concept of violence that can be translated back to biblical Hebrew, the book reconstructs distinct patterns of divine violence and offers close readings of certain episodes of this violence as a way to decipher the logic of power imagined and claimed to be invested in that violence and expressed through it.

This brief introductory note suffices to make one realize that pitfalls of historicism loom large over this book's project. Like many others, I read the Bible as a rich depository of various strands of political thinking that originated, found expression, and were revised, compiled, and edited at a certain moment in antiquity (however long that moment lasted). This moment is separated from us not only by millennia but by the same traditions and translations that make the Bible legible for us today. The "*logic*" of divine rule and the "*violence*" at its center, "modes of ruling," "governmental practices," and even an old term like "theocracy" belong to various lexicons of postbiblical political thinking, ancient, modern, and contemporary. Using them necessitates interpretive, conceptual, and philological work that seeks to demonstrate the legitimacy of their application to the biblical texts even when they have no straightforward biblical equivalents. At the same time, such work must also involve a constant effort to identify, acknowledge, and deal with moments of untranslatability and, in their light, to make amendments and revisions to the concepts and presuppositions used in the unfinished process of translation. Recognizing and accepting this challenge is the necessary first step in a work that studies the textual acts as historical documents.

Mere awareness of the traps of untranslatability and the pitfalls of anachronistic reading cannot save one from naïve realism or an uncritical positivism. The risk is all the more pronounced when one consciously departs from a long, rich history of the reception of the Hebrew Bible among rabbinic Jews and Christian Catholics. This reception history consists of readers who did their best to ignore, bracket, or marginalize the historical setting of the biblical texts, the changing contexts of their composition, and the worlds in which their various layers first made sense; they therefore can be of minor help here. And the risk I am taking is even greater than seems at first because by bypassing the history of the Bible's reception, I have inevitably allied myself with dubious predecessors and contemporaries who have taken the same approach in the service of goals I do not share.

The Hebrew Bible has been cut off from the history of its interpretations and has become a historical document in several distinct but tacitly related ways. Let me present them schematically, in broad brushstrokes. A modern philological tradition that was part of Renaissance humanism challenged both Jewish and Christian nonliteral—midrashic, figural, and allegorical—readings of the Bible. The humanists historicized the Bible, detached it from its afterlife, and preserved the Old Testament as a document attesting to the rise and fall of a great Hebrew culture in the ancient Near East. Luther and Calvin, who were indebted to this tradition, made the unmediated access to the biblical text—*sola scriptura*—a battle cry and a basic principle of the Protestant revolution and rejected the canon of allegorical interpretations of the Catholic Church for the sake of a literal and historical reading of the Old Testament: "It is the historical sense alone which supplies the true and sound doctrine."[1] In the eighteenth and nineteenth centuries, Christian nationalists in Europe, Britain, and the United States drew from Hebrew Bible models for their visions of national renewal, in their own land or in others'. Nineteenth-century critical scholarship of the Bible combined historicism and philology to discern and reconstruct the Bible's multiple "schools" or "doctrines," trying to fix their dates of composition, ascribe author-ship, and identify the ongoing interventions of compilers and editors. Finally, in the wake of the last two modern traditions, Zionist scholars and intellectuals read the Hebrew Bible as the founding document of the modern Jewish nation, telling the history of its birthplace and providing the ground for its claim to re-turn to its homeland.

A contemporary, critical student of the Hebrew Bible has good, distinct, and interrelated reasons to take a clear distance from each of these traditions, and I have taken mine. Taking such a distance, however, does not mean a wholesale rejection of the philological-historical approach. It certainly does not mean an a priori rejection of any approach that bypasses, as this book does, most of the history of the Bible's receptions and iterations, with its various traditions that have never stopped reworking the texts, ignoring their discursive formations, and altering the worlds imagined and described by their authors. Obviously, even a text that has been read and interpreted, revered and worshiped by hun-dreds of millions for over two millennia can still be studied as a multilayered document where distinct discursive structures and theopolitical imaginations left their marks during a long period of composition, editing, and compilation. To reconstruct these traces without falling into the traps of anachronist, un-critical realism but also without museifying them has been one of my main chal-lenges in this work.

I met this challenge by paying most of my attention to formations of theo-political imagination captured in the biblical texts and to the worlds these texts constructed. The theopolitical imagination at stake here is the one centered on the figure and position of God as a supreme power, a ruler and a judge, and the extreme violence he used in these capacities. The worlds at stake here refer to the horizons demarcating the totality of the lived experience, including memo-ries and anticipations, within and through which divine rule was experienced or imagined according to the testimony of the various texts. I assume that the theopolitical formations are enacted as the world is unfolded in the text, serving the narratives and law codes, speeches, and actions of which this world is made as a set of enabling conditions. These formations and those worlds attest to theo-political imagination as a historical reality in the same way that they and other elements of the texts may attest to the history of their composition or to the historical reality within which they were composed. But unlike historical reality, these formations and worlds are not external to the interpreted text; rather, they are enacted in it the way a discursive formation is enacted through the text it enables, serving it as a kind of infrastructure.[2] The reconstruction of the theopolitical formations that subsist in the historical document involves hypothetical, speculative claims about a certain reality that existed at different moments in the history of the texts' composition and was captured in the interpreted texts. This reality is the product of discursive, psychological, cultural, geopolitical, and other dimensions, including, if the reader chooses to believe so, the marks of divine interventions. But in the text, this reality subsists as a theopolitical formation, and this is what the analytic, conceptual interpretation seeks to reconstruct. The search for such a formation is a search for a recurring form, a certain set of relations among distinct textual elements of which that form consists. At this level of abstraction, the form would emerge at the surface of the interpreted text as a result of the conceptual reading and would be relatively independent of the style, mode, and linguistic materiality of its expression. Once the form emerges and is analyzed, however, it stops being only a relic from an ancient culture, for it immediately joins our contemporary archive of political formations, with which it may interact in various unexpected ways.

The theopolitical formations I reconstruct here are not sketched as such in any of the Pentateuchal narratives or envisioned by any of the Pentateuch's codes of law. But the theopolitical imagination at play in both narratives and laws, as well as in their intertwining, can be reconstructed, as is often done with any set of documents in which relations of power, modes of ruling, and practices of governance have been recorded. Theocratic formations of power are shown to underlie the Pentateuchal theopolitical imagination and to be inscribed in various layers of the texts. It is important to clarify that the historical reality of the reports, or the question of whether certain laws were ever enacted, is irrelevant to the existence and persistence of the imagined formation of power. The only factual-historical question of concern for this study is whether such formations of power were ever imagined, and the answer is to be found in the texts, articulated and delivered in the process of its reading.

The intervention this book offers in biblical studies and in the history of political theory consists in this reading, which is guided by the assumption that at the formative stages of its editing, most of the Pentateuch was not simply a collection of stories and laws but the careful assemblage, juxtaposition, and sometimes interweaving of distinct models of divine rule. The textual traces from which these models are reconstructed are conceived here—and this assumption is a key to my reading—as remains from at least two rival thought experiments. In some cases, the texts were probably experimental as they were initially composed; in others, they assumed the role and structural complexity of thought experiments through the way they were adjoined to and intertwined with other texts coming from different Pentateuchal sources. These experiments consisted in evacuating a certain space-time from existing political institutions and in efforts not only to imagine divine rule but also to place every aspect of reality in its context and read that reality from the point of view of that rule. In their attempts to conceive of theocratic systems of power, the Pentateuchal authors included accounts of how they could have emerged and been constituted in a no man's land where no political power held sway. They imagined the obstacles such formations of power must have faced and how they should have handled these obstacles. Violence in all its forms, effects, and temporal manifestations—threats, lethal eruptions, and traumatic memories—played a decisive role in these accounts. But it was also here that divine violence found its most elaborate political context. Tacit assumptions and explicit claims about divine rule and the theopolitical imagination that sustains them can be found across the entire biblical corpus, but I have assumed that the Five Books of Moses, and especially the last four, present the most concentrated effort to think about God's mode of ruling and to assume theocracy as a framework for narrating history and proclaiming the law.

The reader may identify here an echo to a seminal early modern political study of the Hebrew Bible, Spinoza's *Theological-Political Treatise*, particularly its seventeenth chapter. Mixing the accounts of revelations in Exodus 19 and Deuteronomy 5:20ff., 18:16–18, Spinoza suggested that after their liberation from Egypt the Hebrews found themselves in "a state of nature" and freely transferred their rights to God, who became their true sovereign. He projected onto the Pentateuch his own model of the social contract and saw the biblical narrative as a historical account of the constitution of a short-lived theocracy, which was soon replaced by a human (Moses's) rule because the Hebrews were terrorized by the intimate proximity of their God (Spinoza 2001, 206–8).[3] But the Hebrews came from the "house of bondage," from under the yoke of a great king, and when they left Egypt, they were already subject to God's rule, an essential part of the narrative that Spinoza ignores. My suggestion is similar to Spinoza's but differs in two key respects. Instead of reading the Pentateuch as a (phantasmatic) historical account that might inform contemporary political theory, I analyze it as a set of thought experiments undertaken by the biblical authors, whom I take to be political thinkers in their own right. And instead of positing a state of nature in which submission to authority can be freely and rationally chosen, I assume that the biblical authors looked for a space free of preexisting institutions to enable laboratory conditions in which God's ruling power could be grasped clearly, imagined to be instituted, envisioned as it was displayed, and examined through a collection of narratives and codes of law.

In other words, I propose to read the biblical authors and redactors as trying to build a city of God on earth and to build it "in speech" (*en logoi*), "from the beginning," as Socrates proposes in Plato's *Republic* (369c). The Pentateuchal city was but a moving camp, and the main architectonic enterprise was to imagine it unfolding in time, not in space, but it was no less separated from its surrounding environment than a new Greek colony. Bearing some obvious differences in mind and focusing on the imaginary constructions, the Pentateuchal text, with its multiple authors and redactors, should be placed alongside that of a single author, Plato, who, one or two centuries later, recounted how Socrates invited his friends to build a city in words from the beginning. This moment, which opens the constructive part of Plato's *Republic*, shaped the future of European political theory and its inheritors across the globe. In a way that was more devious and contentious but no less forceful, the biblical authors and redactors who envisaged the Pentateuchal theocratic formations built the environment where the rule of God could be imagined. This had been a zone of indistinction between the political and the theological; only later did it become the theological infrastructure that has explicitly or implicitly undergirded political theory wherever the Hebrew Bible has been treated as Scripture.

The biblical authors left very few traces that might indicate what they were *trying to do* by writing what they actually wrote. They told stories, listed laws, proclaimed injunctions, composed or reported prophesies, recorded family lineages, mapped territories in words, and more. But *why* they or some later editors put these together in the way they did, they did not tell. This book does not try to decipher a hidden plan behind the composition of the Pentateuch or locate the historical circumstances that gave rise to it. The plan is attributed to some of the texts assembled in the Pentateuch by way of a hypothesis, a thought experiment of my own: to read the texts as *engaged in such a thought experiment themselves*, while looking for evidence that would not only allow such a reading but make it compelling. The idea that the Pentateuch can be read as a series of attempts to imagine divine rule is offered here as a way to make sense of the violence (the exact meaning and adequacy of this term will be examined later) that the biblical texts attribute to God. Divine rule, I argue, is not only *my* framework for explaining divine violence but also the way the Pentateuch's authors and redactors tried to make sense of the violence already attributed to God, and, perhaps, to justify the violence they wished to attribute to Him.

Thinking about the Pentateuchal formations of divine rule as thought experiments is an interpretive construct for making sense of divine violence. This construct relies on textual, not historical, evidence, but it is not historically implausible. Accordingly, "making sense" here should mean first and foremost reconstructing what could have made sense for the authors and their audience, in their world. In this attempt at reconstruction, I assume that in the world *of* the text—both the world imagined in and depicted by the text and the world of those whose imagination was at work as they were writing the text—the violence attributed to God was not the solution but the problem. It is this problem, I suggest, that competing stories about the emergence of theocratic regimes and rival depictions of their features, as demonstrated in relation to constitutive events and reflected in codes of law, sought to address.

The rationale for the interpretive framework sketched here is presented in the book's first two chapters with some additional conceptual and methodological clarifications, aided by brief glances into various biblical texts outside the Pentateuch. Each of the three remaining chapters is dedicated to interpretive reconstruction and theoretical analysis of a different theocratic formation. Roughly speaking, the three formations are associated with three groups of sources identified by historical philologists working with and often against the "documentary hypothesis": pre-priestly writings (the so-called Jehovist [J] and Elohist [E] sources) in Genesis, Exodus, and Numbers; priestly writings (P) across the first four books of the Pentateuch; and Deuteronomic writings (D), which make up the Pentateuch's last book, Deuteronomy.

The reading proposed in these three chapters is led by an admittedly speculative and risky hypothesis, but one that is continually informed by close reading and that takes note of some of the vast literature recently produced in the field of critical Bible studies. A brief comment about my use of this body of research is now in order.

Many contemporary critical scholars of the Hebrew Bible approach the texts as historians who use philological tools to examine the history of the Bible's composition, redaction, and canonization and, often ignoring the hermeneutical circularity of their reading, use their findings as a basis for their interpretation of the narratives, law codes, and prophetic writings. Many others who are mostly interested in particular themes, and not necessarily in mapping the sources and excavating the chronology of the Bible's composition, take seriously and often uncritically the historicity of their sources. The history of composition is examined along two parallel routes, separable for some, closely related for others: an "internal" literary history and a sociopolitical history (where archaeological findings join the philological efforts). I have not been trained as a Bible scholar, and my questions as a reader are not historical. Only the objects of my interpretive work are: the theopolitical formations that subsist in the texts and serve as their infrastructure. To respect the historicity of these objects, I had to rely on the work of historians and philologists. I have been following an eclectic group of Bible scholars belonging to different schools of interpretation, and I have used their studies as signposts and as strictures on my own reading. I have paid close attention to the main fault lines distinguishing several distinct biblical sources according to recent versions of the documentary hypothesis and to the different layers of editing that intervened in earlier texts or stitched them together. And yet, in identifying the three theocratic formations I always tried to weigh the philological putative fault lines against the findings of my reconstructive work and the distinct theopolitical formations and figures of divine rule this work helped bring to the texts' surface. More than once I offered two alternative interpretations of the same formation according to two conflicting datings of the texts at stake and irreconcilable determinations of their provenance.

At the same time, I have also examined the literary composition and architectonics of certain distinct episodes in the Pentateuch, which I studied more closely than others. Reconstructing tensions among conflicting voices; assessing the impact of repetitions and differences, of an abundance or lack of details, or of positions changed in the middle of a story; deciphering how putative interpolations reframe a story and how such reframing conceals, emphasizes, or undermines earlier meanings—all play their part in unpacking certain self-contained texts. These texts were chosen because once unpacked they display, with unusual intensity and clarity, key aspects in the configuration of divine violence and the theocratic formations that underlie it. Such, for example, are the stories of the flood in Genesis 6–9, of Korah's rebellion in Numbers 16–18, or of the covenantal ceremonies in Deuteronomy 28–30 and Joshua 24. One of these stories—that of the disastrous expedition of the twelve scouts to the promised land—appears in different versions in Numbers (13–14, interweaving pre-priestly and priestly sources) and Deuteronomy (1). Reading these versions together allows for a simultaneous display of all three theocratic formations and provides a key for their differentiation.

Once the three formations are reconstructed and laid alongside one another, new questions quickly arise. Some of these are plainly historical, relating to the composition of the Hebrew Bible: Was there a time when these formations really coexisted and competed to capture the imagination of the communities that composed, edited and read the Hebrew Bible? Was a later formation a response to an earlier one? What were the historical circumstances that gave rise to a certain formation or marginalized it? Other questions relate to the postbiblical history of the theocratic formations. Why were they abandoned or repressed in a variety of postbiblical discourses, among Judeans in the late Second Temple period and later among Jews and Christians alike? Were they replaced, and by what? If they were indeed repressed, is it possible to locate particular moments in the two-and-a-half millennia of the Bible's reception in which certain returns of the repressed are discernible? And if the ancient theocratic formations antici-pate features of the blueprint of the modern state, what role did they play in the emerging discourse of the modern state?

These questions lie beyond the scope of my scholarship and certainly beyond the scope of this book; I hope they will be taken up by others. I was mainly oc-cupied by another question: What can the putative transfer of theocratic forma-tions to the heart of modern political imagination, to the state's legal discourse and its governmental reasoning, teach us about the urgency of a theopolitical critique of the contemporary state? My reflections on this question are scattered across the book, accompanying the close readings of biblical texts and the re-construction of their theopolitical imagination. Some of these reflections are collected and rephrased in the book's Afterword. The deification of the mod-ern state with which the book concludes sketches a beginning of a project of a wholly different kind.

1

STAYING WITH THE VIOLENCE

DIVINE VIOLENCE—A TRAILER

Imagine this sequence.

In the beginning, he created heaven and earth, outlined an orbit for the moving stars, and established their government. He crafted land and sea, populated them with an abundance of living creatures, and deposited them all under the rule of man. For a very long time, this earth, under those skies, was the stage on which he appeared to whoever was capable of watching. From very early on, many of his manifestations were fraught with disaster. Taking great pride at first in what he created, he was soon disappointed and so habitually disrupted the order of his doing, wreaking havoc and destruction, directly or through his emissaries. Each catastrophic event served as the arena where his power was displayed and his superior might was proven. Calamities were his preferred mode of revealing himself to humans. It has been so since the flood in Noah's time, some ten generations after creating Adam and Eve.

Catastrophes were not his only way of revealing himself to humans or demonstrating his will and might, but the reader of the Hebrew Bible is never too far from them. At first, when humans were few and the task of ruling easy, his response to transgressions was relatively mild. A code of law had not yet been given to mankind, but there were precise instructions and direct commands. Thus, his first traumatic epiphanies were reactions to conscious acts of defiance.

His first sentences were severe, irreversible, and had far-reaching consequences, yet he avoided capital punishment. In the first murder, when Cain killed Abel, he pulled the strings from afar, preferring Abel over his brother, but shared none of the blame for what followed. He then reacted with restraint (Gen. 4:12–15), perhaps because he recognized his part in arousing Cain's envy and rage (Gen. 4:4–5),[1] or perhaps because Cain did not yet have a child and he did not want to cut off human lineage too early. He first tried to prevent violence by instilling guilt (Gen. 4:7). When he failed and the murder took place, he tried to prevent revenge by promising "sevenfold vengeance" to "whoever kills Cain" (Gen. 4:15). Nevertheless, the killings continued, and the next killer, Lamech, multiplied by elevenfold the warnings against revenge-taking (Gen. 4:24).[2]

Soon, however, humans "began to multiply on the face of the earth" (Gen. 6:1). After ten generations, human evil accumulated,[3] and his reaction was the worst of its kind: near extinction of life on earth. Had he ever tried to educate or correct his corrupted creatures? Had they known about him, his surveillance, or his power to punish? Noah—a relatively righteous man, blameless "in his generation" (Gen. 6:9)—was saved along with his family and a sample of all living species. He designed an ark and instructed Noah to build it for the future survivors, as if to save himself the trouble of starting all over again. Correcting humans' ways did not seem a viable option. He could not tolerate the immensity of their evils, corruption, and violence, so when he took action, his force of destruction was unhinged, and havoc pervaded the whole of Creation. When the floodgates of the heavens were opened, no earthly creature (except for the few on Noah's ark) was spared. Soon after, however, he regretted what he had done "to all living things." In a rare moment of reflection, he understood, somewhat belatedly, that "the devisings of the human heart [yetzer lev ha-adam] are evil [ra] from youth" (Gen. 8:21). After all, this was how he created them. He promised to never again annihilate them (Gen. 8:21, 9:12–17).

No one lamented the lives and beauty gone with the rising water. Noah's sons were busy reproducing, and the earth was soon filled with humans working and acting together. Something about this seemed to surprise, scare, or simply make him jealous. Accompanied or aided by an unnamed entourage whose role and power are never mentioned,[4] he ruined a city under construction where people had dared to design a tower, which, as towers often do, intended to reach the sky. These humans worked collaboratively and wished to make a name for themselves and preserve their community. Contrary to many later readings, they were driven by practical wisdom and a wish to preempt foreseeable dangers (Gen. 11:4), but he saw hubris in their act, perhaps recognizing himself in the mirror they posed for him. Other than this hubris, no offenses are mentioned, and the response was not lethal. The human desire to concentrate in one place and speak one language was simply inverted, causing dispersion and making translation, with all its hazards and opportunities, inevitable.

In Babel, understanding and agreement ("one language and one speech") in times of great fear ("lest we be scattered abroad over the face of the whole earth") served to generate action ("let us build us a city") (Gen. 11:1–4). Is this not the key to human progress? Clearly, he was impressed with their feat, but he saw their progress as having no immanent restraint, which was precisely what he feared. "Now nothing that they propose to do will be withheld from them" (Gen. 11:6). Couldn't he foresee this coming? What was it that mortal humans could have done that could have threatened him? Couldn't he see that they are doomed to fail, unable to overcome the various pitfalls that come with their finitude? Perhaps the gap between them and him was not yet settled, perhaps it was even bridgeable still. The short, condensed passage into which the drama of Babel is shrunk leaves us guessing. But one thing has become clear already: Whether motivated by justice or envy, desire for recognition or fear of human competition, he reacted to frustration by changing the course of events, destroying what he created and undoing what he initiated. "What [he] built, he [would] destroy, what [he] planted [he] would uproot, all of that land [was his]."[5] Again and again we meet him as he sows (or threats, or is called to sow) destruction while his subjects plead for forgiveness, mercy, and rescue. His ominous destructive impulse hovered above whatever his humans thought and did.

Let us follow the textual trail of his catastrophic visitations, skipping for now many other aspects of his character and the story of his time on earth. After the great flood, he next unleashed his destructive force in a great spectacle of brimstone and fire, inflicting a calamity that would forever be engraved in the collective memory of all Bible communities.[6] Two cities, Sodom and Gomorrah, thrived as "the garden of the Lord" (Gen. 13:10) but were filled with evil people who committed "very grave" sins (Gen. 18:20). So great were their sins that both cities were annihilated. He wiped out "all their inhabitants"— presumably men, women, and children—and "what grew on the ground" (Gen. 18:25). The cities were crushed with one blow. This time, he expressed no regret. "The outcry of Sodom and Gomorrah, how great! Their offence is very grave," he exclaimed (Gen. 18:20). We know nothing about the nature of that offence, whether the people had ever been warned or could have foreseen what would soon come. Some legends of their sin formed around the violent way they treated a privileged foreigner, Lot, and his guests (Gen. 19:4–11). Lot entertained visitors even newer than himself, and the Sodomites had good reasons to be suspicious (Gen. 19:1–5), as the reader will soon find out. We also know that human innocence was of limited value. He agreed with Abraham that the cities would be annihilated if only nine righteous people could be found there (Gen. 18:32–33). As it turned out, newborns who were not yet given time to become righteous were not counted either. The destruction was total. Except for Lot and his daughters, which he had exempted beforehand, no creature was saved, and "the smoke of the land . . . went up like the smoke of the furnace" (Gen. 19:28).

Total destruction, on the one hand, and the rescue of a few individuals, on the other, are the two Janus-like moments of revelation in time of disaster: calamity for the multitude of evildoers, rescue for his few privileged favorites.[7] But the separation between disaster and rescue had to be complete. In Sodom and Gomorrah, only the dying could witness the destruction; only the survivors and the bystander (Gen. 19:28–29) could witness the ashes.[8] Lot's wife, who was curious to see the disaster, could not remain alive. She missed an opportunity to be saved, as did Lot's sons-in-law, who did not even bother to leave. Others were offered no such chance. The catastrophe erupted without warning, and the end came abruptly and swiftly. It was governed neither by divine laws (which have not yet been given) nor by "laws of nature" (a term the Hebrew Bible does not recognize). The singularity of the event embodied the singularity of his will and power, at the same time setting a precedent for a pattern of separations between the doomed and the saved.

His destructive force would be unleashed again in a similarly excessive and spectacular way, this time in Egypt. But for the first time, both the excess and the spectacle served some goals. His excessive power far outweighed that of Pharaoh's and cannot be simply measured against the latter's crimes, for it also had a special role in the educational theater staged on the Nile. Both parties were in the audience. The Egyptian masters had to learn that he and only he was *the true Lord* (Ex. 7:17),[9] while the Hebrew slaves had to learn that he, not Pharaoh, was *their true master*.[10] The victims on both sides played an important role in this series of calamities—the plight of the Israelite slaves had called forth his appearance and acts of deliverance; the pledges of Pharaoh's servants (Ex. 10:7) and the outcries of the stricken Egyptians (Ex. 12:30–31) finally convinced Pharaoh to let the Israelites go. In the final episode of Exodus, when "all Pharaoh's horses, his chariots, and his horsemen" were drowned in the Sea of Reeds with "not so much as one of them remain[ing]" (Ex. 14:23, 28), the entire international community—Philistines, Edomites, Moabites, and Canaanites—joined the audience and watched from afar. They were terrified spectators, quaking and quailing. "Shuddering seized them . . . fear did fall upon them"; they were "melting away" before the spectacle of his "arm [as] it loomed big" (Ex. 15:14–16).[11]

During the flood and at Sodom, Gomorrah, and Egypt, his eruption into presence was traced by the extreme violence of the elements—water, fire, darkness, beasts, and insects. Each of these early catastrophes was an intense, excessive display of his superior power and ferocity. Abraham called him "the Judge of all the Earth" (Gen. 18:25), but for readers who had only the Bible's reports to rely upon, he could have been as well crowned as the Lord of all Disasters. How else could his mastery be demonstrated at that stage? For when he was truly present— not speaking from afar or in dreams by a few individuals but rather heard clearly by a large public—he appeared in or through the figure of a looming or actual catastrophe. The number of people who experienced his catastrophic presence was far greater than those who witnessed all his other epiphanies. In this sense, at least, disaster was his primary mode of "being in the world."

The Egyptian calamity, however, marks something new. It clearly displays a shift in his concerns and, as he performed "all [his] scourges [*magefotai*]" (Ex. 9:14), a more nuanced use of his destructive power. The drama started as a power struggle with an earthly king and ended with the liberation of the Hebrew slaves, whom he would later promised to turn into "a kingdom of priests and a holy nation" (Ex. 19:6). From their redemption onward, those liberated slaves, who were gradually developing into a people, became the main target of his ferocity. The possessor of the entire earth became the lord of one elected nation. Only now, a genuine kingship could be established and a true political community forged. Before Egypt, violent destruction could hardly be understood as a mode of ruling. The earlier catastrophes are not depicted as elements in a system of power and domination but rather as sporadic acts. Genesis 1 describes him as the architect of heaven and earth who created a complete order so as not to intervene in it further. He separated the elements, put boundaries to the waters and placed the stars in their routes, gave two heavenly bodies dominion over the day and the night, and ordered humans to "conquer and hold sway" over every living creature on land, in the sea, and in the skies (Gen. 1:16–18, 28). In the earlier catastrophes, he demonstrated similar disinterest in the art of ruling; destruction was total, a pure means that consumed its end. Only in Egypt was destruction instrumentalized, becoming a phase within a larger plan. Until that point, he had demonstrated a capacity to create, possess, plan, destroy, and coerce but did not govern.

His supreme lordship was recognized early in the biblical narrative (Gen.

14:22, 18:25). The political nature of his rule may be indicated by the two early covenants he unilaterally declared. The first was entered with "all flesh that is on the earth" (Gen. 9:16–17), while the second was entered with a single individual, Abram, a married man about whom virtually nothing is known when the reader first meets him. Covenant is basically a form of political relations, but his first two were exclamatory; they did not grow out of or lead to any kind of political relations.[12] It was only in the wilderness, as he was leading Israel out of Egypt, that he practiced the art of governing. Only then a space for political action could be opened for his subjects too. As a space for public action, this option rarely materialized, but its possibility was never ignored, only clearly and violently rejected. In the few episodes when his subjects insisted on publicly challenging him or his delegates, the consequences were catastrophic.

His arsenal of governing tools included more than a mighty hand and the capacity to mobilize all the elements. After all, he announced (in an act that would only later be interpreted as a gift) laws, provided instructions, and even responded to several questions (Num. 15:32–35; 27:1–11). Some of his interventions were constructive, even providential, supplying the people with water, manna, and quails—but even then, according to some reports, salvation went hand in hand with disaster (Num. 11:32–34). More foundational perhaps were the two pillars of fire and cloud that gave shape and presence to his invisible power to guide, protect, and rescue. Some texts say that the pillars were a means of communication and transport (e.g., Num. 9:15–23), while another claims that they served as a screen behind which his mighty hand destroyed the people's enemies (Ex. 24:17–18).[13] This almost immaterial screen formed the partition separating and connecting catastrophe and rescue.[14]

None of these nonviolent means sufficed, however, and disaster was always an available tool at his disposal. He used it not only to strike but also as harrowing threat and chilling memory. Yet those who walked the long road from Egypt to the promised land often failed to recognize this. Neither side learned the lesson. Their recurrent failures to grasp his power reflected their "stiff-necked" nature, so he thought, and Moses concurred.[15] (The voices of those who thought the failures rather reflected a desire to stay free of his yoke were usually silenced.) But there was another failure, on his part, to extract their recognition, and this, an unbiased reader may conclude, reflects a poor calculation of how to use that mighty force. How can a power so deeply in need of his subjects' recognition, so quick to resort to violence, willing to destroy his own creations or change his plans, how can such power be conceived omniscient or omnipotent?

It is not clear that he could create everything that (or as) he had wanted. His aggressive response to the builders of the tower at Babel shows quite clearly that he had overestimated the generative power and improvising skills of humans and underestimated their destructive potential. Had he been omniscient, he would have known that sooner or later those humans would be overpowered by their inclinations, destroy what they had built, confuse their own languages, and scatter on their own to all corners of the earth. And certainly, if he was omnipresent he would not have had to descend to Sodom and Gomorrah to investigate whether their vices were indeed so terrible (Gen. 18:21), and he would have known how many righteous residents lived in those cities, saving Abraham the argument.[16] And how to account for the inclusion of all the innocent lives of infants and animals annihilated in the deluge and in the two sinful cities? Benevolence is certainly not the right term.

Indeed, it was neither his omniscience nor his omnipotence that marked him.[17] Those who conversed with him, from Adam to Job, certainly did not experience him as such. We do not know what he was in his own realm, if he ever had one. Since the sixth day of creation we could only follow him among humans and in relation to them.[18] There, in the realm of human affairs, the radical difference between him and humans lies not in his absolute power but in that invincible superiority. The difference cannot be reduced to that between mortal creatures and an immortal being, however crucial this difference is.[19] The latter dichotomy does not structure the biblical narrative or shape the relations between humans and their creator, as happens in various ancient mythologies.[20] The foremost difference resides in their *relations of power*, in the disparity between, on the one hand, the immeasurable excessiveness of his power and the absolute impunity granted to his actions and, on the other, humans' frailty, their inclination to transgress the rules meant to bind them and to discover in those transgressions their limitedness, finitude, and, sometimes, their vengeful creator, too.

He completed creation in six days, but in the centuries that followed, the only skill he would perfect was that of destruction.[21] The most elevated beings he had created betrayed him, disrupted his plans, and failed to live up to his expectations. And only rarely could he bring them to mend their ways.[22] In his fury, there was not a thing he could not demolish. When it came to destruction he was creative but not mindful of the trail of unaccounted collateral damage his disasters left. An army of devoted commentators would later make sure that no recorded horror be left unjustified, but for him (or for his biblical narrators), most of the details that made his actions palatable to human understanding hardly mattered. His ability to annihilate knew only the ever-changing bounds he set for himself, and this pattern would persist long after he began ruling over his own people. Catastrophe, the form of violence that characterized his rule more than any other, was for a long time the main governmental technology at his disposal.

Shortly before setting to annihilate Sodom and Gomorrah, a striking moment of mutual recognition between him and Abraham took place. He recognized Abraham's righteousness (Gen. 18:19), and Abraham recognized him as "the Judge of all earth" who would surely "do justice" when visiting the two cities and "[would] not slay the righteous with the wicked" (Gen. 18:25).[23] The two interlocutors seem to share a common sense of just ruling, as both ignore the wider meaning of the imminent catastrophe hovering in the background. Abraham never objected to the clear, causal relation between his judgment and his capacity to destroy. This, in fact, was the signature of his rule and what distinguished it from the rule of humans, who often destroyed without judgment and judged without immediate recourse to destruction. Even more significantly, the two ignored the implications of the loss of nonhuman lives and the lives of humans too young or weak to sin. Their negotiation presupposed a common moral sense, an agreement on a threshold of harm and suffering that legitimized total destruction.[24] The threshold, characterized as *mishpat*, "just ruling" in this context, was introduced now into the heart of a power whose destructiveness could be unlimited. In establishing the threshold, some details had to be fleshed out: When is it applied, and how many innocent lives lost as collateral damage are justifiable? This exchange betrays a *sensus communis* shared by most biblical communities throughout the ages, where total annihilation was seen as divine justice and the unnecessary loss of life need not be questioned.[25]

This kind of common sense was expressed by many of the prophets, and the tale of Sodom and Gomorrah was a recurring parable for describing the forthcoming fate of sinful nations.[26] The noncanonized, apocryphal writings inherited the idea of a total and just destruction *tel quel*, and the apocalyptic literature experimented with its imaginary, fantastic figuration. When Paul made Abraham, whose righteousness lay in his faith (Rom. 4), the kernel of the new ecclesia and of the inclusive exclusion of Israel within it, he too shared the apocalyptic imagination and accepted the same old common moral sense.[27] Regardless of how the distance between him and mankind was conceived across this vast corpus, it did not reside in the willingness to accept the catastrophic mode of action but in the capacity to generate and execute it. This capacity, we know well, was not fixed in creation but grew and developed as generations passed, and the distance gradually eroded. Was the man created in his image doomed to become as destructive as he was? Have humans become that destructive geological force because he created—or they imagined him creating—them in his image? As we know today, the cumulative effect of this human force that works on a geological scale might be a partial or even total extinction of life on planet Earth. Is the difference between the two forces then one of speed—150 days of flood (Gen. 7:24) versus millennia of human development and centuries of colonial, racialized capitalism—rather than a difference of scale and precision?

A BRIEF NOTE ON COUNTING AND EXPLAINING AWAY

If divine violence could inspire a movie, the preceding pages could be the trailer's script. Alas, movie trailers seldom do justice to the films they trail, and ours is no exception. Divine violence—the violence perpetrated or instigated by God or attributed to his command[28]—does not fully capture the drama of God in the Hebrew Bible, the contours of his figure(s), or the meaning of his acts. Divine violence is not a microcosm of the divine macrocosm, not even a secret clue for deciphering the biblical plot. At the same time, it is hard to imagine a reader of the Hebrew Bible—whether they be novices or scholars, whether they read the Bible as a scripture and testament, a literary treasure or a historical archive—who has not come across the spectacular displays of the violence God directly perpetrated or commanded or indirectly instigated and inspired. At least since the Christian heretic Marcion in the second century CE and the Christian author and apologist Lacatantius in the late third century CE, God's excessive use of force was a basis for a fierce critique of "the Old Testament," its God, and the Jews who adhered to it. Recently, however, the critique of divine violence in the Hebrew Bible has been placed within a larger critique of religious fundamentalism, and of monotheism more broadly, which coincides with a growing post-Holocaust theological interest in the Hebrew Bible, on the one hand, and in acts of terror associated with Islamist, Christian, and Jewish fundamentalists, on the other.

In 1978, the Swiss theologian Raymond Schwager counted approximately one thousand passages in the Hebrew Bible that mention God's "bloody works."[29] Steve Wells, a professed atheist and author of the *Skeptic's Annotated Bible*, counted 135 events in which the Bible's God or those acting in his name killed (by Wells's calculations) 2.5 million victims and countless others in which mass killing is reported.[30] Terence Fretheim, a liberal Protestant, surveyed the entire biblical corpus for its violent episodes and found that divine violence is always a response to human violence.[31] Richard Dawkins, another professed atheist, rejects such excuses, instead stating that God is arguably "the most unpleasant character in all fiction . . . bloodthirsty, ethnic cleanser, racist, infanticidal, genocidal," and much more.[32] Theologians and professed atheists alike are obviously bothered by the numerous instances of biblical violence attributed to God or carried out in his name. Yet this abundance of violence, which has so often been embraced without being questioned and sometimes used to incite violence or justifies it, has been quite systematically—and symptomatically—understudied, either ignored completely or asserted and then ignored or explained away.[33]

Theologically motivated authors, regardless of religious denomination, have been interested in reconstructing a figure of God to whom they can pray and with whom they can live, more or less peacefully, ultimately giving meaning to their lives and their world. For some, this has meant embracing and sometimes even celebrating his violence, especially if it targeted people they learned to hate or despise.[34] Others looked for ways to bracket divine violence within the early stages of God's personal history,[35] perhaps to make peace with or even forgive him. Sometimes this was done by accepting the contradictions that run through his epiphanies or even his being. As the rabbinic midrash did since antiquity,[36] God has been described as being both "kind and cruel, good and genocidal,"[37] protested and excused in the same breath. A different strategy, also known since antiquity, was to avoid the problem altogether by rejecting a literal reading of the text. This rejection had a variety of hermeneutic and epistemological rationales, ones not directly related to the question of divine violence but more generally to the anthropomorphic representations of God in the Bible. It goes at least as far back as the second century BCE, evidenced in the Jewish-Hellenist *Letter of Aristeas* and the teachings of the Jewish-Hellenist philosopher Aristobulus. In the first century BCE, Philo of Alexandria used elaborate allegorical readings to bracket the question of divine violence,[38] and a few centuries later, early Christian readers of the Old Testament developed similar and other strategies for systematically deliteralizing the scriptures, much of it done as a polemic against Marcion.[39] Among Jewish scholars, the rejection of literal readings of biblical depictions of God received an authoritative rabbinic, albeit rationalist, version in Maimonides's twelfth-century *Guide for the Perplexed*.[40] In the early twentieth century, the literal reading was rejected from the opposite direction by the antirationalist theology of Rudolf Otto, who associates divine violence with the mysterious dimension of God's being.[41] Biblical description of this violence should therefore be read as the Scriptures' way of conveying this inconceivable dimension of God.

Even if one sticks to the letter of the text and does not skip what seems to contradict one's beliefs or affronts one's faith and sensibilities, some ways to avoid dealing with divine violence are still open. One may, for example, declare that God has evolved and changed since his early outbursts or that the text is merely a parable on the reader's own limitations. Or perhaps, one may read the text as meaning exactly what it says and, in the impossibility of these accounts, thus cannot be trusted as a straightforward description of God's ways and deeds. In this view, "the real God" could not have authored all that violence. This was basically Marcion's point, according to recent reconstructions of his mostly lost writings, as he read from the Scriptures "a consistently negative [story], of a God who repeatedly demonstrates himself to be weak, unreliable, self-contradictory, and given to irrational acts of anger and wanton cruelty."[42]

A different strategy to deal with divine violence, shared by theologically and nontheologically motivated readers alike, is historicization, which neither explains the violence away nor really thinks it through. The thrust of the historicist effort is to identify similar figures, language, and justifications of divine violence in the ancient Near East that could be considered as direct or indirect sources of influence to biblical authors. Historicization (like its twin, psychologization) does not justify violence but rather relativizes it and shifts attention from the event and its effects to a context of origin that makes it appear understandable and easier to exonerate without being thoroughly examined. Writing as a historian and a Bible scholar while addressing theologically concerned readers, Thomas Römer exemplifies this common ground. He insists on the necessity of "a historical investigation" that would allow the reader "to place oneself in the conceptual and ideological context of the authors of those [biblical] testimonies" and then of following God's "biography," to relate his various figures to the historical setting in which they were composed.[43] When doing so, one finds the proper context for the appearance of God as a genocidal warlord. Thus, to describe the God of Israel, the authors of Deuteronomy adopted the figure of an "Assyrian overlord," and those who composed the book of Joshua, the figure of "an Assyrian-style God," but both needed to show their God's superiority.[44] This reasoning would also explain why it is so often the case that the hyperbolic depictions of violence collected in our movie trailer often seem to surpass those left in inscriptions describing imperial violence in the ancient Near East.

The putative Near Eastern origin of many biblical texts was often used to better understand the violence they ascribe to God but also to make the more abhorrent depictions of that violence more palatable to sensitive contemporary readers, especially those who wish to trust their God as a God of peace and justice. But the true impact of such historicization is often to keep divine violence close to its origin and sealed in a remote past. Furthermore, even for historians, the study of origin and the reconstruction of the conditions for adopting and preserving certain (discursive and/or nondiscursive) practices fall short of the study of the economy of the violence depicted. To take one example, the prolific, fascinating discussions of the Mesopotamian predecessors to the flood story in Genesis (and the two sources combined in it) cannot replace an analytic approach to God's destructive power or to the ancient effort to contemplate the first mass extinction.[45] For, in order to study violence—human or divine—it is not enough simply to study the history of its representations. What is required is a phenomenology of the violence depicted and a reconstruction of the world in which it could have made sense. It is thus quite surprising that even when we look for such reconstructions—where the investigation is neither shaped by an interest in a preconceived figure of the divine nor content with the historicist reduction of violence to its putative sources—we find little scholarly patience for or interest in dwelling on the violence itself. Without dwelling on it, however, one cannot observe the patterns of its unfolding or follow its transformations throughout the biblical narratives.

It is quite rare to find a study of violent biblical episodes where violence is the focus of the interpretation. Many of the episodes where violence is depicted allow for and require a close, thick reading that would take into account the text's literary and rhetorical elements, its functioning as testimony and warning, the legal codes to which it may refer, the justification built into or missing from its description, and the various points of view—of the instigator, perpetrator, collaborators, victims, spectators, and narrators—recorded in it. Furthermore, there may be discernable patterns beyond the isolated episodes, and their reconstruction requires a synoptic view and an intertextual reading. Pairing of this sort of synoptic view with a close reading is rare in Bible studies and even more difficult to find when divine violence is concerned.[46] This book seeks to open a path for a synoptic view of divine violence in the Hebrew Bible through close readings of some major episodes depicting its unfolding in the Pentateuch.

VIOLENCE, AS IT IS UNFOLDING: A PHENOMENOLOGICAL SKETCH

Does the divine origin of violence necessarily change the way it unfolds? It may. The magnitude, scope, and swiftness of destruction might be perceived as utterly extraordinary. But this was not always the case. When Jacob wrestled with God, who looked to him like a man, he hurt his hip (Gen. 32:25–32); the first two plagues in Egypt were something Egyptian magicians could also conjure (Ex. 7:14–8:12); and many of Israel's wars were fought like any other. Much of the violence described in the Hebrew Bible is attributed to or inspired by God, but this violence unfolds like it often does, sowing terror, harm, and destruction. The main difference, I suggest, is a matter of scale. There are few important exceptions to this rule, when it is not only scale but the form of violence that is extraordinary, but these stand out precisely because so much of the violence attributed to God is ordinary.

Hence the study of divine violence is first and foremost a study of violence. The very concept of "divine violence" is a modern one, and we must ask ourselves whether "violence" itself is a category or a concept recognized by the Bible, and whether it was associated with God. The term, which seems to us a straightforward category essential for any account of human affairs, may not be so neatly translated backward onto biblical texts. And this term is hardly ever isolated; there is an entire semantic web associated with it, connecting various kinds of actions, means, and targeted objects, as well as kinds of agency and responsibility, terms for describing boundaries, excess, violations, and the like. We therefore begin with a sense of *décalage* between our own contemporary discourse and that of the ancient texts we study. It is built into our inquiry, but we do not yet know how wide the gap is. Worse still, we cannot even assume that today, in the American academic English of 2021, "violence" is a category we—whoever "we" are—share and use in the same way. It is necessary to begin, therefore, with violence as this book means it.[47]

"Violence" will be understood here as the operation of any force that violates, harms, injures, dissociates, destroys, dismantles, uproots, or annihilates what is affected by it, whether targeted or not, whether that be bodies, psyches (through humiliation, insult, or denial of recognition), solid structures, or landscapes and entire environments where humans and other beings dwell. Harm, destruction, and loss are not always caused by violence, and violence does not always end in destruction and loss, but it is always potentially so. Violence is an act and an event in which objects, bodies, psyches, or persons are violated (or under such threat). The kind of entity affected (objects, bodies, etc.) does not matter here; what matters is the effect of the violating force on the ability of that entity and its right to stay what it is and act as it wishes.

But this is not enough. For violence to take place *the violation must be related to some prescribed norm, rule, or law.* Our guide here is the opening of Walter Benjamin's "Critique of Violence": "The task of a critique of violence can be summarized as that of *expounding its relation to law and justice.* . . . A cause, however effective, becomes violent in the precise sense of the word only when it bears on moral issues."[48] This means that before engaging in a critique of violence, one must assume that violence exists in relation to some expectation of how things are or ought to be, according to custom, law, or justice,[49] and this relation is at the heart of the critical interest in violence. In other words, violence is the infliction of harm by a force, where the power to authorize or prohibit the use of said force exists or even where, by virtue of law, tradition, or custom, the use or restraint of this force falls within the realm of the justifiable. Hence, violence's very existence and manifestation are discursive and institutional and therefore cannot be limited to a phenomenal plane of forces and the affected objects, bodies, or souls.

We assume—as Benjamin must have done—that no violence takes place unless law or justice (or other binding criteria) are invoked and an authorizing power is presupposed. An act does not assume its violent nature until such invocation takes place. That is why there is no violence in "nature," at least as long as nature is thought as outside the human domain. Floods or fires cause harm, of course, but unless one invokes the governmental effort to regulate humans' relations to their environment and insists on describing the natural events as symptoms of malpractice, negligence, or failure to be cautious and prepared, to act or to perform one's duty, the description of the natural forces as violent is strictly figurative. Such figurative language implies a wish for—but not the existence of—a norm that would render the harm unacceptable and a tribunal where the demand for repair and compensation could be heard.[50] The wish may be strong enough so as to call into existence the rule, and even the power, to enforce it. The question is not whether a god or a government capable of helping exists but whether they are imagined and attributed with such power and whether the attribution is followed by an expectation to use that power according to moral judgment or legal duty. Violence is the forceful infliction of harm that takes place in the purview of a demand for or a question about its authorization and justification.

To establish a case as violent, one does not have to show that it has been authorized or not, that is, that it has or lacks justification, only that the case requires authorization and justification and that it is meaningful to judge the act accordingly. We may envision a backward movement: from the torn flesh to the bullet; the trigger of the gun; the shooter's hand, eye, and mind; to the order or the right to shoot, or to the law that forbids the shooting, and the authority that lets or makes it happen, or is responsible to prevent it from happening and to respond when it does. This line is schematic, the series may be set in a different, nonlinear order, but all these elements must be there to make violence happen. The discourse of violence extracts harm and loss, destruction, pain and suffering from their "natural" scene and places them in discursive and political contexts.

Broadly speaking, "law" should be understood to include any recognized binding standard to which the perpetrator and the victim may appeal to justify or protest the violent act. The exact distinction between justice and law—a thorny issue—need not bother us at the moment.[51] Suffice it to say that invoking justice implies a real or desired moral tribunal to which one may appeal when the law itself allows or sanctions use of force one deems unjustifiable. In the same vein, the exact distinction between law and known rules, customs, or norms that have not been formally coded is insignificant here, as long as the latter exert or are ascribed with authority to allow or to forbid the exercise of force. The justifiability of the forceful act is crucial, but justification itself—on either legal or moral grounds—does not make the harm not violent. It is the other way around—an act or an event becomes violent when the attribution of responsibility, and hence the justifiability of the act, are possible. It is not necessarily the intention of a perpetrator that decides the violent nature of an act or an event but rather the possibility of demanding an account for it. In other words, violence is a specific, forceful impact on one's flesh, psyche, property, and physical environment that cannot take place without passing through the flimsy medium of a certain prescriptive discourse.[52]

Violence is a use of force whose legality and morality may yet to be determined and, even if determined, may always be contested. The legal and moral determinations may not be congruent, and even when they are and the use of force is both legal and morally justified, the use of force is still a case of violence because a harm has been inflicted and a norm or law invoked. Shooting a person in self-defense is still an act of violence. An ideal police department in which the use of harmful force is strictly limited to cases sanctioned by just laws and where the use of such force is always a last resort carried out in the most moderate ("proportional") manner still inflicts harm and is thus violent. The same is true for a just God who acts according to (his) laws or his sense of justice. Even a perfectly benevolent God may act violently. We must extract from the text how God's qualities, however superb, directed his violence or are reflected in it, not project a construct of violence according to some anachronistic conceptions of benevolence or justice. In the case of both a local sheriff and of the lord of heaven and earth, it is not the nature of the actor but rather the relation of the act to authority, law, and justice that renders the harmful act violent. This relation cannot be simply presupposed. It may be introduced in anticipation of the violent scene, invoked as the violence is unfolding, but also, as we will see below, belatedly, by the victim, perpetrator, spectator, or the reader.

The relation to the law is further complicated by the violence inherent to

the law itself, in the form of its constitution (constitutive violence) and enforcement (the force of law). Even when no violence is actually exercised, law
enforcement—in distinction from the written laws or those advocated in public
discourse—is both a substitute and a supplement for violence. "Law" is an institution founded on and sustained by violence and a mechanism that serves to
control, reduce, channel, and manage the distribution of violence. Thus, to the
extent that God's catastrophic visitations can be related to his laws, they should
be interpreted along the same lines. Yet whereas violence without any recourse
to law or justice is a contradiction in terms, the opposite is not true. A rule of
law with neither a history of nor an actual recourse to violence can be (at least)
imagined, conceived, and hoped for without a contradiction. It may be hard to
find an actual case of a nonviolent rule of law, but it is not impossible to imagine it. We will later examine one clear biblical attempt to imagine such a case.[53]

The relation between violence and law (in the term's broadest sense, which,
in our context, encompasses every domain of government in which an authority
to use force is claimed)[54] goes much further than this, of course.[55] Any critical
account of law, governance, and order must include an account of the violent
ways these are inscribed onto human affairs, including the bodies and souls of
the governed subjects, for the work of the law, the life of the ruling power, and
the daily business of government are all channeled through multiple displays of
force (mere threats included). There are veins of violence through which rule
and government are practiced. From education to capital punishment, from tax
collection to the military draft, and from gender to labor relations, violence is
distributed unequally and affects differentially those subjected to the powers
exercising it.

For a scene of violence to become legible and for its pattern to be properly
recognized, the scene must be placed on a map that traces how violence circu-
lates and is distributed. Scenes of violence have a place in a general economy of
violence, from which they draw their general conditions of possibility, meaning,
and value.[56] In this economy, patterns of violence involve distribution, cycles,
accumulations of means and effects, investments, benefits, and losses. But the
forces used and the harm caused can never be measured by any economic calculation, and the gap between the "use value" for the "consumer"—the victim—i.e.,
the value of the collateral effect of the harmful strike, and the exchange value for
the producer or the user—the perpetrator—is not a contingent matter but what
defines the objective value of the violent act in the first place. Furthermore, and
even beyond the immeasurable terror and trauma, violence also concerns the
harm generated when it is withheld and suspended, hovering without erupting,

acting through a series of threats, simulations, or flashbacks that break through the repression and denial of the violent scene.

The way violence is represented cannot be separated from its actualization and its differential distribution and repercussions. In fact, the role of "representation" in the general economy of violence cannot be overstated. It is involved in the circulation of violence and its conversion into threats that can both reduce or encourage further violence. Iconic depictions of violence tend to generate imitations, guide interpretations of future violent scenes, and become inseparable from the justification or censor of violent acts. Sodom and Gomorrah, the drowning of the Egyptian army chasing Israel, and the plague in Baal Pe'or are such iconic events of extreme violence in the Bible. More generally, the biblical texts provide us with ample examples of representations of acts and events that we would recognize today as violent. These texts record, imagine, fantasize, and warn against acts of "murder" (*reṣaḥ*), "outrage" (*ḥamas*), "destruction" (*sh'mad*), or "wiping out" (*makkha*), and a whole gallery of other atrocities executed by the use of force. Leaving aside for the moment the question whether the authors or protagonists of these texts would have recognized our concept of violence (see the following section), what we find in these texts is enough to start mapping the distribution of biblical violence and reconstructing at least some of its elements and the general patterns of its economy. Not surprisingly, we will see that each theocratic formation is characterized by a distinct economy of violence.

No matter how dense and terse the biblical depictions of violent scenes are, they should be treated like any other historical, legal, or literary source. We may find there sudden blows (with their own patterns) and the almost imperceptible spread of slow violence (with its own surprises).[57] Each form has a different impact on the patterns of violence's unfolding and the wider context within which they become legible. Furthermore, beyond the micro scale of any particular event of destruction, the violence consists in the macro scale, with the spread of shock waves; the articulation of pain and loss; its circulation, reiteration, and inscription in collective, long-term memory; the invocation of justice and law; and the assertion of the agency of victims and perpetrators. The phenomenology of violence should thus expand to cover a long span of time, stretching as long as violence's wake keeps moving, chasing its waves. In chronic, "slow," or "systemic" violence, it is not easy to separate an "original scene" from its long wake.[58] This may well be the case with an abrupt event extended indefinitely into the future through its traumatic reverberations and the ongoing struggle to overcome the denial and suppression of the victims' outcry.

The violent event activates and puts into motion an entire configuration of relationships between elements that belong to different registers: bodies, language, memory, patterns of distribution, modes of subjugation and subjectification (the perpetrator, the survivor, the witness, the one who provides aid and shelter, etc.). Once the strike occurs and harm is registered, violence becomes a communicative act involving inter- and apersonal relations, not only intrapersonal affects and experiences (suffering, loss, rage, jealousy, greed, desire, etc.). The act intensifies or disrupts encounters, suspends habits and practices, violates bounded spaces and scheduled times, unties and ties, throws and crushes, and tears apart existing assemblages of things, living beings, words, signs, and images.

By definition, this complex configuration must relate to law and justice, but it also relates to a variety of other, more contingent elements: social distinctions, external and internal boundaries, distribution of sources of power, the arsenal of violence's means, and the differentiation of their effects. The configuration is recognized by characteristic interplays between violence's display and its withdrawal, its spatial-temporal dispersion, its verbal articulation during and after the event, and more. Furthermore, the violent event supports, exposes, undermines, or deconstructs spatial-temporal organizations, the orders of ruling, and the rationality of governance. And because violence is so often perpetrated by a ruling power, directly or with its tacit consent, or exercised by those whom the ruling power ignored or failed to stave off, the scene becomes an arena in which the ruling order is illuminated from multiple perspectives at once.

The search for patterns of unfolding violence is an integrative inquiry that seeks to bring into relief the relations among all the relevant elements of this unique, reproducible, and ever-changing configuration. "The configuration of violence" is a conceptual construct, drawn according to the relation between the identifiable elements, concepts abstracted from the records and traces of violence in various media of representation. It is a scheme of relationships among all the elements that the violent event affects and brings together, even as it tears them apart. This can hardly ever be grasped by those involved at the scene but may be reconstructed, more or less dimly, by an analytical gaze that looks for traces of recurring relations among similar elements.

Both the conceptual configuration and the imagined-narrated world rely on and subsist through a discursive infrastructure. Without passing through discourse, the harmful force cannot be identified and attributed to an agent; the act cannot relate to authority, law, or justice; and the survivors cannot make sense of their experience, learn their lesson, cry out for justice, become better subjects, identify a target, take revenge, or find the goal and means for their resistance. Hence, shattering the ability of *some* subjects to make sense of their violent experience may be one of the most consequential means, effects, or explicit goals of violence. For the perpetrators and their collaborators, making violence illegible for its victims and witnesses is a means for perpetuating the destruction; for the phenomenologist as much as for those trying to resist the violence, it is a crucial element in the overall configuration of violence. In the event of extreme violence, concepts, even language itself may become useless or inaccessible. Arriving belatedly, the analytical gaze seeks to make sense of what the survivors might experience as ineffable. It does so by placing that experience in relation to the conceptual construct called here "configuration of violence," not in order to give words to an ineffable experience but to grasp its function and conditions of possibility.

Discourse (in the strong, rigorous sense Foucault gave to this term)[59] is the regularized, recurring, and more or less distinct pattern of the pragmatics of a language. Its regularities include the relationship between words and things; the limits of what can be said and what can appear, be recognized as this or that, and be shown as such; the subject's position and authority to say, listen, and show, interpret and learn, justify and disagree, evaluate, command, or be addressed and commanded; and the concepts that may be clustered together to explain, justify, predict, or authorize and those that should never be associated. I assume that transformations of the entire discursive formation are not frequent events, that discursive regularities exist and last for a significant length of time, as they are practiced by a certain community of speakers (with many local variants). Given more or less stable discursive regularities, the configuration of violence embedded in a certain discursive infrastructure is relatively stable and persists over time. This relative stability allows the recurrence of the configuration of violence and of the figure of rule that comes along with it, both being recognizable and shareable within a distinct community discourse. The violent acts are always contingent and variable, but as they take shape and continue to circulate—in and through discourse, in memories or through the effects of their traumatic repression, through imitations or counterviolence—they make sense within the same configuration that they keep reproducing, at least for a while. This lasts until a new configuration of violence is introduced, with the advance of a new discursive infrastructure and new events that make a discursive shift necessary. Breaks between discursive regimes mean breaks between configurations of violence, which the ritualized reiteration of the narrations of violence and the unbroken chains of traditions of their interpretation cannot overcome. Hence the necessity of structural historicization and of dissociating later strata of ritualized narratives and their interpretations from the earlier records of violence.

In *Discipline and Punish*, Foucault paved the way for reconstructing distinct configurations of violence that corresponded to and were integrated within distinct discursive formations.[60] Read in this context, the "configuration of violence" may be understood as a possible interpretation of Foucault's concept of power, which underlies that book. Foucault famously displaced violence from the center of power to its periphery and foregrounded nonviolent practices in the exercise of power, yet he did pay close attention to particular displays of violence (most notably the public execution of Damiens, the man who attempted to assassinate King Louis XV, which opens the book), as well as to the setting in which an apparatus of meticulous disciplinary coercion held violence in suspense without renouncing it altogether (in the modern prison) or reigned more freely (in the punishment colony). His close readings of Damiens's public execution or Bentham's papers on the "Panopticon" offer exemplary reconstructions of configurations of violence and their discursive infrastructure. Reading a very different set of documents, I will try to follow the trail Foucault blazed.

Through its undecided or unsettled relation to law and justice, violence implicates political relations. A violent act may be domestic, erratic, systemic, and calculated or unpredictable, expressing an outburst of uncontrolled emotions or a psychotic breakdown. Nonetheless, its setting is always one that involves the authority to use force. Such an authority—or lack thereof—may be claimed by the perpetrator, the victims, or those who tried to protect them; thus the possibility to contest authority is also implied. Said authority can be called upon and questioned in different ways and for different purposes, when the violence occurs or is later recounted. When the authority to use force is publicly questioned, contested, or asserted with a view to its potential problematization, a political setting is created and a stage opened for performative acts of *public problematizations of power* of any sort.[61] Contestation and problematization are performative actions that need a stage of their own, whether within the violent scene or in its wake. The political scene resides in the performative space opened by the dissension such actions reveal.[62]

Problematization may be thwarted and the space for dissent shattered and denied, but as long as its possibility is not completely eliminated, its suppression can still be traced to the preemptive, repressive actions of the ruling power. In these cases, power itself, anticipating dissent, presents its questionable justifications and authority to use force, thus keeping alive the potentiality of a political mode of action. By publicly anticipating its own problematization and working to make it impossible or superfluous, power's performance betrays the fact that its force and authority have not yet been naturalized. The political aspect of power disappears only when the use of force is finally naturalized, somehow made transparent, or silenced altogether. It disappears along with violence, which may then turn into a transparent friction of forces. Violence brings back the political opening; whatever is at stake, it invokes a questionable claim for the authority to use harmful force. Wherever there is a victim or a bystander who screams "*Gewalt*," there is a political opening.

The situations to which I allude here are familiar and may appear specifically modern if not strictly contemporary. And the fact that biblical Hebrew had no term equivalent to "politics" and no way to articulate the specific political aspect of power and action might only increase the sense of an anachronistic conceptual framework prepared here to be imposed on the biblical text. The impression is inevitable, but the difficulty is not unsurpassable, I believe. Terms designating power, rule, and authority abound in biblical Hebrew, and no power, including divine power, is described as fully immune to problematization, secure and indifferent to its recognition and legitimization among its subjects. In fact, for biblical authors the public problematization of power was part and parcel of its description and characterization. Notably, they did not only criticize kings' and princes' abuse of power but put in question the very idea of kings' unlimited power, as well as the principle of hereditary rulership. In a few critical moments, they—or their protagonists—dared to question the moral and political judgment of God himself.[63]

In this sense of "the political," the political aspect of numerous biblical texts is undeniable. There are ample examples of shifting power relations, institutions that used force and claimed authority for doing so, rituals in which power was displayed or challenged and authority was granted or denied, and numerous struggles that reshaped the ways by which people were ruled and governed. And all these, as the texts to be discussed will demonstrate, apply for both humans and divine power. Whatever gap separates the divine from the human in the Hebrew Bible, it is not reflected in the "politicality" of power. The problematization of violence does not become *a*political when the violence is attributed to God. The "theologization" of violence goes together with the legal and moral injunctions invoked in God's name, in the wake of his violence or even as it unfolds, and hence is thoroughly political.[64] There is no reason to assume that the theologization of the power to which violence is attributed (as it occurs, or belatedly) comes at the expense of power's political dimension.[65] On the contrary, this theologization stretches the potential reach of the political to include the most powerful nonhuman actor and a host of his heavenly delegates. This expansion is itself a political move because it involves contesting and redrawing the boundaries where power is exercised and its authority may be questioned.

As we shall see, in all the biblical texts that will concern us here, God is always already political, and this theopolitics resists readings that try to separate the theological and the political.

We have noted that violence may be contested as it unfolds but also long before or long after it is exercised. The coexistence of both options is inherent to the nature of violence as much as it is inherent to the nature of the political. Many biblical depictions of violence problematize and politicize it as it unfolds, in a synchronous manner. In other cases, the political moment follows soon after the event or is anticipated in advance. Sometimes, however, the problematization lags far behind or is performed long before, by way of warning or prophecy. Taking a more general perspective, however, the (non)synchronicity of the problematization of violence appears within specific *textual* features, effects of narrative structure, composition and editing of specific episodes, and the intertextual networks that permeate the Bible as a whole. This derives from the nature of the slow, prolonged process of the Bible's composition and editing.

This also means that the problematization of violence may be an effect of the act of reading itself as one moves back and forth along the chronologies of the depicted events and the transmitted enunciations but also along the textual layers and the intertextual veins that connect and separate events, depictions, and enunciations. As such, in its very textuality, openness, and readability, the Hebrew Bible is a site for the ongoing problematization—hence politicization—of the violence put there on public display. It is the particular textuality of the Bible that overdetermines the political nature of the violence depicted in the text. The phenomenologist shifts the contours of the text and of the worlds portrayed in it as she reads and interprets, and with these shifts, new moments of problematization and politicization of the power at stake may be exposed and described. If the description invokes the reader's outrage and interpellates her judgment, it is a mark of the phenomenologist's success. Violence is a "moral phenomenon," not only a political one, and this is how it needs to be addressed.[66]

Here lies a real challenge. It is not the anachronistic use of terms like "political" or (as we will see) "violence," not even the (inevitable) opening of biblical violence to new moral and political problematization. The difficulty is not intrinsic to the Bible (or any other ancient text) but rather belongs to the very temporality of language and the way this temporality is both activated by and reflected in our reading of the depictions of violence in the (here ancient) texts. The relative *synchronicity* of the discursive formation—the fact that the same discursive formation remains relatively stable or reiterates over a relatively long time—makes possible a distinct configuration of violence and modes of ruling to persist within a certain source and sometimes across sources. This synchronicity clashes, however, with the inherent *nonsynchronicity* introduced by the flux of meanings and formations that characterizes the life of language, the multiplicity of languages and their untranslatability, and the ongoing problematization of political power.

The *synchronicity* of a discursive formation means that the indeterminacies and fluctuations of words' meaning are arrested within certain limits, and these make possible a common sense, a world of recognizable objects and relations, and spaces where people can do things with words in a more or less coordinated way. Following Foucault's conception of discourse, I assume that the referential function of language, the capacity of words "to stick" to things, states of affairs, and personal affections and generate the impression (and illusion) of their sameness depends on the relative persistence or recurrence of these formations. This persistence is crucial for the regularity of any human interaction, for the recognition of order, and the ability to give meaning to the irregular. When violence is concerned, recognition of the regular and giving meaning to the exceptional are matters of extreme urgency, of life and death, of tormenting pain and inexpressible suffering. The point is not that words really stick to what they stand for when violence is at stake but that they must be assumed to mean what they say, "literally." Plays of words, intertextual thickness, metaphoric flights, and poetic pleasure must be postponed, or at least ignored and pushed to the background, or assumed to have been thus displaced at the moment when violence unfolds. Otherwise, if their referential function does not become both predominant and widely shared, the words would become useless.

Nonsynchronicity may be introduced by a contemporary critical reader capable of escaping the gripping power of active discursive formations. But as time elapses, meanings fluctuate, and discursive formations become inoperative, nonsynchronicity is not merely a possibility, the position of an "untimely" reader, which one needs to work hard to realize, but a condition no reader can escape. A two-thousand-year-old discursive formation may still be operative (this is not *logically* impossible), but it is unlikely and cannot be presupposed—that it is still operative must be shown. In reading the Bible, nonsynchronicity must be one's point of departure.

Hence the well-known clash. This clash has been noted by many but never been resolved, and it is often denied or ignored. Let me reiterate it. A contemporary reader of the Bible must presuppose at one and the same time, first, the alien nature of the text that was composed and that made sense within a discursive formation he or she does not share and, second, the persistency of that discursive formation (and the configuration she seeks to reconstruct) in the world of the text's authors, redactors, and early readers.[67] The distance must be crossed, the discursive formations should be retraced, a literal sense of bodies and actions, threats proclaimed, orders decreed, and authorities announced must be assumed as shared—at least by protagonists in the world described by the texts, by the authors who composed them, and, probably, for a relatively long time, by their earlier readers too. Apparently, the nonsynchronous problematization of political authority, moral judgment, and meaning more generally seems to owe nothing to the pressing urgency that called forth the referential function of language and relied on a common, literal sense of words. Such a problematization does not need to relate words to an (assumed or imagined) original moment of utterance. But if we use this as a pretext to free words from any literal meaning we will never be able to understand the violence in the biblical text (or any other document for this matter) as a political and moral phenomenon *in the world of the text and its authors*. In other words, we will undermine our ability to answer the question of divine violence as we have posed it—a question that must be addressed and answered in terms of the world(s) in which that violence was first problematized—the world(s) of the biblical text.

Insisting on the texts' historicity I will argue in what follows that the problem appeared early on, as demonstrated by the discontinuity between the biblical configurations of divine violence and those shared by readers of the canonized text in late antiquity, like Philo, Paul, and Josephus and their followers. This does not mean, however, that the biblical configurations remained sealed in a pre-Hellenist Judean culture. When we complete their reconstruction, it will be possible, albeit in a sketchy manner, to grasp the recurrence of these configurations in the modern European states that have become the contemporary universal form of political power. It will also become clear that paradoxically the configurations, which are relatively recognizable for a contemporary reader, have remained hidden in the biblical text because readers have given up grasping how alien it is. The clarity of the vision in which this recurrence will be grasped in the book's final chapter may be nothing more than that of a daydream, but its allure will be strong enough, I hope, to invite readers to a new path of inquiry.

LITERAL READING AND THE BIBLICAL LANGUAGE OF VIOLENCE

The clearest indication of a discursive break between biblical and postbiblical texts belongs with the Hebrew Bible's major protagonist. He assumed many figures and was called by many names but all too often appeared or was conceived as the architect and driving force of the story, the writer of some of the scripts and the director of many of the dramas, the one who proclaims the law, the one to whom all prayers and requests are addressed. In many of the stories, certainly in the Pentateuch, this is a protagonist whose overwhelming presence could be sensed. His dreadful proximity was often tangible and transforming, and his speech was sometimes heard with no mediation. The disappearance of this God was a slow process that began in the Hebrew Bible itself. A distance grew, his nonmediated presence diminished, his nonmediated words ceased to be heard, and hyperbolically metaphoric depictions of his abstract qualities multiplied.

The Hebrew Bible says very little about *what* God is ("Yahweh is one") but is preoccupied with *who* he is ("I am Yahweh, your God, who . . ."). Postbiblical, Jewish, and Christian writings were split over the second question and became gradually more interested in the first, which they answered in radically different ways. When the question "*dignus* or *indignus*" (worthy or unworthy) with re- spect to God and his violence could be pronounced (by Tertullian, at the begin- ning of the third century CE, in his polemic with Marcion and rejection of the latter's claim that the God of the Old Testament is evil),[68] it was only because the abstractions and distancing had long taken over and God had assumed a new cluster of qualities, which a question like this must assume. As if to counter this tendency, rabbinic midrash indulged in unabashed anthropomorphic legends. As far as biblical texts are concerned, however, both the abstract figure of a tran- scendent, omnipotent, benevolent, or omniscient God and the midrashic figures of an all-too-human, caring, and compassionate king and father are anachronis- tic. Assigning him to a realm of his own where he surveils (always from above, of course) the division of human affairs into distinct "spheres" obfuscates the reader's ability to reconstruct (that is, imagine and critically evaluate) the violent scenes in which he was involved. Violence is a messy business, and God, however distant he was when his forces hit, must have been imagined as somehow taking part in that mess. At the same time, neither his otherness—however he appeared, he was always other than human, even when first encountered in human dis- guise (for example, Gen. 32:25–31; Jud. 6)—nor his lethal zeal could be ignored. The biblical authors who questioned God's use of extreme violence could ask for more of it, not only for less.[69] It did not occur to them to doubt the literal sense of phrases like "Yahweh of armies (or hosts)" or wonder whether such a title fits with their notion of God's character. The reason, I dare to assume—and this is a "metaextrapolative" assumption—is that these authors did not deprive God from a place in and an access to the myriad of human relations. Some of the Bible's protagonists could question the concrete presence of God in their midst in a specific time and place but did not count such a presence as the end of a world and an opening to another.[70] Even when he was assigned with "a dwelling place in the heavens" (e.g., 1 Kings 8:49; 2 Chron. 6:21, 30, 33), he was still fully responsible for causing or preventing every scourge on earth (1 Kings 8:37) and for the triumphs and losses his people endured in their wars (1 Kings 8:46–47). The difficulties that ancient Jewish, pagan Greek, and Christian readers had with everything that seemed to contradict their view of the biblical God (that he created evil, changed his mind, let the Israelites take Egyptian property on their way out of Egypt, or let his prophet kill dozens of young children)[71] generated various interpretive methods. These include allegory; creative midrash; a search for esoteric, hidden meanings; or simply a sort of dismissive derision. When taken together, they signal a dramatic discursive break that directly affected God as an *object* of discourse, that is, a radical shift in what could be said about him or how he could have appeared and been envisioned.[72] Only when aided by these hermeneutic, rhetorical, and logical devices could pious readers entertain stories about the ways God used to mingle among humans. Within the new discursive milieu, the filter provided by these hermeneutic devices was necessary for handling texts that "showed" close-up pictures of God and put his violence on (literary) display.

The break, which was probably a result of the encounter with Hellenist philosophers' critiques and reinterpretation of Greek mythology, was already discernible in some Second Temple Jewish writings that introduced allegorical readings of biblical narratives and became prominent in the works of Philo of Alexandria at the beginning of the first century CE.[73] Philo's sophisticated use of allegory turned many biblical narratives into philosophical parables and was part of a concerted effort to reconcile a perfect and transcendent God with the mess of the human condition portrayed in the biblical texts. Violence, always a key element in that human mess, served biblical God as a common medium of interaction with humans, and it had to be allegorized to let the new, idealized figure of God appear. The heretic Marcion was controversial among Christians who read or heard about him because he insisted on literal readings of the Old Testament God, which undermined the character of the God imagined and promised by contemporary Christian thinkers. Marcion's insistence on God's evil and his rejection of allegorical readings that could explain away his outpouring of violence were two sides of the same coin. The reluctance of *our* contemporary scholars (like those we will encounter in the next chapter)[74] to study divine violence and follow it as it is depicted in the biblical text (that is, before the discursive break) is testimony to the lasting effects of that break and of the hermeneutic devices used to divert attention away from God's tangible presence among humans in general and his violence in particular. Whether driven by theological interest or by "reason alone," these scholars have all fallen prey to a secularizing process that, if it did not kill God with Nietzsche, has certainly distanced him from the world of humans. God has been relegated to a metaphysical sphere of pure transcendence or to one of myth and religion, and these often seem to be the only legitimate contexts available for scholars who want to talk about him. Once placed in the realm of "religion," divine violence as the Bible portrays it has already been obfuscated. To understand the Hebrew Bible and its God(s), one must stay with his violence, bringing it down to earth, following it in the domains where it issued forth, among the people who lived under its shadow.

The biblical configurations of violence seem so foreign to us not because of the violence employed, its means and effects, but because of the radical change that the main figure who authored, authorized, and commanded it underwent. It is not the descriptions of the drowning, the burning, the slashing of the flesh, not even of the earth that opened its mouth that seem untranslatable; it is not there that a sense of anachronism lies. When reading these descriptions, we should learn to stay with the violence (in our sense of this term) that transpires, and for this one must first stay close to the text and follow its referential arrow—that is, try to imagine the world described in it—before looking anywhere else. And we should always remember to figure out what God's role was in the spectacular or slow unfolding of that violence. For without him things could easily become all too familiar.

Let us recall here a pattern that characterizes many biblical narratives: a description of an abrupt and immense violent strike, followed by the establishment of its ritualized memory, which, in its turn, determines how the violence is to be represented for years to come. The paradigmatic scenes (the first murder, the destruction of Sodom and Gomorrah, the drowning of the Egyptians in the Sea of Reeds, the destruction of Jerusalem) come with their "memory capsules" that structure the way one experiences violence and misrecognizes its patterns in one's own time. The study of the periodic, ritualized reciting of violent scenes in the collective memory and the various political and ideological uses of this memory has become popular of late, but for us it is a trap that must be avoided. A collective memory of violence so far removed from the "original scene" obstructs access to the phenomenology and logic of the violence unfolded there.

We have only textual records of biblical violence, and no text, especially no canonized text, can be conceived, "in itself," as completely bounded and separated from its intertextual network and the histories of its reception. Yet this is what we must strive to do—we must separate the "original scene" and its biblical wake from their manifold later receptions. For us, the closest we can get to this scene is to read its description in the earliest extant text. The fact that this text is neither original nor homogenous should not obscure its distinction from later revisions, borrowings, commentaries, midrashic interpretations, prayers, and so forth. The boundary between the text that became part of "the Scriptures" and the history of its reception is hard to draw, especially since it is often already erased in the biblical corpus, due to the many layers of which it consists. But if we do not want to read the violence in Egypt through the perspective offered by the Passover Haggadah at this or that Seder table (and study the countless differences among these numerous tables) or if we do not want to read the massacre that followed the rite of the golden calf through the perspective offered by contemporary atrocities of so-called religious fundamentalists, we are drawing that boundary anyway. We should be prepared to draw it properly.

But how can we stay with the violence depicted in the Hebrew Bible if we come to the text with our own contemporary concept of violence (presented here as an Americanized blend of European streams of thought, with a strong Israeli flavor)? We need a biblical term that is at least "partially congruent with the way 'violence' and 'to act violently' is used in contemporary American English."[75] The biblical lexeme *ḥamas* (חמם) comes close to this.[76] It occurs eight times as a verb and sixty times as a noun, covering a wide range of violations, including destructions and damage, theft, stealing, and bloodshed. The words first appear in Genesis to designate the evil deeds of the flood generation (6:11, 13), and many of its other occurrences capture the intimate link between the use of brute force and the invocation of (in)justice, the crossing of a threshold, excess, or the transgression of the law. This link between force and injustice is most explicit in the idiomatic phrase *za'aq ḥamas*, which literally means the vocal expression of a moral outrage, an outcry in front of an evil generated by force. The phrase appears three times, each time with a different verb designating a slightly different vocal expression—a cry, a shout, or a scream—of outrage.[77]

However, the semantic field that permits an intimate link between the use of force and moral outrage is a bit more complicated. The idea can be phrased in a variety of ways without using the term *ḥamas*. Indeed, when the evil of the wrongdoing is great, the outcry could come out of the evil deed itself, as happened in Sodom and Gomorrah, when the people's offense was so great that it reached God and interpellated him "to go down and see" the extent of "the destruction they have dealt" (Gen. 18:20–21).[78] Nonetheless, *ḥamas* may occur as one among many ways to generate evil and injustice, some of which rely on the use of force (hence modern violence) and others on lies and deception. Jeremiah

(22:3) places *ḥamas* somewhere between cheating and bloodshed, while the prophet Zephaniah (1:9)—places it alongside deception.[79] A passage from Isaiah (59:6–8) captures this polysemy well:

> What they make are deeds of **vice** (*aven* אָוֶן), and the work of *ḥamas* in their palms. Their feet run to **evil**, and hurry to **shed innocent blood**: their devisings, devisings of vice, **wrack and ruin** (*shod vashever*) upon their paths. The **way of peace** they **do not know**; and there is **no justice** (*mishpat* מִשְׁפָּט) where they go. They make their courses **crooked**—who trade on them **knows not peace**.

As a whole, the cited passage stands for the tenuous relationship between the harming act and the moral outrage. In this sense, it captures an essential aspect of violence's contemporary conceptual configuration. Isaiah needs a few verses and a set of closely related terms to express this. But, as we have seen, that relation may also be designated by "*ḥamas*" when the word stands alone. *Ḥamas* appears in moments of iniquity, evil, the shedding of innocent blood, wasting and destruction, and veering one from a straight path. In such a cluster of partly overlapping terms, the use of force, as well as deception, are associated with injustice and, implicitly, through the prophet's speech act, with an appeal to justice and law (often contracted in the Hebrew *mishpat*). *Ḥamas* may be translated as "violence" in this passage, but its resonance with "crooked [or twisted] path" cannot be overlooked. The clear line separating lying and swindle from the use of force in the modern concept of violence is not respected in biblical Hebrew. When *ḥamas* is rendered as "violence," the inherent link between violence and deceit suggested by the word is lost in translation.

There are at least two additional serious problems with accepting "violence" as a straightforward translation of *ḥamas*. First, biblical Hebrew is rich in terms that describe all kinds of what we would understand today as violent acts, without necessarily clustering them under one concept.[80] The metonymic use of *ḥamas* for designating the entire cluster is rare and indecisive, and, as we saw, it would include lying and deception. Second, each and every occurrence of *ḥamas* is a case of injustice, an unjustifiable use of force or words. The term never describes a justified use of force or a use of force whose justification is still in question. *Ḥamas* is a form of injustice generated by violence or deceit; when the term is used, the act's justification is no longer in question. Violence, in our strict sense of the term, is a use of force that calls forth and questions claims for justice and legality, but the injustice or illegality of an action may be still undecided. In this sense, violence is not *ḥamas*.

This is probably the reason why God's massacres, inflictions, plagues, famines, or abandonment of the Israelites are never called *ḥamas* by biblical narrators. The same goes for bloodshed perpetrated in his name, on his behalf, by zealots like Phinehas and Elijah or in the course of a sanctioned war when the genocidal ban must be enforced.[81] Only once is *ḥamas* used by a victim of divine violence, Job, who uttered the word, yearning to be corrected: "Know, then, that God has undone me, and encircled me with His net. Look, I scream *ḥamas* and I am not answered, I shout and there is no justice" (19:6–7). And even in Job's outcry, *ḥamas* can be read as injustice, or outrage, as Alter has it, not as violence, and it is only one in a long list of terms that describe Job's devastation, humiliation, loneliness, and alienation.

Together the two incongruities between "violence" and "*ḥamas*" expose a distinct characteristic of the biblical language describing violence in our sense of the term. It is one bifurcated between divine violence (and violence perpetrated on God's behalf) and all other kinds of human violence, and *ḥamas* is the mark of the split. Both God and humans may kill and destroy, but only humans commit *ḥamas*. It is a human, all-too-human injustice or evil, generated by force or deception, and it is emphatically used to characterize the gravest offenses that justified the most extreme forms of divine violence (Gen. 6:11–13). As far the narrators are concerned, God never deceives or uses his might unjustly, and the same goes for his human enablers, the zealots who brutally enforce God's will. Even if wrathful or zealous, God and his faithful delegates never commit an act of *ḥamas*.

God is never found to be unjust, but the Hebrew Bible is not Pollyannaish, even when God is concerned. Tacitly the Bible reflects—or invites its readers to reflect—on the violence of its God(s) whenever the redactor leaves traces of conflicting accounts of an event involving divine violence (for example, Num. 13–14, 25). By virtue of telling the story differently, and without ever accusing God of using force unjustly, the biblical authors or redactors created openings for problematizing God's use of force. God himself might question the zealots who kill in his name.[82] More explicitly, humans may question his use of lethal force. This does not happen frequently, but when it happens the dissenting voice comes from God's most obedient and trustful disciples. Abraham does this in his negotiation with God over the number of righteous people whose existence in Sodom and Gomorrah would justify the plan to wipe out the two cities: "Will you really wipe out the innocent with the guilty? . . . Will not the Judge of all the earth do justice?" (Gen. 18:23–25). Moses is more diplomatic when he twice questions God's plans for genocide (Ex. 34:5–9; Num. 14:13–19), and Jeremiah dares to "speak against" him and articulates boldly the contradiction between his righteousness and the prosperity of the wicked (12:1–3).

As for Job, the book as a whole questions divine justice. "Though in the right I can't make my plea, I have to entreat my own judge . . . the blameless and the wicked he destroys, if scourge causes death in an instant, He mocks the innocent's plight" (9:15, 22–23). When God answers Job from the whirlwind (9:38–41), he never bothers to explain or justify Job's awful fate. Hiding behind the rhetorical display of his superior, spectacular power, he simply proclaims justice as humanly incomprehensible. God's ways, including his violence, are beyond mortal reasoning, so says God. It is only because Job accepts this incomprehensibility that he decides to "recant and repent" (42:1–5). As long as he demands reasons for becoming a victim of divine violence, the wretched righteous man could still desperately "cling to [his] innocence," as his wife remarks incredulously and impatiently when she asks him to "curse God and die" (2:9). The book creates a *différend* between Job's demands for justification and God's insistence on its incomprehensibility, which only power can bridge.[83] Even if one sides with God, one cannot forget Job's outcry and demands for explanations.

Questioning God's use of force does not necessarily mean condemning his violence. In the verses just quoted Jeremiah is asking "to draw [the wicked] out like sheep to the slaughter, set them aside for the day of killing" (12:3). The crucial point from our perspective is that even when it comes to God, and even though God's righteousness is presupposed, the use of force is placed in an unsettled relation to law and justice: "Righteous are you, Yahweh, when I dispute with you, yet my brief [or 'charges'] I will speak against you" (12:1). This fact has two important and related implications. First, it means that even without a fully congruent term for translating the contemporary "violence" into biblical language, our use of the term is not inadequate and is not forced on the text. Harmful use of force calls for justification, even if God is involved and even when he refuses to provide it. The use of harmful force is expected to be authorized and justified, and if it is not, it needs to be censured and rebuked. This basic aesthetic of violence,[84] which knots the sensual, most painful experience with the invocation of justice and law and makes this invocation part of one's experiences at the violent scene, was active among the prophets and the narrators of the Bible's historical accounts. Understanding how this aesthetic of violence was active with respect to divine violence is necessary for explaining how the extreme violence that the Bible attributes to God could be legible within the world constructed by and in the text.

The second implication of those moments of questioning of divine violence left by the Bible's authors and redactors is even more significant. Clearly, divine violence is more often justified in the Bible than it is questioned. But that God's use of force *could* even be presented as a problem is a decisive indication of the proper context for studying divine violence. The space in which an authorized use of force can be questioned is a political space, and God, who authorizes the use of force, exercises it as a political power.

The world in which divine violence was exercised was one in which God acted as a ruling power, assumed or sought recognition for his authority, and used violent means to enact his plans. His violence was inherently political because it needed justification and could have been questioned in public; his subjects' violence was political either because he commanded and directed it or because it was carried out against his will or laws and hence considered rebellious. The problematization of his use of force could always be suppressed, but once this suppression was recorded, the problematization was recorded with it, thereby politicizing his repressive power. Job, unconvinced by his four pious friends, challenged God as long as he could: "Far be it from me to declare you right, till I breathe my last I will not renounce my virtue. To my rightness I cling, I will not let go" (27:5–6). Then God silenced him, as many sovereigns, having the right of the last word, do. But many readers of Job kept the text, and Job's questions with it, open till this day.

For us, staying with God's violence means staying in the space opened by Job's questions without, however, repeating the questions themselves. Job's courage is admirable, but his questions are not mine. God is not my missing interlocutor but the central figure (in fact, a collective name for a set of figures) of a theopolitical imagination to which the Book of Job and the entire biblical corpus more broadly attribute the use of extreme violence. Job asked "why." "Why do you hide Your face and count me your enemy?" (13:24). Why did God use his force the way he did? Job looked for reasons that would justify his violence or for an admission of the wrong committed. This book asks: How was divine violence exercised? What were its configurations? How was it articulated in biblical discourse? Violence's reasons and justification will be considered here as but one aspect of the event of violence and its mode of being, and not necessarily—certainly not always—the most important one. Framing the question in this way, the book further deviates from Job's dissenting voice. The question is introduced against a long tradition of scholarly interest in divine rule, which, while being interested in God as a political persona and an object of a theopolitical discourse was symptomatically oblivious to God's violence in general and to the phenomenal aspects of this violence in particular.

2

THEOCRACY: THE PERSISTENCE
OF AN ANCIENT LACUNA

THEOCRACY, WITH AND BEYOND FLAVIUS JOSEPHUS

Throughout the Bible, God is recognized as the supreme ruling power, a lord, a king, the judge of all the earth, and the people who accepted him as their God saw themselves as subjects and slaves (*avadim*) under his rule.[1] Divine violence is an element and aspect of this rule and must be read politically in all its manifestations, even when the documents are poor in details. This does not exclude considerations of God's temper, jealousy, and uncontrolled rage and of human personality complexes projected back onto God. What may seem from a psychologist's point of view like an overflow of rage due to loss of control should, from a political point of view, still be acknowledged as a specific manner of ruling. When wrath, jealousy, or grace are associated with the way a ruling power uses its force, they are not merely personal traits but manners of claiming, expressing, and enforcing authority and sometimes means of governance too.[2]

The reports about divine rule are not different in this respect from the reports on ancient tyranny or modern liberal democracy. The reconstruction of the ideal type is likewise indifferent to the question whether the chronicles are true historical accounts or mythological fantasies. A form of rule, the regime formation, is reconstructed on the basis of these chronicles of ruling and governance, but, being an abstraction or an ideal type, it should be clearly distinguished from them. The chronicles are used for reconstructing the form of rule, which, in its turn, must be presupposed, however vaguely, for making sense of the chronicle. Since many of the chronicles are concerned with divine violence, tracing divine violence is both legitimate and necessary for interpreting divine rule. The hermeneutic circle is unavoidable here.

The first thinker who presented divine rule as one form of rule, or one *politea* among others, was the first century CE Judean historian Flavius Josephus. A brief look into his concept of theocracy will help shape my own. It will also show that at the very moment the concept of divine rule appeared, divine violence exited the scene.

Following the Greek names of other political regimes, like "democracy" or "aristocracy," Josephus called divine rule *theocracy*, to help his Hellenist and Roman readers understand the kind of *politea* their empire had just vanquished. Josephus added God to the list of possible recognized rulers, which the Greek thinkers characterized according to their number and quality: the demos, the rich, the aristocrats, or the single monarch. Like monarchy and tyranny, theocracy too was based on a single ruler. Unlike those systems, theocracy was ruled by a deity, and its rulership was not despotic but ingrained in a system of just laws attributed to him. As a matter of historical fact, however, these rules were actually given to the ruled people by Moses, "our legislator." For Josephus, divine rule was a historical phenomenon and, like any other form of rule, established by a human being:

After the successful outcome of some great deeds, [Moses] naturally concluded that he had God as his governor and adviser. Having first come to the conviction that everything he did and thought was in accordance with God's will, [Moses] considered it as his prime duty to impress this notion on the masses; for to those who believe that God watches over their lives, do not allow themselves to commit any sin. . . . There are infinite varieties in individual customs and laws among mankind as a whole, but in summary one may say: some have **entrusted** (ἐτέρεφαν) the power of government [*politeuma*] to monarchies, others to the rule of the few [*dunasteia oligon*; oligarchy], others again to the masses. But our legislator [Moses] took no notice of any of these but instituted the government as what one might call—to force an expression—a "theocracy," **ascribing** (άναθείς) to God the rule and power (*ten archen kai to kratos*) and, **persuading** everyone to look to him as the cause of all good things, both those that are common to all mankind, and those that they themselves received when they prayed in difficulties, and that neither any deed nor anything that anyone thought in private could escape his attention. He represented Him as single and uncreated and immutable through all eternity, more beautiful than any mortal form, known to us by his power, but as to what he is like in essence—unknown.[3]

Josephus, it should be clarified right away, cannot guide us in our reading of the Hebrew Bible. While the latter portrays more than one figure of God (hence more than one theocracy), none of them resemble Josephus's God. By granting Moses the power of legislation, stewardship in war, and care for every Israelite through their journey in the wilderness,[4] Josephus relieves God of the duties of human governance and presents him as the ruler and cause of the entire universe and his sovereignty as provident and omniscient.[5] Adopting a Hellenized version of the Hebrew Bible's God, like Philo before him, Josephus already stood beyond the fault line of the discursive shift noted previously. In his discussion of biblical theocracy Josephus also avoids literal readings of passages that depict God and his actions as violent, thus obscuring and transforming his figure as a supreme ruler.

Despite all this, the text just quoted includes two insights that I find highly significant for our study. First, Josephus explicitly searched for a new word and concept to describe the Judean *politea*, which had just been dismantled by the Roman Empire. He did without such a term when writing his comprehensive account of Judean history, the *Antiquities of the Jews* (much of which is based on a carefully worked-out exegesis of the Bible).[6] There he uses other known Greek terms—hierocracy, aristocracy, or kingship—to describe various biblical regimes and their transformations, always emphasizing the importance of the regime's judicial component and ascribing the origin of laws to God.[7] Theocracy appears only in *Against Apion*, an apologetic text in which Josephus defends the reputation of the Judean *politea* and clarifies its distinct (and quite idyllic) structure. Josephus uses here the reflexive, meditative features of the apologetic genre to bring into relief the theopolitical thought that runs throughout his historical oeuvre[8] and presents not the historical but the original, purposefully and systematically idealized Judean *politea*. In naming this ideal type of *politea* a theocracy, Josephus presents God as the *differentia specifica* of this type of rule. Judean kingship, hierocracy, and aristocracy described in *Antiquities* would now appear as variations on or deviations from the rule of God.

Second, when he includes the Judean polity as a new member in the family of regimes known in the Hellenized world, Josephus inserts a tacit distinction between those already established and the one he introduces, which, he argues, precedes them all. The difference is subtle but clear: In the Hellenized world,[9] "the power of government" is "entrusted" (ἐτέρεφαν) to a certain known and concrete individual or group; in the Judean theocracy, "rule and power" are not "entrusted" but "ascribed" (or accredited) (ἀναθείς) by Moses (but initially neither by the people nor by the narrator) to God,[10] and this ascription involves "persuasion." God is not *entrusted* with power and authority by humans but is rather recognized as always already having such power and authority. The term ἀναθείς implies here what is already taking place, for Moses recognizes God through his success and from this infers that God is behind the laws that he, Moses, gave to the people. The attribution of the laws to God is an act of recognition in the double sense of this term—inward realization, the perception of something as existing or true, and outward acknowledgment of that which has been understood. Moses, the real author of the laws, attributes them to God, and the attribution is willingly shared by the people.

Furthermore, while in Greek cities, legislators sometimes "attribute[d] (ὑπο-τίθενται) their laws" to the gods,[11] these attributions were instrumental and made in bad faith. They had little to do with the cities' political regime and the real site of power in each and did not bear on the differentiation among their regimes.[12] In the case of the Judean polity, there was no power beyond the power attributed to God, embedded in his laws, and actualized by the people who learned and taught them, abided by them, and enforced them when they practiced the law. Moses instituted this form of government so the form itself could last when its founder is gone. Therefore, no real transition of power took place with the death of Moses or the death of the judges and priests who practiced the law after him.

Judean theocracy was sustained by the power of divine law alone, without recourse to divine violence. In *Against Apion*, Josephus does not invoke stories about God's direct intervention in human affairs. This becomes both unnecessary and impossible, since Josephus's God is already "a philosophers' god," a perfect being, and the cause for all good things, his laws included.[13] Because he found the laws he devised to be perfect, Moses believed them to have originated from God and managed to "implant that belief . . . in the [people's] descendants of all future generations."[14] He persuaded the people not only to accept the attribution of their laws to a perfect God; he made the constitution such that by its "very shape . . . *it was always employable by everyone.*"[15] The laws included a whole body of rites and practices that taught the laws and reinforced their memory together with their rationale and attribution, and these "practices and occupations, and all speech"[16] cultivated piety, a single virtue that included all others, and guaranteed the reproduction of the theocratic order. Virtuous, law-abiding Judeans were not only loyal to their constitution but ready to fight for it to the death.[17] Hence, *God ruled by the power of the people* who attributed to him Moses's laws and imagined him as the architect of their polity.

With these seemingly benign distinctions, Josephus gives his own nonbiblical version of the birth of biblical monotheism, while covering its story at the same time.[18] The Hebrew Bible never presents Moses as the party responsible for attributing rule and power to God or as the founder of the Judean polity. Josephus attributes the founding act to a human leader who attributes the constituted power to God, while the constituting power rests with the leader's persuasive talent. One miracle—a divine rule that comes into being through an act of self-constitution—is replaced by another, which is somewhat less mysterious—a lawgiver constitutes power and attributes it to another without taking any credit for himself.

Here as elsewhere, Josephus is clearly a postbiblical author. He does not presuppose what his account is set to explain (the attribution of power to God), as so many biblical stories do. Biblical stories of revelation, public as well as private, tend to tell of an encounter with God's agency, power, and authority, where these are already taken for granted and demonstrated, not explained or questioned. Once agency is properly attributed, it is immediately followed by the acceptance of its authority. From God's words to Abram, "go forth from your land and your birthplace" (Gen. 12:1), through Moses's encounter with the burning bush (Ex. 3:2) and the Mountain that was "all in smoke" as "Yahweh came down on it in fire" (Ex. 19:18), to "the sound of minute stillness" on Mount Horeb (1 Kings 19:12), for the biblical authors, the only question open is one of the proper recognition of a vision or speaking voice as God's. The first moment of an encounter is usually followed by an order, promise, or threat, which are never questioned, even when God's addressee tries to resist, negotiate, or evade the command, as Moses does near the burning bush (Ex. 3:11–4:17). In Josephus's account, however, God, who is not a speaking subject, emerges as an actor ("the cause of all good things") only through Moses's reflection on his success as a leader and a legislator.

Thus, in humanizing divine rule, Josephus encloses in a black box what, as a historian, he would have studied closely for other formations of power (where power is "entrusted" rather than "ascribed"). For the success of such a novel, unprecedented constitution and attribution of power calls for an explanation.[19] Moses—or anyone else, for that matter—could have succeeded in establishing a Jehovist theocracy only through a general acceptance, and the frequent reiteration of the *attribution* of power and authority to Yahweh in all matters of rule and governance, regardless of first impressions. In a world where power and authority were attributed to local chieftains and lords or to kings and emperors and where loyalty was demanded accordingly, the attribution of supreme authority and the origin of immutable laws to one, invisible God could not have occurred without a struggle. The process, which Assmann calls the "theologization" of ruling power and the law, must have been a laborious, contentious undertaking and could not simply have been a matter of "persuasion," as Josephus had it.[20] The attribution of power and authority was transferred to Yahweh (or Elohim) by a group of people who accepted—or were called to accept—him not only as their God but as their lord, king, and supreme judge. In other words, in the world Josephus describes, there must have been a significant and ongoing effort to instill this attribution in the governed subjects and make it seem "natural" or "self-evident." Such an effort would have demanded denial of other options that could undermine it and a radicalization that urged people to fight for their laws unto death.

This argument is not new. "The people are fickle," wrote Machiavelli in *The Prince*.

> It is easy to persuade them about something, but difficult to keep them persuaded. Hence, when they no longer believe in you and your schemes, you must be able to force them to believe. If Moses, Cyrus, Theseus and Romulus had been unarmed, the new order which each of them established would not have been obeyed for very long.[21]

Machiavelli was probably the first to write against the European tradition (which Josephus inaugurated) that celebrated divine laws and ignored the forces behind them. Emphasizing the teaching of the law, Josephus did not say much about the labor of unlearning the laws of others, whether of kings or gods, and about the violent oppression that must have been involved at the institution of theocratic rule and as long as it had lasted. Ascribing to Moses a success story, Josephus concealed a long history of violent struggle, without which his theocracy could not have taken place.

Note that the argument here is not historical. For this theocracy to make sense as *a real possibility* for Josephus's readers in Josephus's time, a struggle of the kind to which I allude here must have taken place *within the world portrayed by Josephus's utopic theocracy*.[22] Josephus makes the transfer of attribution explicit but allows its occurrence to remain as mysterious as the attribution itself. He conceives Judean theocracy as a form of rule dissociated from both human and divine violence and, as Flatto puts it, "does not explicitly address the manner in which God governs."[23] Moses managed to turn a group of freed slaves into the law's "good subjects" through a laborious education and a peaceful transformation of their theopolitical imagination, not through coercion. The interiorization of the law was sufficient to guarantee order and stability to the Judean polity. This idealized picture cannot be taken as a description of God's rule, not even of an ideal type of a theocratic regime extracted from the Bible. It is hard to believe that Josephus tried to do justice to the biblical text or to a postbiblical Judean history. Rather, Josephus seems to use the authority of the scriptures to construct an ideal type of theocracy that could be imagined as the best possible *politea* for the Judean community *after* the destruction and loss of Jerusalem, the temple, and the entire Judean polity.

Josephus's historical works were read by Christian scholars throughout the Middle Ages,[24] but his contribution to European political theory came later. In the late sixteenth and early seventeenth century, as the biblical "Hebrew Republic" was added to the classic Greek and Roman models of political systems, Josephus's work became a main source of inspiration for radical political thinkers, Calvinists, political Hebraists, and others.[25] I am interested in this moment of Josephus's reception here because his "black box"—that is, the story of a nonviolent emergence of a theocratic regime—survived the transmission intact and unopened. The ideal type, a regime formation where an idealized rule of law is attributed to God and functions without recourse to violence, surfaced after centuries during which it was missing from the political lexicon and the arsenal of political imagination. In the Netherlands, Petrus Cunaeus was the first to use *Against Apion* as a main source for studying the Hebrew Republic, and in his account of Moses as the legislator who attributed the laws to God he "follow[ed] Josephus' phrasing cunningly."[26] Soon after, it was Spinoza who knew better and seemed ready to debunk the legend. He communicated with some of the political Hebraists and used Josephus in his political reading of the Hebrew Bible, but his account of emergence of a Hebrew theocracy in chapter 17 of his *Theological-Political Tractate* reads like a critique of Josephus (whom Spinoza quotes elsewhere but not in that chapter).[27] In the chapter's title, Spinoza identified the biblical Hebrew Republic as a *"Respublica divina,"*[28] but instead of turning to Josephus he turned to Hobbes. He modeled his own version of biblical theocracy on the idea of the social contract in a state of nature, where every member freely transferred his rights to the divine sovereign while God's laws and commands became the laws of the republic. At the same time, like Machiavelli, Spinoza acknowledged the role that brute force played in cultivating God's good subjects. Yet he limited this role—and with it the true theocratic moment—to a brief instant:

> On this first appearance before God they [the Hebrews] were so terrified and so thunderstruck at hearing God speak . . . [so that] overwhelmed with fear, they went back to Moses, saying: "Behold . . . why should we die? For this great fire will surely consume us. . . . Go thou near therefore and hear all that our God shall say. And speak thou [not God] to us." . . . By this they clearly abrogated the first covenant, making an absolute transfer to Moses of their right to consult God and to interpret his decrees.[29]

God's saving power, that is, the crushing of the Egyptian oppressors, was essential for instilling in the ancient Hebrews the beliefs that He alone could save them, and by virtue of this conviction the covenant God made with them was "fixed and binding."[30] But the same mighty power was eventually responsible for replacing the first covenant with another, this time with Moses. Soon after entering the scene of the first covenant, God recedes into the background, and theocracy became an affair between Moses and the people. Thus, when Spinoza wanted to "explain in an orderly manner how the whole state was governed," he, just like Josephus, referred to the laws and their interpretation, to judges and priests, to the division of power among different human authorities, and to the transition of power without assigning God any active role.[31] Theocracy, for Spinoza, as much as for Josephus, was a regime in which everything was done in God's name and where using this name was the highest political asset but also how the presence of God was bracketed, as it was no longer needed or, in fact, possible. The real theocracy was actually only a mere opinion, "a matter of theory, not of fact."[32] The black box that seemed for a moment to be opening was sealed anew, now much more forcefully, by Spinoza's rationalist, materialist discourse.

Puzzled by Josephus's silence on the use of force in his theocracy, some contemporary scholars have suggested that Josephus described a religious phenomenon, not a historical political structure. As a political reality (at least in Josephus's time as a Judean citizen), the Judean theocracy, if there ever was one, relied on the policing force and the foreign policy of their Roman authority.[33] In other words, Josephus's theocracy in *Against Apion* should be freed from both textual and historical pretension and left to do its work as an idyllic, counterfactual construct of a theopolitical imagination, for only in that realm the rule of God could rest on the power of education and persuasion. After the crushing of the Judean rebellion, with the Roman Empire stretching over both geopolitical and temporal horizons, divine rule could rest on nothing else.[34] As a new figure in the Greek lexicon of regime formations, Josephus's theocracy was not a way to use the Hebrew Bible as a cluster of documents recording God's rule but, on the contrary, a perfect distraction that prevented this from happening. In fact, Josephus's account of the Judean *politea* is far more phantasmatic than the biblical accounts from which it diverts. Certain elements of this account are taken from the Bible—especially the Deuteronomic emphasis on Moses's role, the administration of justice, the teaching of the law, and the practice of memorizing the founding narratives of the people of Israel—but, and this will be significant for my argument, these elements do not amount to a reconstruction of the Deuteronomic theocratic vision; they are rather extracted and separated from it. Josephus cleansed the Deuteronomic vision of God's rule from all the traumatic memories of violence and from the great fear of its recurrence. As I will show in Chapter 5, these memories, fears, and threats had sustained Deuteronomic theocracy in ways that, for Josephus and later readers like Spinoza, became completely obstructed.

It is a sign of the enormous success of centuries of persuasion that, as people became accustomed to attribute power and rule to God, the attribution itself became transparent. When Josephus attributed this persuasion to a single man, Moses, he closed the history of persuasion until Machiavelli reopened it. Early modern political thinkers turned to the Hebrew Bible to find inspiration for new formations of power and rule, but the violence that accompanied the persuasion was either ignored or ascribed to humans, not to God.[35] As Hammill notes, apropos Machiavelli, "divine violence is only rhetorically divine."[36] And this is still the case today, with the recent resurgence of interest in the political theology of the Hebrew Bible and the Jewish political theory indebted to it.[37]

I have dwelled briefly on Josephus's notion of theocracy less because he was the first to coin the term and more for his role in cleansing it from divine violence and obstructing any serious political consideration of its depiction in the Hebrew Bible. Besides this ongoing obstruction, there is little the tradition that followed Josephus can teach us about the place of violence in God's rule. Instead of following this tradition, I will demonstrate its long shadow by examining three contemporary works written by scholars with a keen interest in the way violence is depicted in the Hebrew Bible.

THE BLIND SPOT: THREE CONTEMPORARY READINGS OF BIBLICAL VIOLENCE

This section is a digression into the works of three scholars who approach the Bible equipped with distinct theoretical toolboxes and hermeneutic skills developed, unsurprisingly perhaps, outside the philological-historical field of Bible studies. All three combine, in very different ways, close readings with a synoptic point of view.[38] Despite this promising combination, and regardless of their different approaches, they all avoid analytic confrontation with the logic, rationale, and mode of operation behind God's use of lethal force. Regina Schwarz uses literary theory and psychoanalysis, Michael Walzer combines political theory and intellectual history, and Jan Assmann engages in Egyptology, the history of ancient religions, and the study of collective memory. They are all interested in violence and insist on understanding violence in the context of the psychological economy of the biblical protagonists; their political and theological imagination, political institutions, and cultic practices; and the system of meanings that sustain them.[39] In other words, they seek to relate the violence depicted in the Hebrew Bible to a world in which it could make sense, and they have at least two distinct worlds in mind—the world of the biblical authors and their own world. And yet, the lacuna they share is symptomatic of a long scholarly tradition that shies away from confronting divine violence altogether.[40]

I first follow Regina Schwartz's literary and psychoanalytic readings of biblical stories plagued by lethal identity politics, which she associates with the Bible's monotheist credo and program.[41] I then compare Michael Walzer's two political readings of the Bible and look at the way he deals with divine violence while searching for biblical politics in *In God's Shadow*.[42] Last I examine Jan Assmann's series of readings of the Hebrew Bible as a testimony for the emergence of monotheism and the legacy of its violent propensity.[43] These works have often served me as guides, and my critical engagement with this sample of works, which cannot do justice to their richness and complexity, should be read as a tribute, not only as critique. Here I am interested however not in their hermeneutic and theoretical insights but in the blind spot they share. The boundaries of this blind spot demarcate the uncharted territory this book is set to investigate.

Regina Schwartz

Regina Schwartz's *The Curse of Cain* (1997) has been for many years a model for "postmodernist" writing on the Bible. Seamlessly combining a blend of psychoanalysis, poststructuralist literary analysis, and feminist critique, Schwartz proposes a sophisticated theory of biblical violence. She reads the Bible as a literary text and reads the literary text as a testimony to a mostly repressed and displaced set of emotions involved in a specific type of antagonistic identity formation. This identity formation, Schwartz claims, is responsible for the kind of violence that populates most (or the most remembered) biblical stories and vibrates throughout the history of their reception. Introducing the book, she states bluntly:

> This book is about violence. It locates the origin of violence in identity formation,
> arguing that imagining identity as an act of distinguishing and separating from others,
> of boundary making and line drawing is the most frequent and fundamental act of
> violence we commit. Violence is not only what we do to the Other. It is prior to that.
> Violence is the very construction of the Other. . . . Outside by definition but always
> threatening to get in, the Other is poised in a delicate balance that is always off balance
> because fear and aggression continually weight the scales. (5)[44]

This type of identity formation works by way of a series of negations of an individual or a group designated as "the Other," namely, separation, exclusion, denigration, denial of any resemblance, refusing contact, abolishing shared grounds and conditions of coexistence, targeted killings, and wholesale elimination. When an identity is thus constructed, it is conceived "in violence" from its inception, and the violence is both discursive (cutting discrete identities off from whatever is not properly theirs) and somatic (cutting bodies and destroying lives and conditions of living). Antithetical identity, which is set against an imaginary Other, is at one and the same time the origin "of the laws protecting men from violence against one another" and what "sets in motion a cycle of violence that no legislation can hold" (37). The construction is imaginary and discursive, but the worlds in which it is put to work are full of bloodshed.

The Bible is a testimony to this bloodshed not because the recorded events "really happened" (Schwartz declines to entertain this question) but because the Bible was put to work in the service of different powers, which imitated biblical violence and replicated its logic. The story of Canaan's conquest and all its horrors, for example, is "a wild fantasy"; the real issue is not its authenticity but the effect of telling this story about a people created "through the massive displacement and destruction of other peoples," taking their lands and slaughtering them "under the banner of divine will" (57).

But this is not the whole story (we would not need the Bible if it were), for the violence involved in this antagonistic construction of identity would not be chronic, systemic, and catastrophic as long as there are only two parties to the game. Antagonism between the Self and its Other is neither enough for deciphering biblical violence nor particular to the Bible. It takes a triangular configuration between Self, Other, and a third party that sets the lethal relation in motion and guarantees its relentless reproduction. This third party, either God or a father, is an authority, a source of terror and protection, whose attention, love, and support are given to some and denied to others. In the history of the Bible's reception, these two figures, God and father, would later be joined or replaced by others—the nation, republic, constitution, or flag (xi, 12–13)—but this would not change the basic scheme: an antagonistic identity formed under the stricture of an authority that both constructs and incarnates a "metaphysical scarcity . . . a finite supply of whatever" (33), including the scarcity of identity itself. The acts, efforts, or events of construction are repressed and denied. The effect is an imagined scarcity that is conceived as "metaphysical" (or, one may say, "transcendental"), and the negative, exclusionary relations driven from it are presumed inevitable. Schwartz is not concerned with real scarcity and its impact in the form of competition and rivalry. The scarcity of property in the biblical stories is rather "perceived" so as to "[necessitate] the distinctions: inheritors and outcasts, kin and nonkin," us and them, leading one to believe that "at the top of the power heap" there is room "for only one" (106).[45]

Insecurity, jealousy, greed, guilt, and anxiety are built into this configuration from the very beginning. And desire too. Schwartz follows a mosaic of stories, metaphors, and themes to reconstruct a filial logic that dominates the text and the history of its reception: a father or a God, afraid of his sons or his servants,[46] commanding love and respect but also obsessed with competition and betrayal. He secures his superior position by setting one son against another or one group of servants against others, forging the identity of the one through the exclusion and negation of the others. This is how it was from Cain and Abel to Judea's exile, from Noah and his sons to David and his, from the Fathers to the prophets, from the rejection of Esau to the banishment of the "foreign women" by Ezra. Violence between the inheritors will never end; it can only be displaced. When scarcity is metaphysical and identity is established against the Other, violence is systemic and its replication unavoidable. The inevitable betrayal of the strict separation commanded by the antagonistic relation to the Other will ensure—and also justify—the curse and punishment meted out to the elected and rejected alike.

Ham, Noah's son, discovered his father drunk and naked in his tent. Sober again and furious, Noah cursed Ham's son, Canaan: "The lowliest slave shall he be to his brothers." (Gen. 9:18–27). To Schwartz, this story serves as a key text for establishing the filial logic of the Bible, and in doing so, she ingeniously adopts and subverts Freud's speculative reading of Moses's murder in *Moses and Monotheism*.[47] She offers a daring correction to the ur-myth of psychoanalysis: a Noah complex instead of the Oedipus complex, where desire and mutual fear between men (father and son) replaces a son's desire for his mother and fear of his father.[48] From Noah through Abraham, to Sinai and beyond, the covenant is the legal articulation of metaphysical scarcity. It establishes the necessity of and quest for an antagonistic identity and at the same time sows the seeds for failure, betrayal, and disaster. It was never a covenant among equals. Scared of the rivalry of sons or subjects, the father/God establishes his authority through the rivalry he creates among them by introducing a covenant with one privileged (elected) individual or people. Sooner or later, the elected will fail to remain faithful to their superior or become hated by their peers, and this hatred will perpetuate the violence.

The scarcity of love, attention, protection, and other resources, and the preference of one over the other, are two sides of the same coin. "When everything is in short supply, it must all be competed for . . . In many biblical narratives, the one God is not imagined as infinitely giving, but as strangely withholding" (xi). In other stories, it is the father who withholds—his love, as Abraham or Jacob did; his blessing, as Isaac did; or his crown, as David did. The structural analogy between the partisan father and the God of election, where the claim of the third party (God or father) for absolute exclusivity is the condition of the violent, antithetical identity formation, runs throughout Schwartz's book. But more is at stake here than a mere analogy between theological and kinship relations.

First, if "monotheism is a myth that forges identity antithetically—against the Other" (16), then patriarchy is the kinship structure that could best fit it, providing it with ever more occasions for articulation and reaffirmation (117). More importantly, with Marx, Nietzsche, and Freud, Schwartz inverts the direction of creation, suggesting that an ancient patriarchal society created a God that claims exclusivity for himself, instilling his servants with antagonistic identities forged in a double-blind process. The "Noah complex," she writes, turns "love/hate for the father" into "an intolerable guilt . . . *a guilt projected onto an omnipotent monotheistic deity* who punishes" (115, emphasis mine). A dominating father who fabricates a scarcity of resources (thereby introducing competition) and becomes the object of love/hate or fear/desire is the origin of monotheism. Projection is its mechanism, and a punishing God is its result. Listing a series of forms that scarcity takes, Schwartz concludes that it "imposes patriarchy . . . monotheism . . . and transcendence," all of which are designed "to enforce the separation between the Creator and his Creation" (116).

Scarcity is the original sin in this story, and its construction is responsible for one sort of plenitude—that of violence, suffering, and loss.[49] Now let us look more closely at the fate of divine violence in *The Curse of Cain*. It is mentioned rather briefly as Schwartz concludes her exposition of the "Noah complex":

> A regime of monotheism that presumes scarcity [yields narratives that] tell of God punishing Man with mortality . . . crushing man's heavenward ambitions . . . and punishing . . . the sons of God with mortality for cohabiting with the daughters of men.[50] . . . The entire nation of Israel is punished . . . at the instigation of an angry Father. (115)[51]

No episode of *divine* violence is read closely enough to support Schwartz's general scheme of human violence, shame, and guilt. All we have is the general formula: "a guilt projected onto an omnipotent monotheistic deity" (115) resulted in a punishing (hence violent) God. No variety is allowed in this formula, no way to distinguish between punishing Israel and destroying its neighbors, between an outpouring of wrath and a calculated execution of a plan, between threats of destruction and its actual happening. When approaching scenes of divine violence, Schwartz seems to look the other way. Noting the dreadful atmosphere in Sinai, as the covenant was "given amid a huge display of terrible power with the full fanfare of fire, brimstone, thunder, and lightning" (30), she is reminded of the moment in *The Wizard of Oz* when Dorothy exposes the Wizard as a simple hot-air balloonist from Kansas (30). Two cases where God inspired violence are examined briefly (2–4, 24), but neither places him as the main perpetrator. Schwartz is very interested in Noah but not at all in the flood. Other catastrophes are mentioned without any reference to their divine origin.[52] The plagues that terrorized Egypt and forced Pharaoh "to let [his, i.e., God's] people go" are recalled, but only to emphasize (correctly, of course) "the pivotal place of memory in the narrative" (151–52).[53]

There is something puzzling about a book on "the violent legacy of monotheism" that consists entirely in reading the Bible and that pays close attention to human violence—but never to the violence perpetrated by God. Was divine violence of a different kind? Schwartz does not say so, and anyway it would be hard to make such an argument, given that divine violence is considered a projection. She is interested in the figure of God not as an independent actor who perpetuates violence but only when scarcity, difference, and exclusion are ascribed to his preferences. That he uses extraordinary means of destruction unavailable to humans but also humans as a means and that sometimes he even acts like a violent human[54] have no bearing on these choices. More generally, the means of violence, so crucial for understanding violence's effects, are left outside the interpretative frame. The psychoanalytic attention to the phenomenology of violence is limited to a symptomatic reading, a reading *through* the violent acts, words, and gestures, a reading aimed at discovering the repressed mechanism that produced it. Divine violence, so it seems, is nothing but the amplification and projection of the mechanism that produces scarcity to generate antagonistic identity. But even if there is nothing in it beyond this projection, could we not learn something about antagonistic othering ("other gods"), rage, jealousy, the desire to be loved and recognized, or the construction of that imagined "metaphysical" scarcity by looking more closely at some of the scenes in which God is the major protagonist?

Throughout her exposition, Schwartz associates scarcity with the exclusivity of the father/God. Only one God should be recognized, and only one people are elected; only the father blesses, and only one child is blessed. Schwartz says that "all of those constructs of the One and the Many [that oppose it] . . . presuppose a kind of metaphysical scarcity" (33). But "metaphysical scarcity" neither presupposes nor implies oneness, for oneness is not the only way to conceive or manage it. When scarcity reigns, there could be less for everyone or a little more for a few; authority can be shared at the top while protection and provision, as well as precariousness and suffering, may be shared at the bottom. The Bible can provide us with examples not only of plenitude, which is the alternative sought by Schwartz,[55] but of plurality at the top: Abraham and Sarah together decide the fate of Hagar and Ishmael; Rebecca, Isaac's wife, helped Jacob undermine seniority among the couple's two sons; Jezebel shared Ahab's kingly power and murderous corruption; and even God deliberated with others (with "the sons of God . . . and the Adversary among them," Job 1:6–13) over the fate of Job. Ruling power and authority, whether in the family, nation, or the earth, can tolerate plurality without dissolving or stopping to generate scarcity, and scarcity may be a reason to replace this One with another.[56]

The origin of violence to which the Bible gives testimony is, therefore, an imaginary discursive configuration that links scarcity to oneness, or, rather, violence is linked to oneness through a particular construction of scarcity. Since scarcity does not yield oneness on its own, it must be the other way around: The claim for exclusivity and demand for oneness are specific ways to construct scarcity and justify it, and scarcity framed by claims for exclusivity turns out to be a terribly efficient way to replicate the authority of the one. But whence came the demands for oneness? The answer can be found neither in the Bible nor in Freud, but it may be found in the politics of the ancient Near East, which provided plenty of monistic authorities to draw from. The centralization of power in Egypt and Mesopotamia and its representation as supreme and far reaching did not yield monotheism (except under the short reign of Akhenaten) but did give rise to different sorts of monistic political imagination. Once authority was reimagined as an exclusive and divinely appointed oneness, the one embodying it sought to rule indefinitely. With one ruler at the top and a general scarcity of political authority, the imaginary scheme of antagonistic identity formation rooted in scarcity could find a fertile ground and enter the vicious circle with the One that presupposed it and disseminated it to perpetuate its rule.[57]

We must think about the ruler—father or God—in clear political terms, then. The One should be a self-constituting authority with a claim to the subjection of others, a will to power, specific modes of ruling, and even techniques of governance. Schwartz is not oblivious to the political context of the monotheistic or patriarchal One, but while she exposes and brilliantly analyzes the political dimensions of kinship and its entanglement with kingship, she is oddly silent about the politics surrounding and emanating from the divine monarch. Had she done so, she would have taken a close look at divine violence. By not engaging with a study of divine violence, she chose to ignore the logic of divine authority that allowed for or necessitated that violence and was supported by it.

It must be stressed that the reason for avoiding stories about God as a perpetrator cannot be related to the fact that God is considered to be nothing but a projection of the human imagination—in fact, all the subject positions in the scheme excavated by Schwartz are. In other words, one could extend her theoretical analysis to include divine violence without compromising the overall theoretical framework. The omission, we must conclude, in the spirit of Schwartz's reasoning, is symptomatic. As we will encounter similar omissions in the works of Jan Assmann and Michael Walzer, it will become evident that the myopia is a collective phenomenon.

Michael Walzer

Michael Walzer is a prolific and influential political theorist, a historian of political thought, and an engaged intellectual who has dedicated two monographs to the Hebrew Bible. In his early work *Exodus and Revolution*,[58] he reads the story of Israel's Exodus from Egypt "in the light of its political interpretations," which understood "the Exodus as we know it . . . as a liberation and a revolution—*even though* it is also, in the text, an act of God" (7, emphasis mine). Here is Walzer's framing, in a nutshell: Exodus has always been read in these political terms despite and not because of God's role in the drama. His presence in the text is an obstacle to a political reading, a sort of distraction, or at best some sort of a supplement. The thrust of the story, at least in some strand of its reception, lies with the people's progression from bondage to redemption.

Liberation and revolution both involve violence, just like Egyptian oppression and slavery did, and the Bible generously displays it, on both sides of the aisle. Walzer is interested in the violence of the oppressors, sorting out its physiognomy with evidence from the biblical texts and from its commentators, starting with ancient rabbinic Midrash. Pharaoh's oppression plays an important role in the history of readings that Walzer reconstructs, and he, for his part, explains how the revolutionary emancipation relies on correctly interpreting the pharaonic oppression as an injustice and moral scandal (40). He also traces ancient memories of this oppression in the progressive aspects of the biblical laws concerning slavery and wages to laborers (26–31). But when it comes to God's violence against Egypt, Walzer takes his distance. It is "in the text," so it must be accounted for, but it all comes down to one statement: "God is a greater warrior [than Pharaoh]" (32). For example, in Exodus 15:1, Miriam says of the defeated Egyptians, "horse and its rider He [God] hurled into the sea." About this, Walzer writes with a midrashic flavor that the horse-rider pair symbolizes Pharaoh's tyranny and that this "symbolism recurs throughout the Bible" (32). Were the chariots and horses only symbols to the biblical authors? Was Pharaoh's tyranny the only thing that was "hurled" or "pitched" (Ex. 15:4) into the sea? And if one insists on symbolic reading, what would the act of throwing tyranny (or a whole army) into the sea symbolize? Can the meaning of the symbol be read while ignoring the literal meaning of the signifier?

The recourse to symbolism at this decisive moment is revealing. Two kinds of violence portrayed in the Bible are discussed in *Exodus and Revolution*. The first is demonstrated by the Israelites' "crushing labor" [*'avodath parekh*] in Egypt, which can be traced back to some probable historical circumstances that would grant the interpreted text with an "effect of the real."[59] Like Schwartz, Walzer has no interest in establishing the truth of the biblical story, but he claims to know something about the world that inspired that story, about the violence of bondage and repression and its memories that persisted in the worlds of the story's ancient readers. The second kind of violence, perpetrated by God, only exists within the story. God destroyed the Egyptian army by himself (and Walzer spares us the details), but many political readers, he reminds us, drew from his triumph a call for humans to resist all tyrants (33). Their point was not to obey God or wait until he demonstrated his superior power but rather to imitate him in the struggle against oppression (33). The model for the historical struggle was a story about another struggle in which only one of the parties involved could have been read literally. The allegorical reading of divine violence in the history of emancipatory struggles frees Walzer of the need to question it in the world of the text.

There are no revolutions without a purge, and the Exodus was no exception. Walzer carefully reads the purge of the idolaters initiated after the Israelites worshiped a golden calf while waiting for Moses to return from the mountain, the place where God had recently revealed himself to the people and offered them a covenant. More than a month had passed since Moses left, and they already felt lost and were looking for a substitute for their missing leader (Ex. 32:1). Along with the sources he tracks, Walzer reads the following brutal episode mainly through the lens of the purge, "a summary justice . . . without warning and without judgement" (60), which loyal Levites executed on Moses's command (Ex. 32:26–27). He stresses that unlike the suppression of other cases of disobedience and transgression in the wilderness ("the murmurings"), this punishment was dealt by human hands.[60] And it is the history of much more recent revolutions, and of Machiavellian politics (32:58–61), that makes the brutality of the killings—of "each man . . . his brother and each man his fellow and each man his kin" (Ex. 32:27)—familiar and credible.

But there were other violent instances at the scene of the golden calf—a genocidal threat that Moses averted (Ex. 32:7–14), and later a plague, about which little is said (Ex. 32:34). Of this, Walzer mentions in passing the genocidal threat only to move quickly to Moses's rage, the smashing of the tablets, and his call for the purge (32:55–56); the plague is not mentioned at all. This omission is in line with the missing account of God's violence—feared, imagined, or actually perpetrated—when discussing other episodes: the manna, the twelve scouts, and the Sinai revelation. The erasure of divine violence is joined by the familiar claim that the Israelites entered freely into the covenant at Sinai, never questioning how their consent was obtained. "Slavery [to a human tyrant] is begun and sustained by coercion, while service [to God] is begun and sustained by covenant" (74). But how was the covenant itself sustained among mankind? Walzer limits the scope of his answer. He says that the text "poses a clear question of political violence and the agents of violence, and so it has been read for years"—or avoided for the same reason (61). Indeed, it is a serious question that centers on the motivation, justification, and limitation of the use of human violence against kin and neighbors when a lofty cause is at stake, a question about the cultivation of subjects capable of such violence. But isn't the invocation of God, his laws and threats, part of the discussion? For some of the readers Walzer follows, it certainly was.

In God's Shadow, a text Walzer published almost three decades after *Exodus and Revolution*, is a new political reading of the Bible. It is more comprehensive and ambitious and presents a marked revision in the way the author approaches his corpus.[61] The Bible is no longer read through the history of its reception,[62] and Walzer, who is still interested in "what the Bible's authors thought had happened," not in what "really happened," is free to ask these authors—not their later readers—how they interpreted what they thought had happened.[63] The most substantial difference between the books, however, is that now God has come to occupy center stage.

> What makes the literature of ancient Israel especially interesting, and worthy of close study, is that all this [instituting a new, exclusivist religion; bitter internal conflict; wars with other nations; disputes on authority, policy, and legislation; and more] takes place in the shadow of an omnipotent God. . . . How much room for politics can there be when God is the ultimate ruler . . . [and] for prudential decision-making in a nation that lives under divine command and divine protection? (x–xi)

The gist of Walzer's answer is: not much (xii–xiii). It is a very complex answer, though, for Walzer mines the entire biblical corpus and examines whatever he deems political: the covenants, codes of law, equality before the law, elements of a welfare state, kingship (with a certain role to the elders), the priestly elite, the prophets (as both critics and court intellectuals), seizure of power, international relations, and various cases of internal unrest and resistance. But wherever he turns, he finds that the biblical authors were uninterested in, indifferent to, or outwardly against "politics," both within and beyond the Israelite group. In fact, Walzer argues, there is no political theory in the Bible, since all forms of human power and institutions—kings, judges, elders, priests, and prophets—are over-shadowed by God's kingship, whether actual, desired, or feared.

At the center of the book and of the biblical politics it portrays, Walzer finds a void created by the shadow that the supreme sovereign casts over every sphere of human activity, and he insightfully delineates its contours. If biblical politics could take place, it was assumed, it is only *under* that shadow, which, by definition, left God outside the shadowed realm. The judge of all the earth cannot become a player in the political field; at most one can think about him as creating and severely limiting the conditions for the political existence of humans. This, however, is Walzer's presupposition, not something he learned from the text. I see no reason to accept this presupposition and exclude God from the political realm. We should be interested in the shadow itself no less than in what takes place under the shadow, which, after all, is formed by the way God rules over heaven and earth, or his own people. This shadow consists of the manner by which he governs, punishes, and protects his subjects; his tendency to resort to violence; and his modes of using it. For the people who imagined themselves living under God's shadow, this violence must have been part of the fabric from which it was made. But on this Walzer has little to say. God is said to be eternal and omnipotent,[64] and the origin of his shadow over human politics is allegedly transcendent or extraterrestrial. This understanding of God underlies everything Walzer says about divine rule and frames his reading: "the rule of the true Sovereign is not, properly speaking, political," his kingship was not thought politically, while human kingship was thought from a human perspective (xiv).[65] The Bible as a whole "is, *above all*, a religious book," but, Walzer adds, "it is *also* political" (xii, emphases mine). In other words, for the Bible, religion comes first, while politics are an aside, an "also," which somehow made its way and survived in the void created by God's shadow.

The Hebrew Bible never attributes omnipotence or transcendence to God, and much of what it tells about his actions may give us a clue why it does not.[66] Walzer, however, ascribes to God a figure that fits his modern-liberal perspective

and guides him as he categorizes, separates, and structures the hierarchy between religion and politics. In this imported framework, it is understandable
how he states, in the book's conclusion, that politics is "largely missing" from the
Bible due to "the religious culture itself, [to] the powerful idea of divine sovereignty" (202). The biblical texts, he contends (rightly), dedicate very little space
to popular participation or procedures of decision making and (this is questionable) are not interested in constructing ideal regimes (202, 205–6). In other
words, they are oblivious to what is crucial for politics and to the Western tradition of political theory. In short, because "the central concerns of political philosophy as the Greeks understood it . . . were never central in Israelite thought"
and because God "did not decree a politics" (206)[67] there was no politics under
God's shadow.

The book ends where it begins: at the antagonistic intersection of divine sovereignty and human political culture. For a moment, one could hope that once
God was recognized as "the true Sovereign," the *sense* of his excessive violence
would be redeemed or at least its senselessness acknowledged. But according
to Walzer, "the doctrine of God's earthly kingdom . . . is an apolitical doctrine:
it denies autonomy to political actors," and the use of his mighty hand, whether
to help the Israelites or to crush them, "represents a loss of political control" by
human agents (66). Humans may still call upon God's mighty hand and even get
its help if they follow God's laws, but when put to action in the realm of human
affairs, God's might always made humans' actions and virtues redundant. Hence,
God is not recognized as a political actor, and so his use of force is not examined.

Walzer follows Martin Buber's model of divine rule,[68] which Buber drew from
the Book of Judges and the opposition created there between hereditary kings
and temporary judges. Walzer agrees that this opposition "is not, until the end
[of that book] at least, wholly unattractive" and acknowledges that "the idea that
God's rule is better than the rule of kings survives the highly problematic experience of divine governance" (60). One may wonder whether it survived precisely
because divine governance and its problematics were excluded from the discussion, as is the case in both Buber's and Walzer's readings. The two seem to agree
that when "theopolitics" is established, human power struggles and earthly interests lose their purpose.[69] But what is that theopolitics? In Buber's *Kingship of
God*, divine rule is presented as an "expression of a disposition" of those who
yearned for it and believed in its possibility. Only as such was the expression historically real.[70] But in order to maintain theopolitics as a historical "disposition,"
Buber had to separate the judge Gideon's renunciation of power and assertion
of God's rule from the "legendary" narrative of Gideon's "calling, conflict, and

victory,"[71] that is, from the display of violence, both human and divine. The idea of renouncing earthly power is discussed by Walzer in the context of the prophet Isaiah, who pleads to the king to leave the confrontations with other kings to God and renounce international power games (to "be quiet" and "do nothing"), even in times of oppression by a foreign power (100–8). This advice was "purely religiously motivated," Walzer says, quoting Max Weber approvingly, reiterating the separation between religion and politics (102).[72]

Both Buber and Walzer bracket divine violence by a decisive separation (the legendary and the historical layers of the Bible, religion and politics). The categories are different, but the logic is the same. To Buber, what Walzer calls "religious" is still politics, albeit theopolitics. God has been stripped of the spectacular violence attributed to him by various biblical texts but remains within the realm of power. Adding God as a political partner, Buber distinguishes between *two kinds of politics*, two forms of rule, and two modes of power relations and relations *to* power. But he also limited his claims about biblical theocracy; to him it was not a real regime where God was supreme sovereign but one imagined and prescribed by humans.[73] Walzer calls this position religious (which he studies mainly in order to establish his point about the absence of politics in the Bible) because the separation (Weberian in spirit) between the two spheres, religion and politics, is presupposed and frames his entire investigation.[74]

Thus, for example, the ban (*ḥerem*) in wars sanctioned by God (the command to destroy all property and kill every living being of the vanquished enemy) was not fully enforced, and the failure to do so was "religious, not political" (39). In other words, the extreme violence sanctioned by God concerns Israel and their God and is thus not a political matter.[75] Kings exercised realpolitik, while the radical, warmongering "literati" that called for the ban (like the Deuteronomic scribes or the prophet Samuel) did so because they were "farthest from the trenches"—and from "actual political or military engagement" (46). Negotiations over the use of divine violence and the nature of divine rule recorded in different layers of the Bible are hardly mentioned. So too are God's own quasi-political gestures, like taking counsel, seeking recognition and legitimization, decision making, and changing policies (all these will be discussed in what follows). The different, conflicting accounts of divine violence in various biblical sources are not addressed at all. All these may be ignored, so it seems, because divine rule is seen as antithetical to politics and divine violence exiled to the realm of religion. The problem with this view lies not only in the anachronistic and questionable division of two spheres (religion and politics), which some of Walzer's critics questioned,[76] but also in the tacit assumption that what "we"—from classical

Greek philosophers to contemporary liberal intellectuals—consider "politics" is a realm of power relations free of invisible entities that exercise the kind of excessive power that the Bible attributed to God.

Jan Assmann

Jan Assmann, an Egyptologist and historian of memory ("mnemohistory") and ancient religions, came to the issue of violence through his study of the monotheist iconoclastic revolution of the pharaoh Akhenaten in the fourteenth century BCE and the dramatic counterrevolution that followed it. Initially he was interested in the immediate memory of this period, its long repression and distorted survival in antiquity, and its resurrection by Egyptologists at the turn of the twentieth century, when Akhenaten was conceived as a predecessor to Moses.[77] Assmann reconstructed the history of this (unfounded) association (on which Freud based his *Moses and Monotheism*) as part of the European imagination of Egypt. He claimed that there could be no way that biblical authors could learn their "Yahwehism"—the insistence on revering a single deity with whom they entered a covenant—from the repressed Egyptian monotheistic movement. He searched the Hebrew Bible for key differences between Akhenaten's imposed worship of one God, Aten, and the "monotheistic revolution" in ancient Israel.[78] But Assmann was also attracted to the common structure that characterized both monotheistic revolutions. In both cases, the iconoclastic fervor and the violence involved in the institution of monotheism were grounded in a social structure quite similar to the one identified by Schwartz, of fundamental, binary, and exclusionary othering, which Assmann called the "Mosaic Distinction."[79] The repudiation of "the others," members of outside groups, was translated into a systemic colonization of the surrounding counterculture, repression, and widespread destruction.[80]

The theoretical framework of Assmann's studies in this context is a historiosophical thesis concerning the so-called Axial Age and the process of "the theologization" of history, politics, morality, and the law.[81] Politics was theologized with the introduction of "the model of political alliance as a new form of relationship between god and man . . . as the political theology of Assyria was adopted by way of 'subversive inversion,'"[82] and much of what was originally part of politics—domination, war, laws, and judgment—was gradually absorbed into what became a separate sphere of the divine. The divine, which could not be materially represented, became "transcendental," "independent of political institutions," and separated "from the overall system of culture, politics, morality and law." But by setting the ultimate criteria for interpretation and judgment of human action in every realm of human affair, everything that was separate from the divine became subject to God's rule and hence practically absorbed into its own distinct, "autonomous sphere."[83]

For us, the implications of these bold, far-reaching observations are crucial: With the theologization of politics and law, violence of all kinds (sanctioned or not) was now conceived in relation to God, his judgment, and his laws, while divine violence became a practice of deliberate engagement in human affairs. This seems to be a proper starting point for closely examining the logic and meaning of the proliferating violence, which the Hebrew Bible attributed to God.

Initially, Assmann proposed some rather simplistic observations. He identified the exclusivist, violent tendencies of biblical monotheism with the book of Deuteronomy and the prophets associated with its tradition. The God portrayed in priestly writings (which Assmann conceives as a "primary religion" that did not undergo the monotheistic revolution) is the creator who cares for everything he created and is thus served through an elaborate cult that shapes human's worldly experiences. In the "counter-religion" developed by the Deuteronomists,[84] God is transcendent and exclusivist and must be served by following "the outwardly order" of his laws, whose "revolutionary character" is expressed in the hitherto unparalleled command "Thou shall have no other gods."[85] The relation to this God is based on the basic "Mosaic Distinction," which underlies "more specific distinctions such as Jews and Gentiles, Christians and pagans, Muslims and unbelievers. Once the distinction is drawn, there is no end of reentries or sub-distinctions. . . . Cultural or intellectual distinctions such as these construct a universe that is not only full of meaning, identity, and orientation, but also full of conflict, intolerance, and violence."[86]

The Mosaic Distinction drew criticism for privileging the true/false binary, as well as for linking biblical monotheism to Islamic fundamentalist terrorism.[87] Assmann kept revising the basic distinction but continued to insist on a binary logic that shaped the emerging monotheist discourse and determined its fate. The revised distinction—where loyalty (to God) and betrayal (epitomized by the metonym "Egypt") replaced truth and falsehood—emphasized even more the violence implicated in it.[88] Assmann insisted that the opposition between loyalty and betrayal is a "deep structure concept" that carries with it a series of more contingent distinctions "on the surface of articulate speech."[89] The revised distinction is relatively flexible and could be shared across different religious systems, always ready to demand commitment and sacrifice from the faithful and, occasionally, a struggle unto death against their "Others."

Violence, both human and divine, is studied in this context as part of the "cultural semantics of monotheism," as a matter of representation where the only significant reference is human violence. At the same time, the phrase "the language and imagery of violence" is left as a general formula that guides Assmann's reading. He uses it to examine two "types of religious violence":[90] first, the violence that targeted external enemies in sanctioned war against the Canaanites and became a divine injunction for total extermination in the ban (*herem*) on captives and captured property and, second, internal violence that targeted idolaters and was driven by divine jealousy and human zeal.[91]

In both cases, Assmann stops short of reconstructing the imagined world in which such violence could have made sense. In fact, he goes out of his way to make clear that no such world ever existed, taking great care to separate the actual use of violence from the violence that populated the Israelites' theopolitical imagination. "No traces exist of a major invasion, destruction, and superimposition" in Palestine in the contemporary period.[92] The Deuteronomic law that sanctioned the ban was "fictitious and utopian," and "one ought not to think that [it] . . . was ever put to practice." Limiting the discussion to one group of texts clearly separating the "cultural semantics of monotheism" from the actual acts of the monotheistic zealots, let alone their God, serves the same purpose: to absolve the Israelites—and by uncritical intimation the Jews who inherited the Hebrew Bible—from any blame for taking part in the actual violence in their sacred book, while recognizing the dormant potentiality waiting for actualization.[93] After all—and this is Assmann's main interest—the words were uttered, and the acts they portrayed became imaginable and could be made into models of the commanded practice. Indeed, the stories about zealous actions against idolaters "stem from *an early phase* of monotheism, when the gods were still conceived of as actual rivals of Yahweh and not as fictitious, imagined entities." Beyond its apologetic tone, and just as we saw in Buber's reading of Judges, the insistence on relegating certain elements of the text to a legendary realm reveals a commitment to what really took place in the Bible's world—the gradual development of monotheism, in this case, and, by implication, the emergence of a community of discourse that carried a monotheist system of beliefs and its underlying discursive formations.

Assmann's preoccupation with the justifications and excuses for the violence depicted in the Hebrew Bible proposed by biblical narrators and their readers[94] comes at the expense of any attempt to study that violence. This is most evident in *The Invention of Religion*, Assmann's book on Exodus. From the beginning of his interest in the Hebrew Bible, Assmann placed great importance on the opposition between Egypt and Israel and saw it as crucial for the emergence of monotheism as a counter-religion and for the mnemohistorical thread at its core. "Moses is a figure of memory but not of history, while Akhenaten is a figure of history but not of memory."[95] In *The Invention of Religion*, Exodus is presented as interweaving both aspects of monotheism, and violence becomes one of the main themes in its study, both as corollary to the antagonistic structure of monotheism and as elements in its culture of memory.

The revised Mosaic Distinction runs through the three theological dimensions of the Exodus story—liberation, covenant, and cult.[96] The distinction assumes three specific articulations, corresponding to the three dimensions: Egypt and Israel, or captivity versus freedom; Israel and the nations, or the elected people and the others; and friend and foe, or loyalty and betrayal.[97] Each axis of opposition hinged on divine violence, and one could use the scheme Assmann proposes to map its unfolding in the entire Exodus-Deuteronomy corpus: the destruction of Egypt as the other side of liberation, terrifying and punishing the people as the other side of the covenant, and crushing idolatry as the other side of a properly functioning cultic sphere. But when Assmann comes across these moments of violence he almost always finds a hermeneutic or rhetorical strategy to deflect his discussion elsewhere.

The strategies differ. The boldest one is a straightforward declaration: When "the world splits into Israel and the nations . . . [the] distinction has *nothing whatsoever* to do with intolerance and violence" (80, emphasis mine). With this emphatic negation, the Sinai event of election and covenant (Ex. 19–20, 24) is cleansed of all traces of violence.[98] Assmann insists that the Israelites entered the covenant voluntarily, implying—as many other commentators do—that refusal was a real option.[99] Once the covenant and its distinction between Israel and the nations are ruled out as (textual) sites of violence, the two other moments of the Mosaic Distinction (Israel vs. Egypt, captivity vs. freedom) neatly reflect the dichotomy between external and internal violence, the idolaters from outside and the idolaters from within (punishing both the pagan Egyptians and the golden-calf-worshipping Israelites with plagues). Here, violence cannot be simply denied. Let us see how it is accounted for.

Egypt first. Assmann devotes a whole chapter to the spectacle of the plagues and the crossing of the Sea of Reeds (138–78). He retells the story, follows the process of the redaction, places some of its elements in the Egyptian context, and captures some moments from its long afterlife. He also leaves the door open for the possibility of a real event at the origin of the plagues story and considers some possible realistic explanations for the crossing of the sea (147ff.). Mnemohistory should let "realistic reporting, theological interpretation, and

poetic stylization . . . exist side by side in the depiction of a single event" (151).
But this kind of mnemohistory does not shed much light on the violence at its
center. Two genocidal acts perpetrated by two great powers that confronted
each other—Pharaoh (Ex. 1:15–22) and Yahweh (Ex. 12:29–30, 14:21–30)—
frame the story, and a litany of the suffering and misery these powers ordered
is recounted, then celebrated. Biblical monotheism, certainly the version encapsulated in what Assmann calls "the Exodus tradition," is based on a radical
and absolute separation of these two powers, but this separation grew out of
the confrontation between them, in which the superiority of Yahweh over Pharaoh was demonstrated. In Egypt, at least, the controlled and calculated use of
violence was the only medium through which this superiority could be articulated. In other words, and contrary to Assmann, the monotheism that grew out
of the Exodus story was *not grounded in a violence that arose as a response
to disloyalty and betrayal*. It was the other way around: The violence depicted
in the Exodus story opened the space in which the distinction between loyalty
to God and his betrayal became possible. In the world of Exodus, monotheism
did not precede the violent clash between God and Pharaoh but rather was its
result. In other words, before instigating violence, the Mosaic Distinction was
born from violence. This other violence, from which the monotheistic violence
originated—if origin is still a valid term to be used here—is left outside Assmann's
field of vision.

Assmann's vision is framed by the opposition between loyalty and betrayal,
which could not have appeared before the people entered the covenant.[100] For
the history of Exodus's memory, as well as for the history of monotheism, this is
the only kind of violence that should be of real concern, Assmann seems to assume, because this has been the violence replicated in God's name throughout
the ages. "Religious violence" would be the violence of the fundamentally faithful who slaughter the idolaters, pagans, Jews, or the infidels, all in God's name.
This kind of violence is clearly distinguished from the violence demonstrated, for
example, in the ten plagues, which was "purely divine violence," devoid of any
human involvement, and also unrelated to divine wrath.[101]

It is hard to miss here the Schmittian logic famously articulated in *The Concept of the Political*. A radical opposition that places "us" against "them," friends
against enemies, can be easily translated into all kinds of oppositions, which
articulate the basic political opposition in concrete situations. This opposition
is both strictly binary and hierarchal, with a positive and a negative side. It delineates the rigid boundaries of the theopolitical community and allows, if not
actively generates, exclusions and cleansings of the idolaters, "the enemy from

within," as well as preemptive attacks on the enemies from without—the people who worship "other gods"—far beyond the boundaries of the community of the faithful. These attacks are associated with other terms on the negative side of the opposition (impurity, desecration, treason, wickedness, etc.). Lastly, loyalty to God and his disciples overruns all other commitments, much in the same way that obedience to the political imperative in Schmitt trumps all other commitments and interests articulated in other spheres (loyalty over truth, justice, economic profit, etc.).

Assmann's made his debt to Schmitt explicit a few years before the German publication of his book on Exodus (2015), in a lecture he delivered at the American University in Cairo in 2012.[102] He also drew there their differences, and these seem quite striking. Most importantly, his own theopolitical scheme amounts to an explicit inversion of Schmitt's famous claim that "all significant concepts of the modern theory of the state are secularized theological concepts."[103] Assmann's basic insight is that the monotheist revolution was a theologization of politics, morality, and law that took place through a "transposition of an original political concept to the religious level, transforming god-king, king-subject, and king-vassal relations into the relations between god and man as well as God and Israel."[104] With this "transposition," the Mosaic Distinction can be applied not only to politics but also to morality and law and, in fact, to every human realm. This, then, is the "deep structure" that generated the "language and imagery of violence" at the foundation of biblical monotheism and, most importantly, generated "the narrative self-representation" of the monotheistic revolution and the Deuteronomic version of the saga of Israel's liberation from Egypt.[105]

We have already noted the importance of Assmann's inversion of Schmitt's secularization thesis; in the present context, we are concerned only with the way this theoretical construction has framed and narrowed Assmann's interest in divine violence. In the Cairo lecture, the reliance on Schmitt opened a clear path for dealing with it. For a moment, violence is at the center of attention. But it turns out that it is not what we are interested in. The Mosaic Distinction is described as capable of generating a Schmittian *Ernstfall*, literally "the serious case," the state of emergency, which reveals, according to Assmann, the religious equivalent of the "being unto war" in the Schmittian conception of politics.[106] Using again his two favorite cases—the worship of the golden calf that led to the massacre of thousands of idolaters in the hands of the Levite zealots (Ex. 32:26–29) and the killing of the idolatrous couple in the sanctuary of God by the high priest Phinehas, "who zealously acted for [God's] zeal"

(Num. 25:7–11)—Assmann finds this violence paradigmatic of the Bible. Violent zealotry of this kind, Assmann argues (rightly, I believe), "belong[s] within the frame of the idea of the covenant . . . [and] impl[ies] the employment of human violence that fights for God." And he adds: "Human violence . . . is exactly what we are interested in, and this appears only after entering the covenant at Mount Sinai."[107]

Using Schmitt to frame his concept of "religious violence," Assmann explains away divine violence, omitting God's role even in the two cases he discusses, explicitly bracketing that "purely divine violence," of the kind exercised in the ten plagues, for example. But how can the story of the theologization of politics be completed without accounting for that other, "purely divine" violence, which Assmann mentions without addressing? Why must it be excluded from the investigation when the political merges with the theological—if the two have ever been separated? Can the "legendary" element be dissociated from the imagination of the perpetrators? And how can we account for the occasions in which the two kinds of violence ("religious" and "theopolitical," that is, human and divine) worked together, complemented each other (Ex. 32:26–29, 33–35), or worked in opposite directions (Num. 14:11–12, 40–45)? Addressing this last question with respect to the violence against the idolaters in Numbers 25, where God's wrath accounts for twenty-four thousand dead and Phinehas's zealotry for two, Assmann writes: "I am focusing here not on the plague and its twenty-four thousand victims; *this is normal, so to speak,* in the ancient world. I am focusing on the deed of Phinehas . . . this is new, even revolutionary."[108]

If this were normal, then God could not reclaim the position of Schmitt's "secularized" sovereign in the new religion, operating the distinctions on which it is based. Was not Egypt, where God, acting alone, decided on both the enemy and the exception, a perfect case of *Ernstfall,* with God simultaneously playing the role of the sovereign and the sovereign's army? But, strangely enough, for Assmann only those humans who claim to speak and act in his name (for example, Moses, Phinehas) hold the sovereign position, proclaim the community's boundaries, announce who must be excluded from it, and order their destruction. With this, God has not only been exonerated of his pure violence, but divine violence has been altogether made exempt from the critical scholarly gaze.

Soon after that series of lectures in Cairo, when Assmann came to work on the book of Exodus, he could no longer ignore this "purely divine violence." There, the distinction between loyalty and betrayal is the pretext and structure of divine violence in most of the fourteen cases of resistance—murmuring, lack of trust, flawed initiatives—to God's rule and to the missions carried out by his delegates, which Assmann diligently counts, classifies, and analyzes (253–71).[109] Now, divine violence is registered but almost always presented as a punishment for this or that form of disloyalty—and, once registered, it dissipates. More precisely, divine violence is addressed only in the context of biblical texts that document the theologization of politics, law, and history, where violence is driven by the biblical version of the Schmittian opposition (loyalty vs. betrayal).[110]

At first, the shift of the scholarly gaze away from divine violence is subtle, almost imperceptible. It starts with foregrounding the case in which "God's wrath appears most prominently," when the Israelites "actually worship another God, Ba'al-Peor" (268; Num. 25). When Assmann mentions again the "normal, so to speak," extreme violence brought about by God's fury, it is only to note that the text "expresses the mirror-image relationship between God's jealousy and human zeal" (269).[111] He immediately looks forward to a mythologized-historical moment, depicted in the first book of Maccabees, when the scene of Ba'al-Peor is evoked as inspiration for *human* zealotry in the beginning of the Hasmonean rebellion against the Seleucid Empire (269–70). Looking back at the murmuring in the wilderness (270–71), Assmann notes the violence that was necessary to crush "the resistance" that threatened to imperil "the project," that is, "the departure from Egypt" (270), but that violence does not find its way to the table that Assmann constructs to aggregate and classify the episodes of resistance (271). In the history of memory, the ultimate framework for Assmann's narrative and interpretation, divine violence is merely a transitory stage between popular resistance to, or a foreign campaign against, the "unappealing, inconvenient and unpopular" (282) demands of monotheism and the human violence mobilized to crush that resistance. In the thickness of the history of memory, God's wrath and violence are lost again.

The point is made in a less subtle way as Assmann moves into the next sections (271–86), reexamining speculative theories (by Goethe, Sellin, and Freud) concerning the murder of Moses and less speculative claims (by Baltzer and Steck) about the tradition that passed down stories of the persecution of early monotheistic prophets, from Moses to Jesus. He grants the latter historical feasibility (283) and combines it with a common hypothesis about the postexilic redaction of the Pentateuch. With the destruction of the First Temple and the Babylonian exile, as the threats and warnings of the preexilic prophets came true, there emerged the "post traumatic" Deuteronomic view of history (284): Divine violence was retroactively projected onto the mythical history of the people in order to frame the recent catastrophe as part of an ongoing pattern of catastrophic events, which always followed rebellions against God. The stories that present this violence as punishment for disloyalty kept it within the framework of a theodicy, in which the distinction between God's blessing and curses was mapped on that between friend and enemy (285).

But there is clear difference between the two distinctions and the violence associated with each of them. The friend-foe distinction involved real, human violence, brought about by the rise of monotheism as a counter-religion, first (probably) when the adherents of a full-fledged monotheism were persecuted by the dominant, nonexclusivist, syncretic Yahwists and later (and quite certainly) by zealous monotheists against their rivals. Divine blessings and curses (hence divine violence), on the other hand, were projected backward to explain and justify the downfall of God's people, its destruction and exile. It was part of a new theopolitical imagination that had to suit the new condition of the Judean community. The reason and meaning of the former violence was rooted in the antagonistic nature of the new counter-religion; the reason and meaning of the latter was contingent, driven by unfortunate historical circumstances, and was never a necessary component of the monist God and his exclusivist covenant.[112]

According to this interpretation, the theopolitical imagination associated with divine violence was a response to the specific historical conditions of the Judean community, not a necessary aspect of the monotheist ideology and practices themselves, while the *potentiality* of human violence is inherent in monotheism's exclusivist, antagonistic structure. If monotheism was violent, one should blame humans and their historical conditions, not their God. For human violence is not a necessary corollary of monotheistic religions but merely *one* of its forms occurring in *some* of its manifestations. Theoretically, monotheism can be purged of its violence. As for divine violence, it turns out to be no more than a background, a mythical phase and imaginary excuse for what really took place on the main stage: a series of mythologized stories transmitted through various memory practices as part of the reproduction of some major binary distinctions, which have kept alive that version of monotheism where violence is an inherent propensity.

ON THE ATTRIBUTION OF POWER AND AUTHORITY

In one way or another, Schwartz, Assmann, and Walzer fail to take notice of the violence perpetrated by the God(s) of the Hebrew Bible. They fail to do this even though God shares with humans the same forms and frameworks of action that generate violence, according to our authors. For God has his own psychodynamics and modes of forming identities (Schwartz), his own strategies of inscribing himself in collective memory for the sake of reproducing the legitimacy of his authority (Assmann), and his own ways of giving laws, judging and claiming justice, instituting authority, and repressing resistance (Walzer). The scholars' gazes focus on the people who projected that violence onto God, the violent language they used to describe him, or the human problems that were either solved or generated by this violence. In different ways, each one of them has failed to understand that the imaginary violence attributed to God in the biblical texts was not only an enlarged projection of human violence but played a crucial role in *generating* and *shaping* it, in the text and beyond it, and that it was not simply the memory of that violence but also its form and place in a general economy that must be accounted for. Despite all their scholarly depth and theoretical sophistication, Schwartz, Walzer, and Assmann have not departed significantly from the long-held tradition of explaining away the question of divine violence.

This tradition, as I showed, goes all the way back to Josephus Flavius's *Against Apion*. The text that introduced the term and concept "theocracy" to describe the biblical *politea* was also the first to cleanse it from the violence of its ruling power. Both the conception of divine rule and erasure of divine violence tacitly hinged there on a key idea noted earlier—the attribution of power and authority as a condition for the very existence of the theocratic regime. We need to attend to this idea and spell it out beyond what can be found in Josephus, in order to resist the blind spot he instilled and mark a clear departure from the tradition that has preserved it.

Attribution of power and authority takes place in any form of ruling power. A ruling power (*shilton* in Hebrew, a combination of *archē* and *kratos* in Greek) is a publicly known, or presumed (hence also imaginary), and in any case attributed capacity to command and extract obedience via a potentially harmful use of force, and to get away with it.[113] The use of force is always potentially harmful, even when it is used for the benefit of some, whose protection, survival, or well-being is at stake.[114] The authority (or right) to use force and the responsibility for the actual use of force (agency) are aspects of a ruling power but physical strength or military might are not qualities that necessarily inhere in the persons or institutions that hold power. These aspects of power must be *attributed and recognized by many*. Without such attribution, or when attribution fails to generate public recognition, power becomes mere force, and the responsibility of the acting agent remains unaccountable. Power needs both attribution and recognition to function, and neither can be self-granted—they must come from others. For this reason, because of their power to attribute, the many have a share in power. Their share consists in their power to withhold attribution and recognition from an acting agent.[115] This may be the only power they have, but it is precisely what is necessary for distinguishing power from force.

Attribution is all the more crucial in a theocracy because the ruling power is mostly invisible, its appearance is unpredictable, and its recognition is uncertain. Public performances of attribution and their possible contestations are therefore given a special weight. In theocracy, the people's political imagination is not simply instrumental but constitutive of their political regime. This form of rule is instituted by an attribution of power and authority to a mostly invisible powerful agent that is said to already be at work. The putative omnipresence and unsurpassable power of this agent could only be inferred from the interpretation of the phenomenal traces left in the realm of human affairs, incarnated in individuals, artifacts, or natural phenomena. In their turn, the identification of these traces and the validity of those interpretations must themselves be recognized as authorized by the represented authority or its authorized delegates. Because they speak and act in the name of an invisible agent and are authorized to interpret his words and deeds, the delegates' own power increases at the same time as their direct responsibility decreases, for it can always be alleviated by turning to the power they represent. For this to happen, however, they must be bestowed with recognizable marks of the ruling power and attributed with the authority to incarnate, represent, or interpret the ruling power.[116] They too, must be recognized by many.

The stronger the *power of attribution* is, the less likely it becomes that the *attributed power* or the agent's very existence will be questioned independently of the discourse that enables the attribution and requires it. Josephus provided a safeguard against such questions. This agent, that is, God, "is known to us by his power but as to what he is like in essence, unknown."[117] To know an agent by its power means to know it by the revealed effects of the actions attributed to it, without ever knowing who or what the agent behind them is; we know only what the exercise of its power reveals. All that one is left with are attributions, *which are not a matter of belief but of linking*—of phenomenal and experiential effects to imagined or concrete agencies, of instructions to the authority that issues them, and of actions to the power that commands them and gives them sense and direction. The difference between the biblical texts and most other documents recording political events is the rarity of the public visibility of the main agent to which power, authority, and responsibility are attributed. But as Josephus understood well (and the three authors studied in the previous section missed), for a rule of God to be imagined, the rarity of God's public epiphanies should be compensated by a consistent, well-orchestrated, and persistent labor of attributions.

Reconstructing this system, Josephus did not follow any biblical text. In the story he tells in the passage quoted earlier in this chapter, the development of the system and its success are ascribed to Moses. Let us read this again:

> After the successful outcome of some great deeds, [Moses] naturally concluded that he had God as his governor and adviser. Having first come to the conviction that everything [Moses] did and thought was in accordance with God's will, he considered it as his prime duty to impress this notion on the masses; for to those who believe that God watches over their lives do not allow themselves to commit any sin.[118]

The first attribution was a personal matter, based on Moses's interpretation of his own experience, reflecting his success as a leader and legislator. Then he moved to instill the same attribution in his people, teaching them to take his (Moses's) laws as expressions of God's will. Since the laws were so perfectly made[119] and were designed to serve the people, not their leader, having everyone share in Moses's attribution of power was not too difficult to achieve, or at least to imagine,[120] and a perfect rule of law according to God's will replaced the biblical rule by God's mighty arm.

Attribution, not theocracy, is the main concept I would like to take from Josephus. Turning back to the biblical text, we will henceforth follow the trail of attributions they trace. Like readers of literary texts, from fairy tales to science fiction, one may be totally immersed in imagining the God(s) the text tells us about without projecting his existence beyond it. One may leave God in the text because one is theologically indifferent or because, like the midrashic commentators or the early Christian theologians cited earlier, one may have another image of God in mind, to whom the power and the glory are attributed. Most importantly, as a political theorist, one may gain insight from learning how the attribution of God's authority was naturalized or how it moved people to act.

Whichever one's position is and however one follows the trail of attributions, respect for the biblical texts forces us to accept that, contrary to Josephus (and the long tradition that followed his steps), for whom theocracy true *archē* was the rule of (divine) *law*,[121] in biblical theocracy everyone was potentially subject to God's *violence*, not only (or not at all) to his law. Divine violence in the Bible is not only an embarrassing residue (embarrassing by modern moral standards, of course) of divine rule that somehow cannot be explained away but an integral part of God's rule. As is the case with other formations of power, certain economy of violence was indispensable to it. The omission of this violence is an ideological idealization of power relations, which takes part in their reproduction and obfuscates their effects.[122] Looking for the veins of violence that run through any system of power is crucial for grasping the form of power at stake. Hence, while divine rule is the proper context for explaining divine violence, a proper understanding of divine rule requires an account of the distinct configuration and economy of violence characterizing that rule. In the worlds portrayed by the biblical texts, formations of divine rule provide the proper framework for rendering divine violence legible, both for us as readers and for the text's protagonists, in the world of the texts and in our own. At the same time, the scene of violence and the aftermath of its events will help to identify distinct formations of rule in which God is attributed with supreme power and authority. My distinct intervention in the study of biblical theocracy consists in this insistence on the role divine violence played in the formation of divine rule.

When we find evidence for the attribution of violence and rule to God, we should be careful to not attribute this attribution to the *beliefs* of the biblical protagonists or to the authors who composed and edited these writings. It is their *theopolitical imagination* with which we are engaging and the imagined worlds reproduced and transformed in the transmission of their texts. Imagination does not imply belief (in the cognitive, modern sense of the term). The authors of *Frankenstein* or *Peter Pan* did not have to fear or admire the figures they created. But they did have to let the protagonists in their stories attribute extraordinary powers to these figures and perform these attributions whether or not they believed in those figures.[123] Furthermore, literary work—and the biblical texts are no exception—is a medium of experimentation. Writers and readers, story tellers and listeners, prophets and their audience are parties to a contract in which one is called to imagine a being-in-the-world depicted or created by the text. The biblical texts may always be read as doing this as well—experimenting with the figure of God and the imagination of living under *his rule*. The invitation to such an experiment is an aspect of the text that readers should accept, at least as long as they are willing to stay in the world of the text. Staying in that world, if only briefly, is necessary for understanding the text, however critically. Many biblical texts interpellate their readers to stay forever in the world they created, an offer the reader is always (or should always be) free to decline. Our problem, however, an obstacle we need to overcome, is the reluctance of so many readers, ancient and modern alike, to stay in the imagined world without taking shelter in categories like myth or religion and to stay there long enough to study the impacts of divine violence and reconstruct its raison d'être, that is, the theocratic formation to which it belongs.

KINGSHIP, ANARCHY, THEOCRACY

Theocracy is the name of a distinct type of regime, a specific formation of power. Neither the name nor the concept of regime has any equivalence in the Hebrew Bible. With some minor, late, putative exceptions, its authors did not think in Greek. Ancient Greek philosophers took great interest in the typology of *politeai*, or forms of rule. They classified all known regimes and invented some others, but divine rule was not among them. Such a quest also required a keen understanding of the art of ruling and an interest in its basic principles, not to mention the justifications for and limitations on ruling practices. This kind of intellectual interest and philosophical reasoning is generally missing from the Bible; where it did surface, it was never articulated as a philosophical inquiry. The biblical narrators (prophets included) do not reflect on the concept of theocracy (in fact, they hardly reflect on concepts at all). But even without conceptual reflection, many among them still thought that divine rule was superior to other forms of rule, and they desired to teach this to others. This is most evident in relation to the covenant, a paradigmatic institution of political rule and the dominant term characterizing the relations between God and his people and mankind more generally. When a covenant, *brit*, is used to describe God's relation with mankind, with his elected disciples, or with Israel,[124] God is clearly placed in the position of the supreme partner, the king or suzerain. The formula itself was borrowed from the Mesopotamian treaties, but putting it into practice as the decisive scheme for describing and prescribing the people's relationship with their God was the unique achievement of the biblical authors. The term *brit*, one should remember, was used numerous times throughout the Bible to describe the relations between human allies in a variety of contexts. There was nothing obvious about adding God as a partner to a covenant, not alongside the king and on his behalf but rather in his place, and doing so, as far as the Pentateuchal texts are concerned, without ever calling God a king.[125]

Coming from various sources, the Bible provides ample evidence for different perspectives on God's presence among humans. In Babel (Gen. 11:1–9), the human entrepreneurs feared other humans, not God, and he was worried about competition, not loyalty and lack of submission. He did not want them to attribute to him any power and did not need their recognition; all he wanted, so it seems, was to fail them as competitors in world making. When he revealed himself to Jacob in a dream, he promised him a great future (Gen. 28:10–16), but Jacob, who recognized Yahweh's presence, conditioned his allegiance to God on the safe completion of his journey (28:20–22). In Joseph's novella (Gen. 37,

39–48), God worked behind the scenes, giving Joseph clues that would help him rise to power and govern successfully, but it was Joseph, not God or Pharaoh, who governed Egypt. In the first chapters of Exodus, when God orchestrated the clash between Pharaoh and his magicians, his authority was not recognized by the Egyptian king, and the Israelites' recognition was hard and slow to win. The shift from obeying a human ruler to a godly one had to be learned. The prophets were adamant about this shift and kept scolding the people for failing to live up to it, for placing their hope, trust, and loyalty in human powers, both foreign and local, rather than in God. As Isaiah proclaims (8:13): "The Lord of Armies, Him shall you hallow [and not another king or sovereign], and He is your fear and your terror." Despite all this, the prophets never pondered on the adequacy of a political treaty as a model of relationship between God and humans. They spoke as if it was "natural" for a god, for Yahweh at least, to enter into a political contract with a human partner, and they mainly described *how* he entered covenantal relations with his people. They often used nonpolitical metaphors to illustrate and explain the political relationship but never to replace or displace it.[126] Finally, and most clearly, each of the versions of God's revelation in the covenant ceremony (Ex. 19, 24; Deut. 4:9–40, 5:19–30) and many of the accounts of dissent and rebellion in the wilderness can be read as acts in an educational theater, in which the people in the show and their spectators are taught theocracy's basic principles and initiated into covenantal ideology.

This educational effort was clearly necessary. The voice of the idolaters is not heard often, but when it is heard, it betrays a real resistance. In the opening scene of the golden calf (Ex. 32:1), the people ask Aaron: "Make us gods that will go before us, for this man, Moses . . . we do not know what happened to him." They had not yet learned the distinction between Moses and God or between a living god and handmade one. Ezekiel reports on a clandestine paganist ritual that the performers, "the elders of the house of Israel," justify by saying "Yahweh does not see us. Yahweh has abandoned the land" (Ezek. 8:12). In a rare episode in Jeremiah that takes place in Egypt, the speakers, a group of refugees from Judah, explain that when they, like their fathers, kings, and nobles "in the towns of Judah and in the streets of Jerusalem," served "the Queen of the Heavens," they "were good, and evil [they] did not see" (Jer. 44:17). Since their cult came to an end, however, they "have lacked everything, and by the sword and the famine [they] have come to an end" (44:18). Furthermore, the idolaters refuse to acknowledge their obligation to Yahweh, as well as the prophet's authority to speak in his name: "The word that you have spoken to us in the name of Yahweh we will not heed you" (44:16).

We must remember this resistance and the stakes of educational theater when we reconstruct the formations of God's rule and the place of violence within it. As far as the biblical narrator is concerned, God initiated the contract, set its terms and later changed them, chose his partners, decided when it was breached, and punished the offenders. When Israelites insisted on serving other gods, they never had an alternative tribunal to look for. Confronting a straightforward rejection, like the one reported by Ezekiel in God's own words—"you say, 'We shall be like the nations, like the clans of the land, to serve wood and stone'" (Ezek. 20:32)—Yahweh simply and vigorously reasserts his force and authority in words that recall the crashing of Egypt: "'By My life,' said the Master, Yahweh, 'with a strong hand and with an outstretched arm and with outpoured wrath, I will surely reign over you'" (20:33).

The cults of other gods are almost always presented and reproached in terms of the covenant, never as a claim regarding the covenant itself. The limits of what could have been questioned reflect God's discursive position and legal status as the covenant's senior partner. But even if not challenged in a straightforward manner, the submission to God was interpreted in a variety of ways, and when they clashed, a clear moment of reflective political thinking emerged. Scattered few and far between, such moments are inserted into segments of narratives, poetry, and prophetic orations, offering elements of abstract thinking about rule and power, mainly in the context of kingship and some of its alternatives. The topic has been widely studied,[127] so I will limit myself to the juxtaposition of kingship as a form of rule distinct from the rule of judges and priests, on the one hand, and to the absence of any rule, a state of anarchy, on the other. Even a quick glance at the relevant passages is sufficient to reveal an awareness of the differences between distinct forms of rule and their respective (dis)advantages. Without being named, divine rule is certainly included in this silent typology.

Our guide is the relation of divine rule to kingship, which is either contested (Judges, Samuel) or conspicuously understated (Deuteronomy, Judges). When an old Samuel is asked by the elders of Israel to appoint a king (1 Sam. 8:4–5), God instructs him to "solemnly warn them and tell them the practice (*mishpat*) of the king" (8:9). *Mishpat* is untranslatable in this verse, for its entire semantic field—which includes justice, judgment, the practice of judging, and the mode of operation of the ruling power—may be implied in this context. For us, it is crucial that the term is impersonal and indifferent to the qualities of the man who will be anointed. In fact, in the way it is used in this passage, *mishpat* comes close to the Greek *politea*. What Samuel then describes (8:11–17) is indeed the king's rights and mode of operation, the range of his power to subjugate and exploit the people whom he will govern (*shaphat*), judge, and lead to war. The king's *mishpat* is clearly the epitome of an injustice that could send the people crying back to God (8:18).

The narrator of 1 Samuel 8 gives a clear background to the elders' demand. As he got older, Samuel "set his [two] sons as judges for Israel," but they turned corrupt, taking bribes and twisting justice (*mishpat*) (1 Sam. 8:1–3). Placing the elders' request right after the short account of the transition crisis implicitly questions God's actual role in Israel's political affairs. Since Samuel did not wait for God to appoint his sons to judges, he "overstep[ped] his mandate as *shofet*" (a judicial authority and ad hoc political leader).[128] Because of this, both the narrator and the people blamed the corrupted sons for failing to follow their father's—not God's—way (8:2, 5). For the elders, God does not provide the standards for the rulers' proper manners, nor is he asked to appoint or anoint a king. For them, Samuel's authority sufficed. They hoped that the king would take Samuel's place, not the place of God, who seems absent from their model of the political hierarchy. Obviously, they did not have God and his ways on their mind when they asked to be ruled "like all the nations" (8:5).

In the background, there is a noticeable cycle of corruption among the heirs of judges and priests.[129] But this pattern indicates a clear form of rule: Priests (Eli) and prophets (Samuel) could become judges (rulers), while some outstanding ordinary Israelites (like Gideon, whom God chose as a judge) could fulfill some priestly roles (Jud. 8:24–27). In this form of rule, the transfer of power was never guaranteed, let alone institutionalized. God occasionally appointed judges without promising a hereditary succession of power. When such a succession was attempted, it ended in corruption and disaster.[130] In the interim periods, the Israelites turned away from God and were oppressed by their neighbors, and God "left aside" hostile nations "to test" them (Jud. 3:1) and to force the people to repent. Throughout Judges, God is presented as the one who orchestrates the back-and-forth between oppression and redemption. Salvation and oppression were two sides of divine rule, and Israel had to rely on God's guidance and assistance in its wars (Jud. 2:11–23). Hence, when God tells Samuel that "it is not you they have cast aside, but Me they have cast aside from reigning over them" (1 Sam. 8:7), he may mean that the Israelites have forsaken him to serve other gods but also that they have rejected the form of rule in which he had formerly delegated his authority and power to temporary judges.

Either way, Samuel seems to have missed this subtext, and he certainly forgot God's role in appointing Israel's leaders. After decades of being Israel's judge, he could have mistaken the administration of justice and leadership to be his own domain. And yet, when the elders mistrusted his judgment and rejected the hereditary rule he tried to institutionalize, he consulted God, for even when he erred, he was a committed servant and a "stalwart [or trustworthy, *neeman*] prophet to God" (1 Sam. 3:20). Quick to respond, God corrected the prophet's mistake, revealing the true nature of the event *from his point of view*. God is portrayed here as the only one who insists on understanding the elders' demand as a rejection of divine rule, at least one form of it, and he immediately indicates that he is willing to walk back from his position: "Heed the voice of the people in all that they say to you" (3:20). Up to that point, it was God himself who heeded the voice of the people when they cried out to him, sent them a rescuer (Jud. 3:9, 15), "sallied forth before" (Jud. 4:14) one elected warlord, and bestowed his "spirit" on another (Jud. 6:34). The appointment of judges, priests, and prophets was part of the order of divine rule, not external to it. But now, when the elders turned to Samuel, God—or the narrator—seems to contrast the appointment of a king with God's own rule. Kingship would have deprived God of an important leverage on the people for the first time since he appointed Moses to lead the people out of Egypt. He would be like the English monarchs who were forced to yield their power to appoint a prime minister to Parliament.

This is precisely Gideon's point in Judges 8:22. After saving Israel from their Midianite oppressors, the people offered him a hereditary form of power, which he readily refused: "I will not rule over you nor will my son rule over you. The Lord will rule over you" (8:23). The world portrayed in this episode and elsewhere in the Book of Judges (1–16) is one in which God reigned over Israel through periodic abandonment, while strengthening their oppressive neighbors and occasionally empowering individual warlords who rose to their rescue. Thus, when Martin Buber claims that Gideon's response expresses a wish for a rule of God, not the reality of living under God's rule,[131] he may be overstating the historical evidence but understating the literary one. Gideon is in agreement with God in 1 Samuel 8, and what God describes there is not a human wish but the state of affairs up to that point. The two agree that hereditary rule is antagonistic to divine rule, and it makes little sense to interpret the rejection of hereditary rule as a rejection of God if divine rule is not assumed as a matter of fact.

Gideon's voice is also in line with the historical pattern described explicitly in Judges 2:11–23 and reiterated succinctly in some of the following accounts of the various judges. The formula is famously countered by a Deuteronomist (or some like-minded) editor, who interjected a voice-over into the narrative: "In those days there was no king in Israel, every man did what was right in his eyes."[132] The verse juxtaposes kingship and its absence, which it captures as anarchy, the absence of any ruling power. What the elders of Israel rejected when they requested a king, according to this counterformula, was not a different form of rule but the danger of no rule at all, into which a corrupted, lawless rule might easily deteriorate. Anarchy is not analyzed; instead, it is shown through detailed accounts of its disastrous consequences: the horrendous civil war between the tribe of Benjamin and the rest of Israel (Jud. 19–21), to which one may add the massacres and wars initiated by Abimelech (Jud. 9), and the Danites' destruction of a peaceful town in the north and the massacre of its people (Jud. 18).

The transition from judges to kings is inscribed in the canonical order, as the book of Judges is followed by 1 Samuel. This is usually understood as a response to anarchy, which is certainly part of the story, but such understanding leaves out God's role. In fact, the alleged transition from anarchy to kingship is thwarted if God's continuous involvement in the affairs of power and ruling is taken into consideration. Samuel was the last judge and the one who anointed and enthroned the first king. During his judgeship, God's ark indiscriminately sowed terror and death, bringing havoc to the Philistines' camp (1 Sam. 5) and killing tens of thousands of Israelites (6:19–20). Later, after the Israelites repented and abandoned yet again their pagan gods, God took part in a decisive war against the Philistines and helped Israel rout their enemies and restore control over the towns they had lost to them (7:3–14). He was still involved in Israel's wars when Saul became Israel's first king (14:23, 15:1–3). He ordered and directed Saul's election and crowning and soon after oversaw his downfall and the transfer of the kingship to David, the first king of the lineage that would last till the fall of Jerusalem. God claimed responsibility for the split of the kingdom into Israel and Judea and remained involved in the fate of their kings until the end of the two kingdoms.[133] Before the fall of Samaria and Jerusalem, he orchestrated two great catastrophes, one to punish Israel (2 Sam. 24; 1 Chron. 21) and the other to save Judea from an Assyrian onslaught (2 Kings 18–19; 2 Chron. 32).[134] He empowered two exceptional miracle-making prophets, Elijah and Elisha, who, in his name and on his behalf (and sometimes on their own) instigated human and superhuman violence.[135]

It is against this background that we should read the brief yet highly significant discussion of kingship in Deuteronomy.[136] Despite clear overlaps with 1 Samuel 8, kingship is not presented as coming at the expense of God's direct engagement in human affairs, and the initial danger of anarchy, which allegedly motivated the quest for monarchy, finds no trace here. A *politea* based on a combination of a judge and elite priests—"Levitical priests and . . . the judge who will be in those days" (Deut. 17:8–13)—is presented alongside, not in opposition to, kingship (17:14–20).[137] Kingship is not the narrator's (or Moses's, or God's) first choice, but it is still a legitimate form of rule that the people *may* call for once they settle in their land (17:14).[138] The popular demand is a legitimate, unproblematic option, as long as the king is conscious of not acting like the kings of other nations. The Deuteronomist turned Samuel's critical description of the way kings ruled into a set of injunctions prescribing how they *should not rule* (17:16–17).

The king cannot be a non-Israelite, and *his election must be left to God*.[139] His rule should be guided by the same book of laws (which the Deuteronomist both wrote and wrote about) in which kingship appeared as an option and where its rules were set. The king should read this book all his life and study it closely (Deut. 17:18–20). He is subject to God's laws, which he must not change.[140] Thus defined, kingship can easily be understood as a soft version of divine rule (just like the rule of Judges described in Jud. 2:11–22), at least as long as the king subjects himself to God, whom he "may learn to fear . . . [and] keep all the words of this teaching (*Torah*) and these statutes" (Deut. 17:19). Deuteronomy does not state this explicitly, but, in fact, nothing said about the king could not have also been said about the priests and the judge that the king would replace (16:18–20, 17:8–13). In that regime, a judge and Levitical priests were appointed to mediate all "matters of judgment" according to God's teaching (Deut. 17:9–11). Two forms of rule were designed for the time the Israelites would conquer and inherit their promised land and present different forms of subjection to God's laws—in the first, the priests instruct God's teaching to the people and judge them accordingly (17:10–11); in the second, the king is commanded to study God's teaching all his life and "swerve not from what is commanded" (17:19–20). In both cases, human power followed and enforced the rule of (God's) law. Human violence was explicitly prescribed only in the first rule (17:12); restraining it was implied in the warning to the king not to get many horses (17:16) and not let his heart be "haughty over his brothers" (17:20). Divine violence was insinuated in both: The people should "listen and fear" the king (17:13), while the king should "learn to fear Yahweh his God" (17:19).

These two models of rule can be read as two versions of "indirect theocracy," where human power is institutionalized to mediate, not replace, God's laws and force.[141] Linking the law with the force of its enforcement is the hallmark of political rule, but as we will see in Chapter 5, the way this link is portrayed in Deuteronomy is markedly different from the way it is displayed in the history of the monarchical period in Samuel and Kings. By proposing the establishment of kingship in a code of laws presented in the wilderness, the Deuteronomist authors did not try to anticipate, emulate, or improve upon the principles of king-ship one could adduce from Samuel and Kings. Instead, they proposed a coun-terfactual alternative in which kings, just like priests and judges, the personae and the institutions, played their part in an imagined polity ruled by God.

But if both kingship and hierocracy were imagined theocratic formations, readied for the time when the wandering people would settle in the promised land, who ruled Israel in the meantime, on the way to Canaan, in the present time of the Deuteronomist narrator? Or when the laws were pronounced or re-called? The Deuteronomist's answer was straightforward: "Yahweh your God led you these forty years in the wilderness. . . . And you knew in your heart that as a man chastises his son Yahweh chastises you. And you shall keep the commands of Yahweh your God, to walk in His ways and to fear Him" (Deut. 8:2, 5–6). In other words, Israel lived under divine rule from the moment the people were ordered to leave Egypt (Ex. 12). While the Deuteronomic vision of kingship under divine rule (Deut. 17:14–20) is idyllic, a kind of legal utopia,[142] the direct theocracy in which Moses was but a mediator with no decision-making power is presented as a relic of history. But an idyllic legal vision of kingship was part of the legal code encapsulated in the Deuteronomic *historical narrative*, which, in one respect at least, is far more "counterfactual" and at the same time far less idyllic than the Deuteronomic *law of kings*: the narrative sketches four decades in the life of a people that went from slavery to freedom and traveled through a relatively empty desert, during which they were fed, protected, ruled, judged, and pun-ished by God. Moses, who, for the most part, tells this history and pronounces these laws, takes little credit for initiating any of this, except for one crucial mo-ment in which he convinced God to avert his genocidal plan (Deut. 9:12–29). Theocracy is not an ideal formation for Deuteronomy but a lived, contentious reality, as well as the underlying structure of its historical narrative. It is also the proper context for explicating the Deuteronomic conception of divine violence.

HYPOTHESIS, METHOD, AND STAKES

Despite several layers of redaction, Deuteronomy is attributed to one school or tradition of authors. It is one of the most coherent texts in the Bible, and in the Pentateuch, it is certainly the most coherently structured. Since the Deu-teronomic code addresses various authorities and political institutions—kings, judges, priests, prophets, overseers, and military commanders—the rule of God is articulated through the prescription of each authority's rules and limitations. Furthermore, much of the historical narrative that frames the code is concerned with instituting Israel as a people and conceives Israel's peoplehood from within a covenantal framework that determines the juridical rhetoric and the theopolitical ideology. In other words, the institution of Israel as a people is the institution of God as its ruler and of divine rule as its formation of power. Everything the Deuteronomist authors borrowed from whatever legal and political documents with which they were familiar was geared to this purpose, revised, reframed, and weaved into a new fabric that would fit it. As a result, the outline of Deuteronomic theocracy is relatively accessible for the analytical gaze. It is also quite specific to Deuteronomy. It cannot be found even in the so-called Deuteronomic History books, from Joshua to 2 Kings, for there, with relatively few exceptions, God acts through human violence; direct theocracy is presented as an anarchic precursor to kingship; and the reign of kings, for the most part, is presented as the inversion of the idyllic vision proposed by the king's law (*mishpat ha-melech*) in Deuteronomy 17.[143]

Once the Deuteronomic theocracy is properly delineated, however, others may be grasped as well. Deuteronomy's bold, experimental attempt to project a theocratic formation of the history of God's people, situating it in the wilderness between Egypt and Canaan, has at least one additional version in the Pentateuch and other, more and less fragmentary traces in the Latter Prophets. The theocratic rule portrayed by the priestly sources (in Exodus, Leviticus, and Numbers and the priestly interpolations in Genesis) was centered on God's sanctuary, mainly the moving Tabernacle, and is significantly different from the Deuteronomic one centered on the code of law, and yet it is no less discernible.[144] Like the Deuteronomists, priestly authors integrated narrative and laws, prescribed a theocratic code while describing a theocracy in action, and located their theocratic formation in a distant past, in a no-man's land, a space free of existing political institutions.[145] Here too, God is the supreme authority, and others— Moses, Aaron, and his sons—to the extent that they have any authority, are subjects to his command. The priestly interpolations in Genesis, from creation and the flood through the stories of the Fathers and the descent to Egypt, can be read accordingly as fragments describing a primeval stage of this theocracy, carefully tracing a well-crafted story about the transformation of God from the creator and judge of heaven and earth to a sovereign preoccupied with ruling one people, a tribal society he turned into a nation.

We may take this reading one step further. Once the two theocratic formations are recognized, a third formation may be extracted from the pre-priestly sources in Exodus and Numbers.[146] With their own narratives and code of laws,[147] they are set in the same emptied space and distant time, and the only author-

ity they recognize other than God's is that of Pharaoh, whose total defeat in
gigantomachy on the Nile and the Sea of Reeds is at the center of the Exodus
drama. The pre-priestly fragments are a major source for dissenting voices and
the crushing of the opposition to God's rule in Egypt and throughout the journey in the desert.[148] Furthermore, against the backdrop of the priestly interpolations in Genesis, the pre-priestly accounts of primeval history in Genesis (1–11)
and some of Abraham's stories may be read as fragments coming from several
attempts to imagine a prehistory of divine rule, which would eventually lead to
the pre-priestly descriptions of the formation of the Israelite theocracy on the
journey from Egypt to Canaan. It may well be, however, that the retrospective
outlook is not only ours but one that guided priestly or Deuteronomic editors
of these texts.

I have finally come to my working hypothesis, which the following three chapters seek to corroborate. I assume that a theocratic theopolitical imagination is
shared by all five books of the Pentateuch, regardless of the different sources and
layers of which these books consist, but that this imagination is activated differently through three distinct theopolitical formations. These formations roughly
correspond to three key groups of sources: pre-priestly, priestly, and Deuteronomic.[149] In all three, Egypt and the desert serve as the stage for experimentation
in political imagination, where the story of God's rule unfolds. An odd textual
finding, which, as far as I know, has never been noted, may support the claim
about the experimental setting. From the moment God is revealed to Moses
at the burning bush (Ex. 3) and the Exodus drama begins to the last verse of
Deuteronomy, there is hardly any mention of a person, an artifact, an animal or
a plant, a particular site, or an environmental or meteorological phenomenon
that is not related to God's words and deeds, his laws, threats, and promises.
In Genesis, and certainly outside the Pentateuch, there appear ample details
from everyday life, sometimes whole episodes, that lie outside of God's shadow.
The reader encounters people working in the fields, accompanied by animals;
eating and drinking; getting drunk; making love; raping; meeting each other
incidentally; helping or killing each other—and often they do this without fearing God, looking for him, or consulting him.[150] This is the case not necessarily
because these people do not know God but because their world has not been
emptied of that which is not related to him. But this emptying out is precisely
what takes place from Exodus 3 to Deuteronomy 34. The Israelites depicted in
these texts walk and camp, but they do not work for their living; they get their
provisions from God and live in a kind of an autarkic system, and they do not
make their clothes, build their tents, or even prepare the stuff needed for their

cultic practice. It is this emptying out that creates the counterfactual alternative setting for the stories through which the theocratic experiments unfold and the Pentateuchal political thinking is displayed.

This reading will be extended to parts of Genesis, focusing on those passages where God's supreme power and extreme violence are displayed. It may not be a coincidence that of the various displays of divine violence described in Genesis, none took place in Canaan. Sodom and Gomorrah, which could have been considered part of the promised land, are explicitly taken out: An allegedly priestly redactor was careful to note that the land Abram ceded to Lot (Gen. 13:10–11) was not part of Canaan.[151] The other calamities take place in a post-Edenic no-man's land, in the nonplace of the entire earth (the flood), or in the lands of the most significant others—Babylon (Gen. 11:1–9) or Egypt (12:17).

My experimental hypothesis could be extended to the book of Joshua as well, for it too is emptied of everyday details and takes place in the liminal space created in the promised land during the war of colonization.[152] But the scope of this study does not even allow me to do justice to the full corpus of the Pentateuch. Beyond Joshua, there are other attempts in Prophets and Writings to envision the kingship of God, but none share the setting, the intensity, and the expansion of the Pentateuchal thought experiment. For nowhere else do those unique conditions—a remote time combined with a no-man's land and a political space devoid of political institutions—hold.

Politically speaking, the Pentateuch presents the Bible's equivalent of "a state of nature," a tabula rasa where a new political structure can emerge—in fact be patently imagined as being created forcefully—and where the Bible's clearest thinking on divine power, authority, and violence takes place. Stated more cautiously, I am proposing to take this approach to the Bible seriously and experiment with it. I am proposing to read the Pentateuch as recoding the biblical authors' own experiments in theopolitical imagination. They envisioned a polity under God's rule and sought to establish it *en logoi*, in discourse, "from the beginning," as Socrates suggested in the second book of Plato's *Politea* (369a). Unlike Socrates and his interlocutors, however, the biblical authors did not construct an ideal city from the basic elements of the human condition, which Plato observed and analyzed according to principles of reason. Instead, they unfolded the contours of their polity gradually, by means of sophisticated historical narratives combined with various codes of law. They forged a collective memory for the nation that God chose to be his and told a history that started with creation and ended when the elected people arrived to their promised land. They did not set their experiment in a miraculous future or in a contemporary fictional place but rather imagined a past time that could be conceived as real (probably integrating rich oral traditions) and placed their plot in a relatively familiar, close by, mostly uninhabited area. To a putative history of a people formed and ruled by God they attached a more speculative account of the origin of humans on earth. The opposition that made this an experiment in counterfactual thinking was not one between the actual state of human affairs and a hypothetical, ideal one. Indeed, the legal codes in Exodus, Leviticus, and Deuteronomy imply visions of an emergent ideal state, where people would live under God's laws in their promised land, but God's rule was already in place when the laws were given. The opposition was between the authors' current polity, shaped and ruled by humans, and an imaginary past polity in the wilderness, formed and ruled by God.

There was nothing truly "ideal" about this divine rule—its many failures and setbacks are well known and will be explored in what follows. But the relatively empty, remote, or undefined spaces in which God displayed his power (as depicted in the Pentateuch) were fertile grounds for the theocratic vision. The empty desert provided a perfect space for what Seth Richardson called, in the context of ancient Mesopotamia, "a presumptuous state," a state formation imagined before—or, in this case, without—being materialized. Richardson describes Mesopotamian polities as striving to achieve "uniform territorial control, legally constituted political rule, and political membership identities" and doing so in part by acting, discursively, as if they had already achieved those goals. They promulgated law-codes as a way to imagine the power necessary for enforcing them and cultivating the subjects ready to obey; they competed for "clientele" of obedient subjects (for a long time this competition was more important than rivalry over lands); and they presented claims for authority and attributions of powers as facts with dire consequences, and were busy imagining the peoples subjected to these powers, their lands, histories, and genealogies. These aspirations and discursive strategies were precisely those which the Pentateuch transposed to God.[153]

In that semi-utopic space, Israel was ruled and governed by a power mostly but not entirely invisible, certainly audible, and to a certain extent tangible. This power often used lethal force but was also preoccupied with justifying its violent acts and securing the recognition of its subjects. Here, God could communicate daily with the few privileged individuals who would then speak and act on his behalf, but occasionally he would also reveal himself to the people as a whole. The forms of subjections and modes of governance that would sustain order in that *politea* were outlined, various patterns of limited distribution of power within its small governing elite were envisioned, and the (doomed-to-fail) resistance, dissent, and fragmentation this *politea* might incur were narrated. Extracting recognition, deterring dissent, crushing rebellions, and protecting against enemies meant an extensive use of force. Reading the episodes in which violence is depicted in their proper theopolitical contexts will help us reconstruct three different economies of violence and, accordingly, three distinct theocratic formations. Of special importance in this context are the stories envisioning how theocratic regimes were inaugurated or reinaugurated. Hence, we will pay close attention to stories about the consolidation—gradual, abrupt, or renewed—of the theocratic formations. We will see that these are the episodes where divine rule is most intimately associated with violence.

The analogy drawn between the Pentateuch and Plato's *Politea* must be qualified in one important respect. None of the five books can be compared to a Platonic dialogue, certainly not to one as magisterially designed as *Politea*.[154] Each of the five books is multilayered, composed by multiple authors, and was changed through both oral transmission and written interventions over many centuries. If the analogy with Socrates's idea of constructing a city *en logoi*, from the beginning, can hold, it must be ascribed to the later stages in the history of the Pentateuch's composition and the formative stage of its editing. The origin of many of the Pentateuchal texts probably goes back to a pre-exilic period, with some building blocks (oral stories, which later became "documents" or "scrolls") dated to the early centuries of the first millennium BCE.[155] But a solid body of scholarship over the last three decades suggests that the formative stage of editing (not necessarily the final one) of each of the five books did not take place before the middle of the sixth century BCE, after the Babylonian conquest and subsequent exile.[156] Furthermore, many have claimed that in its final form, the Pentateuch was a reckoning with the destruction of the Temple and loss of political freedom. The idea that God punished his people and withdrew from his land was implanted in texts that were allegedly pronounced long ago in the desert as a threat for the future (Lev. 26:27–41; Deut. 28:61–68, 29:21–27). The authors aimed to explain how the disaster took place to counter the claim that Yahweh was defeated by Assyrian and Babylonian gods but also to anticipate the possibility of return and a renewal of the covenant (Lev. 26:41–45; Deut. 30:1–10).[157] The hypothesis guiding this book may contribute to a reformulation of this idea. The main theopolitical strands in the Pentateuch do not simply try to offer a metanarrative that enables the Jehovist community to come to terms with its own disaster. To do this, the Pentateuch's authors and redactors first would have had to contend with the nature of divine rule and the logic of its violence. Hence the experiments in theocracy. There is no direct evidence that these experiments were explicitly reflective. But both biblical narratives and legal thinking had to operate within a relatively consistent image of divine rule, force, and justice. Such images may have been implied in older stories and prophetic writings, but sometime between the late sixth and the fourth centuries BCE, some patterns emerged, as older segments and new passages assumed their place in the biblical oeuvre. Working at the pragmatic, discursive layer of the biblical language, the different emerging patterns, most importantly the configuration of divine violence and the figures of divine rule associated with them, so I assume, played a decisive part in the formative stage of editing. The task is to reconstruct them.

I assume that an exilic or postexilic date for the formative stage of editing the Pentateuch is most likely. I believe that such a dating provides a most plausible context for the Pentateuchal theocratic formations and that the theoretical analysis proposed here may even lend it some support. But I am aware of the tentative nature of such suppositions. Different timetables are possible too.[158] The categories used to differentiate the theocratic formations would still make sense if the dating would change, albeit with different theopolitical consequences (I will account for these in a few specific contexts; see especially the fourth section of Chapter 5). Once the formations are recognized as acceptable textual constructions, they may pose new questions and contribute new evidence to the historical research.

At this point, the relation of this study to the "documentary hypothesis" should be reiterated and clarified. Throughout my reading, I have assumed the broad outlines of the differentiation among pre-priestly (Elohist and Jehovist, to the extent they are distinguishable), priestly, and Deuteronomic sources. Working from the perspective of divine violence and looking for figures of rule and the configurations of violence, I found that the distinct patterns that emerged fit the main differentiation of the documentarists in recent scholarship.[159] I relied on a variety of relatively recent studies without pretending to exhaust the vast literature and numerous debates on the identification of any particular segment. I used claims about the differentiation of the text into sources and the editing of narrative units that supposedly integrate segments coming from different sources as pieces of a map that may help me identify elements of distinct discursive or theopolitical formations. But I used the map cautiously, following the logic of the emerging formation more than the strictures imposed by the differentiation into sources.[160] The main philological labor was invested in recurring forms at the text's surface, not in identifying their putative sources. It may well be that future changes in the scholarly conception of the topography and history of the edited text will affect the sociohistorical aspects of my findings and raise new questions about the forms that have emerged, but such changes will probably have little to do with the forms themselves and their theopolitical ramifications.[161]

The theocratic formations to be reconstructed here will not be presented as a system of beliefs or ideologies but as linguistic forms that can be located at various textual planes, between discursive formations, at the pragmatic layer of the text, and the recurring figures and forms that transpire at the text's semantic layer. Such forms consist of the persistence or recurrence of certain relations among a given set of identifiable, recurring elements in the world to which the text refers. This is the world that the reader is invited to imagine, and these are the forms she is supposed to recognize in order to find her way there. These recurring forms are reconstructed patterns of *textual phenomena*. Although I have spoken about the "theopolitical imagination" and the imagined "world" in which violent episodes depicted in the text make sense, this "imagination" and that "world" are studied here as real effects of certain discursive patterns. From a methodological point of view, these patterns have the same status as patterns of natural phenomena from which a law of nature is inferred. In distinction, "source," "school," or "tradition," a community or a lineage of thinkers and a chain of transmission, are *extratextual* entities that are usually inferred or reconstructed by following different textual phenomena, like a distinct lexicon, doublets, contradictions, or differences in names of people and places, dates, and age, often with the help of other historical documents and archaeological findings. For the most part, however, the theopolitical formations we are after are not imprinted at the level of the text's semantic or grammar and certainly not in documents and archaeological remains that did not find their way to the biblical text; they must be excavated from the worlds described in the texts and their discursive infrastructure. We are, in other words, in the domain of literary analysis that knows the extratextual world only through the traces it has left in the text but is occupied with that world to which the text refers or which it implies. At the same time, and despite our interest in forms, our reading is not formalist; we will never forget that the possibility of the violence depicted in the text *was meant to be imagined* as extratextual.[162]

Literary analysis has been an important aspect of recent studies seeking to revise the documentary hypothesis and prove its viability against its many critics.[163] The revisionist assumption is that the original sources were basically coherent, organizing their narratives in a rather strict chronological order and inserting there their legal and other non-narrative segments accordingly. This assumption guides the revisionists' identification of the various sources as well as the reconstruction of whole segments of each source used in the final text. Such a literary reading, claims Joel Baden, a prominent advocate of this approach, can reconstruct—and at the same time limit itself to—four independent, perfectly reasonable sources (J, E, P, and D) and the work of one compiler who wove them together into the final edited text.[164] Baden insists on a sharp distinction between the literary analysis and the historical investigation interested in the internal development of each source, its external context, and the dating of its various stages.[165] If such a distinction can be maintained, "sources" and "compiler" have here the same ontological status as our theopolitical imagination and their correlated worlds—they are textual effects of a literary analysis. "The documentary hypothesis in general and in its particulars, is a literary solution to a literary problem, and no more than that."[166]

Baden looks for a thematic, coherent story in each of the sources that make up an episode, while I look for the structural coherence of the theocratic formations and figures across episodes. In both cases, coherence is what needs to be demonstrated. But the coherent units sought here are not a narrative with a plot and characters, a problem and a moment of dénouement. They are recurring forms that transpire across episodes, narrative units, and sometimes even across schools or sources. In the search for the forms, the putative identity and coherence of the sources serve as road maps and guides, but (hopefully) not as constraints. As theopolitical formations are reconstructed according to some version of the documentary hypothesis, the crossing of putative boundaries between different sources is not necessarily an illegitimate move. When it happens, it means that the force of the discursive or theopolitical formation trumps the narrative of one source and strips its fragments of their theopolitical logic, so they can be integrated with fragments coming from another source. The general pattern seems to be the following: **J and** E sources share the same theocratic formation even when they seem contradictory at the thematic level; when they are combined, the logic of the shared formation is amplified (e.g., Num. 11); when the redactors of Genesis combine P and J sources the pre-priestly formation is maintained (e.g., Gen. 6–9); elsewhere in the Pentateuch the priestly formation prevails (e.g., Num. 16–17), with the exception of the story of the scouts (Num. 13–14), where the distinct narratives keep the distinct features of the two formations; whatever non-Deuteronomic sources found their way to Deuteronomic, the Deuteronomic formation prevails.

Our attention here is limited to the recurring forms—regime formations and the configurations of violence. Most of the theoretical work is invested in grasping their theopolitical rationality. Schools of thought, intellectual communities, and traditions of reading and interpretation, to the extent that they can be reconstructed historically, may explain the persistence of forms over time, sometimes even their condition of possibility, but taking them as given textual facts may also obscure the forms' recurrence in the text and beyond. Such putative extratextual entities are neither sufficient nor necessary for the recurrence itself. Forms can cross traditions and intellectual communities, and the latter may work to suppress certain forms and advance others. Occasionally, I will be tempted to entertain some speculations about those extratextual entities, but mostly tentatively, always going back to the emerging theopolitical formations, asking how different historical assumptions affect their theopolitical rationality and significance.

Even more important, however, is the room this assumption leaves for future recurrences of the forms long after the community of discourse that first introduced them has ceased to exist. That they may emerge anew, however disguised and without any discernible line of transmission, is crucial for the most important finding in this book, namely, the idea that key elements in the formation of the modern state are prefigured in the Pentateuchal theocracies. The discursive and figurative lenses employed here are indispensable for recognizing this because they are independent of the continuity of transmission and its piecemeal transformations, accepting of long intervals and irregular recurrences, and relatively indifferent to changing lexicons.

With this in mind, let me clarify that the Pentateuch is not presented here as the origin of the modern European state, not even as an early phase in its genealogy. It is not a genealogical research that is offered here but rather a reconstruction of the political aspects of divine rule in the five books of Moses, which results in three theocratic formations (presented in the next three chapters) that foreshadow in different ways the logic of the modern state. The rest of this book is a contribution to understanding a crucial moment in the state's prehistory, which still belongs to its present. The critique of the state needs to come to terms with the long-repressed theological dimension at the state's heart. Uncovering this dimension goes far beyond recognizing the modern sovereign as a secularized political concept. A systematic politicization of the divine sovereign is where such a critique should begin.

3

THE RULE OF DISASTER: EXTINCTION, GENOCIDES, AND OTHER CALAMITIES

BECOMING POLITICAL

When did God become a political being? "Political" is understood here as a mode of being-together, where many publicly engage with, address, question, and challenge the power that rules them (the ruling power) and where that power is not completely indifferent to the many it rules. For God to be considered political he should be recognized as a ruling power by the many who are affected by this power. In this sense at least, his rule before Egypt was mostly a prepolitical one. Clearly, he was never one of those deities who preferred not to deal with humans and be left alone for their own divine pleasures, rivalries, and trivial quarrels. According to the priestly version of creation that opens the book of Genesis, he gave humans the whole earth to "fill . . . and conquer" and "to hold sway over" (Gen. 1:28) all other living beings, and he has been engaged with and cared for the ways humans conducted themselves ever since. But neither priestly nor pre-priestly sources describe him as occupied with the everyday business of ruling. When he acted, he responded to violations of rules clearly set (in the Garden of Eden) or to excesses of evildoing, for which no standard was set in advance. His authority, however, was not thematized, let alone questioned, until Abraham named him "the judge of all the earth"[1] and challenged him to agree in advance what such a standard should be. The issue was discussed privately between the two protagonists. The multitudes were exposed to his power only when inflicted by one of his calamities.

In the priestly version of Genesis, the very idea to create humans, the only act of creation that is preceded by a reason, seems motivated by an aesthetic pleasure or an emotional comfort—creating something "in our image, by our likeness" (Gen. 1:26)—a desire for the company of others, or perhaps a desire to be recognized by some other whose recognition counts. A more practical reason is also implied—humans will rule the domain of the living, relieving him from the ongoing labor of caring for and ruling over the life he has created. The Jehovist version (Gen. 2–3) offers a far more political scene, however. There were rules of conduct in the Garden of Eden, some clear duties and responsibilities (2:15), and one famous prohibition. Once the prohibition was violated and the transgressors caught, their cunning, duplicity, fear, and vulnerability were exposed, together with the preexistence of surveillance and the subjects' tacit recognition of his authority. The punishment that followed consisted not only in expulsion but also in a reordering of creation's most primordial arrangements (3:14–19). Even before it was meted out, a clear relation of power was set: "I heard Your sound in the garden and I was afraid, for I was naked, and I hid" (3:10). This relation needs to be qualified, however. Adam spoke disingenuously, perhaps, but he invoked his own shame, not God's authority, which he neither challenged nor explicitly acknowledged. And while the three verdicts God pronounced (3:14–15, 16, 17–19) unequivocally set the submission of the three creatures—Adam, Eve, and the snake—to their maker, the expulsion that follows (3:22–24), reveals God's—not Adam's—acute sense of rivalry and premonition of threat: "Now that the human has become like one of us, knowing good and evil, he may reach out and take as well from the tree of life and live forever" (3:22).

Immortality was not something to be shared, and it was on this, before anything else, that the hierarchical relations rested.[2] But it was this very radical difference between the mortal and the immortal and the need to guarantee that difference, which undermined the possibility of a shared space in which God could rule over humans. Political authority requires the recognition of those subjected to it, and this recognition cannot be taken for granted. It is neither born or dies like a living being nor is constructed to stay like an artifact; its temporality is that of human action.[3] The recognition must be sought and protected, renewed, and reformulated, in constant reference to a changing world that a ruling power and its ruled subjects share. This presupposes the possibility of misrecognition, unrecognition, denial of recognition, or a qualified and conditioned recognition.

Adam's and Eve's sin embodied the potential for the problematization of authority, which political relations presuppose and which an Edenic world could not tolerate. God wanted human recognition without human competition. For this, human mortality had to be guaranteed, and the first couple had to leave the garden.

At first, he was recognized by very few men and women, whom he guided
by explicit, precise injunctions. He affected the lives of many more, but the vast
majority of these had never recognized him as their Lord, and most of them
probably had not known his name. His interventions in their affairs took the
form of disaster-generating violence. Very few of the survivors could ascribe the
calamities to his power.[4] Even his clash with Pharaoh in Egypt did not materialize
as a truly political moment. Throughout the confrontation, when both parties
still used some diplomacy (with Moses, Aaron, and the Egyptian soothsayers
and magicians as mediators), the Egyptian god-monarch related to him as the
alleged god of the Hebrews, an alien power to be ignored first, then (when
recognition became unavoidable) as a power to be appeased and maneuvered,
or as an invisible and unpredictable mighty force that must be somehow contained or repelled, without losing grip on the enslaved Hebrews. On his part,
the Lord of Hosts launched his plagues like surprise attacks and used camouflage
and deception (Ex. 14:19–21) to implement his final strike at the Sea of Reeds.
Between violence and diplomacy, each party recognized the other as a force to
be maneuvered and reckoned with but not as an authority that one must, even if
temporarily, recognize and contend with. Pharaoh never recognized the God of
the Hebrews as the sovereign power behind Moses's demand to free the Hebrew
slaves, and God in turn never recognized Pharaoh's legitimacy as a sovereign;
the latter was nothing but a means for his grand plan, an instrument he could
tune as he wished.[5]

Still, pre-priestly sources in Genesis do record some protopolitical moments.[6]
In what follows we will look in some detail at one such moment—the story of the
flood—but for now it is enough to consider a general feature of his mingling in
human affairs. No matter how spectacular or trivial the show of force and how
lethal the violence, God's interventions were never carried out without purpose
and justification, and their very enunciation implied the possibility of disagreement and problematization, both in the world of the text and for its readers. This
possibility is crucial, for, as argued in the first chapter, the political moment is
introduced with a public problematization of a ruling power or an existing order
of power relations. We already saw one such brief moment, on the eve of the destruction of the two cities, in a private encounter between Yahweh and Abraham.
Other, less distinctive moments come to mind as well. Responding to Cain's envy

and rage, he sowed guilt and displayed the arbitrariness of his rule. He did not protect Abel from his brother's rage, but he did look after the assassin. Furthermore, Cain's complaint and request after being sentenced to nomadic life (Gen. 4:13–15) implies both a recognition of his highest authority as well as a certain space for negotiation,[7] and God's response expresses a certain interest on his part in limiting bloodshed among humans.[8] Another story, of the Tower of Babel, reveals his sense of insecurity in the face of competition with other political forces. When he scattered the builders, he prevented the creation of a public space in which power and authority, the Lord's promises and responsibilities, could be shared with others, acknowledged and problematized by many. Without this shared space (even if only partly shared), he could neither turn humans into his subjects nor become their Lord.

For power to become political, its *claim* for authority—the authority to give and take, lead, direct, and prevent—must be presented in public and recognized by many. One should bear in mind the distinction between the recognition *of the claim as a claim for* "the authority to do *x*" and the recognition *of the claimant as having the authority* he or she claims. The former is necessary for the politicization of power,[9] the latter for its legitimization as a political authority or a ruling power. In the Exodus story, from the burning bush to the revelation in Sinai, God is a power driven by the quest for this second recognition. For this he needs to convince Moses—despite his protests and disinclination[10]—that he can and should be his messenger and representative. God taught Moses how to do this and guided him as Moses delivered his master's words to Pharaoh. He had to help Moses teach both the Hebrews and the Egyptians how to read the spectacular events that had unfolded since the latter returned to Egypt[11] and to let his name "be told through all the earth" (Ex. 9:16). The last point is especially crucial. God could create and destroy heaven and earth, issue forth disasters and bestow prosperity on people and nations, and be the mastermind behind everything that takes place under the sky, but he could be the Lord and assume the power and authority of a sovereign only as long as his claims to hold this position were put on a stage in a public space and recognized by many. Egypt was where this stage was first set, and Sinai was the site where public recognition was gained.

FROM EXTINCTION TO GENOCIDE

Among the means most ready to God's mighty hand were large-scale disasters. As we saw, however, those appear on the narrative stage—if one reads Genesis and

Exodus "chronologically," according to their order in the redacted text—early on, certainly before he gains his position as a recognized political sovereign. The first catastrophe was the most horrific. Responding to the multiplication of human evils, he brought about the deluge. Only a few generations after creation[12] he already "regretted that He made humankind on earth" (Gen. 6:6) and decided to wipe them out, together with animals, creeping things, and the birds in the skies, saving only a handful to start anew.

Stories of mass disasters were not unknown in the ancient Near East, and the story of Noah and the flood has several antecedents.[13] These catastrophes were usually ascribed to the unusual and earth-shattering forces put to work by numerous deities for a variety of reasons. Calamity was perceived as punishment for injustice or for neglecting to worship a deity. In other cases, it could be related to struggles between gods or their irritation with human hustle and bustle—as was the explicit cause of the flood in the epic of Gilgamesh.[14] In this respect, the biblical depiction of divine violence has clear precedents, which have often been noted. Biblical authors, so it seems, inherited famous themes from ancient Mesopotamian, perhaps even Indian, myths of the deluge, and they most probably responded to some of these. What most significantly distinguishes the biblical story of the flood (in both its Jehovist and priestly versions) from more ancient myths, it has often been noted, is the appeal to human depravity as a justification both for the mass extinction and for the promise never to repeat it.[15]

Frymer-Kensky identified an interesting similarity in the way the deities' exterminatory acts are presented and explained in Mesopotamian myths and in Genesis. The gods, she argues, react to an excess that they cannot tolerate; the crossing of an imaginary threshold unleashes their catastrophic rage.[16] This "theological-physical" mechanism was already recognized and contested in the Mesopotamian myth. In tablet XI of the epic of Gilgamesh, the god Ea revealed to the mortal Utnapishtim that his fellow god Enlil had conspired with other gods (Anu, Ninurta, and Ennugi) to flood the old city of Shuruppak to punish humanity for making excessive amounts of noise. To save him, Ea commanded Utnapishtim to dismantle his house and build a boat, abandoning his earthly possessions while gathering living creatures to take aboard. Once Enlil realized that life had endured the flood, he was furious. Ea defended his betrayal of the gods, arguing that their exterminatory act was far too excessive a punishment and that instead of destroying all of humanity in the flood they could have settled for minor afflictions, such as unleashing wild beasts, famine, or disease.[17] In Genesis, it is God himself who has second thoughts about the magnitude of the extinction (Gen. 8:21), and his sense of intolerable excess on the humans' part is clearly expressed, but it is an excess of evil and injustice (6:5), not a benign nuisance like noise.

Unlike most biblical narratives of crime and punishment, here, facing the worst eruption of divine violence, no specific evil (*raa*) is mentioned, only their accumulations. God "saw" that their deeds were always ("all the day") evil and that "every scheme of [their] heart[s'] devising"[18] was "perpetually evil" (Gen. 6:5). Did they understand that their use of force meant injustice? Did he ever try to warn them? Were they really incorrigible, deserving to be perished? The humans' point of view, or their awareness of what he ascribed to them, is not part of the story. The priestly source's emphasis on the *immensity* of humans' corrupted ways and injustice generated by violence (*ḥamas*) (Gen. 6:11–12) and its affective impact on God ("He was grieved to His heart"; 6:6) may be read as an attempt to circumvent this difficulty in the J source. The priestly interjection underlies both the crossed threshold and its specific moral nature.[19] At the same time, the priestly explanation of the moral outrage shifts the focus from the devising in the humans' heart to the effect of their deed: "The earth was corrupt and filled with *ḥamas*, for all flesh had corrupted its ways on the earth" (6:12). Human misconduct has affected the entire earth and every being living on it, producing a disaster on a "global" scale; the response should therefore be directed at the earth as a whole. The effect of God's justness in this context would mean the restoration of an earthly equilibrium that had gone unhinged. Enlil only cares for his ability to sleep, but Yahweh is concerned with the corruption of the entire earth. In both cases, the human victims could have been as ignorant about the disturbing or corrupting effects of their deeds. The justification for the calamity, as Frymer-Kensky showed, is nothing more than the deity's subjective reaction to an excess of a disturbing substance, which the Mesopotamian myth imagined as noise and the Bible conceived as evil.[20]

The clear-cut distinction between the "moral" version of the biblical flood and its "amoral" version in Mesopotamian myths is further undermined if we remember that the figure of a threshold and the excess created by its crossing are not foreign to the author of Genesis, but there the figure is deployed quite differently. In a few stories, both Jehovist and priestly, that involve a massive exercise of divine violence, the drawing of the threshold is a reasoned, reflexive operation, and the proper response to it involves a cautious calculation. In Genesis 18 (a J source), Abraham convinces God to set the threshold quite high (ten righteous persons would have saved the two cities no matter how terrible the accumulative sin), but at the same time he leaves out the lives of innocent babies and animals whose righteousness could not be established and whose death made no difference. Likewise, the return to and conquest of Canaan had to be delayed until "the iniquities of the Amorites [would be] full" (Gen. 15:16; a priestly source). The theme recurs in Isaiah: God orders the prophet to prevent the people's repentance to let their sin accumulate, so he can justly lay waste to their cities (Is. 6:9–13). In all these episodes, a moral calculus is at play. And in both versions of the flood story, the missing moral calculus and the excess of the divine response is corrected explicitly by reflection, a sense of regret, and a commitment to not generate again extinction at such a scale (8:21–22 [J]; 9:9–17 [P]). This moment of self-reflection is the way the biblical story preserves the protest and criticism of the Mesopotamian god Ea in a fashion appropriate for a God who is on his own and who acts alone.

Some scholars offer a psychological reading of God's outburst of wrath and his later regret. Following Muff, Handel, and others and relying on a cluster of midrashic interpretations of the flood stories, Yair Lorberbaum argues that God's bouts of rage should be read as expressions of adolescence and their gradual overcoming as a coming of age—the story is read as a "bildungsroman" in which God learns to recognize the fundamental flaws of his making, overcome his disappointments, and conquer his ferocious rage.[21] Lorberbaum's close reading of the flood stories has interesting affinities with the symptomatic interpretation of divine wrath suggested by Peter Sloterdijk.[22] The latter critiques the emotive reductionism of psychoanalysis and of the philosophy it has affected. Instead of an emotional economy rooted in the ever-renewing libidinal passion and the regular failure to satisfy it, Sloterdijk suggests that the erupting rage and its related states[23] should be understood as a part of a separate emotional economy that operates according to its own set of rules of accumulation, exaggeration, a crossed limen, and eruption. It is within such a separate emotional economy that the two biblical sources of the flood story offer "mechanisms for the management of jealousy," according to Lorberbaum, the sacrificial incense (J) and the rainbow in the clouds (P). Jealousy is thus a dynamic, not a fixed, category, but the whole affair, according to Lorberbaum, is "internal" to God's personhood. Even the rainbow, he argues, is a semiautomatic device placed "in the cloud," facing God and visible to him, not necessarily to humans, to remind *him* of his promise.[24]

This is an insightful and compelling reading, which, when left alone, is misleading. For even if the management of rage is a process that is internal to God (in the J source he speaks to himself [8:21]; in P he establishes his covenant with humans unilaterally, without waiting to hear from them [9:11–17]), it takes place between the wrathful actor and his creation, the whole earth, and the remnants of humanity who have survived the deluge. The internal affair is played out on a "planetary" stage—"the earth," is mentioned forty-two times in the story (Gen. 6–9), always referring to the whole earth, not to any particular region within it—and this has a clear political meaning.

If the real distinction of the biblical flood story lies in God's concern for the whole earth (which both sources share), the stake of the decision "to wipe out from the face of the earth all existing things that [he] has made" (7:4, a J source) is located in a realm beyond good and evil, namely, the realm of power. In the eyes of the narrator, God acts as the sovereign of all the earth. Four features mark God's first epiphany as a supreme ruler. The first is the attention to *all* the earth and to *all* creatures living on it[25] and the frequent recurrence of and variations on holistic phrases that signal an interest in a strong, synoptic, totalizing point of view that characterizes a supreme ruling power.[26] The second is the clear decision to take a radical action that would affect almost all living creatures—to wipe out everything. The decision is clearly articulated and presented as reflecting regret and grief over a previous act, "that he has made humankind on the earth" (Gen. 6:6). The decision is followed by a plan, which is carefully executed. The third feature is the fact that God's two cardinal decisions—to change course and wipe out life on earth, as well as the commitment never to repeat the genocidal act—are explained and justified in nonpersonal terms (6:5, 8:21). The reasoning is the same in both (Jehovist) cases, and its wording is almost identical, referring to the evil "devisings of the human heart." The difference between the two is small but decisive. Before the flood, God sees the human heart as "evil all the day," while after the flood he comes to understand that it was evil "from youth."[27] In other words, God seems to accept responsibility for a certain bug in his own design. The fourth feature is the commitment itself, to never "again strike down all living things as I did" (8:21). The priestly version goes further; it places the commitment at the core of a covenant, the first of many, that sets new terms for the relationship between God and all living beings (Gen. 9:9–12),[28] and it adds the rainbow, a meteorological device to guarantee that the promise will never be forgotten (9:12–16).[29]

Implied in the promise and included in both versions of the story are the unity and durability of his authority, without which the promise could not be kept—and no relation of ruling and submission could be sustained. The covenant added in the priestly version seems to underscore further the political nature of his ruling after the flood, when life was made possible again. The two versions of the story share the general scheme (an all-encompassing outburst of divine violence and a restart for life on earth) yet differ in many details, which have some "local" ramifications (the sacrifice, Noah's age, the number of animals

brought on the ark).[30] But the addition of the covenant in Genesis 9 rewrites the
political meaning of the story as a whole. The story remains protopolitical in
both versions (this feature of divine rule will not change before the revelation
in Sinai), and the covenant does not change this (after all, unilateral promises to
silent creatures who are not even aware of their entering into a binding relation
with their master fall short of what could count as political). What the priestly
addition of the covenant transforms is the nature of divine rule. It turns the
flood retroactively into an inaugural event, setting new terms for the relationship between the creator and his living beings, and it places the great extinction in a prepolitical era to which there is no return. This aspect of the priestly
version is far removed from both the Mesopotamian flood myths and from the
Jehovist version. At the same time, however, the editorial intervention that inserts claims for divine justice and divine care (the promise) into fragments of
the ancient myths renders calamities of mythical proportions integral to a certain
conception of divine rule. Total extinction is a divine potentiality that was clearly
demonstrated but is now indefinitely suspended by a sovereign decision, while
all lesser calamities remain active threats. For the Jehovist version there is no
such rupture and no such restraint—the promise is not formalized in a covenant
and remains closed within an internal dialogue, a promise that the divine ruler
makes to himself ("and God said to [el] His heart"; Gen. 8:21). Given the four
political elements contained in the J version—decision, synoptic point of view,
justification of the genocidal act, and a long-term promise—it is clear that total
extinction was the first exercise in divine rule over the entire earth. Total extinction may not recur, but its possibility was established, and limited mass extinc-
tions of entire human groups (cities, nations, and peoples) will be the hallmark
of the Jehovist conception of divine rule, while its consistent absence is that of
priestly theocracy.

The second act of mass extinction, of the two prosperous cities "in the land of
the plain" (Gen. 19:28),[31] was justified by an ascription of guilt that was vague
but somewhat more concrete than the accusation of the flood generation. The
residents of those cities were "bad and sinful" (13:13), their "outcry" was "great,"
and "their offense" was "very grave" (18:20). The decision to exterminate was
not taken lightly. God investigates and deliberates ("let me go down and see,
whether as the outcry that has come to Me they have dealt destruction"; 18:21).
He even shares his plan with Abraham, but it is hard to say whether it was a
courtesy to his disciple, a call for a check on the justness of his coming deed, or

simply the need for a witness who could fully appreciate the display of his destructive power. Like in the flood story, the totality of the destruction is emphasized (19:25). The point, so it seems, is not merely to demonstrate the immensity
of divine power but to use destruction as a means for achieving the totalizing
effect of power. Only in destruction is this ruling power capable of articulating
its claim for the exclusivity of its control, possession, and dominion. The exchange with Abraham highlights this point because what is at stake is phrased
in terms of all or nothing: to destroy everything or not to destroy at all ("I will
not destroy for the sake of the ten"; 18:32). Collective punishment or collective
forgiveness: This is the question. Annihilation is one of his potentialities, and he
has full control over it. He is capable of total destruction, and he is capable of
not destroying at all.[32]

BEYOND DESTRUCTION

Beyond this, his mode of ruling does not seem very flexible. In the negotiation
with Abraham, the option of a selective extermination is not raised.[33] But he did
make some exceptions on his own. In Sodom and Gomorrah, just like in the
flood, these exceptions were preconceived decisions to refrain from exercising
the full scope of his violence and allowing a few to be saved—Noah, his family,
and the animals he brought to the ark; Lot and his family. The exceptions were
part of the initial plan, not a concession or an expression of mercy. The exercise
of extreme violence and its withholding take place at one and the same time,
manifesting both sides of his destructive potentiality, pointing to the totality of
his destructive power on the one hand and, on the other, to his unbounded capacity to care for those he chooses to spare.

No law was suspended, for no law was yet announced. The actualization
of his power in total destruction seems a radical interruption of the regular
course of affairs, executed with the most uncommon means to achieve unprecedented effects—weeks or months[34] of uninterrupted rain that "covered all the
high mountains that are under all the skies," eliminating all living creatures "that
[were] on the dry land" (7:17–22), a rain of "brimstone and fire" that "overthrew
all those cities and all the plain, and all the inhabitants of the cities and what
grew in the soil" (19:24–25). But, in fact, neither the flood nor the destructions
of the two cities were exceptional stories in the cultural milieu from which the
stories are drawn. Flood myths were associated with Mesopotamian deities, and
the complete destruction of rebellious cities was the ultimate symbol of earthly

imperial power.[35] Unprecedented as the events were for humans, God acted as gods and great kings were supposed to act, and in this context he did make an exception for the sake of the few survivors whom he spared.

Between these two cases of extreme, genocidal violence, there is a case of the ruination of a city and a tower that has just been built, where Yahweh combines in his own action the power of a deity and the cunning of a shrewd political actor who outwits his rivals.[36] The figure of Yahweh that overshadows the first half of Genesis thus combines the lethal power of a deity with the destructive might of an earthly emperor, and it is this very combination that presents Yahweh as a ruling power and shows his power to be that of a supreme ruler. He began to rule—and appears to the reader at least—as the Lord of the earth not when he created it and all livings beings on it but when he performed its destruction. He reasserted his rule over the particular region in which his chosen man was wandering not when he promised Abraham would inherit it but when he displayed his capacity to destroy any part of it he saw fit.

That combination between the lethal power of a deity and a deep sense of earthly political rivalry was not entirely successful, one must admit. He was in the company of humans and communicated with them from the moment he created them, but he acquired his first loyal disciple and subject only many generations later. Except for the few he saved from annihilation, his relationship to mankind in the flood generation, to the industrious people of Babylon, or to the wicked residents of Sodom and Gomorrah was unilateral. He revealed himself to them—if they were able to understand his catastrophic epiphany—only at their very last hours, as they were perishing, or losing the world they had shared. The same is true in Exodus. He had not revealed himself to the Egyptians before he began torturing them and outmaneuvering their king. They were cruel enslavers, but he was not their God.

His relationship with his few disciples were intimate but included cruel and dangerous tests—testing their loyalty (commanding Abraham to sacrifice his son; Gen. 22) or courage and strength (fighting with lonely Jacob; Gen. 32:24–31). Most of his earthly subjects knew little or nothing about him, but we read more about his dealing with them (Babel, Pharaoh) than with other deities. These, rather than other gods, were his rivals. He probably had some nonhuman company,[37] was mostly indifferent to other gods, never demanded exclusive worship, and even tolerated the presence of idols in Israel's camp (Gen. 31:19, 30–35). The narrators who recorded his affairs among humans were neither monotheist nor monolatrous, yet they depicted him as violent all the same. The demand for exclusivity embedded in the monistic theopolitics (as Assmann has it) or the

logic of scarcity that he cultivated (à la Schwartz) cannot explain the outpouring
of violence with which he visited those who did not worship him and with whom
he never established ongoing relations. Schwartz is right to observe that scarcity
in paternal love may explain the brotherly rivalry, hatred, and cruelty running
through Genesis from Cain and Abel to Joseph and his brothers. But God was
directly involved only in the first confrontation, and his name was never invoked
in the worst case of extreme human violence recorded in Genesis—the massacre
in Shechem committed by two of Jacob's sons, taking revenge over the rape of
their sister (Gen. 34). Unlike monotheist zealotry, there was nothing mimetic
in the violence of the Jehovist God. Except for the murder of Cain, his name
was never invoked in stories of cruelty, greed, and jealousy (Sarah and Hagar;
Rebecca, Jacob, and Esau; Laban and Jacob; Joseph and his brothers). The issue
with his violence was bad governance of an incompetent ruler who knew little
about the means of domination, let alone techniques of governance. After creation, his main claim to fame was destruction and the use of lethal force. If rulership were an advertised job and Yahweh a newcomer who took possession of it,
we would have said that the new appointee simply did not fit the job description.

In the beginning, he sought neither to educate nor to govern. If he ruled the
earth, this rule did not demonstrate a will to govern; if deliberation with others
was involved, it concerned only some unnamed, undisclosed deities (implied
in Gen. 11:6–7)[38] and, less obliquely but still not publicly, his disciple Abraham
(18:17–33). In Sodom and Gomorrah there was a carefully drawn plan: Its necessity was examined (18:21) and then executed with precision, attention to detail
(19:29), and a capacity to improvise under changing circumstances (19:10–22).
But at other times the Lord appeared more anxious and less confident ("now
nothing that they propose to do will be withheld from them"; 11:6). He was preoccupied with control rather than the assurance of proper life under his dominion, mostly opting for reactive force over proactive actions. The generation of the
flood and the residents of Sodom and Gomorrah were under his jurisdiction but
apparently not directly ruled by him; their evils were recorded and weighed, and
then they were wiped out. If they were ruled, we know nothing about that. The
epiphany of divine rule (for the texts' reader) almost coincides with the demise
of the entire population subjected to his rule. If the momentous catastrophes left
any lasting impression on the survivors and bystanders, that impression was not
recorded.[39] And it may not be a coincidence that both men chosen to be exempt
from total destruction—Noah's on account of his own virtue and Lot on account
of his uncle's—ended up stoned in a temporary shelter, one naked in front of
his children and the other sleeping with his daughters. The two episodes mark

an anticlimactic and embarrassing end to momentous events that should have inspired awe and reverence. It is almost as if the narrator signals to the readers that they should not look in these stories for a lesson about Yahweh's greatness, but they should certainly remember his tremendous destructive power to undo something that went terribly wrong with the humans he had created.

Destruction for the sake of replacement was not his only mode of action. He provided private, direct guidance and protection to his faithful disciple and some of his kin and often intervened in a nonharmful way in family affairs, saving the women (Sarah, Hagar, and Rebecca) from their men's misconduct or their own.[40] He also made a series of promises with far-reaching geopolitical consequences— "I've given this land to your seed, from the river of Egypt to the big river, the river of Euphrates" (Gen. 15:18). These promises implied a clear plan and a series of future actions: When the time comes, he would expel ten nations (15:19–21) from their lands, destroy, and annihilate them. Abram only wanted a son and was not invested in this futurist politics. He did not care to ask at what cost his descendants would inherit a land that was not theirs.[41] The priestly source inserted at that point (15:13–16) sought to make clear that God was already envisioning a different political scene.

This came about only when he delivered the twelve clans of slave workers from their bondage and turned them into a nation. In the process, the pattern of an extensive use of force became all the more prominent in the overall configuration of the divine rule. In this respect, the recurrence of violent outbursts is more important than the differences between them. At the same time, the relatively frequent recourse to violence attests to the shortcomings of his rule, to the failure of internalizing his authority, or perhaps to the fact that this rule simply subsisted in the excess of his violence. One may trace in every catastrophic outpouring the crossing of a threshold of evils that could not be contained or tolerated any longer, while such crossings came along with ineffective threats, messages that did not get transmitted, and expectations that were not met. Even in the most dramatic event of all—the Exodus—the extravagant, hyperbolic display of his power was insufficient to teach both the Egyptian masters and the Hebrew slaves their lesson. While the masters were ready to rise from their mourning immediately after their firstborns had been slaughtered in order to chase their fugitive slaves (Ex. 14:5–7), the liberated slaves were prepared, when faced with the first serious danger on their journey, to return to their house of bondage (14:10–12). If in devising that ambush to Pharaoh and his army at the Sea of Reeds the Lord had hoped to demonstrate his might to his new subjects, it is not clear how impressed they really were (or how impressed the reader was supposed to be). For soon after the echoes of the hymn chanted by Miriam had faded, Egypt was again imagined as a land of plenty (Ex. 16:3).

In Egypt and at the Sea of Reeds, he revealed his destructive power through devastating plagues and one ostensibly miraculous and unprecedented strike. Catastrophization appeared now most clearly as his mode of ruling, as well as his favorite form of epiphany. Soon one realizes, however, that the plague and the drowning of the Egyptians in the Sea of Reeds were but a prelude to the most important revelation of all—the revelation at Sinai. This sublime moment of awe and wonder was not without its own display of violence, which remained virtual till Moses came down from the mountain and materialized only then (Ex. 32). Memories and images of catastrophe were hovering above the gathering crowd like the clouds of his glory, as the two parties, the Lord and his subjects, prepared themselves to enter into a covenant. The preamble to the covenant (Ex. 19:4–6), that is, the verses that can be read as the covenant's prerequisites, contain the three temporal dimensions of divine rule: a violent *past* ("You yourselves saw what I did to the Egyptians") that generates the people's separation as a ruled community ("brought you to Myself"), a *present* of all-embracing domination ("for all the earth is Mine"), and a conditional *future* that encompasses both sanctity ("and you shall be to Me a kingdom of priests and a holy nation") and an implicit warning ("if you will indeed obey My voice").[42]

What is presented here is not the form of his theocracy but rather his claim to an unbounded authority. There is nothing about the responsibilities this authority involves, merely a decisive aspect of the way it musters obedience—an unsurpassable force and threats of catastrophic violence. It is a self-constituting rule that proclaims itself and its community; determines the conditions of their contract, their subservience, and His promises; and presents the range of his rule in space ("all the earth") and time (between a well-defined past and an indefinite future). The divine rule further defines the source of its authority: the Exodus, the redemption of the People of Israel, and the disaster of the Egyptians. They became his subjects because he delivered them from slavery. Exodus was a transition from one Lord to another, executed through a spectacular display of violence—the mark of all revolutions to come.

The seed of calamity was sown in each of the three temporal dimensions. The covenant between God and his people resided in the space that spans between the memory of disaster and its expectation. The conditions of the covenant were set in the wake of a catastrophic redemption from slavery, while anticipating the recurrence of violence in case the conditions were not met—a threat that would soon be materialized (Ex. 32:15–35). And in between a recent past and an unknown future, at every moment during the event of revelation itself, an immediate, imminent threat is being invoked. God declared the mountain at Sinai a closed territory and a potential site of disaster, creating the conditions for hallowing the mountain and avoiding the danger of his revelation: "Take heed to yourselves that you do not go up to the mountain or touch its base. Whoever touches the mountain shall surely be put to death. Not a hand shall touch him, but he shall surely be stoned or shot with an arrow; whether man or beast, he shall not live" (19:12–13).

The spatial separation separated life and death. Then, as if this was not clear enough, Moses, who went down with the instructions, was called back on the third day, to receive another warning, "lest they break through to gaze at the Lord, and many of them perish. Also, let the priests who come near the Lord consecrate themselves, lest the Lord break out against them" (19:21–22). It seems that Moses did not understand what else was required of him, since the sanctification ritual had already taken place and all the preparations completed: "The people cannot come up to Mount Sinai; for You warned us, saying, 'Set bounds around the mountain and consecrate it'" (19:23). After all these warnings, the entire people, even the mountain itself, trembled (19:16–18).[43] Yet God was not convinced, so He called Moses to return with Aaron and the priests and repeated his warning. Like a boastful bully who indulges in the effect of his threats and begs others to restrain him, he warned Moses yet again: "Do not let the priests and the people break through to come up to the Lord, lest He break out against them" (19:24).

Obedient and trembling from thunder and lightning, a blast of that trumpet, a thick cloud, a kiln-like Sodomite smoke,[44] and the fire on top of the mountain, the people were introduced into the covenant with God. Is it surprising, then, that when the memory of the menace faded, so many acted as if they had never really agreed to the terms presented to them in Sinai? When violence is divine rule's primary mode of acting and presence, that rule is internalized according to the living memory of violence.

The catastrophe on the mountain's slopes was avoided, as both sides had succeeded in restraining themselves, only to erupt after forty days in response to the rite of the golden calf. Moses had disappeared for weeks, and his absence made the people anxious. They may have felt abandoned and vulnerable and so sought protection in a figure substituting for the vanished God or for his emissary, in turn violating the first and (or) second commandment.[45] Did they already forget both his laws and his threats, as well as the catastrophic performances of his power, which they had recently witnessed? Or did they err in their understanding of the law? God, for his part, was not interested in finding out. The revelation ends in disaster, with human violence joined to divine violence. First Moses commands the sons of Levi to launch an indiscriminate killing of brothers, fellows, and kin (about three thousand men were executed; Ex. 32:26–28), then God unleashes a plague that caused an unknown number of victims (32:35). However, this catastrophic eruption of violence, performed by divine power or carried out in his name ("whoever is for Yahweh, to me"; 32:26), was the lesser evil, a substitute for wholesale annihilation. It was only thanks to Moses's pleas that he abstained from letting his wrath "flare against them and . . . put an end to them" (32:10). Like the flood story, the genocidal plan was announced along with a plan for a restart, and Moses had to play the role of Noah, the remnant who would become the progenitor: "I will make you a great nation" (32:10).

The threat of total extinction—both the idea and the speech act—recurs several times in the Bible, with respect to Israel, Amalek, and other nations.[46] In most cases the threat is general, and no action is taken. But twice in the desert, a concrete plan to annihilate the people of Israel and replace the seed of Abraham with the seed of Moses was proposed, and taken seriously, by Moses, at least, as he pleaded with God for forgiveness.[47] The second time took place after the return of the scouts' expedition to Canaan and the people's rebellious response to the disheartening news they brought with them. Twice the threat was aborted after Moses's pleas to God. A third genocidal threat is described, but only retrospectively, after an act of great sacrilege, as "the scourge was held back (Num. 25:9), and the difference, as we will see later in the fourth chapter, is important.

Unlike the total extinction of all life on earth, which according to both versions of the flood story ends with a divine promise never to be repeated, the plan to wipe out the people of Israel was abandoned but never completely renounced. There will not be another flood, but the fate of Sodom and Gomorrah forever looms over Israel (Deut. 29:22).[48] God will always be blessed not only for all the good things he did to his people but for what he was about to do but at the last minute gave up doing: As Nehemiah recalled in his brief summary of the people's history: "In Your great compassion You did not make an end of them [our fathers] or abandon them, for You are a gracious and compassionate God" (Neh. 9:31).

Within the economy of violence and law established by the Jehovist model of divine rule, genocide—a limited form of total extinction—does not stand apart from other catastrophic forms of violence, a doomsday strategy limited to the apocalyptic end of history; it is rather an integral part of God's arsenal of violent means and of the narratives that chronicle their uses and an existing possibility invoked more than once after the flood. If total extinction inaugurated divine rule, then local or partial genocides, threats of genocide, and revoked plans to execute genocides structure divine rule from then on, and they must be accounted for when the logic of pre-Priestly theocracy is reconstructed and its recorded memory is recalled. Jacob Taubes grasped this well and articulated it compellingly when he linked his radical interpretation of Paul's Letter to the Romans to a reading of the opening of the Yom Kippur *Kol Nidrei* prayer and based both on the genocidal threat in Exodus 32.[49] Paul, Taubes explains, reenacts the scene in which Moses was offered to become a progenitor of the new people of God, instead of the old one doomed to annihilation. Unlike Moses, Paul accepts the offer. A new ecclesia will replace the old one, linked to Abraham not by seed ("father to a multitude of nations"; Gen. 17:4–5) but rather by faith (Rom. 4:13–25). While Israel will not be annihilated, they were erased as a chosen nation from the new covenant, and their role as the people of God was revoked; unless they joined the new ecclesia, they were spiritually, if not physically, doomed. In the opening of Yom Kippur's evening ritual, according to Taubes, the community as a whole takes Moses's position and reenacts the moment of Moses's plea to God as he tries to change the Lord's heart and prevent the looming catastrophe. Taubes proposes that both the founding moment of the Christian faith and one of the most important, cherished, and enduring rituals of the Jewish people reanimate the same traumatic moment that has accompanied Israel ever since its inauguration, as the catastrophic prospect that accompanied the covenant with God became concrete and imminent.

One may regard Taubes's reading of Paul and its juxtaposition with the Jewish ceremonial prayer of *Kol Nidrei* as an anachronistic projection onto the remote biblical scene of the trauma that he and his generation lived through, a genocide that did take place, which Taubes clearly invoked when he delivered his seminar on Paul in Heidelberg, Germany, in 1987. Nevertheless, this reading should be embraced, I believe. Taubes does not offer a comparison between the two genocides—one virtual, even within the realm of the biblical myth, and the other historical and real, one divinely made and the other a specific, humanly executed, regime-made disaster.[50] And he does not call on us to hold God accountable for crimes against humanity. That is the business of those who address a living God. Taubes's task is to understand their political imagination. What Taubes suggests, in fact, is that it is in the wake of the Jewish genocide—that Jews are reading their Bible and practicing their prayers and that in this they are placing themselves in a long tradition of life in the wake of past and future genocides (or other forms of mass extinction, if one cares for the γένος in genocide).

We too cannot extricate ourselves from the wake of these genocides,[51] a long wake to which one should add those that took place before and after the Jewish genocide and are often overshadowed by it, as well as those that might be generated in the wake of ongoing climate catastrophes.[52] But at the same time, we should avoid the risk of overlooking the specificity of different genocidal events, whether real or imaginary, and the historicity of the conditions that made them possible. We do not live in the wake of one long catastrophe. Our task is to add those catastrophes associated with divine rule to a general typology of regime-made disasters. For the biblical genocidal disasters with which we are concerned were imagined, in some detail, and retold; for many centuries they have been considered as real or as real possibilities averted at the last moment, and at the same time they have become iconic. Once humans devised, built, and accumulated enough destructive power and assumed enough hubris, these disasters were no longer simply imaginable. They could be planned and executed with new technologies, as indeed they were and might be again, while being rationalized and justified along patterns of thought that bear significant resemblance to those reconstructed here. It is a resemblance we must attend to.

SEPARATION AND DISASTER

Before Sinai, God had no special relation to those whom he struck, destroyed, or wiped out. His use of force rather reflects an acute intolerance to evil or competition more than an interest in ruling and government. But early on he established a special relationship with one man, Abraham, and later with one of that man's sons, Isaac, and one of his grandsons, Jacob. The logic of selection and separation (*havdalah*) was already at work.[53] In fact, it was at work from the very beginning (of the Jehovist source), and it was usually followed and sometimes preceded by disastrous consequences. In two distinct acts of creation, he created man as a creature different and separate from all other creatures (Gen. 2:7, 19–20) and placed him to guard a Garden where two trees stood separate from all others (2:16–17). This generated a desire for the fruit of the forbidden tree before desire was even known and opened the gate to lethal violence. He discriminated between Adam's two sons, Cain and Abel, and created the conditions for the first murder.[54] Noah, the sole righteous man of his generation, was selected by God to survive the deluge and to select the animals that would restart life on earth; the foreigner Lot was separated before the destruction of Sodom and Gomorrah; God respects Sarah's request from Abraham to separate Ishmael from his half-brother Isaac and expel him; he does not intervene when Jacob's mother helps her young son steal his father's blessing, which was meant for the older brother, Esau. Jacob preferred Joseph, then Benjamin, over all his other ten sons. And when the extended family settled in Egypt, in a segregated area, Goshen, a new drama of separation began.

Disaster struck either as a result of an act of separation or in order to maintain separation and crush the forces that threatened it, as if the distinction could not appear otherwise and a distinct identity could not be forged without an act of violence that safeguarded the articulation of that distinction and the identity established through its reiteration. Each act of divine *havdalah* in the pre-Priestly source was engraved on the human body through some catastrophe.[55] In the beginning, the violence involved was either the form of his revelation (in the flood and Sodom and Gomorrah) or its dark side—he only appeared to and spoke with people associated with a looming disaster—Cain, Noah, Lot. This pattern changed when he revealed himself to Abraham with no immediate threat or associated eruption of violence. But his violence was never far away, following Abram and Sarai to Egypt (Gen. 12:17–18, 20),[56] hovering above the covenant scene (15:9–10), and then again when he orders Abraham to sacrifice Sarah's son, Isaac (15:22), an order revoked and displaced at the last minute. The violence in Egypt was meant to protect both the life and the separateness of the nomadic couple and their household, and the disaster befell their innocent hosts. But in the two other cases, new motives appear that deserve our attention.

God's revelation to Abram (Gen. 15) is the first moment in which God's people appear in the Bible. The people was still a remote promise: Abram's "seed" would become numerous as the stars in heaven and will inherit "this land," where Abram dwelled as a guest at the time (Gen. 15:5, 7). Abram asked for assurances (15:8) and was ordered by God to slaughter a heifer, a she-goat, a ram, a dove, and a pigeon and to cut the cloven-hoofed animals into two. A carrion bird swoops down looking for prey, and Abram has to drive it off. The scene is bloody and ominous, and Abram is engulfed with anxiety, "great dark dread came falling upon him" (15:12). As he falls into "a deep slumber . . . a smoking brazier with a flaming torch passed" between the animals' cut parts (15:12, 17). The violent cuts through which the cutting of the covenant was performed heralded the emergence of a nation that would come to inherit a wide, clearly designated piece of land at the expense of all its indigenous peoples (15:18–21). All that Abram wanted was a sign that his own son, springing from his own seed, would inherit him (15:2–3). But what God saw in the vision of his own "com[ing] to Abram in a vision" (15:1) was the future separation of one people from among all the peoples, to inherit one land from among all the lands.[57]

The violence of the cutting that runs through this scene, far into the future, from the slaughtered animals to the people of Canaan to be uprooted by Abram's descendants, cannot be dissociated from the divine selection of one man (Abram), his descendants and his people, and the promised land they are to be given by God. "The Cutting covenant has cut the people off," Schwarz states succinctly.[58] This combination of separation and violence embedded in a promise was given a name: *bĕrîth*, covenant. The conjunction of these two terms is embedded in the Hebrew word, an anagram of the verb *b.t.r*—to cut. There was no covenant that did not separate the cutter from at least part of his or her surroundings,[59] and there was no covenant ceremony that took place without spilling blood by cutting animals (Gen. 15:9).[60] In the Sinai covenant, the spilled animal blood was literally *dām habbĕrît*, the blood of the covenant, as Moses tells the people in Sinai (Ex. 24:8).[61] Further, covenants usually contained recollections of earlier covenants and an ominous threat of a future cut. The covenant and the violence of separation are both etymologically and thematically linked. The covenant presupposes, requires, performs, and generates the violence of separation in order to eventually provide protection from the violence of the others who will have to pay its price.

The other scene of violence that marks Abraham's relationship with God, which is even more dramatic than the covenant of the cut pieces, is the revoked sacrifice of Isaac. Abraham is ordered to sacrifice the son to whom he waited for many decades. The sacrifice would jeopardize the promise of the covenant, and the obedient disciple and the bereaved father would be abandoned by, but still be left with, a senseless Lord. Abraham complies silently. The text does not record any emotion, complaint, or inner dialogue on Abraham's part, only the gentle words he speaks to his lads as he leaves them behind and to his fearful, inquisitive son, whom he takes with him (Gen. 22:5, 8). That Isaac is finally released from the altar and replaced by a ram does not dissipate the violence. The angel's last-minute intervention displaces part of the violence (to the ram) but also hides another part of it, which cannot be revoked—the infinite pain that must have accompanied Abraham for three long days and nights, all the way to "the place that God had said to him" (22:9), and Isaac's nameless, inexpressible dread. This is the price God was willing to pay for getting a proof of Abraham's loyalty: "for now I know that you fear God (*y're Elohim atha*) and you have not held back your son, your only one, from Me" (22:12).

We are bypassing the countless readings of this famous passage and take from it only one motive: God was in need of a proof for Abraham's loyalty. The (Elohist) story betrays a deep sense of insecurity and a craving for recognition, which reflects and counters Abram's sense of insecurity expressed in the (Jehovist) covenant scene (15:8). There Abraham is asking for an explanation and reassurance of God's promise to be his "shield" and multiply his "reward" (15:1). What these could mean for a ninety-year-old man who does not have a child, he asks. He seems to be reassured when God promises him to multiply his seeds as the countless stars in Heaven (15:5), though this is told by the narrator: "and he trusted in Yahweh and He reckoned it to his merit [or righteousness, s'daqah]" (15:6). But when promised to inherit the land Abraham asks for another sign and reassurance (15:7–8), and it is in response to this that the covenantal ceremony and the revelation in the dream take place. God does not take Abraham's second request for reassurance as belittling his trust but as a reason to formalize their relations. What is decisive, however, is that both stories place trust in God as a pivotal moment in the narrative. Once it is established, there is a turning point in the plot—a promise displayed in heaven is replaced by a formal covenant sealed in a dream; Isaac is released from the altar and replaced with a ram.

Though different in intensity and implications, the two stories express the importance of God's need to reassure the trust and loyalty of his first elected disciple. Before Abraham, in the first cycle of stories in Genesis, God's relation to humans was guided by the latter's wrongdoing and potential rivalry. The need for recognition and demand for loyalty appear only with the intimate relation with one man, some of his offspring, and later the clan of his descendants. Perhaps the selection of an individual and then a whole people was his way to guarantee and control trustful recognition. He needed subjects (subordinates) who would recognize his authority and owe him allegiance. The enslaved Israelites in Egypt, who already served a great lord, might have seemed worthy candidates. What were the plagues of Egypt if not a show of force for the purpose of recognition? Why did God harden Pharaoh's heart? In order that he "may know that I am Yahweh in the midst of the Land" (Ex. 8:18) and "so as to show My power, and so that My name may be told through all the earth" (Ex. 9:16). This is an expression of a need not for loyalty but for recognition. This recognition is emphatically celebrated in the song that concludes the plagues drama, after Pharaoh and his army are trapped and drowned in the Sea of Reeds:

> Peoples heard, they quaked. Trembling seized Philistia's dwellers. Then were the chieftains of Edom dismayed, the dukes of Moab, shuddering seized them, all the dwellers of Canaan quailed. Terror and fear did fall upon them, as Your arm loomed big they were like a stone. Till Your people crossed over, O Lord, till the people You made Yours crossed over. (Ex. 15:14–16)

In the priestly source, recognition in the plagues drama includes Egypt as a whole, not only its Pharaoh (e.g., Ex. 7:5) but, like the pre-priestly (usually identified as E) source, it does not claim to gain *a trustful* recognition from the Egyptians nor to achieve it from the Hebrew slaves before the spectacular display of horrors (Ex. 6:9). There was no trust or loyalty in that recognition, only terror, to which, according to the pre-priestly source, the people of Egypt succumbed before their lord (Ex. 10:7). They recognize the Hebrew's God as the cause of their misery; they call him by his name and attribute to him their calamities. But they do not recognize him as *their* Lord; they have never been asked to do so. In fact, the Egyptian terror was but an element in the display of divine violence that was meant to secure a trustful recognition from the Hebrew slaves.

We should draw here a distinction between a recognition that secures the recognized self-identity and a recognition that establishes relations of power, domination, and subjection between the recognizing and the recognized parties. In the Hegelian drama of gaining self-consciousness, these two moments are inevitably linked, as the first moment—establishing one's self-identity through the recognition of another—presupposes the second—subduing the other; in due time the second moment is negated, and the power relations it implies are undone in a mutual recognition between equals. The priestly source of the creation story was interested only in the former moment, while the second, which conditions the first, is taken for granted. God is not a master who subdues a fearful other and reduces him to slavery but one who creates his own other, whose inferiority has been established in the very act of creation. On the sixth day of creation, before creating the humans, male and female (Gen. 1:27), God offered or declared "Let *Us* make man in *Our* image by *Our* likeness" (1:26). Readers have long asked whether he was addressing some other unnamed deities or speaking of (and to) himself in a plural form. For us what matters in this ambiguous and intriguing statement is that the addressee's or addressees' recognition of him is taken for granted but does not seem to be sufficient. God speaks to someone— himself or others—who knows who he is, but what he suggests or proclaims is an act that would produce a new creature that would reflect his image and thus grant him self-recognition, which is seemingly indifferent to the relation of power between the two parties. Creation enters here its "mirror stage," for the new creatures would be made "in Our image, by our likeness"—note how the doubling effect of the reflection is reflected in the phrasing of the verse—"and God created the human *in His image, in the image of God* He created him"— and then doubled in its content: *"male and female* He created them" (1:27).

God, so it seems, understood that in order to establish and assert self-identity he needed the recognition and affirmation of creatures of a different kind but similar enough so he could see himself in their response to his words and acts.

He, who had never been born and did not have, properly speaking, a childhood, had to create man as his reflection in order to achieve mutual recognition and, through it, self-consciousness. Reading his Hegel, or writing him avant la lettre, he knew that without recognition from others like him (who were not total aliens to him), even he would be unable to know himself. But as he never gave up on the inferiority of his other, it seems that he never read Hegel carefully enough, or beyond that famous chapter on master and slave. He conceived the mirror without taking account of the potential contradiction between the image of the other who would return his gaze and that other's freedom *not to*, his freedom to not recognize.[62]

The priestly version of creation presents therefore a quest for trustful recognition that both relies upon the power relations between the recognizing creature and God and represses their role in achieving it. The next intervention of the priestly source in the Genesis narrative, the priestly version of the flood story, suggests that God soon gave up on the promise of that mirroring image he created. The only humans to survive the deluge were Noah, a "righteous man" who "walked with God," the best in his generation (6:9), and his family. But the promise he made and the covenant he established with the survivors did not address trustful humans like Noah only or his entire family. The promise was extended far beyond the human survivors and all their descendants, the future human race, to "all living creatures, all flesh that is on the earth" (9:16). This promise was as unilateral as the act of creation. Humans were ordered not to eat "flesh with its lifeblood" (9:4), but the covenant was not conditioned on this law. His expectations from those created "in our image" were low. Clearly, as far as trustful recognition was a persistent desire on his part, he had to gain it in a different way. That way was proposed by the pre-priestly sources.

If one assumes that the sources identified as pre-priestly were indeed composed before the priestly writings, it is clear that the suppression of God's desire for recognition in the priestly version of the primeval era, after creation, expresses an acceptance of the pre-priestly reasoning and a coming to terms with it. Trustful recognition is possible for pre-priestly authors only when the recognition comes from a creature who recognizes himself as God's obedient subject, forever living under his or her master's authority.

For the pre-priestly source, this was clear from the very beginning. Its version of the creation story (Gen. 2:4–3:21) leaves no doubt that the first humans created were not yet ready to secure trustful recognition and the loyalty and obedience it implies. On the contrary, the prohibition not to eat from two clearly designated trees generated desire and shame that soon overcame God's

commanding voice. It may well be that subsequent failures, with the generation of the flood and the thriving, ambitious polity of Babel, taught him the
danger of human freedom and entrepreneurship. Trying to secure a universal
recognition, he may have understood, would mean that once they turned away
from him, he would have to annihilate humanity as a whole and begin anew,
betraying his postdiluvian promise to never again curse the earth (Gen. 8:21).
And if, as a result, he opted for a limited contract with one group of humans,
he probably knew that he had to select them according to some initial trustful-
ness and raise them up to become obedient. To start with a group of people
who had already been enslaved is not a bad idea in this respect. It was right
after the disaster in Babel (Gen. 11) that God found his significant Other (Gen.
12)—that is, the Other whose recognition counted and whose misrecognition
would have been perceived as a betrayal. But it took many generations before
he came back to Abraham's descendants, who grew up to become a recalcitrant
and opinionated people, hoping they could offer a meaningful, trustful recognition. Such recognition would count for nothing if it were not based on the
freedom to deny it, hence the importance and danger of choosing a stubborn,
"stiff-necked" people,[63] a people unruly enough to call forth the full scope of
his ruling power.

From this perspective, selection was not simply an expression of divine
whimsical desire for company but part of the development of God's self-
consciousness, and this development was neither external nor anterior to the
divine rule. He did not come of age, develop self-consciousness, and *then* seek
to constitute his rule. From its very inception, his consciousness and personal
tendencies were shaped as aspects of his ruling power—and not the other way
around. Ever since he encountered Moses near and through the burning bush,
the "others" with which that self was confronted and whose recognition was
sought were chiefly subordinate subjects who could disobey his commandments
and ignore his expectations. And the power to subordinate and demand recognition had always been marked by catastrophic violence. As an event, disaster
was always a takeover, his takeover, a means to regain control over his people
and eliminate those who dared rebel. At the same time, as a memory and a testimony, disaster constituted the very work of ruling. He extracted obedience and
imposed his government through the memories of past disasters and the images
of calamities to come—hence, he was always helped by those who recorded and
recited those testimonies and disseminated those images.

Once the group was designated, those who had failed to provide proper recognition were usually doomed, whether as a result of his ill temper or because

he found it so difficult to reconcile and forgive. However, with the narrowing down of the significant others to one people, the scope and intensity of the disasters were significantly reduced. From that moment onward, his destructive force was directed mostly at his own people and occasionally at the peoples that stood in their way. Through their loyalty and suffering, destruction and salvation, his people were expected to witness his disasters and miracles as displays of his power and demonstrations of his might and glory. The recurring references to past and future calamities seem like the ongoing work of an insecure power that must appear invincible in order to sow fear and that cannot dominate without reactivating traumas. Out of the prohibition to recreate God's image, pronounce his name, or utter it in vain, disaster emerges as the first tangible and scathing approximation to everything that may be said of him later. His majesty, heroism, vengefulness, generosity, military successes, grace, mercy, and salvation can all be deduced (and more effectively so) from the spectacle of disaster, the hideous torments, the cries and the screams, and the depths of grieving that follow them.

In Egypt, God found the descendants of the favorite "fathers" as an already segregated group. "The sons of Israel," Pharaoh's welcome guests, were given "a holding in the land of Egypt, in the best of the land" (Gen. 47:6, 11), where they tended to Pharaoh's cattle and their own. Once Pharaoh's generous hospitality turned into enslavement and the ever-growing Israelite community became a community of indentured laborers, their spatial segregation became part of the Egyptian political economy and allowed a cruel biopolitics and a genocidal practice (Ex. 1:22) that affected every Israelite.[64] The same spatial segregation played an important role in the Israelites' liberation. The series of disasters inflicted on Egypt to convince Pharaoh to let the Israelites go struck only the masters, not their slaves. Except for the first plague, which turned the Nile's water into blood, each plague marked anew the Israelites' segregated dwelling place, inscribing the calamity on "the Land of Egypt," on their masters' "dwelling places," bodies, and livestock (8:19, 9:6, 10:22–23). This was a difference of sickness and health, darkness and light, and ultimately death and life, as the series of disasters culminated in the tenth plague. Yahweh "passed over" the Israelites' houses, which had already been marked, to distinguish them from those of the Egyptians, and only struck down the masters' firstborn (12:23).

But like a coda in the divine symphony that refuses to come to its end, Pharaoh recovered from that blow, too. The vitality and power of the persecuting Egyptians are a crucial part of this story, and the tables were almost turned until Yahweh intervened at the very last moment and brought the art of separation to its sublime apotheosis. The last act and event of *havdalah* was at once both redeeming and disastrous, saving the Israelites and completely eliminating the army that chased them. A pillar of cloud "came between the camp of the Egyptians and the camp of Israel," giving "darkness to the one, and . . . light by night to the other," preventing the former camp from "coming near the other all that night" (14:20). Then the sea parted, and its waters served the People of Israel as "a wall on their right hand and on their left" (14:22) as they passed to safety. Israel was thus saved by the separation between two columns of water, and the two sides of the same cloud that acted like a screen and a torch, blinding on the one hand and illuminating on the other, while the trapped Egyptians drowned.[65] Saved and relieved, the Israelites (and the "motley throng" that joined them),[66] were finally left alone in the wilderness, alone with God for the next forty years, under his rule.[67] With Pharaoh's doom, a new regime of generative separation was established. Israel had to be *physically* separated from their oppressors before entering the covenant with God and being declared "a *treasure among all the people*" and "a *holy* nation" (19:5–6), two expressions that actually imply and presuppose their exceptional status in God's eyes,[68] hence their *theological* separation. The separation became a condition and effect of Israel's submission to their God, a new form of relation that the revelation in Sinai sought to articulate and establish.

Two principles converge here, intersecting through their inner development and granting the story its unique structure: spectacular catastrophe that works through and guarantees separation as a site and form of his revelation and separation through disaster as his mode of action. The destructive force that wreaks havoc operates in order to separate. Separation is the supreme principle, and disaster is the ultimate manifestation of his rule. Separation is first perpetrated by way of disaster and then animated by the imagery of disaster, presented as memories and threats. The two principles merge in the covenant, when the chosen Israelites become subjects under his rule, and hence the main object of his power—they are his to save and destroy. He is theirs to acknowledge, trust, and obey, lest they too be destroyed, and this they can do only through their proper separation. The convergence of separation and destruction unfolds through a web of loyalties and betrayals, promises and disappointments, between the senior party and his chosen partner. The web holds an ever-suspended promise to protect the junior partner, who dwells—now and always—in a world of suffering and trouble, where a foretold disappointment of the Lord and his emissaries is caused by the junior partner's failure to meet the conditions set by the contract. The Lord always appears to be surprised and incensed by his people, as if, from its inception, sin had not been the other side of disaster and new or renewed separations—the other side of every promise.

If finding a partner capable of trustful recognition was what motivated God's strategy of selection (one man, one sibling among his descendants, and then one nation separated from all others), if this was his way to satisfy his desire for recognition, he seems to fail miserably. But perhaps it was the other way around—that desire for recognition, which was fully acknowledged in the pre-priestly sources, had to be insatiable, so as to always allow for a recourse to extreme violence, which was his main way to assert his rule. Within this setting, the need for recognition is not disingenuous; it simply serves a higher need, the need to rule, to dominate, and to assert one's ultimate superiority. Both the subjects' recognition and their failure to remain loyal work in the service of ruling, the first by acknowledging it as the framework of the relations, the second by making the show of force, the other side of power, both legitimate and necessary.

Was this pattern itself necessary? Must divine rule combine destruction, by which it asserts itself, displaying its force, and separation, by which he demarcates the domain where God exercises his dominion? The pre-priestly sources recognized the possibility of another option. They embedded an inversion of the pattern described here in the novella of Joseph that occupies a large part, about a quarter of Genesis (37, 39–50). The novella includes an elaborate account of a time in which God ruled through this able man, whom he guided in devising a whole governmental apparatus that served to preempt a looming human catastrophe for the benefit of all, rather than generating one for the benefit of a few (Gen. 40–41). Divine intervention brought that Hebrew foreigner, the once chosen then lost son of Jacob, to become the second-in-command and the actual governor of Egypt, and divine intervention helped him preempt the foretold catastrophe of a seven-year drought. In Joseph's government, the only divisions that counted were driven by the effort to avoid the catastrophe and live in peace and prosperity despite extreme scarcity. There was no dread or violence when God revealed himself to Joseph and guided him, only private dreams and their divinely inspired (40:8, 41:38–39)—and public—interpretation (40:5–19, 41:1–37). The interpretation included a detailed plan on how to run the kingdom and avert the disaster Joseph foresaw. In this plan, Egypt would become the supplying market for the entire region ("the whole land"; 41:57). Both Egyptians and foreigners who sought provision could buy it without discrimination (though at a high cost: The Egyptians had to sell all their property and later their land too; 47:13–26). Two lines of separation that existed before these events were eroded in its course: As the story ends, the lost, betrayed son reunites with his family (45), and, soon after, the hospitable Egyptians welcome the entire Israelite clan to dwell among them, offering them an arrangement for cohabitation (47:1–6).

The drought was an act of God (Gen. 41:25, 32) but not a devastating calamity. It generated severe famine and widespread suffering, in Egypt as well as in Canaan (41:56–57; 43:1; 47:13, 19), but not without cure. The famine was a problem, and its resolution, which had been foreseen, had a clear purpose—to lure Jacob and the clan of his descendants to Egypt. Here, like in Sodom and Gomorrah and Noah's flood, there was a plan at work, which had been designed by God and produced excessive suffering and loss. Only now the famine was not genocidal, a wholesale disaster was foreseen and preempted, the suffering was relieved according to the plan, and its unfolding was conceived as an act of providence performed in a kingdom whose elite could capitalize on the administration of welfare distributed to the entire community. The welfare system was run by Joseph, who, singlehandedly, executed God's plan (in distinction from the genocidal events where God acted all by himself). Joseph, an unusually wise man animated with divine spirit (41:38–39), implemented a politics of disaster that favored the ruling elite and their guests—Joseph's entire clan—while impoverishing the multitude but at least letting all of them survive the calamity.

This was the least violent episode of divine rule the biblical authors describe in detail (as actual history, not mere promise or praise). It was a configuration of divine power that contained—but also inverted and subverted—many of the elements of divine rule we have encountered in previous sections, including recognition, trust, and obedience, and it neutralizes the dread associated with them.[69] The contrast between the ruling power that lured the Israelites to Egypt and the one that ultimately drove them out is sharply drawn, but the two contrasting configurations of divine power belong to the same theocratic formation—God directs the course of events through the orchestration of disasters, which humans can prevent or mitigate if they act properly. The unfolding of the disaster was carefully organized—spatially, when he punished and destroyed, or temporally, when he protected and saved—and it always concerned the creation and distribution of excess, which could not have been avoided but could be redistributed. Disasters were planned, and the planning included making them known in advance to a few—those who would be spared, or those responsible for the saving. And they ended up in a reorganization of the relations among humans, which was lasting in some cases and short lived in others.

The contrast between the two configurations of divine rule is clear: genocidal catastrophes for the elimination of evil, on the one hand, and providential administration of scarcity for a political purpose, on the other. Furthermore, in the first case, disaster takes center stage, and everything else takes place in its shadow; in the second case, an ongoing disaster is the stage on which another drama takes place, that is, the relationship between Joseph and his brothers. And while the catastrophic God is directly involved in almost every detail of the plot, the providential God recedes to backstage and does not play any direct role in the drama.

And yet the two configurations have still more in common. In both, God's rule extends over an indefinite space that he does not try to subjugate, his recognition is not at stake, and he is not asking for loyalty, obedience, or anything else. This feature of his rule was radically transformed in Egypt. In fact, only there his rule became truly political. The real contrast is not one between a catastrophic God and a providential one—both are equal aspects of his power—but between a God who used his power to intervene dramatically but briefly or to direct humans behind the scenes and a God who was fully immersed in establishing his power and authority, that is, in the politics of his own power. Before Egypt, trust, recognition, and loyalty played roles only in the interpersonal relations with the very few humans he singled out, and the exercise of violence had nothing to do with his quest for recognition. In Egypt and afterward, the quest for recognition became public and its relation with extreme violence predominant; in fact, the two have come together to form the backbone of his politics. The narrative of Exodus opens (after counting the Israelite families in Egypt) with marking the shift: "And a new king arose over Egypt who knew no Joseph" (1:8). There will be no Joseph in post-Joseph Egypt, Moses will not be Joseph's substitute, but God will soon take the place of the Egyptian Pharaoh.

We have read Genesis retrospectively, from the point of view of the new stage that was set in Egypt and, soon after, in the wilderness, looking for precedents for the political formations found there. In what follows, we will see how the pre-priestly sources that followed Israel's emancipation from Egypt and into the wilderness weaved together God's quest for recognition and loyalty with divine violence, creating the problem with which both priestly and Deuteronomist authors tried to contend.

VIOLENCE AND LAW

When the time came to return the Israelites to Canaan after four generations of indentured labor in Egypt (Ex. 6:16–20),[70] the Israelites were forced into a rebellious act in which they had no interest. Moses did not grow up among

them and had never spent a day in crushing labor. His first attempt to resist
Egyptian oppression, initiated by his first exposure to the slave's suffering, was
not well received, and, fearing for his life, he fled to the desert (Ex. 2:11–15).
When he reluctantly came back, following God's instructions, and was joined
by his brother Aaron, the two were rejected by the people for making them "re-
pugnant in the eyes of Pharaoh and in the eyes of his servants, putting a sword
in their hand to kill us" (Ex. 5:21). When the plagues were unleashed on Egypt,
we learn nothing about their impact on the enslaved; all we know is that they
reluctantly accepted Moses's leadership, followed his instructions (12:21–27),
and prepared themselves for their departure. Upon hearing Pharaoh's order
(12:31–32) and under the pressure of the panicked Egyptians (12:33), carrying
their "kneading pans wrapped in their cloaks on their shoulders" (12:34), they
went away, but not before borrowing ornaments, gold, and cloaks from their former masters, "despoil[ing] Egypt" (12:36). All those plagues did not help them
trust God's power to rescue them from Egypt's avenging wrath. When Pharaoh
and his army were seen from afar, rising on them in the desert, the end looked
nearer than ever: "Was it for lack of graves in Egypt that you took us to die in the
wilderness?" (14:11). Only after the complete demise of the Egyptians was a clear
change of mindset and a rare expression of trust in God recorded, immediately
followed by an even rarer moment of joy: "Israel saw the great hand that the
Lord had performed in Egypt, and the people feared the Lord, and they trusted
in the Lord and in Moses His servant. Then did Moses sing, and all the Israelites
with him, this song to Yahweh" (14:31–15:1). But in light of what follows, these
two verses and their conjunction seem more like the narrator's wishful thinking,
for very soon the mistrust and disobedience recurred.

The desert's first episode of mistrust came right after crossing the Sea of
Reeds (15:22–26). After walking three days in the desert without water the
people found water, but it was undrinkable. Their outcry was directed to Moses,
but God was quick to respond, instructing Moses to perform a saving miracle
and sweeten the water. Then comes a verse that reads like a reflection on the
first episode of unrest in the wilderness: "There did He set him a statute and
law, and there *did he test him*" (15:25b). The distress was a test; God was experimenting with the people—or with Moses. It is not clear who was tested and
what was at stake, but we know that God's wrath did not flare and that he saved
the people without even reproaching them. In the two pre-priestly episodes
that immediately follow (16:4–5, 17), the testing recurs, and again no violence
erupts. In Exodus 16, God tests the people's respect for the Shabbat: He was going to give them bread from the sky but expected that they would avoid gather-

ing their manna on the Shabbat; in Exodus 17, it is the people who test God by asking for water (17:2, 7). The very fact that the people could test God, staging an event that would provoke him to react, to see "is Yahweh in our midst or not," should be understood as evidence not only of their "stiff-necked" nature but of their relative freedom as God's subjects, as well as of their failure to understand his rule. For this was the last time that their failure to meet his expectations did not provoke his lethal reaction.

This series of "tests" is crucial for countering the image of a God who is quick to violent anger. God decided to use violence only after his restrained reaction had not been appreciated and the evidence for the miserable condition of his people had accumulated. If Baden is right, that the Jehovist account of the revelation in Sinai should be read as basically a response to the people's experiment ("is Yahweh in our midst"),[71] then God's initial moderation and the people's ongoing shortsightedness should be even more pronounced. When God's fury and violence finally burst, it must be seen as a calculated response to an accumulated frustration. The formula that guides his judgment was announced in a statement that wraps the narration of the first testing episode, whose first words were already quoted earlier:

> There did He set him a statute and law, and there did he test him. And He said: "If you really heard the voice of Yahweh your God, and do what is right in His eyes, and hearken to His commands, and keep all His statutes, all the sickness that I put upon Egypt I will not put upon you, for I am Yahweh your healer." (Ex. 15:25–26)

These verses bewildered commentators, especially since the emphasis on "a statute and law" (*hok vemishapt*) and "commandments" (*mitzvot*) before Sinai seems out of place, and the conjunction of lawgiving and the expectation of obedience with people's (or Moses's) testing seems awkward.[72] This awkwardness is symptomatic for all the testing episodes where the Israelites' discontent is rebuked. In two of them (15:22–25a, 17:7) no specific law or statute is invoked at all; in the third (16:4–5), resting on the seventh day is assumed as a law but introduced as a testing instrument. In all three cases, the people are under great distress of thirst and hunger, and the injunction of the law probably seemed to them out of place and ill-timed. When God (15:26, 16:4), Moses (17:2), and the narrator (17:7) present these situations as cases of testing, disregarding the people's distress, they insist on something more fundamental than the law, which conditions its possibility, namely, heeding the voice of God no matter how dire the situation seems to be.

God never offered explicit warnings of the risks they were taking when they complained; or talked highly about Egypt, expressing remorse for embarking on the journey; or clashed with their leaders. They were a group of recently liberated slaves who probably found it difficult to understand his injunctions and expectations. He was by no means a remarkable educator, nor was he an effective governor. Neither his early moderation nor the wrath, impatience, and violence that characterized him later had a lasting effect on his subjects. Their capacity to learn from experience was rather limited. He, on the other hand, was capable of some reflection and could even change his mind and mend his ways, as he famously did after the deluge (Gen. 8:21–22) and also after the sin of the golden calf (Ex. 32:14, 34:10). Then, recognizing how disproportionate his responses to their failures were, he appointed a deputy, a substitute, to lead that "stiff-necked people, lest I put an end to you on the way" (33:2–5). He withdrew from dwelling in the camp, which he had led with a pillar of fire and cloud since they had left Egypt (13:13–14, 21–22), and talked about the people as if they were Moses's, not his, and as if it had been Moses who had "brought [them] up from the land of Egypt" (33:1).[73]

The narrator presents God's withdrawal and the appointment of a substitute as motivated by his harsh judgment of the people's "innate" unruliness, but we may read here God's recognition of his own shortcomings as well—they repeatedly failed his tests, and he was either incapable or not interested in further investing in their upbringing as "good subjects." Moses, however, refused to accept any of this. He understood the appointment of a substitute as an expression of mistrust, perhaps even his own demotion to a lower rank ("yet you, you have not made known to me whom you will send with me . . . if your presence [*paneicha*] does not go, do not take us up from here"; 33:12, 15).[74] Moses insists on regaining God's trust (33:13a), rebranding the people as his (33:13b), and keeping God's presence in the midst of the people without exposing them to another threat of annihilation (33:15–16). He lures God to grant him a private session of theophany (33:18–23), receives brand-new tablets (34:1–4), and uses another closed meeting with God (34:3, 6) to turn God's words on their head and argue that precisely because God's people are stiff-necked, he needed to be "slow to anger," be "abounding in kindness," and not reckon "the crimes of fathers with sons and sons of sons" (34:7–9).[75]

This fascinating exchange between the Lord and his major servant reveals two related features of his rule: First, as despotic as he might seem, and as superior in any respect to any of his subjects, he was not alone and never too far away. He was always assisted by some company, and, second, even after a major case of offense and breakdown of trust, he left some room for negotiation. This negotiation was not carried out alongside any preestablished procedure but was left entirely to the ingenuity of his trusted servant Moses, just as it was with Abraham before him. These negotiations did not aim for any structural changes to God's rulership but rather affirmed its basic configuration. While Abraham failed to curtail God's violence, Moses managed to do so (preventing the genocide), but neither the catastrophic nature of divine violence nor the unpredictable manner of its use had been affected. In fact, this was the case in every episode of dissent and discontent recorded in the pre-priestly sources. It is through them that Yahweh's rulership is displayed. Let us read closely one such typical episode, in Numbers 11.[76]

"The people became complainers of evil in the ear of Yahweh" (Num. 11:1). God's anger flared, and he set the outskirts of the camp on fire. The people cried out to Moses, and the fire was extinguished. The people were hungry. The whole congregation joined the riffraff (*asafsuf*) in whining about their sparse diet: How long could they live on manna? Whether ground on millstones, pounded in a pestle, or cooked in a cauldron and made into cakes, it always had the same dreadful taste of "the creaminess of oil" (11:8). God was angry, and Moses was exhausted, unable to care for them on his own. He spoke like a broken man: "I alone cannot bear this people, for they are too heavy for me. If thus You would do with me, kill me pray, altogether" (11:14–15). Trying to assist Moses in the work of governance, God asks him to gather seventy elders and officers to stand by him and share the burden (11:17). For his part, he promises a didactic miracle: He will give them meat, a lot of it, so much that it will "come out of [their] nostrils and become loathsome" (11:20). Meat for a whole month? asks Moses in wonder. Where are the flocks and the herds? Where would he catch the fish? In his distress, the prophet has underestimated his master's capacities. The Lord notices this lack of trust ("Has the Lord's hand been too short?") without taking action against Moses.[77] Assuring him with a "you will see . . ." (11:23), he focuses on the task at hand and sends quails in immense quantity to the camp (11:31–32). The saving miracle happens, but for numerous (and unnumbered) gluttonous people who gathered more than ten homers (a fantastic volume—about 2,200 liters, or 580 gallons) of quails, it was their last supper. Then and there, "the meat still between their teeth, they are struck by His very great blow," lending the site its proper name, "graves of lust" (11:32–34).

What made hoarding the quails such a sin? Was it an expression of lack of trust (which they shared with Moses) or of anxiety? Did they misread the message coming, literally, from the sky and fail to realize the danger of that abundance? Was this failure entirely their own? Couldn't he have done better in communicating with them? Was gluttony only a pretext? Moses and God became angry when, across the camp, the people were "weeping by its clans, every man at the entrance of his tent" (10). This was clearly an act of widespread but non-rebellious mournful desperation,[78] but we may equally see here an orchestrated political rally. The dissidents created a public space and made a public statement by simply presenting themselves at that space's threshold, "at the entrance" to their private domain. They acted as demonstrators in an autocratic regime where access to the public space is limited and cannot be taken for granted. They hoped to be protected by staying at their tents' entrance but letting their voices be heard. Was not it the form of their protest—the very existence of a public complaint—that arose God's anger and Moses's frustration? We may infer this from the fact that they immediately displaced the complaint itself, reading it as a symptom for an extensive opposition to the present leadership. Moses, in a whining mood, saw himself as a caring nurse who lacked the proper means to fulfill his task. God too thinks only of himself, viewing the recurrent protests as an expression of revulsion to his rule, not just to his underwhelming menu.[79] Hunger made Egypt appear as a land of gourmet food, and its fancy diet is invoked in detail (Num. 11:5; cf. Ex. 16:3). The immense supply of quails was given to the Israelites in response to their regressive mood, which preferred Pharaoh's Egypt over God's wilderness. Both his miracle and his blows express his counteraversion. On both sides, revulsion was a political affect embedded in a political action. In fact, from its very beginning, the whole episode was a political clash; no specific law was transgressed.[80] He was relatively tolerant with the whining protesters and the nostalgic invocation of Egypt but unforgiving toward those who amassed too many quails. Apparently, they had satisfied their hunger without restoring their trust. Just like the first blow (11:1), the last one (11:33) too was God's response to a breach of trust. What was at stake was an unconditional acceptance of his superiority and rule.

Education and persuasion were options not available to God, and mitigating consequences—the heat of the desert, the toil of the journey—were never considered. He wanted his recognition and trust wholesale and permanent. Its denial ignited rage and frustration as much as it was an occasion to demonstrate his force and superiority.[81] He was impatient with their complaints from the beginning (11:1) and throughout this incident. The quails were brought from the sea not as a gift but as a trap. Their excessiveness, as they piled on the ground "about a day's journey on this side and a day's journey on the other side, all around the camp" (11:31), foreshadowed the excessiveness of the violence to be exercised. The narrative's structure reflects here the logic of his rule. And we may note that in both cases, excessiveness was displayed without being questioned. Given the nature of the governed and the stakes of the crisis, was his response effective or rightful? Is it possible that in losing his temper, he acted unjustly, punished excessively, and caused superfluous suffering and loss? Or was this excess his own "way . . . to do righteousness and justice" (Gen. 18:19)? For if he was just, indeed—we have to take the narrators and protagonists at their word on this matter—then excessiveness was built into his conception of justice, an aspect of its appearance to human eyes. He was explicit about this when he explained the ultimate sin, the worship of other gods: "For I am Yahweh your God, a jealous god, reckoning the crime of the fathers with the sons, with the third generation and with the fourth, for My foes, and doing kindness to the thousandth [generation] for My friends, and for those who keep My commands" (Ex. 20:5). When Moses repeats these words, he adds, as if to soften their impact, "compassionate and gracious, slow to anger and abounding in kindness and good faith [*emet*]" (Ex. 34:6–7). But he repeats his description as a jealous god all the same, almost verbatim, sending it to reverberate throughout the Bible.[82]

THE SOVEREIGN'S MOMENT

In the Bible, both compassion and jealousy tend to overflow, respecting no boundary or measure. They are two modes of going out of one's way, albeit in opposite directions. Often, God was compassionate precisely after (and because) he was excessively jealous, failing to find the right balance in his response. He was capable of multiplying his strikes, extending and prolonging their effects, but also of suspending them; the justness of his deeds always evaded human judgment. "No judgment of the deed can be derived from the commandment. And so neither the divine judgment, nor the grounds for this judgment can be known in advance," writes Walter Benjamin in his "Critique of Violence."[83] But in fact, they cannot be known posteriorly either. If he were to strike a fine balance, a measure for measure of human transgression weighed against a divine rebuke, the exact measure could only be presupposed, while that which had been measured could only be guessed. And when he withheld his violence, pardoned or gave a second chance, this too could not be explained; it could only be added to the expressions of his justness, as we will see in more detail in what follows. God's justice appears deus ex machina. If God is just and calamities are God-made, it follows that when the justice was executed through calamity, calamity was justly executed. The repeated rebellions against his rule indicate that many remained unconvinced of this logic.

Among the nonpriestly desert tales, the quail episode is emblematic.[84] The recurrence of its main elements allows us to see here a distinct recurring configuration of divine rule: the people's grievances and lack of trust; the problematization of God's or Moses's authority (or God's through that of Moses) in the absence of specific breaches of the law; Moses's weakness as a leader and deputy; Moses's recurring calls for help and God's ultimate resort to (usually extreme and often miraculous) violence in response; and ineffective ruling and failed governance (God hardly succeeds where Moses fails). God seems incapable of or uninterested in political or governmental reforms, and even when he implements one—by calling seventy elders to the Tent of Meeting, where they are allowed to prophesize, and placing on them some of the spirit that is upon Moses, so they can "bear with [him] the burden of the people" (Num 11:16–17)—no real change is recorded. In fact, for the author or redactor who linked the elders' episode to that of the gluttonous quail hoarders and their grotesque end, the point of the reform is completely lost. God supervises, cares, and salvages with his miracles, guiding the people with the pillars of fire and cloud, but he always pulls the rope a little too tightly. He demands excruciating patience (the need to wait for Moses, the monotony of the manna), endurance of many hardships (hunger, thirst, persecution), the ability to overcome anxiety under these conditions (the pursuit of the Egyptians), and full, unconditional trust. He acts as a despot who promises to protect his people and wishes to gain their loyalty but can tolerate no dissidence and is often overcome by fury. Only coincidental interventions like Moses's pleas (Ex. 32:11–14) can appease his rage. Saving miracles and devastating disasters are his main tools. But as a means of supervision, care, direction, warning, or punishment, they are usually not well suited for the task of full control over his subjects, which is already implied here.

Even after the law was given and the rites were institutionalized, the divine ruler continued to encounter difficulties. Of course, the people could always be blamed. They have had enough of God and were impatient, critical, and lustful. But is it right to blame these recently freed slaves? Slavery had made them dependent and lacking in initiative, now the desert scares and tires them, the promised land is a legend they find hard to believe, and in any case it is still too far off to encourage them in their arduous journey. Confronting these difficulties, God reacts like a prickly, irritable father. Each story evokes the same familiar, sour taste of the frustration experienced by a father who is ashamed of his parenthood and of his children, who fail to please him, a father who constantly projects his emotions on his children. He tends to strike them even though he could foresee their trespasses, and he does not bother to prevent them; as previously noted, he needed them not only to vent his rage but to demonstrate his invincible power.

He tried to bring up his subjects and accommodate them to his rule through miracles and disasters, which were mostly unusual but by no means rare events. They might have come as a surprise when they occurred, but from the narrator's point of view they do not seem unexpected, and they usually failed to change the course of events or introduce a real change of mind. The Egyptians could witness in awe the angel of God or the column of cloud that moved to protect Israel (Ex. 14:19),[85] but as out of the ordinary as these epiphanies were, for Moses, Aaron, and their people they were signs of his enduring presence and close movements, which often functioned as guiding signs and a means of communication.[86] Apart from the voices and visions in front of the Mountain (Sinai or Horeb), the pre-priestly sources do not record great astonishment, incredulity, or fear when the exceptional occurs, and, as the golden calf clearly demonstrates, the awe-inspiring impact of Sinai was short lived. Moreover, these miracles could not generate that primordial sense of guilt that, as Agamben explains, "refers not to transgression, that is, to the determination of the licit and the illicit but to the pure force of law, to the law's simple reference to something."[87] Without such a sense that precedes every deed and compels obedience, neither law nor sovereign authority could function. It seems that the miracles and disasters failed to imprint that which direct divine speech had not been able to achieve since Cain, that is, an understanding that sin always crouches in wait for humans, tempting and elusive, and they must recognize and rule over it (Gen. 4:7). The vigilance required to recognize and avoid the trespass depended on this sense of a priori guilt that enabled individuals to become addressees of a decree, prohibition, or law that had always preceded them. If they were old enough and capable of avoiding bad faith, they could have known that sooner or later they would fail to obey him.

Indeed, the displays of horror reflect the might of an unsurpassable ruling power, but they alone could not ensure that the loyalty and obedience that this power demands were properly internalized. Without an a priori sense of guilt, no act of grave violence, no threat, no rescue, let alone the proclamation of the law, was sufficient to instill his authority. His invincibility ensured the crushing of all dissenting voices, if he so pleased, and yet he repeatedly complained about the people's disloyalty and disobedience, which leaves one wondering what pleased him more, obedience or his bursts of anger. They did not hear his voice when they were thirsty, or fed up with the manna, or scared to death by the report brought by the scouts who had been sent to spy on the Promised

Land (Num. 13–14). Acting as lost children of a terrorizing father, they did not even call upon him when they were thirsty, hungry, or scared (Ex. 15:24, 17:2; Num. 11:2), while he, on his part, heard any complaint as directed at him, even when his name was not invoked (for example, Num. 11:4–6, 10, vs. 11:18). Not heeding his voice was the recurring excuse for the eruption of violence; it was also one of the main forms for displaying his power and reaffirming his authority. He had great interest in finding out when and where his subjects failed to heed his voice but little interest in finding out why. He preferred subjects who knew him through disasters and lived under their shadow, wake, and anticipation. His failure—or reluctance—to assert his authority could only provoke more violence but ultimately prepared the way for his later withdrawal. His repeated attempts to use violence in order to extract full recognition and punish disloyalty were, after all, inseparable from the economy of violence that thrived under his rule.

This was a rigid theocratic formation. Despite the great prize promised to the obedient subjects, they did not succeed in freeing themselves from old habits, overcoming old anxieties, or relinquishing their childish demand for immediate gratification. They did not even try. They were caught in a typically patriarchal family dynamic that set an irritable father and unruly children in opposition, a pathological self-perpetuating pattern of "call and response" where a lack of (human) trust and loyalty was met with outbursts of (divine) violence, which sowed only fear without cultivating trust. Even after the covenant was established and the law given, power continued to be enacted through miracles and disasters, and the violent enforcement of the law was too sporadic, too extreme and unpredictable, to be counted as a rule of law. If the person of the king in Egypt was the incarnation of the "living law," God's lawgiving was the exact opposite. The law was meant only for his people, not for him, who remained entirely external to it,[88] exercising extrajudicial violence as he saw fit. At Sinai, he declared the law but did not embed it in a system that would be able to adjudicate and enforce it.[89] Negotiation on the use of his force took place only in two extreme occasions, when the very survival of Israel was at stake. The first occasion was the sin of the golden calf and the second the rebellion after the return of the scouts from Canaan, a notorious case of a sheer breakdown of trust to which I will return in the next section. In both cases, in order to change God's heart, Moses appealed not to the recently established covenant but rather to old promises God had made (Ex. 32:13; Num. 14:16) and, even more emphatically, to his reputation among the nations. The Egyptians might say, "'He brought them out to harm them, to kill them in the mountains, and to consume them from the face of the earth'?" (Ex. 32:12); other nations might suspect that God had "killed

[His people] in the wilderness" only because he "was not able to bring [them] to the land which He swore to them" (Num. 14:15–16).[90] The excessiveness of his violence was not restrained by reason or law but mainly by appealing to his sense of self perceived through the eyes of others.[91]

In this theocratic model, which probably belongs to the more ancient layer of the Bible, divine violence was never conceived as a continuation of politics by other means, and the political space opened when the subjects talked back to the power that ruled them was meager indeed. Even when erupting in response to a clear breach of the law, this violence was already indifferent to the law at the moment of its eruption. In the two great catastrophes described in Genesis, the flood and Sodom and Gomorrah, divine violence was a reaction to an undefined yet apparently grave accumulation of violence and injustice, but it was also a way to curb human ambition (Babel) or to protect Abram and Sarai from their Egyptian hosts. Divine violence assumed new roles when God's rule was defined by his relation to his elected people. It became a means for the display of God's superior power and claim to fame, a machine of war, and a technology of governance. Above all, what this violence sought (and failed) to institute was not law but rather a recognition of the supreme, exclusive authority of its author and source.

What violence was set to destroy was not any previous law (of the Egyptians or the Canaanites, for example) or law in general (as Benjamin had it when characterizing divine violence as "law destroying"), and God did not try to clear the ground for his own laws (as revolutionaries often do).[92] Rather, in the pre-priestly theocratic model, divine violence aimed at life itself, the life of those whose recognition he sought and failed to get. In eliminating those who denied him recognition, he hoped to instill it in others. But fear of death could not break the circularity of his demand; he had to be trusted in order to be followed, because too often his promises seemed no less dangerous than his threats: "Why is this that you brought us from Egypt: to kill me and my children and my cattle with thirst?" (Ex. 17:3). It took "another spirit" (Num. 14:24), not sheer violence, to generate a leap of faith, and this could only happen if God was already present in the people's hearts or in their midst. This intimacy could only benefit those who fully and continually trusted him but was a mortal danger for all those who did not. Intimacy presupposes mutual trust, which requires intimacy in its turn, and only a supernumerary divine intervention, an arbitrary, unsolicited bestowal of "the spirit," could break this vicious circle. This may be the main motivation for his order to Moses, in an episode attached to "the menu revolt": "Gather Me seventy men of the elders of Israel . . . and I shall hold back some of the spirit that is upon you and place it upon them" (11:16–17).[93]

As we have seen, not all expressions of mistrust ended in divine retribution. In the pre-priestly theocracy, the eruption of divine violence is always preceded by a trigger and sometimes followed by a justification, yet it never follows a preexisting rule of its own. When dissent and rebellion were punished, the divine scourge was almost always performed as a mass killing. In these cases, the magnitude of mass killings appears to reflect the depth of the people's mistrust and misrecognition, and thus a balance of some sort seems to have been struck. The sinners must be annulled with the sin,[94] and avenging violence is justice in performance. But there is another compelling option, though used more rarely—pleas and supplications may bring God to forgive the sin and revoke or reduce the people's punishment. In the two cases of reversal of a genocidal plan mentioned earlier (Ex. 32:7–14 and Num. 14:11–20), his judgment was not executed. In the case of the golden calf, there was no forgiveness, only a change of heart ("and Yahweh relented from the evil that He has spoken to do to His people"; Ex. 32:14) and a limited "wiping out" of only "he who has offended against Me" (32:33, 35). It is almost as if God admits that the plan he had in mind involved excessive killings, which he has now decided to avoid. After the outrageous reception of the scouts, however, God did respond to Moses's pleas with an unambiguous forgiveness ("I've forgiven according to your word"; Num. 14:20). The plague that was supposed to obliterate the entire distrustful generation was replaced with a nonlethal punishment (Num. 14:22–23). Forgiveness here needs to be taken with a grain of salt, for God actually curses the people he had just forgiven to "never see the land that I swore to their fathers" (Num. 14:23). Their sin will be absolved only when their entire generation of sinners dies. God's forgiveness in response to Moses's pleas amounts to an act of pardon of a collective capital punishment and its commutation to life in prison, the wilderness.

What is crucial about and common to these two episodes is neither forgiveness nor the avoidance of the use of lethal force—both remain optional—but rather the very possibility of revoking the execution of divine judgment. If God's justness is accepted as an axiom, then both the execution of punishment and its revocation, commutation, or indefinite deferral must be considered as performances of justice. When violence is attributed to God, it must be just. Benjamin noted that while divine violence must be just, its attribution to any specific case cannot be certain. The idea should be accepted in principle without being applied to historical cases.[95] The authors of the Pentateuch wrote as if attribution was never *their problem*, and they used *their attribution* confidently to explain the course of human affairs under God's rule. But they also placed the deferral of divine judgment and its violent execution as a means to perform justice.

An echo of this conception may be heard in God's words in the Decalogue (Ex. 20:6), reiterated in his exchange with Moses in the aftermath of the scene of the golden calf: "And I shall grant grace to whom I grant grace and have compassion for whom I have compassion" (Ex. 33:19). The statement was uttered in a moment of reconciliation, shortly after granting grace to the entire people he had not wiped out. But just like in the Decalogue, the statement was addressed to no one in particular and did not refer to the moment of its utterance, thus opening up both the time and the identity of the one who receives grace. The openness and indeterminacy of this proclamation balances the terror of divine violence and could give those living under its shadow a certain hope. It was unknown who would be granted grace and compassion, or when, as it was similarly unknown when the execution of violence would take place, because it may be deferred to the sinner's third and fourth generation (Ex. 20:5). Under this condition, attributing (or not attributing) violence to God is not only necessary for recognizing divine justice (or negating its realization in a specific case) but becomes an element in divine rule. God cannot rule without his scribes and narrators, the clerks who register his deeds in "the Book of the Battles of Yahweh" (Num. 21:14), and all those who officiate the memory of the affairs in which he was engaged. With all his unsurpassable power, God's rule was a collective enterprise.

In an early, short, and fascinating reading of the book of Jonah, Gershom Scholem interpreted God's indefinite postponement of the execution of divine judgment as the mark and essence of divine justice.[96] The Book of Jonah, a legendary story about a peripheral prophet and a unique literary piece, was presented by Scholem as a reflective text whose role is to teach the meaning of prophecy: the opening of a space in which attribution has not been decided yet, the deferral of the execution of judgment is still possible, the deferral itself is indefinite, and the "return" (tshuva) can still make a difference, as it did for the residents of Nineveh.[97] Two comments may be added to Scholem's brilliant reading. First, the linking of God's justice to the indefinite deferral of the execution of divine judgment is found not only in the writings of a minor prophet but also at the heart of the pre-priestly narratives about God's covenant with Israel. Second, and perhaps contrary to Scholem's underlying message, the idea cannot be separated from its inversion: The execution of divine judgment is no less just than its deferral, even when the indefinite temporality of the suspending act is countered by an unpredictable, sudden blow of the violent retribution. The two may appear together, as they do in the scene of the golden calf, where a genocide was declared and then revoked but a limited mass killing was nevertheless executed (Ex. 32:35). The same duality is captured in the image of the angel or messenger introduced at the same scene. First the suspension: The messenger will go before Moses and lead the people "to where I [God] have spoken to you [Moses], and on the day I will make a reckoning, I will make a reckoning with them for their offense" (32:34). Then, in the next verse, the blow: "And Yahweh scourged the people for having made the calf that Aaron made" (32:35). Deferring judgment and executing it are two sides of the same coin, two equal expressions of God's justice, linked together without the necessary mediation of any law—violent revenge, on the one hand, and an abundance of kindness and compassion, on the other (20:5–6, 34:6–7). The narrators who attribute the violent scene to God and the prophets who opened the space for its deferral work in the service of divine rule, on the two sides of this aisle.

For the attribution to work not only as part of the terror of violence but also as a way to live with it and have trust in God's kindness and compassion, God must be imagined as just (in order to expiate the excess of violence attributed to him) and capable of revoking his judgment (in order to keep open the space for human hope and divine grace). His sovereignty consists in the power and authority to revoke, the power of the last word (judgment), and of the last stroke (violence), which is also the power of deferring the last word and suspending the last stroke. What gets frozen in thin air between these two possibilities, however, is not the law, as Schmitt and those who follow him have posited,[98] but rather God's own judgment and executive power. Agamben calls the space created by the (Schmittian) sovereign act that renders law inoperative without annulling it a "zone of indistinction"; it is a zone in which the differentiation between fact and norm, right and might collapses.[99] This may still be the case with the divine sovereign of the pre-priestly sources, except that, unlike the Schmittian sovereign, God is not at one at the same time inside the law and outside it[100] but always, unambiguously, outside the law. Whether he has not given the law yet or (after the gift was made or imposed) relates to it as his people's law, his own acts are not mediated through the law and often have no relation to it. Whether he strikes or forgives, executes his judgment or postpones it, the facticity of his act and its justness, his might and his right are indistinguishable, and no law is needed to establish this relation.[101]

For the pre-priestly authors, the commandments and the laws (*mishpatim*) were more of a supplement to divine violence and divine justice than a means for regulating the former and establishing the latter. When considered, out of context, as regulating relations between neighbors, men and women, parents and children, they had tremendous impact, of course, but with respect to these matters God seemed mostly aloof; no act of law enforcement was recorded. In the context of the relation between the people and their sovereign, however, the law is but the most distilled expression of the sovereign's demand for exclusive loyalty, recognition of authority, and consistent attribution of power. The proclamation of the law is merely one among many occasions in which the demand was performed.

The binding of the people and their God was achieved through love and fear, the desire to be recognized, and the wish to be protected. This bond was sealed in covenant, but in the wilderness, at least, the added commandments and laws played a marginal role in the life of the people, as the pre-priestly narratives recorded it. Except for the few commandments that articulate the demand for exclusive loyalty. This demand is not merely a part of a series of articles of law, it is also presented—and must be presupposed—as the very condition for the entire enterprise: the acceptance of God as the ultimate authority that was always already there, with the power to command before giving the law, to decide and execute without reference to the law, to give the law without enforcing it, to mete punishment, or to withhold or revoke it, to gather a multitude and make it into a people, and to wipe that people out.

God promised protection as the covenant was signed. He would direct all his might against the enemies of his people: "I will send My fear before you, I will cause confusion among all the people to whom you come" (Ex. 23:27). Mobilizing his destructive force for the colonizing project, he committed to use it in a measured and calculated way: "I will not drive them out from before you in one year, lest the land become desolate. . . . Little by little I will drive them out from before you" (Ex. 23:29–30). He would do this, however, provided the covenant—that is, his recognition, loyalty, and exclusivity—was maintained. A messenger would guide and guard the people upon their arrival to Canaan and would accompany them through their wars of conquest, but they must "heed his voice; [and] not defy him, for he will not pardon [their] trespass; for [His] name is with him" (23:20–23).[102] The guardian angel, like the hornet that will assist in the colonizing project (23:28), are incarnations of his violence when it is directed against the people's enemies. Protecting Israel or avenging their crimes, divine presence is that *pharmakon*—the elixir of life and death.[103]

Divine violence is one of God's modes of presence, a form of revelation, a technique of governing, a destructive force, and a manifestation of his mood, wishes, and plans. But it is also a medium of communication, an educational tool, a punishing apparatus, and an arsenal of weapons. This violence, its spectacular displays and temporary withdrawals, manifest God's way in the realm of human affairs. Walter Benjamin attributed "manifestation" to *mythical* violence, from which divine violence is distinguished: "Mythical violence in its archetypal form is a mere manifestation of the gods. Not a means to their ends, scarcely a manifestation of their will, but first of all a manifestation of their existence."[104] But when he defined divine violence as the "antithesis in all respects" of mythical violence, "manifestation" was taken out of the equation.[105] We should reinsert and question the opposition, at least with respect to the God of the Hebrew Bible. While mythical violence is "merely" a manifestation of the gods, divine violence is God's primary mode of action *as well as* a manifestation *of his justice* or *his temper*, the difference between which one can never really tell. The present study shows that as far as the pre-priestly configuration of divine rule goes, Benjamin was right to state that divine violence does not establish the law, but, as noted, that he failed to capture its essence. Paraphrasing Benjamin's words, Agamben writes: "Pure [i.e., divine] violence exposes and severs the nexus between law and violence and can thus appear in the end not as violence that governs and executes but as violence that purely acts and manifests."[106] With respect to the pre-priestly theocratic formation, this description should be amended thus: *Since* divine rule had severed the link between violence and law or simply ignored it, divine violence manifested itself splendidly but failed as a ruling instrument. It operated as a flawed means to extract recognition and as an extreme mode of punishing those who refused or failed to provide it.

SCOUTS IN THE LAND OF THE GIANTS: THREE THEOCRATIC FORMATIONS

For the people wandering in the wilderness, the shortcomings of pre-priestly theocracy must have seemed quite evident. Perhaps this was how the texts documenting it were meant to be read. God's rule appeared more oppressive than redemptive. A moment of thankfulness and joy after crossing the Sea of Reeds, in which the superiority and protective power of their new Lord had been celebrated and recorded in a poetic language (Ex. 15:1–21), finds only one brief, pale echo in the collection of pre-priestly sources (Num. 21:16–18), and the two remain outliers.[107] Throughout the journey they are mostly described as ill-tempered, discontent, suspicious, pugnacious, and despondent. Whining and grumbling, they are repeatedly scolded, rebuked, and punished, yet they are unwilling to or incapable of learning the lesson of his violence.

The reception of the twelve scouts upon their return from Canaan is most telling in this respect. It is a story that portrays the most spectacular failure of a divine plan, the plan to lead the people of Israel to their promised land. The story is told twice but consists of three distinct versions: Pre-priestly (considered J) and priestly sources are artfully woven together in Numbers 13–14,[108] and a Deuteronomic version takes up much of the first chapter of Deuteronomy (1:20–46). It is therefore not surprising that the fault lines distinguishing the Pentateuch's three main theocratic regimes stand out here in sharp relief. Let me follow the shared themes first and then reconstruct the differences.

A group of scouts were sent to the Promised Land and returned to the Israelites' camp east of the Jordan River to report what lay beyond the river. The land was "flowing with milk and honey," the scouts told the people (Num. 13:27), but, alas, it was already occupied, inhabited by mighty and fearsome people living in large, fortified cities. Some were even "offspring of the giant" (13:28). This report was challenged by Caleb, a man who went on the scouting expedition "with another spirit" (14:24), who said, without providing any reasons, that the Israelites could "surely take hold of [the land] for we will surely prevail over it" (13:30). In response, the others' reports became hyperbolic: The land "consumes those who dwell in it," and its residents "are men of huge measures." They were not just decedents of any giant but "sons of the giant from the *Nephilim*" (13:32–33). The memory of a primordial sin—the mixing between "the sons of the gods" and the beautiful "daughters of man" that preceded the great flood at the time of Noah (Gen. 6:1–4)—is brought back in the flash of a word,[109] and the allusion to extinction is planted in the reader's mind.

But this was not the case for the people at the scene, for they could not see where their sin lay. They feared the great giants more than they feared God and so remained unimpressed by Caleb's steadfast support of the Lord's plan. They adopted the perspective of the other scouts, who admitted that when looking at the native Canaanites "we were *in our own eyes* like grasshoppers, and so we were in their eyes" (13:33). They feared their mighty Lord more than they trusted him, but they were now facing a more tremendous threat: the prowess of the mighty Canaanites. They preferred to die, in Egypt or in the desert (14:2–3), than fight those giants. Since God's warnings and threats were never interiorized—his genocidal propensity in the desert had so far been revealed only to Moses—they gave up on the entire colonizing project and started organizing to go back to Egypt (Num. 14:4; Deut. 1:26). When Caleb, who was now joined by Joshua, tried to change their mind, invoking God's mighty support and warning them not to rebel against him, the people did not listen and were ready "to pelt them with stones" (Num. 14:6–10).[110]

The people were motivated by the immediacy of their fears and could not grasp the reason of the power by which they were governed. Clearly, they were not fully aware that their actions might lead to their destruction. This is another theme shared by all three versions. After hearing God's verdict, as they understood that they were doomed to end their lives in the desert, they changed their minds, mourned and confessed their sin, but then tried too swiftly to display their new loyalty, and in doing so missed the point (as both J and D narrate it; Num. 14:39–40; Deut 1:34–42). Eager to please God and undeterred by Moses's warnings, the people then insisted on going up, right away, to the high country, toward "the place that the Lord said," where they were attacked by the local inhabitants[111] and soon met their doom. Deprived of God's protection—he assists only the wars he commands—the desperate settlers were struck down by the natives whom they had recently refused to fight (Num. 14:45; Deut. 1:44–45). In all three versions, God's response expresses the same kind of despair—the enslaved people will not be able to complete their journey and reach the promised land. They were not up for the task—in other words, there were no more tools in his arsenal to gain their trust and ensure that they would prepare themselves for the challenges of colonization. His limited governmental talent, not only their obstinancy and "slave mentality," as traditional readers so often have it, doomed the liberated slaves to end their lives wandering aimlessly in the wilderness.

On both textual and narrative levels, the Deuteronomic version of the story clearly stands apart from the one in Numbers 13–14, where the two other versions are neatly woven together. But the general lines of differentiation of J and P sources in Numbers are widely accepted, and the debated passages are mostly irrelevant for our reading.[112] Each of the two segments consists of a more or less complete story, as does the Deuteronomic version. Hence, it is relatively easy to establish the coherence of the three versions and read them separately. When this is done, some differences in themes, style, and tone become clear, and the logic of the composition may be grasped.[113]

The J source is almost cinematic, portraying the whole episode in vivid colors—the land of Canaan and its fearsome inhabitants, the scouters' anxiety, God's narcissistic complaint (Num. 14:11) and frustration with his people, and the people's fear-driven behavior. Like his subjects, the Lord too was driven by emotions. At first, he was outraged and wanted to resort to extreme violence—total destruction—to "strike them with the plague and dispossess them," building Moses "a nation greater and mightier than they" (14:12). But he was also quick to change his mind, as he did when Moses reminded him not only of his steadfast love to Israel but also that destruction would tarnish his reputation among the nations (14:16). Moses's plea echoes the one he pronounced in response to first genocidal threat (Ex. 32:11–12).

The language of the priestly source is formal and rationalizing. The names of all the scouts, listed according to their tribes, opens the account. In this version of the story, Joshua's role is emphasized, Aaron is added, and the people's rebellious response is described in more detail, with their explicit preference of Egypt over Canaan spelled out and presented as unforgivable (13:32, 14:1–4). Note, however, that the people's rebellion did not concern any particular law but the very authority of God and his appointed leaders, his plans and policy, as well as the lives of the two loyal scouts, Joshua and Caleb (14:10). The priestly source is careful to portray God's complaint in a more balanced way (14:27). It describes his punishments in terms of the crime, measure for measure, such as forty years in the desert for forty days in Canaan (14:34–35) and death for the scouts who "put forth an ill report" about the promised land (13:32, 14:37). Although the weapon he used was a plague, only the actual spoilers of God's plan were killed, sparing the two trustful messengers (13:38). No other act of violence is recorded in the priestly source. Despite the harsh language ("in this wilderness your corpses will fall"; 14:29), the punishment to the whole people involved neither violence nor death. Those who had seen his plagues in Egypt and failed to understand their purpose would not see the promised land. Those who cast that land aside and did not want to fight for it would not inherit it (14:29–31). In the longue durée of God's rule, this was an entirely reasonable compromise: The people lived on, and the grand plan was postponed for forty years. They and their children would have all the time it takes to practice service at the Tabernacle and learn the law, and he would have all the time he needed to better educate and prepare them for the colonizing mission.

The Deuteronomic version (Deut. 1:19–41) is not written as a report to the reader but rather as a recollection of past events told to people who might still remember it or had heard it many times over, for they would be the new generation about to enter the promised land. The account repeats most of the themes we have encountered but diverges from a few. Sending the scouts was the idea of the people, which Moses readily accepted (1:22–23); lack of trust is articulated more extensively and more emphatically (1:27–33); Aaron is absent, and Joshua is mentioned as the new leader who would lead the conquest campaign and not as one of the scouts; the priestly, nonviolent punishment was accompanied by the same disastrous epilogue that concludes the Jehovist version—a hasty display of loyalty to God by rushing to a war he did not declare. Like the priestly version, however, here too there is one striking omission: There is no trace of the genocidal threat and its retraction. However, unlike the priestly version, even the killing of the scouts is not mentioned. Thus, in the Deuteronomic

version divine violence plays no part at all—they were defeated and humiliated
in the war against the Amorites because they "rebelled against Yahweh's words"
and mounted a battle he had not declared (1:43), but it was the Amorites who
"pursued [them] as the bees do and pounded [them]" (1:44).

Beyond the various differences among the three versions, a clear pattern
emerges. Almost all major elements recur in the two basic versions with typical
variations, including sending the expedition; bringing back the report; and the
negative portrayal of Canaan, accompanied with one or two trustworthy but
dissenting voices; the people's rebellious response; and the punishment that
follows. Most variations to this general pattern have been explained in terms of
the authors' political agenda and historiography, their normative language, and
the legacy of the "founding fathers" they wished to foreground.[114] One crucial
element, however, cannot be explained along similar lines—the patent difference
in the recourse to violence among the three versions. The threat to exercise the
most extreme form of violence, genocide, along with Moses's plea for forgiveness (Num. 14:11–20), is central to the pre-priestly version but missing from
the two others. Both P and D do not try to supplement for this missing element
or blur the gap using some textual redactions. They contain no trace of the
genocidal threat, even though they probably knew the pre-priestly version.[115]
The genocidal episode finds a clear echo in another text, in Numbers 32, where
Moses understood the Reubenites' and the Gadites' request to settle on the east
side of the Jordan River as a reluctance to join the rest of the people's campaign
of conquest. He invoked the scouts and their sin (32:7–14), associated the two
tribes with the distrustful scouts (32:8), and accused them of the same sin, which
might lead to the same catastrophe, where God would "leave them [the people]
in the wilderness and you would destroy all this people" (32:15). The blame is
on the two tribes, but the cause is "Yahweh's flaring wrath" (32:13). The sources
of this chapter are notoriously hard to map, but we have a good reason to believe
that the echo of the genocidal scene is a nonpriestly source.[116]

Viewed more generally, we can note the stark differences in the way violence,
both divine and human, was deployed according to each version. In the pre-
priestly version, a genocidal threat is invoked, then revoked and replaced by
a nonviolent punishment. In the priestly version, divine violence is limited to
the killing of the ten disloyal scouts. And in Deuteronomy, the entire episode is
narrated without any recourse to divine violence. In both the pre-priestly and
the Deuteronomic versions, human violence abounds, as the Israelites were
"struck . . . and shattered" (Num. 14:45) or "pounded" by their enemies (Deut.
1:44) in the battle into which they rushed unauthorized. In the priestly version,

the only trace of human violence is the threat to pelt Joshua and Caleb with stones (Num. 14:10).[117]

The table below schematizes our results.

	Pre-priestly	Priestly	Deuteronomist
Divine Violence	Averted genocidal threat	Limited targeted killing	None
Human Violence	Nonauthorized war and defeat	A threat of a summary execution	Nonauthorized war and defeat

The distinct patterns of violence distribution are elements in distinct configurations of violence and, hence, of distinct theocratic formations. In this, at least, the scouts' episode is unique, for it offers a rare meeting point of the three main theocratic regimes, as well as a space for their divergence.[118] Without ever understating its catastrophic nature and the threat it posed to Israel's very existence, both priestly and Deuteronomic theocracies revised the pre-priestly figure of God and his mode of ruling and devised ways to tame his violence.

In the pre-priestly sources we found rudiments of theocratic thinking from which I tried to reconstruct a possible, putative model of pre-priestly theocracy. Such a reconstruction was not possible, however, without the integration of these sources in the complete Pentateuchal corpus. The theocratic moments in the pre-priestly sources are too dispersed and variegated to be considered as traces of a preconceived model of a theocratic regime, the kind of thought experiment I hypothetically ascribe to priestly and Deuteronomic writings. The more explicit theocratic thinking, rhetoric, and imagination disseminated in the priestly and Deuteronomic writings help one identify God as a ruling power, follow the political aspects of his interactions with humans, and reconstruct their patterns. From Exodus onward, where priestly and Deuteronomic writings comprise most of the text, things become clearer for the pre-priestly sources as well. The textual evidence is less rudimentary; the analysis of the theocratic logic is supported by ample evidence at the text's surface, including a few intense moments of political clashes; and we see some elaborate displays of ruling power, all of which are more accessible to the formal and conceptual analysis that concerns us here. The next two chapters are devoted to these two theocratic formations.

4

HOLY POWER: STATES OF EXCEPTION, TARGETED KILLINGS, AND THE LOGIC OF SUBSTITUTION

HOLINESS

The Form of His Subjectivity

God's figure in priestly writings,[1] his modes of appearance, presence, and action, are distinctly different from those we have encountered in the pre-priestly sources. His figure is more abstract, much less anthropomorphic, and differently distributed across space and time. Here, God could no longer be described as a superhero endowed with excessive powers; his authority was not secured through private epiphanies and public revelations, accompanied by personal promises and injunctions; and mass destruction was not his main governing technology. In the priestly theocracy, God appears qualitatively and radically different from humans.[2] Simultaneously, an entire army of disciples who knew to appreciate that difference were at his service, ready to articulate, carry out, and impose his rule. At the center of this radical theopolitical shift and the new configuration of power lay the discourse of holiness, with its conceptual grid of divisions and separations and the elaborate practice it guided to regulate both divine and human manifestations of the holy. Our first task is to reconstruct holiness as the discursive infrastructure of priestly theocracy.[3] In the first two sections, I will cover some familiar ground necessary for the analysis that occupies the rest of this chapter, focusing on priestly governance, the divine violence that sustained it, and the acts of misconduct and rebellion that provoked that violence.

In priestly theocracy, ruling was an art of separation:

> And Yahweh spoke to Aaron . . . to separate between the holy and the profane (*hol*) and between the unclean and the clean. (Lev. 10:10)[4]

> I am Yahweh your God who set you apart from all the peoples. And you shall set apart the clean from the unclean beast, and the unclean bird from the clean. (Lev. 20:24–5)[5]

Two distinct but related binary oppositions are implied here—holy (*kadosh*)/ profane or common (*hol*) and pure or clean (*tahor*)/impure or defiled, polluted (*tame*)[6]—and they are ubiquitous in the priestly writings.[7] The imperative to separate the two opposing poles is the arch rule of the priestly code of laws. The two pairs are neither synonymous nor equivalent, and the two acts of separation differ accordingly. Both pairs of opposites are qualities of entities or their states of being, but the first opposition—holy versus profane—is also a division between two distinct domains that stretch over clearly bounded times and places and exceed and encompass the qualified entities they contain. In the second pair, clean (or pure) versus unclean (impure, defiled), the designated quality does not imply a distinct domain—there is no domain of pure or impure things.

As a quality and a domain, holiness is bestowed by God or the men he has appointed;[8] it cannot simply be acquired. Once bestowed, holiness separates an entity from the domain of the common. Profanation, on the other hand, is the outcome of an inadvertent or sinful human act that desecrates the holy.[9] Purity is a necessary but never sufficient condition for entering the domain of the holy and assuming holiness, while impurity is a cause for being removed from the domain of the holy altogether.[10] In the domain of the common, entities may be pure or impure without any consequences; in the domain of the holy, the impure must be isolated and cleansed through rituals or else eliminated. Designated places, even an entire land or nation; periods of time (holy days); appointed individuals; liquids such as wine, oil, and water; food items; artifacts of all kinds associated with service at the sanctuary—all these were hallowed. Purity and impurity covered a much larger scope, including all the known animals (catalogued according to the priestly version of creation),[11] bodily organs (their functions, secretions, various defects, and chronic diseases),[12] bodily movements, clothes and ornaments, ceremonies and practices of birth and burial, fields, plants and their fruits, dietary rules, and sexual practices.

The way these two pairs of binary oppositions apply to a variety of beings, sites, and times can be read as forming a "realm of holiness," an imaginary space—physical, social, and symbolic—formed by the crossing and breadth of these two oppositions. The *domain* of the holy includes everything that is no longer or not yet profane or could be profaned (and vice versa with respect to the domain of the common). But profanity itself, in its most prevalent sense of "the common," does not make sense outside its relation to the holy and could not come into being without asserting the holy as separate. The *realm* of holiness thus includes everything that was explicitly excluded from the domain of the holy or, more generally, anything whose status or mode of being is determined or affected by its relation to holiness. Both dimensions of holiness, as a quality and a domain, are captured by a phrase like "access to the holy." "Becoming holy" (that is, being granted with or acquiring holiness as a quality) is a mode of being that, like one's initial place within or outside the domain of the holy, determines one's access to the holy.

"Realm" and "domain" are heuristic terms not found in the priestly writings, but it would not be incorrect to understand priestly discourse as operating with them tacitly or implying them every time the binary divisions are applied. Thus, for example, while Shabbat is the one holy day of the week and the other six days are ordinary common days, the week itself, like the entire calendrical year, belongs to the realm of the holy. Similarly, settlers and hired workers who are excluded from the Passover ritual (Ex. 12:45) belong for this very reason to the realm of the holy. This is a space opened and delineated by the division itself, where access to the domain of the holy characterizes one's position within it. Thus, the difference between the Levites' and the priests' access to the holy touches at one and the same time on their place within the domain of the holy and the hallowed objects with which they can come in contact.[13]

Introducing the two basic oppositions of the priestly writings, Olyan states succinctly: "The holy/common distinction establishes a boundary around the sanctuary; the clean/unclean distinction determines who or what may cross it."[14] This is a compelling formula that requires some qualifications. The boundary is enacted in time as well, not only in space, across a large territory, not only locally around the sanctuary, and the clean/unclean are activated inside the sanctuary (e.g., Lev. 6:3–4, 7:17, 9:9–10), not only at its entrance. Olyan, who carefully presents many cases captured by his basic formula, portrays a static picture and overlooks the generative nature of the basic oppositions.[15] Thus different segments of the priestly writings, and the entire Holiness Code, may expand or contract to include more or less space, time, and spheres of life without undermining the basic discursive grid of the priestly corpus, that is, the two pairs of contrary terms and the positions of those who operate within the space they define: God, the distinct groups of his privileged servants, ordinary Israelites, and the non-Israelites—the stranger (*nokhri*) and alien resident (*ger*)—in their midst.[16]

God can bestow holiness because he is holy. Holiness is his "most quintessential characteristic [and it] imbues all aspects of His being and presence."[17] As it is the mode of his being, it needs no qualification. He claims it for himself in the first person ("for I am holy") with no reservation.[18] The holiness he bestows, on the other hand, is always qualified. God is holy no matter what, but other entities can only *become* holy through being hallowed by his proclamation, an act that lets them *dwell* in the domain of the holy, and they must become holy if they accidentally get too close to places in which God, his name, or his glory are made present. When bestowed on other entities, holiness is always conditioned and partial. When bestowed with holiness, so long as they remained pure, time, distinct spaces, and finite entities could share the domain of the holy with God. In fact, their sanctification is a condition for their existence in his proximity. These entities include, humans and animals, things and manner of speech, and the entire promised land. When holiness (*kodesh*) is imparted to any such entity, an act or process of sanctification (*kidush, hithkadshut*) takes place, marking the entrance to the domain of the holy.[19] Rituals of purification are required when sanctification takes place but also when ritual defilement occurs to entities that already exist in the domain of the holy. Some sins—murder, sexual transgressions, and idolatry, collectively called "abominations" or "abhorrences" (*to'avoth*)—are powerful enough to work in both directions at once, to desecrate God's name and glory and defile the sanctuary (Lev. 20:3; Num. 19:20) and the land (Lev. 18:24–28; Num. 35:34–35).[20]

The domain of the holy has a clear spatial organization and a centric core. There are gradations of holiness and purification, and they are dictated by proximity to the center,[21] which is defined by the Tabernacle (*mishkan*), literally God's "dwelling place" in Israel's camp, called alternatively "the Tent of Meeting," a name that designates the noncultic function of the sanctuary—the place where God meets Moses and the people. God himself instructed Moses to appoint able men to construct the Tabernacle for him as a place "that [he] may abide in their midst" (Ex. 25:8) and gave detailed plans for the construction of the movable site and all artifacts within it (Ex. 25–31:11). In his dwelling place his glory appeared; the altar supplied him burnt animals' flesh, which his fire consumes,[22] grain offerings, libation, and a "pleasing fragrance to Yahweh" (Ex. 29:41). It is there, he tells Moses,

> where I shall meet with you . . . to speak to you. And I shall meet there with the Israelites and it shall be consecrated through My glory. And I shall consecrate the Tent of Meeting and the altar, and Aaron and his sons I shall consecrate to be priests to Me. And I shall abide in the midst of the Israelites and I shall be a God to them. (Ex. 29:42–45)

The intensification of holiness at the camp's center could not be stated more clearly.

Center and periphery were not fixed places, however. The Tabernacle was a mobile sanctuary; hence the domain of holiness moved with its center, along with the entire camp of Israel,[23] and, in time of wars sanctioned by God,[24] stretched far beyond the site of the Tabernacle. It was a system that had to be reterritorialized every so often, according to changing, contingent circumstances, as the people moved through the wilderness.[25] Without a fixed place for his temple, there was no need for or concern with tying God to a specific site and fetishizing it or with assigning God to an alternative place in Heaven, as did the Deuteronomists.[26] The immanence of the holy was forcefully asserted: It literally dwelled in the midst of the Israelites' camp or on its outskirts and was bestowed on people, things, and the site of its surroundings, unfolding and occasionally redistributed between center and periphery in a real, changing geographic space.

Since the Tabernacle was the site of God's presence and the core from which holiness emanated regularly and intensely, the sanctuary's immediate surroundings and the ark and altar in its midst formed an internal division in the domain of the holy. The sanctuary was divided by a decorated curtain (the *parokhet*) that separated "the holy of holies" (*kodesh kodashim*, where the ark lay; Ex. 26:31–37) from the rest of the sanctuary, and from there to the sanctuary's courtyard (Ex. 27:9) and beyond was a continuum of diminishing holiness determined by distance and the nature of the things located there. Access to the Tabernacle and movement inside it were limited accordingly and determined by other internal divisions among humans exposed to the emanation of holiness.

God separated the tribe of Levi from all the rest of Israel. He then separated one Levite clan—Aaron and his descendants, the priests—from the other three clans. Finally, within the priests themselves, the high priest was given a special position shared with no other priest. On the basis of and supported by the division within the tribe of Levi, a strict division of labor followed, organizing the routine and occasional practices in and around the sanctuary. The service at the sanctuary was guided by a detailed protocol of purity rituals and sacrifices that affected the Israelite camp as a whole. Every member of the community, including circumcised household slaves and resident aliens,[27] was subject to some practices of purification, sacrifice, and other sacral offerings. The state of being pure or impure, or inside or outside the domain of the holy, required a series of separating gestures—through rituals of purification, regulating proximity to the core, and practices of removal, taking a distance, and keeping apart. In other words, holy and profane, purity and defilement were states of being that could not be dissociated from the obligatory norms they immanently implied. Once any of them was declared, it yielded a series of instructions.[28] Inside the domain of holiness, and in lesser or greater proximity to its core, "the holy of holies," everyone had to follow the rules of separation. Practices of separation comprised many realms and aspects of life, applied differently to men and women, differently inscribed in their bodies, following individuals from birth to death, in disease and war, in their contacts with other living beings around them, with the elements in their surroundings, and with the non-Israelites in their midst and beyond their moving camp. Together these practices were woven into one extensive, strictly regulated, preordained biopolitical system, which was detailed, hierarchized, and theocentric.[29]

The Holiness Code (H) takes the prescriptive element—the imperative to sanctify through a series of separations—to its extreme: Becoming holy is a task and a vocation assigned to the entire community (*edah*), and the instructions to separate and purify begin to colonize more spheres of everyday life, more times and spaces of communal life. In this, H extends the priestly discourse and stretches its biopolitical system, and without changing the basic matrix, adds a dynamic aspect to it.[30] But H also brings to the fore an aspect that remains dormant in P. As the entire biopolitical system is now encapsulated by and reiterated through the imperative to become holy (*vehayitem kedoshim*), every instruction is an instruction to perform separation. H thus interprets Israel's exception as a special case of God's sovereign *act of separation*, achieved through their election to be God's people. Separation, the basic priestly principle of creation, appears here as the basic principle of ruling, as well. Once Israel was separated, all other separations became internal divisions within the universe under divine rule, and foreigners living in Israel's midst were allocated specific positions within the matrix of holiness. Some of them were subject to purity rules and took part in the sacrificial practices—another point made by P in a reserved way and extended by H[31]—while others who had no share in the rituals were still acknowledged and included (e.g., Ex. 12:45; Lev. 22:10) in the community, protected by some of its rules (e.g., Lev. 25:6; Num. 35:15).

Combining the three contexts of separation—cosmological, political, and cultic—the Holiness Code directs Israel to imitate God's art of separations: "I . . . set you apart from [all] the peoples . . . *you shall therefore set apart* the clean from the unclean beast" (Lev. 20:24–26).[32] According to some influential readings, Israel's holiness seems to be rooted in a basic analogy. In Jacob Milgrom's words, "the dietary system is thus a reflection and reinforcement of Israel's election. . . . Just as God's holiness is a model and mandate for Israel, so is God's act of separation."[33] Criticizing this, Baruch Schwartz notes that "Israelites are not told to be holy *like* God; rather they are commanded to be holy *because* He is Holy."[34] In other words, the claim that *imitatio dei* is the principle that governs the teaching of holiness in H does not reflect the fact that Israel is endowed with divine qualities on a human scale but that they are ordered to imitate God in performing separations. The verses from Leviticus (20:24–26) clearly indicate that the analogy is not thematic but formal,[35] juxtaposing two different acts of setting apart, not the objects or domains of separation. It is precisely here, however, that a clear difference emerges. *Imitatio dei* is not partial because it is formal. Rather, it is limited and curtailed by the fact that God institutes separations while Israel merely performs them, and performing only those that they have been commanded to perform. God's sovereignty is expressed in his power to institute separations, while he himself is always already separated, and uncompromisingly so. This is the very meaning of his holiness. The Israelites, on the other hand, are commanded to *become* holy by performing separations.

God's holiness, reiterated throughout the priestly writings and the Holiness Code, is an unmitigated aspect of his being and a given condition of his action and presence among humans. The separation this holiness involves takes place in an unmediated, spontaneous manner, somewhat like the *causa sui* with which God will be later associated. It is then imposed or conferred on others by his choice. Israel, conversely, is separated by God and would never imitate him in this respect, for the people cannot be the origin of its own separation or of the separations it performs.[36] For God, to be is to be separated; separation is his unconditional and unchangeable mode of being. This is true even when—or most conspicuously when—he mingles in human affairs and dwells in their midst, even when his voice is clearly heard, his presence clearly felt, and a glimpse of his glory becomes visible.[37] At the same time, separation is one of his major modes of action, in the form of creation or inauguration. For Israel, separation means something else: It is their task and duty, a source of great danger but also a means of survival as God's people. Israel can and should sanctify God's name and glory. This is how God's holiness is made present in public, "in the midst of the Israelites" (Lev. 22:32), and how Israel accomplishes the task implied in its own separation without reflecting, adding to, or subtracting anything from the separateness of God.

Here, H sources express an idea, as stated above, that no other source in the Hebrew Bible challenges: God's holiness cannot be qualified. His holiness is *"imbues all aspects of His being and presence."*[38] Neither transgression nor desecration, nor the attempts to force him into appearance, crying out for his saving intervention, can alter or affect his separateness. In fact, this is the only predicate associated with the figure of God in the Hebrew Bible that may be interpreted as the biblical version of the category of the absolute (which has no equivalent in biblical Hebrew). When the holy applies to God himself, holiness means God's absolute separateness. Anachronistic as it might sound, without assuming something like absolutely fixed separateness, the system of priestly separations becomes untenable.[39] At its core, or when attributed to God, the holy is singular and complete. God may be more or less merciful, impatient, or vindictive (e.g., Num. 25:10–13), but he cannot be more or less holy. In itself, the holiness of God is the purest element of his identity, the one that has expelled any and all differences. This does not mean that God lacks the capability to act differentially, change his mind, or even demonstrate contradicting qualities—he is both vengeful and forgiving, for example, zealous and compassionate. But all these different moments are his own, aspects of his being and action, emanating from his separate oneness. Nothing that was even slightly alien to him could have played a part in his existence.

When on his own, he was pure Oneness, a mode of existence in which no finite entity could survive. Mortal, finite beings of any kind—objects, ideas, people, or a sense of a passing moment—always existed "in the plural." To be what it is, a finite being always requires something different from itself against which it can be differentiated and with respect to which it assumes its identity or unity. A finite being draws and redraws its contours not only against but also while being among and alongside other finite beings, and it has a point or surface of contact with them, a medium, a milieu, a space and time they share. He, however, bestows and denies, gives and takes, but shares nothing except for portions of this very holiness. In his absolute holiness he is unlike any other being. To be what he is he does not need to actively differentiate himself from anything else or be actively differentiated from something, by something, through the mediation of something. He is always already and absolutely differentiated. His holiness is radically antagonistic. It may be imagined as a sensual substitute for the yet unavailable concept of infinity (which would not appear in Hebrew before the Middle Ages). It is a substitute that both anticipates the concept and lends it one of its possible meanings—the radical alterity with respect to anything finite.[40]

In this sense, for God holiness is sameness and not selfhood: It is the nonmediated element of divine separateness. But it is the Form out of which subjectivity emerges. If we take this idea seriously, we can understand creation itself as a work of *imitatio dei*—God sought to create an image that would reflect his own separateness and initiated a series of acts that culminated in the creation of a creature "in Our image, by Our likeness," who would be set apart from the entire order of creation "to conquer it and hold sway" over it in its entirety (Gen. 1:26, 28). And then, when this sovereign subject, immersed as he was in his own holiness, sought to practice his rule in earnest, he again separated one people from the many, followed by one tribe from among this people, one clan from within this tribe, and a few individuals from within this clan, through whom he proclaimed a whole practice of separations to live by. The materialization of his holiness in the realm of human affairs was performed through generating multiple separations, a work that some among his elected people would continue and extend long after his departure from their realm. But as long as he dwelled in their midst, occasional eruptions of violence were needed to sustain some of the main lines of separation. To survive, whatever was imparted with holiness must have been actively and repeatedly removed from the profane and cleansed from the impure.

Risks, Violence, and Some Benefits

The radical separateness of God means that he tolerates nothing except what has been purified and become holy itself. This idea lies at the intersection of the two major divisions that make up the concept of separation in the priestly writings. The first division—holy versus profane—is the raison d'être of the second—pure versus impure. Purity is the precondition for dwelling in the proximity of the holy and being imparted with it. Purity is a necessary condition for becoming holy but not a sufficient one. Conversely, defilement is a sufficient but unnecessary condition for expulsion from the domain of the holy, either by moving back to the domain of the common or by being literally eliminated.[41] Immaterial things, like God's name and his hallowed times, can never be defiled. Instead, they can be desecrated through improper placement in the realm of the common.[42] And whereas desecration may be benign and not all cases of it have grave consequences, defilement is always negative and potentially dangerous. Moving into the domain of the holy is always risky. God seems basically indifferent to what exists properly in the domain of the common but very anxious about what resides in or crosses over to the domain of the holy.

God's response to blurring the distinction between the common and the holy involved a judicial process. Once, in the wilderness, when a man gathering wood on Shabbat violated the day's holiness, he suspended his judgment, but when asked by Moses for guidance, he instructed him to order the community to stone the man to death (Num. 15:32–36).[43] But his response to ritual defilement was swift and unmediated. It took place at or near the sanctuary, where, marked by the rising cloud and glory above the Tent, most of his epiphanies took place. Israel's new neighbor was extremely dangerous, and the proximity to his holiness was life-menacing. But because his violence was mostly limited to the sanctuary and its immediate surroundings, the complicated apparatus of restrictions, lines of demarcation, categories of exclusion, and rules of purification served to keep divine violence at bay and mitigate its catastrophic outcome.[44]

Purity, danger, and distance were intertwined, as all three expressed and reflected one another. Distance and purity defined and ranked danger according to areas and situations: The entrance to and exit from the demarcated areas had to be monitored, and, within the realm of the holy, people's conduct in various situations had to be controlled. Proper cleansing would protect those who wished to or were commanded to come close to or enter the holy site.[45] The rules of cleansing were dependent on the distance from the holy center, with the most desirable distance dependent on the status and level of sanctification of the persons—priests, Levites, or Israel—and their belongings that approached the realm. The sanctuary was the center of gravity that activated powerful forces of attraction and repulsion. The profane surrounded the holy center like a wide periphery; at any moment the core could have functioned as a black hole into which that periphery would tumble or, just the opposite, as a fission reaction that would overwhelm its entire surroundings with lethal energy.

Coming into contact with the holy required purification, but at the same time, contact with the holy was itself a means of purification. A detailed protocol of sacrifices was in place to allow for atonement for impurities and offences of all kinds, including unintentional trespasses (Lev. 4, 5:14–18) and other sins that required confession and reparation (Lev. 5:4–13, 20–26). The unclean person is not necessarily a sinner,[46] but if not cleansed properly the polluted person would contaminate the sanctified place and bring sin into the holy core. The proper performance of ritual sacrifice protected those who had sinned from being harmed; the only blood spilled would be that of slaughtered animals. Cleansing, before and through sacrifice, enabled a certain closeness to the holy, but those who truly came close to the place of his dwelling—the Levites and the priests—required further means of insulation. Because of this, they were experts in spotting traces of impurity among the offerings and people who entered the holy space.[47] The proper and timely removal of the defiling elements was a matter of life and death. God's closeness was deadly, but his instructions were life-saving, so he could have been perceived as life itself.[48] Outside the holy zone, cleansing was charged, but failure to cleanse was not met with God's lethal power: A woman who did not cleanse herself after menstruation or a man who touched a corpse was not sentenced to death; a woman left unclean after childbirth is not a sinner. However, within the sanctuary, impurity was literally lethal, and the act of cleansing meant choosing life over death.

Most people, animals, and things were not inherently polluted; pollution was generated through a relation to the holy, just like toxic materials are only considered toxic when they negatively affect life and its conditions. {I'll keep developing the analogy between holiness and life in the brackets that follow.} Cleansing is both a condition and a practice of sanctification {the analogy prevails—in a toxic environment, cleansing is both a condition and a practice of living}, but neither of these meanings convey the metamorphosis involved in sanctification—the process of *becoming holy*. Something must already be *"in the holy"* {take part in a living environment} *to become* holy {to *be born*}. It is a metamorphosis that an object undergoes so that it may be included in the realm of the holy {of living beings}, or change its place within it, getting as inseparable as possible from the holy {life} and as protected as possible from its lethal proximity {so it won't be consumed or infected by other living organisms}. Like defilement {and pollution with regard to living beings}, sanctification is conveyed by touch, transferring its energy instantaneously—"whatever touches [the grain or the flesh of the offence offering] shall become holy" (Lev. 6:11, 20). The metaphysics of the holy {or life} is ingrained in the physics of objects and the chemistry of the flesh in animate and inanimate matter alike.

Cleansing is a process that had a clear point of departure—a state of impurity—and a clear objective—a state of purity—but defilement is a matter of everyday life and, if nothing else, an effect of bodily function, hence cleansing must be incessantly renewed.[49] The unclean that came into contact with the holy was often destroyed at once {here the analogy breaks, as the impact of toxic pollution on life may take years, even centuries, to show its effects}. The elimination was the result of the encounter between impurity and sanctity, and its materialization is rapid: "And fire came out from before Yahweh and consumed them," it is said of the two sons of Aaron who "had brought forward alien fire before Yahweh" (Lev. 10:1–2; Num. 3:4). Holiness was the utter lack of tolerance toward the unclean. Sanctification, justified by its very process, was the only way of being in holiness' proximity {just as cleansing the toxic materials is necessary for staying alive. If the presence of toxic matter in the environment would have acted as swiftly as did the presence of the holy, environmentalists would have long become our priests}. In this sense, in priestly theocracy, the God's Other, properly speaking, was not "other gods," as the Deuteronomists had it,[50] but impurity itself, which always meant the impurity embodied and proliferated among humans. The two opposites could not coexist; holiness was utter purity, which necessarily implies radical intolerance to anything other than itself.[51] Ronald Hendel described holiness as an antisubstance that destroys every substance with which it comes into contact.[52] But if the impurity that results from abominations accumulates, God might abandon his dwelling place, and the land might "spew out" its inhabitants—as it already did once (Lev. 18:22–28).[53]

Because it had no fixed site, every once in a while his dwelling had to be designated anew in the midst of the Israelites' camp; thus holiness was of this world, both earthly and mobile.[54] But because it could not have been exhausted by any earthly site, this immanence was always in excess in relation to the place of its appearance.[55] There was always more to God—more actual and potential violence, power, and glory—than his epiphanies could have revealed. The need to restrict access to and take proper distance from the place where he resided was an effect of this dangerous excess. At the same time, the materiality of his presence is clearly portrayed. Usually it is indicated by the appearance of his glory (*kabod*),[56] perhaps a radiant, formless stuff, which could be brighter or dimmer, more often "in the cloud" as it descended on, abided over, or was lifted from the Tent of Meeting or covering "the Tabernacle of the Tent of the Covenant . . . like a semblance of fire" (Num. 9:15) from evening to morning.[57] Sometimes it blasts in the form of the "fire [that] came out from before Yahweh and consumed" either the offering (Lev. 9:24) or the agents of defilement (Lev. 10:2; Num. 16:32). The fire, the glory, and the cloud are all atmospheric, not grounded; they are the kinds of misty stuff through which he appears. That misty stuff could appear or disappear out of the blue, but the blue was not of the skies (with which "the cloud" is never associated), as the cloud's movements were fully coordinated with the people's camping in and their advancement through the wilderness (Num. 9:21–22, 10:11–12, 34).

The appearance of the glory and the cloud are often correlated with eruptions of divine violence. Since it erupted at distinct sites, divine violence was strictly related to the earthly cartography of the holy rather than associated with descending from the heavens, from nowhere, or from any nonplace that only he could inhabit. The lethal impact of the holy was inseparable from its other effects: separation, elevation, or consecration. This intimate link is well captured by the textual proximity and use of the same phrase, which describes the killing of the sons of Aaron who offered "alien fire" (Lev. 10:2) as well as God's participation in the ointment of the priests that inaugurated the service at the Tabernacle (Lev. 9:24). The two occurrences of the same phrase are separated by fewer than two verses, thirty-five words, and the book's silent division into chapters.[58]

The danger emanating from the core of the holy domain required not only internal divisions and restriction on access but also layers of insulation fitting the social divisions and various occasions and sources of pollution.[59] Any "stranger who draws near shall be put to death." A stranger, as the Aramaic translation clearly captures, is simply anyone not appointed to serve at the sanctum, and hence he or she does not belong to the domain of the holy.[60] But, in fact, being a stranger was also a matter of proximity and location, not only of status, as the death of Aaron's sons makes clear. The warning was repeated three times in the context of the instructions for service at the Tabernacle (Num. 1:51, 3:10, 3:38) and once again when the order of Levite and priestly service was reinstated (Num. 18:7). The detailed instructions for the kind of sacral garments that the high priest must wear when "he comes into the sacred zone" should be understood in the same way, as well as the bell that announces his entrance to the tabernacle and the incense he must burn so as not to die (Lev. 16:13). The incense was also used outside the tent and far from the altar, as detailed in the story of Korah, when Aaron took the incense "and ran into the midst of the assembly . . . and . . . stood between the dead and the living; so the plague was stopped" (Num. 16:46–48). Like the rainbow Yahweh put in the clouds to remind himself what he promised to humans after the flood (Gen. 9:8–17), the incense served at the altar and beyond as a reminder to assuage his divine rage and as an isolating substance that could abate his violence. Both the rainbow and the incense were visible and olfactory aspects of the misty vapor of his epiphany, the rainbow being a kind of heavenly incense and the incense an earthly, manmade rainbow. Both preserve—and at the same time negate—the possibility of total catastrophe, a kind of priestly *Aufhebung* of divine violence of the type imagined in the Jehovist source.

Sanctification, which cannot be initiated by humans, only by God, generates closeness to holiness, a coming into God's possession, and an exposure to the danger that resides in excessive proximity to holiness. "By those who come near me I must be regarded as holy," God says after consuming the sons of Aaron who put that "alien fire in their pans at the Tabernacle" (Lev. 10:1–3). God orders Moses to "bring the Levites forward before" him (Num. 8:10); therefore they must undergo a range of cleansing rites (Num. 8:5–23). The cleansing rites allowed the Levites to serve as human incense, a partition between the people of Israel and the holy: "That there be no plague among the children of Israel when the children of Israel come near the sanctuary" (Num. 8:19). The Levites were exposed to greater risks than Israel was; the priests, who were all descendants of one Levite family, were in greater danger than the other Levites, and the high priest was the most vulnerable of all. The proximity to the holy clearly reflected a ruling hierarchy (first described in Numbers 3). The elites that served the holy were elected by God, and this structure and authority could not be challenged. Exposure to divine violence was the risk of partaking in ruling, and the task of that rule was to restrain that violence.

Mary Douglas proposed that we should understand holiness as wholeness: The holy is perfect, impeccable.[61] Once mixtures or hybrids are introduced, it would no longer be what it was. Desecration, she claims, expresses the fear often associated with concoctions, hybrid creatures, and acts of crossbreeding. The exceptional, defective, or anomalous is perceived as impure. Holiness is that which remains what it is, in its utterly pure essence. It cannot be desecrated because it does not tolerate foreign elements. However, according to Douglas, the holy is not one element but a whole cosmic order. In order to maintain the holiness of that order, everything should remain in its proper place. The world is divided into different sorts, and the task of the intellectual elite is to represent and preserve that classification. Life is full of defects, surprises, undesirable mixtures, strange pairings, disintegration, and paralysis. The cleansing rites aim to overcome the deviations and offer protection against them. Disorder must not triumph over order. The protection of the holy is ultimately a defense of the cosmic order against the chaos that threatens it from within. In Douglas's theory of purity, the analogy between life and holiness I have briefly sketched here is implied in the notion of the holy itself; being the perfect, cosmic order, the holy is the condition of life. But by generating anomalies, concoctions, and crossbreeding, life introduces disorder, endangers the holy, and contains the elements of its own destruction. Preserving the cosmic order means the preservation of the life that depends on it.

Inspired by and as close to the priestly sources as this concept of the holy is, an important difference must be noted. In the priestly writings, the primary danger to humans does not lie in the immanent hybridity of life but in holiness itself. The defense *of* holiness is merely the effect of the danger emanating from its intensified presence and proximity. The danger is immediate and unmediated, not an estimated risk related to long-term effects of disorder. In order to tolerate the presence of impurity's radical otherness in the domain of the holy, the impure must be properly isolated or concealed. Isolation and concealment (as elaborated by Douglas and Hendel)[62] are necessary for the completion of the cleansing, while practices of sanctification may be read as seeking to bring cleansing to completion. But, in fact, sanctification is an unfinished, indefinite, or renewed process that can never be completed—it is a Sisyphean mission to which those thrown into the realm of the holy are doomed.

At the same time, it should be remembered that only by virtue of imparting on others the same absolute, unifying aspect of his being (holiness) could he have company to enjoy and subjects to rule. Without sharing his holiness with others, he would have been left alone, perhaps even lonely. Ruling was his way of sharing his earth with others. This need for sharing the earth with humans necessarily undermined his aloofness, disturbed the emptiness of his purity, and ultimately provoked his violence, which the regime of holiness sought to contain and appease. Readings like that of Mary Douglas, who sees in holiness a supreme principle of a cosmic order, or that of Rudolf Otto, for whom it is the essence of the numinous—mysterious and transcendent—dimension within the divine, ignore or consciously leave aside this aspect of holiness, both psychological and political, which our reading seeks to foreground.[63]

If the priestly authors were thinking something like a cosmic order,[64] this order should be understood as an expression of a specific form of divine *rule*, *a regime* of holiness. Without assuming his yearning for contact with humans, holiness could not be imagined as a system of rule. The flawless *oneness* at its core is the imagined mode of presence of a supreme authority that serves as a source of catastrophic yet relatively limited violence, of horrifying danger and menace, but also of order, distinctions, and hierarchy and, as long as the people abide by the law, a promise of blessed life (Lev. 22:3–13). At the same time, given its deployment across space and time, along the axes of proximity, time, and purity, the imparting of holiness also offers protection from the immanent violence of holiness itself. Unlike the Jehovist model of divine rule, in which the eruption of violence allows the sin to appear post factum, in the priestly model the risks of impurity are known in advance. The priestly version allows sin, misconduct, and benign negligence to be recognized as they happen, and the danger of both inadvertent impurity and unruly offense can be preempted. How this double-edged holiness is to be imparted is therefore the supreme question of rule and governance in priestly theocracy. In the next section, we will follow the unfold-ing of this question in some concrete episodes recorded in the priestly sources.

REBELLIONS IN THE WILDERNESS

Our reconstruction of the discursive infrastructure of the priestly writings has been driven by an interest in their function within a system of rule, their role in the proliferation of the law, the governance of human bodies and action, and the regulation of divine violence. Questions regarding the origin, structural logic, or symbolism of dietary laws, purity rituals, and sacrificial practices, important as they are, have been bracketed. It may well be that the formation of divine rule imagined throughout the priestly corpus originated from certain cultic laws and practices or that this internal logic may explain the meaning and structure of the latter. We, however, are interested here in this formation only as a recurrent pattern that emerges on the surface of a certain textual corpus, formed by—and revealed as—an assemblage of codes of rituals and sacrifices, depictions of vio-lent events, promises and threats, treaties and betrayals, premeditated plans and unfortunate accidents.

Two complementary, more or less parallel distinctions need to be introduced at this point. At the textual level, we need to distinguish between law and narra-tive, which the priestly writings are known for combining and interweaving in a variety of ways. Within the world of the text, we need to distinguish between an idealized state of affairs and what "really happened." These two layers are often related to each other more or less explicitly. The web of laws and instructions proclaimed are not only conditional prescriptions but also a way to describe various domains of life and human conduct within it, as these ought to unfold among law-abiding subjects. The biblical narrative consists mostly of historical accounts of the journey from Egypt to the promised land. Many of these events concern cases of dissent and resistance to divine rule, and in them one may expect to find offenses that rupture the idealized state of affairs. But this is not the case. Usually no specific instruction is violated, and, as we shall see, at times the law does not precede the dissent of God's authority but rather follows it, ultimately using dissent as an opportunity for proclaiming or reiterating his laws.

More generally stated, the priestly writings in Exodus, Leviticus, and Numbers present a matrix of divine rule made of a code of law and cultic practices, on the one hand, and, on the other, narratives depicting the toil of traveling through the desert, the wars Israel fought on the way to Canaan, and occasional resistance to God's rule. The law is proclaimed in the wilderness,[65] but for the obedient subjects it is offered as a blueprint for an idyllic existence, in the future and else-where, in the promised land (Lev. 25:18–19, 26:3–13). The events depicted in the narratives take place in the wilderness, usually in clearly designated places on a map whose main purpose is to name the events that made these places noteworthy. Against the idyllic land promised to those who abide by the laws, the wilderness often turns into a stage for dystopian dramas where divine violence erupts. These are the sites in which divine rule is described as actually practiced, not merely idealized through a (relatively coherent) system of biopolitical rules and regulations. We should bear in mind, of course, that the distinction between the actual and the idealized are both products and features of the theopolitical imagination of the Pentateuchal texts.

Moving from metatextual considerations to internal ones, let us note again that in the priestly version of Israel's wandering in the wilderness, divine vio-lence erupted in front or within the Tent of Meeting, at the heart of the holy zone. There the transgressors are hit and eliminated on the spot. Aaron's sons were struck before the altar (Lev. 10:1–2); Korah and "his congregation," the var-ious groups of rebels whose stories are interwoven in Numbers 16, were stricken in front of the Tent; Phinehas, Aaron's grandson and a priest, substituted for God and extended his zealotry when he killed an Israelite having sex with a Midianite woman in front of, and later inside, the Tent of Meeting (Num. 25:6–11).[66]

The spatial dimension of the unfolding event is clearly articulated in all these episodes, and the long-term effects of violence go beyond those affected at the site of disaster, serving to reassert or reinstitute the priestly order as a whole. After the death of Aaron's sons, who were killed in a kind of "workplace accident" during the holy site's trial run, Moses explained to Aaron the general meaning of his personal tragedy, presenting the most basic principle of divine (priestly) rule: "That is just what Yahweh spoke, saying, 'through those close to me shall I be hallowed, and in all the people's presence shall I be honored.' And Aaron was silent" (Lev. 10:3). Aaron's silence, we may assume with the Jewish tradition, was a silence of grief, but at the same time it was an emblem of a "tacit acceptance" of divine authority. With no interruption, the text then presents new statutes that clarify the rules of access to holiness and establish the distinction of Aaron and his descendants (Lev. 10:4–20). When Phinehas, the zealous priest, acted as a vehicle for transmitting God's jealousy and killed the licentious couple, he was granted a "covenant of peace . . . and eternal priesthood" (Lev. 25:10–13). But the clearest and most significant case in which disaster is followed by the reinstitution of law and authority is the Korah episode (Num. 16–18).[67] In the aftermath of the annihilation of a group of rebels, Korah and his company, the priestly theocratic order itself was reinstituted and presented extensively (Num. 17:16–18:32). In order to grasp it, we have to unfold the Korah episode as a whole.

The Political Moment

The story opens with an outspoken criticism of the ruling power (Num. 16:3).[68] Whose party it was exactly and what complaints it raised are more difficult to discern. There seems to be three groups of rebels: Korah and "his congregation" (*'adatho*),[69] three members of Reuben's tribe (Dotan and Abiram, sons of Eliab, and On, son of Peleth),[70] and "two hundred fifty men of the Israelites, community chieftains, persons called up to meeting, men of renown" (16:1–2). They are mentioned together at the opening of the story but are later addressed separately or forgotten as the story unfolds.[71] Whether together or separate, they each challenge Moses's and Aaron's authority, but their complaints are quite different in both substance and tone. Korah dares to question the basic hierarchy (first presented in Numbers 3) on which the leaders' authority rests. He claims equal power on the basis of equal share in the holy: "You have too much! For all the community, they are all holy, and in their midst is Yahweh, and why should you raise yourselves up over Yahweh's assembly?" (16:3). Who is this holy community? By including the 250 people of Israel, the author or redactor of this text made it possible to read here a universal claim for equality.[72] Still, Korah could have meant the Levites or even his own clan of Levites, the Kohathites;[73] Moses certainly understood Korah's complaint as related to the "sons of Levi" (16:7–10). Either way, the demand subverts the hierarchical structure and the binary logic that characterizes the biblical text in general and the priestly sources in particular. Korah, in Michael Walzer's words, was "the first left oppositionist in the history of radical politics."[74]

There is, however, another, more familiar line of attack on the leadership, which echoes the story of the twelve scouts. Dathan and Abiram refuse to "go up," to proceed in what seems now a useless journey through the desert, after being taken from "a land of milk and honey" and being denied access to another (16:12–14).[75] They are challenging a failed policy, not questioning a principle of rulership. But their challenge became radicalized because they voiced their protest and refused to continue the argument about it (16:12). Their response to Moses's call can be read as a "we prefer not to," taking the first step on the slippery slope of "inoperativity" opened by Bartleby the scrivener, which, without posing any alternative, would radically undermine order and authority.[76] As they were airing their criticism of their leader, these rebels occupied some place in the camp that they refused to leave, so as to avoid direct confrontation. Moses had no choice but to go to their place (16:25) and call upon God to finish with them there, with an in situ execution.

Korah, for his part, does not invoke matters of policy, scarcity, or the goal of the journey through the desert; he challenges the very principle on which Moses's and Aaron's authority rests and poses a clear alternative. While the Reubenites object to Moses "ruling over" them (*tistarer 'aleinu*) because he led them to a dead end, Korah objects to the very *elevation* of Moses and Aaron to a higher status (*titnas'u al*), over and above the entire assembly of God.[77] Moses's two separate responses reflect this difference well. When protesting to God about Dathan's and Abiram's more familiar complaint, Moses insists that he is a trustworthy leader who has not abused his power: "Not a donkey of theirs have I carried off, and I have done no harm to any of them" (16:15).[78] Yet in his direct response to Korah, Moses reminds the rebels what worship really means— "to do the work of Yahweh's Tabernacle, to stand before the community to serve them" (16:9)—and dismisses their claim for priesthood (16:10). In his view, the Levites should take pride in their separation from Israel and work as ordered at the service of God and his people.

Despite the differences between the complaints and those who raised them, and without eliminating those, the redactor who stitched these fragments together tied the more traditional complaints to Korah's radical challenge. Korah and his congregation were ordered to come the next morning with their pans to the Tent of Meeting and offer incense to God, who "will make known who is His" and "who is holy" (16:5). For Dathan and Abiram, Moses calls for a new form of death, "a new thing Yahweh should create," as a proof of the legitimacy of his authority and the rebels' sin of despising God (16:30). Two ordeals were thus set in which God's spectacular violence, staged and orchestrated by Moses, were to be displayed. In both cases the response was postponed—either for a short while (Dathan and Abiram) or till the next day (Korah)[79]—and its onus was relegated to God. The Reubenites waited in their dwelling place, while Korah and his congregation with their fragrant fire pans came in the next day to the Tent of Meeting. Already before describing God's devastating, stunning response, which eliminates the two groups of rebels, the redactor who mixed the two narratives highlighted (or added) the common themes and structure of the two events.

At the same time, the redactor seems purposefully imprecise about the identity of the rebellious groups. The many names, partial genealogies, and epithets brought together here (16:1–2) seem to be a makeshift fabrication of one rebel-

lious party, rather than two (or three)[80] unrelated groups. The identity of this
rebellious party remains ambiguous even when "the earth opened its mouth
and swallowed them [i.e., the Reubenites] and their households, and every human being that was Korah's" (16:32), while "the two hundred fifty men bringing
forward incense" were consumed by divine fire (16:35). Only out of the ashes,
as the rebels' bronze fire pans were "hammered . . . into a plating for the altar,
a remembrance for the Israelites" (17:4), were their names fixed and sealed in
memory with a dark warning: "None should be like Korah and his congregation"
(17:5). This clear effort to fuse the two stories into one and seal the identity of
the rebels under one proper name, Korah, may betray a deeper understanding
of the logic of political rebellion—the identity of the group does not precede
the rebellious act but is formed in the course of its performance and through its
recapitulation in later narratives.

This political insight may be traced to the careful choice of terms describing
the rebels as a group. Two terms are used in this chapter, *eddah* and *kahal*.
Both *eddah* and *kahal* are nouns derived from verbs that designate the coming
together of many to stay or linger in one another's company, to be witness (*ed*)
to each other (hence *eddah*) or to assemble (*hitkahel*; hence *kahal*). Both terms
foreground the assembling, and neither presupposes the existence or nature of
the group before this assembly. The first is used *by the narrator* numerous times
to designate the group of rebels associated with Korah, but it is also used *by
Korah* to designate the undefined group in the name of which he rebels (16:3).
In that same verse, Korah uses the other term *kahal* in a perfect synonymic paral-
lelism with *eddah*: "All the *eddah*, they are all holy . . . and why should you raise
yourselves up over Yahweh's *kahal*." But when the earth swallowed the rebels,
they "perished[81] from the midst of the *kahal*, and all Israel that was round about
them fled" (16:33). Here *kahal* is clearly used to refer to Israel, the people as a
whole, from which the rebels were subtracted as they were wiped out. And it is
the narrator who finally decides and seals the proper identity of the group as he
transmits the memory of the event.

Looked at from the rebels' perspective, however, it is evident that Moses fails
to address the complaint of inequality raised by Korah. Moses either dismisses
the claim with a question (16:10) or ignores it altogether (16:15). This is not to
say that priestly hierarchy was not at stake but rather that it was not Moses's role
to justify it. After all, it was not he who elevated himself above the people; it was
God who instituted and maintained the hierarchy within priestly theocracy. In
this theocratic system, those sanctified and appointed to serve in worship substituted for the firstborn Israelites who had been consecrated to God (3:11–13),

and, as we have seen, this service involved a certain element of risk (explicitly
acknowledged in Numbers 18:3). It is this form of rule that would be reinstituted
once the rebellion was crushed, including the political and economic benefits
that come in exchange for it (18:31). By then, the rebels would all be dead and
would not be addressed; only the memory of their annihilation would appear as
the other, dark side of the priestly theocratic order.

Whether the rebels recognized the high stakes of their challenge is not clear.[82]
Their complaint was specific and concerned the status and privileges of Aaron
and his descendants. The *public* problematization of these concerns grants the
whole episode its acute political meaning. This is clearly the case if the holy
"congregation" (16:3) is read as standing for the entire people. Israelites who
were not of the Levi tribe had no role within the order of worship, which was
not mediated by Levites and priests, even if they were "community chieftains"
or "men of renown." But this is no less true in the more likely case that Korah
ascribed holiness to the entire tribe of Levi, not to all Israelites, and therefore
protested the exceptional status of one family, Aaron and his sons, the priests,
as Moses understood the claim (16:9–10). In both cases, Korah interprets holiness, which provides crucial access to power and material benefits, as something
intended to be equally distributed among all (presumably male) members of
the congregation but that has been usurped by one of its groups.[83] Korah is as
close as the Bible gets to an Athenian democrat, while Moses, in his assumption that closeness to the holy is the way hierarchy is articulated, is positioned
like a virtuous Athenian aristocrat. The analogy breaks here, however, because
Moses attributes the hierarchy and inequality to God himself, who is the origin
and source—archē—of this particular virtue and the one responsible for its un-
equal distribution. Korah, who never denies God's superiority in the order of
power, understood this superiority differently, insisting on equal distribution of
the holiness he imparts to his subjects. Korah saw no basis for the establishment
of inequality among equals, and it was this claim that he puts forward publicly,
forcing the ruling power to respond.

Korah positioned himself as speaking for a community that was, he claimed,
entitled to take equal share of the holy, and he represented that community in
terms of the holiness of each of its members. These terms were the stake of his
rebellion. But as a member of a congregation that was defined as it emerged
through the rebellious act, he also spoke for the entire assembly, which he defined in the same exact terms, a body politic in which all members are equally
holy. Equating *eddah* and *kahal* (16:3), the rebellious congregation with
the entire people of God, Korah (or the redactor) politicized—and sought to

democratize—the Israelite body politic in a way more radical than in any other moment of dissent found in the Hebrew Bible. Korah speaks here in the name of "a part that had no part," yet he represents a part that, through its resurgence (or rather surge), claims to speak for the whole and forces this (new) whole into (new) presence.[84] By this speech act alone, Korah introduces a political fissure in the realm of the holy, an opening onto a space where relations of exchange and domination can be questioned and negotiated and the distribution of privileges among God's delegates can be challenged.

This political opening lasted only one day. It ended in catastrophe, on the grounds of which the priestly order was reinstituted. This time, divine violence was not simply spectacular; it was a paradigmatic case of constitutive violence.

Responding to the challenge, Moses spoke "to Korah and to all his community" (16:5) and recognized them as a party within the larger party of the holy, the Levites. He first addressed the rebels without excluding them,[85] apprehending the political challenge and the need for a political response. But he also begged the question—the rebel cannot have equal share in the holy because they have had enough—and then set the terms and limits of the debate. Misinterpreting this party's claim to equality, Moses presented it as an expression of envy and greed, as if all Korah wanted was to get the benefit afforded to the priests (16:10), thereby challenging Aaron's appointment as high priest.[86] Neither coercive nor patronizing, Moses's response reflects the wisdom of an experienced leader who has weathered crises of trust. He ignored the gist of the challenge and deferred the decision to the higher echelons: "In the morning Yahweh will make known who is His, and him who is holy He will bring close to Him and him whom He chooses He will bring close to Him" (16:5).[87] After all, the challenge posed by Korah was one that must be answered by God himself, the origin of and final reason for the priestly order under debate.[88] The rebellious party was ordered to go to a designated place with their tools of worship, where they would learn the answer to the question they had forced on Moses and Aaron (16:6–7). Moses (or a narrator or redactor joining the story with a narrator's voice-over) could but did not cite or interpret the already existing rules regulating closeness to the holy and, hence, one's share in power. He brought the case before God, asking for his judgment, a sovereign decision that would only be grasped after it had been executed. In the meantime, the debate was postponed and would not be resumed, because the sovereign would end the debate with an executive act. And the rebels entered the trap—did they have a choice? They accepted the terms of the ordeal and waited for his verdict.

Moses translated Korah's claim to his own idiom, determined its serious implications, and set the terms for settling it, but in doing so he actually gave Korah the ultimate, dispute-settling answer: Closeness to the holy is decided by God and therefore not up for debate. With God's appearance on the scene, the terrain had shifted. Cultic practice was not only the bone of contention but also the framework in which the dispute would be decided—as always, by a sign from God.[89] The rebels who brought the political moment (that is, the event in which power was publicly problematized) into being would soon discover the limit of the political in priestly theocracy. At the same time, by setting the ordeal in terms taken from the realm of worship and sacrifice (16:17), Moses not only interrupted the political dispute but transformed it into a theocratic scandal, thereby revealing the limits of *his own* political authority as well as the *divine* violence at its root. And yet the limits thus discovered, of the space opened for political contention and of Moses's own authority, are not the limits of political rule, and they *do not* reflect a settled boundary between worship and politics. Setting the limits of Moses's authority was a political act that preceded the introduction of the sovereign decision performed in Korah's ordeal. In order to be recognized and gain the effect he sought, the sovereign's decision needed its own conditions of possibility, and these could not have been set without an outside political struggle that had already taken place. And yet, even when the decision was performed and the opening for the public problematization of power was closed, the power performing it did not cease to be political. It was political because it was prompted by a political challenge and then remembered traumatically by a terrorized community who could not come to terms with it: "And all the community of Israelites murmured on the next day against Moses and against Aaron, saying: 'you have put to death Yahweh's people'" (17:6). On this basis the priestly theocracy was reinstituted.

States of Exception

As we saw, the stakes of Dathan's and Abiram's complaint were different from that of Korah's, and so were the stakes of the ordeal into which they were thrown—these did not belong to the order of worship but of creation. Moses called upon God to create a new thing, which would be nothing but an unprecedented form of violence: "The ground (*adamah*) gapes open its mouth and swallows them and all of theirs" (16:29–30). At the textual level, the difference is significant. On the one hand, divine violence operates outside the realm of the holy, adding further support to the hypothesis that the Reubenites' rebellion is a pre-priestly source (usually identified as E). On the other hand, the stage for this nonpriestly divine violence was prearranged as an ordeal, which was set *for* God but not *by* him, calling for his violent intervention according to terms he did not establish. Such a call has no parallel in the Pentateuch.[90] This *form* of (priestly) divine intervention was now combined with a pledge, act, and expectation that were quite unique at the conceptual level. God was called to act in a way that, in the priestly context where creation is limited to the seven primordial days (Gen. 1–2:3), would be utterly exceptional. Called to decide between the two options of the ordeal, God was asked to break the priestly rule of creation and create something new. When he did this he did not simply *declare* the exception but *brought it into being.*[91]

Bringing the two stories together, the redactors of Numbers 16 let God reveal the two sides of the sovereign exception by performing them one after the other (16:31–33, 35) and fused the two together as the climax of (seemingly) the same event. For creating an exception in Dathan's and Abiram's case is on par with the refusal to revoke the exceptional status of the priests and extend holiness to Korah and his congregation. Korah challenges Moses's understanding of the sovereign's decision on the exception, while Dathan and Abiram invoke Moses to ask for a new exception. By including an individual, a family, or an entire people within the realm of the holy, God made those special; by inserting another form of violence into the order of creation that ended after six days, God acted in an exceptional way, and the exceptional violence he exercised rendered the whole event as an exception.

The Tannaitic rabbis sensed the radical nature of Moses's call for God to resume creating. The "mouth of the earth" is listed in the Mishnah as the first of "ten things [that] were created on the eve of the Sabbath at twilight" (Avot 5:6). All items on the list are miraculous or extraordinary material entities, which in today's terms we may call "exceptions" to the order of creation, but they were created, according to this Mishnah, as part of creating that order itself. Each such entity is thus waiting for its moment of apparition from the beginning of time. What ensues when it finally appears, however, is a change in the course of human, not cosmological, affairs. Moses is asking for such a change precisely, but the Mishnah clearly ignores the language of his request. Identifying the stakes of the ordeal, he asks: "If a creature [*briaah*] Yahweh should create . . . you will know that these men have despised Yahweh" (30). Moses does not call for an apparition of something already created but for a new *act* of creation. God's response was not simply to eliminate the rebels in the usual way (as he eliminated Korah and his companions) but to make their death a truly unprecedented event.

Let us indulge here in a short digression. This new thing meets precisely one of Agamben's most striking definitions of the exception, which he elaborates on the basis of Badiou's interpretation of the distinction between membership and inclusion in set theory.[92] For Badiou, to be a member is to be present; to be included is to be represented. "Ordinary" elements are both present and represented, but any element in a set can be present without being represented or vice versa. The exception is still different, however, Agamben insists; it is "what cannot be included [i.e., represented] in the whole of which it is a member [i.e., presented] and cannot be a member [i.e., presented] in the whole in which it is always already included [i.e., represented]."[93] The set in our case consists of all the ways divine violence is exercised. The new form of death Moses calls forth cannot be included in/represented among them, even though it is a member of the set—for Moses does not know yet how to describe it. Yet at the same time, Moses has already anticipated it, hence including it in this set as unrepresentable without it being present. But even after the event, when "the new creation" would be represented as "swallowed by the earth that opened its mouth," it would not be *present* as a member of the set in which it is included. The rebels' elimination would be remembered as the embodiment of the extraordinary, a moment completely outside the regularity of life and death or of crime and punishment.

At a first glance, the end of Korah's rebellion in the priestly version seems to present no parallel moment of exception. The fire that consumes Korah and his congregation breaks out according to sacrificial rules, which Korah sought to violate, and the rebellious company is consumed by fire just like Aaron's sons (Lev. 10:1–2). But the difference is no less clear. Whereas the latter's elimination was a kind of "instinctive," nonmediated response to defilement at holiness's core, Korah's fate is brought on by a demand to change the priestly order (which he challenged but had never violated) and eliminate the exceptional status of Moses and Aaron. Just like the Reubenite rebels, Korah and his company were punished for publicly challenging Moses's authority and his interpretation of Yahweh's ruling, and here too the setting for divine judgment and its enforcement was a public ordeal. The setting of the ordeal, as the two rival groups—Korah and his congregation and Aaron and his—confronted each other, "each man [with] his fire pan" (Num. 16:17), means that divine judgment must pass through the same moment of indecision between the rule and its exception. In this case, an exception already made was at stake—and God refused to revoke it—while another was possible—forgiving the rebels and sparing their lives—and God refused to grant it. The meaning of the ordeal was, however, that either of these options was at stake, and the decision to abort one of them was made.

That no exception was revoked or performed (declared or created) in Korah's ordeal does not undermine the sovereign moment but rather exemplifies its "other half." The power to suspend the rule and bring about an exception includes and implies the power to not do so (only a sovereign who has the right to pardon can refuse pardon), and violence could ensue both ways. Sovereignty lies wherever the *possibility* of the exception exists and becomes operative as such, with or without its materialization.[94] By bringing together the two stories of rebellion, the redactor demonstrates in a remarkable way the political nature of God's sovereignty. Furthermore, the text ties together dissension in the realm of the holy (Korah) and one that concerns questions of leadership and policy (Dathan and Abiram), as well as a response at the order of worship with one at the order of creation. Thus the redactor makes clear that the regulation of the realm of the holy, which was made necessary by God's dwelling in Israel's midst, is but one aspect of God's supreme power—and that the political aspect of his power is inseparable from the cosmic one. In this vein, leading the Israelites to Canaan—or not leading them any longer, postponing the journey for forty years—are but two sides of the same coin, God's sovereignty.

Whether or not the exception was created or declared, the two ordeals demonstrate how, to cite Agamben, "human life is included in the political order in being exposed to an unconditional capacity to be killed. Not the act of setting boundaries [in the realm of the holy] but their cancellation is the constitutive act of [divine rule]."[95] Agamben's words in *Homo Sacer* are purposefully taken out of context here and slightly amended to show how close—and at the same time how utterly alien—to the priestly writings his concept of the sacred in Roman law is. For Agamben, the concept assumes an "originary" political meaning by taking "the form of a double exception, both from the *jus humanum* and from the *jus divinum*, both from the sphere of the profane and from that of the religious."[96] For the priestly authors, holiness is God's mode of being that must be bestowed on anything that has come or has been brought close to him, so as not to eliminate it. But bestowing—or not bestowing—holiness is always already a sovereign decision. The formula "You shall be holy for I, Yahweh, your God, am holy" is the priestly version of election[97] that captures in one stroke the inseparability of God's holiness from his power and also the double-edged nature of holiness: holiness as a state of exception that puts in danger and a lifelong labor aiming to establish shelter in face of that danger. In the constructed realm of holiness, where God can be present among and in the midst of the people he set apart and hallowed (and ordered to become holy), the profane is a constitutive element in the economy and distribution of the holy. *Jus divinum* is the idiom in which the juridical-political is articulated and in which human lives are captured, exposed, made vulnerable, and expiated.

If a distinction between cultic rites and worship (which would later be interpreted anachronistically as "religion"), on the one hand, and politics, on the
other, comes here into play, it is only because it is so performed at the height of
a political confrontation as a way to crash a political opposition. Worship is no
more a realm in its own right than leadership or destruction (to which "a new
feature"—a new mode of exercising violence—was added). Worship is a well-
regulated practice of humans who have found themselves too close to a God
that rules them while dwelling in their midst; they therefore had to insulate
themselves from the lethal effect of his presence. Destruction is a mode of action that God often uses when his instructions are not followed and mistrust
turns into open resistance. The demarcation of worship and its spatial arrangement around the core of holiness is a mode of divine governance, just like the
spectacular and exceptional form of killing. Neither of these separates the divine
from the human realm. On the contrary, they tie them together at the altar and
at the scenes of violence where choice, proximity, and holiness melted together
(Num. 16:5). The epiphanies at the sanctuary, the acceptance or rejection of the
fragrant fire, and the elimination of the transgressors all mark intensive modes of
taking part in human affairs, motivated by an effort to assist Moses to accomplish
his governing—and substituting—mission. After all, the two ordeals were not initiated by God but rather called for by Moses and played according to *his* terms.

This is an important qualification, of course. In both cases, the sovereign
responds but does not initiate; he joins the space of human affairs where a challenge to priestly (or Moses's) rule takes place but where, initially at least, no law
is violated. The stage for his intervention is set by the acting human leader, who
invites Korah and his company to participate in the cultic practice as priests and
leaves to God the decision on the meaning of this act and its consequences.[98]
Furthermore, setting the decision in the frame of an ordeal, Moses actually interpellates God, calling upon him to generate and perform—or refuse to generate—the exception, that is to pass through the singular point of indecision
between the ordeal's two opposite poles, which he, God, did not determine. It
is as if the priestly authors tried to keep the sovereign exception as the mark of
divine rule and its violence[99] but sought to establish for their God a controlled
mode of *performing* it.

Finally, a political power struggle yields a sovereign decision and leads to
the reinstitution of the priestly theocratic order[100]—a new beginning to a course
of events that originated in Egypt. At the same time, however, the priestly version of—and intervention in—the myth of Exodus (Ex. 12:1–20) makes sure to
undermine the originary moment in Egypt by inscribing it in the Passover ritual,
which the people reiterate annually in "sacred convocation" (*mikra kodeah*;

Ex. 12:16). As a political space and a realm of existence marked by God's presence and rule, the holy itself has never been constituted; it can only be bestowed
by God or his hallowed delegates. From the first act of sanctification (of the seventh day; Gen. 2:3) to the minutest artifact in the sanctuary, God's holiness was
always already embodied in time and space, in his sanctuary and in those who
served him, and in the lives killed and captured in the wars he sanctioned. When
embodied, the separateness of the holy annexed to its domain whatever embodied it; whatever infringed on that separation was annihilated. In order to be thus
annexed, that is, imparted with holiness, and stay alive, separation needed to be
commanded, enacted, performed, and demonstrated properly.

With this in mind, we may clarify the distinction of priestly holiness from
Agamben's concept of the sacred. Sovereignty and holiness "are joined," like in
Agamben, in one "figure," but it is the figure of God himself, not of "an action
that [excepts] itself from both human and divine law."[101] The holy emanates
from God and is bestowed on certain portions of space and time, where it is
articulated as divine law that captures human life. When holiness is bestowed
on some humans, divine law is the other side of this bestowal and a condition of
the life captured within it. Divine law thus encompasses both the sacred and the
profane while producing and maintaining their differentiation. And yet, just like
"the sovereign and *homo sacer*," the figure of God that joined sovereignty and
holiness "delimits what is, in a certain sense, *the first* properly political space of
the West."[102] Except that now there is more than one such space, it is not clear
which came first, and there is no meaning to this originary moment anyway.
The political space thus created is *not "distinct. . .* from both the natural [i.e.,
earthly] order and the regular juridical order"[103] but rather *encompasses* both.
Any separation between "politics" and "religion" or worship and cult would obviously be completely alien to this theopolitical configuration.[104]

The sovereign emanates his holiness and sets a grid of separations that enables the use of holiness as a mode of rule and as a form of governing. Korah
failed to understand how his share in the holy was allocated and how limited
was his freedom in its operation. Within that grid, holiness and rule were inseparable. If politics, in our ordinary sense of the term, could have been possible, it
would have consisted in questioning the relations between holiness and rule,
but the crushing of Korah's rebellion demonstrates that the proper articulation
of these relations is an axiomatic principle that cannot be legitimately problematized. Henceforth, problematization of the order of holiness could only be
buried in the texts that preserved the voices of the rebels.

As we shall see, the priestly sovereign was proactive in constituting and then reestablishing the priestly order. But once established, there was no space for sovereign decisions within the realm of the holy. As far as a desecration of the holy sanctuary was concerned, the priestly sovereign was basically reactive. In killing Aaron's sons his reactions were swift responses to defilement, hardly mediated by any deliberative process; in the two ordeals in Numbers 16, there was no defilement that required an instinctive response, and his reactive mode was clearly demonstrated. The rebels did not desecrate anything, at least not before Moses told Korah and his congregation to do so (Num. 16:16–18). Before that, the rebels merely raised a dissenting voice, taking no other action. The ordeal itself was a machine that activated the sovereign, presenting the violence that erupted as a perfect display of a deus ex machina. That violence did not immediately follow the rebellious acts indicates the existence of a potential for the appearance of a political space for matters that do not amount to desecration. It was Moses who could not tolerate the dissent, and it was his intervention that forced God to respond.

Constitutive Violence and the Rule of the Holy

The fire that consumed Korah and his band took place in front of the Tent of Meeting, in the presence of the entire congregation (16:18–19).[105] The congregation itself was saved at the last moment thanks to Moses's and Aaron's pleas and instruction to "move away from the tents of [the] wicked men" (16:20–21, 26). The other group of rebels were swallowed by the earth in their own place of dwelling, as they were surrounded by a large crowd of Israelites who, fearing for their lives, "fled at the sound of them," that is, at the screams of those "who went down, they and all that was theirs, alive to Sheol" (16:34, 33). As Alter explains, "the real thrust of the story is . . . monitory spectacle: terror surges through the whole people,"[106] which is true for both stories. The opposition vanished; its remnants were turned into a memorial and a sign of warning, and the lesson was declared: "No stranger, who is not of the seed of Aaron, should come forward to burn incense before Yahweh" (Num. 17:4–5). The ordeal that eliminated the rebels demonstrated the true origin of the authority they had questioned. It became evident that challenging Moses's and Aaron's privileged access to the holy meant rejecting God's own authority. Clearly, the redactor of these texts was not concerned with Moses's leadership or the people's refusal to continue the journey through the desert, but rather with the priestly order as a whole. From the redactor's perspective, the reinstitution of this order was the function of the two spectacular performances of divine violence. But the terror this violence sowed did not suffice.

There had never been a calamity like these two. Nowhere had the victims been better known to the spectators in the story, as well as to the readers, recognized by their names and infamous for their deeds;[107] nowhere had the form of forthcoming violence been described more explicitly, where it was out of the ordinary, absolutely unprecedented, yet envisioned and requested by God's prophet before it took place. But even with the elimination of the rebels, the resistance was not over. The next morning, the people of Israel, traumatized and angry, gathered near the Tent of Meeting and resorted to their familiar way of expressing their grievance, which the narrator designates derogatorily as "murmur" (17:6). Without joining the rebels' cause but also without learning any lesson from their demise, they stage another scene of popular protest. They understood the genocidal threat ("You have put to death Yahweh's people"; 17:6) and refused to put up with the scale of violence, blaming it on Moses and Aaron. They misunderstood the terms of the ordeal or perhaps protested its setting and the invocation of the divine response in the first place; they did not acknowledge the divine judgment that had been revealed through it, and even if they did, they certainly refused to accept the limits set on their political space. God's response is swift but not immediate, for he halts his strike to warn Moses and Aaron and let them separate themselves up "from the midst of this congregation" (17:10). His verdict, not merely his laws, was thus questioned, and this time the eruption of his violence was neither requested nor orchestrated by Moses. Before long "the fury (*ketzef*) has gone out from before Yahweh, the scourge (*negef*) has begun" (17:12b), and 14,700 people were annihilated—many more than the two groups of rebels together. If it were not for Moses, who ordered Aaron to run through the camp with the fire pan, on which he put incense and fire taken from the altar, many more would have died (17:11–13).

Twice did God call upon Moses and Aaron to separate themselves "from this congregation" so he could "put an end to them in an instant," first in the midst of the ordeal (16:20) and then the next morning in response to the popular protest (17:9–10).[108] In both cases, the instant resort to a familiar mode of operation, the elimination of the entire community, was imminent. In the first case, God was willing to listen to Moses's and Aaron's appeal: "Should one man offend and against all the community You rage?" (16:22). When the verdict is executed, only "the two hundred fifty men offering the incense" were consumed in God's fire (16:35). No genocidal threat is mentioned in the case of Dathan and Abiram; the many bystanders simply ran for their lives at the right moment (16:34). In both scenes, however the offenders are separated (cf. 16:24, 27) and targeted, killing proceeds apace. When the protest persists and the genocidal threat repeats, no appeal is made, no negotiation takes place, and only the two leaders are warned and, presumably, separated. For the people, violence took place abruptly, spread fast, and hit indiscriminately, and the death toll was immense. Only the insulating power of the sacred elements activated by the high priest managed to protect Israel from the divine wrath. Twice an explicit genocidal threat was made, and twice it was averted, first blocked by Moses's words and then by Aaron's deeds, killing many but not destroying the people as a whole. And in both cases, the site of the drama was in front of the Tent of Meeting.

We may now return to another catastrophe already mentioned several times. A nonpriestly fragment (Num. 25:1–5) reports how, while camping in Shittim, "the people began to go whoring with the daughter of Moab . . . and . . . bowed down to their gods. And Israel clung to Baal Peor." Yahweh's "anger flared," and he ordered Moses "to impale the chiefs of the people before the sun,"[109] and Moses thus sent "the judges of Israel" to carry out the execution (25:4–5). A priestly fragment attached to this scene records another scandalous case of prostitution and sacrilege—a sexual encounter between an Israelite man and a Midianite woman inside the Tent of Meeting—which triggers a devastating "plague" (*magefa*), killing twenty-four thousand Israelites. The plague comes to a halt only when Phinehas, Aaron's grandson and a priest, follows the couple who entered the Tent[110] and executes both with one blow of his spear (25:6–8). Outside, the Israelites gather at the Tent's entrance and weep to mourn the dead.[111] Both the scandalous sacrilege and the gruesome killing took place inside the sanctuary, so holiness was likely responsible for the plague and redemption alike. And as if the scale of the catastrophe was not enough to indicate the genocidal potentiality of the plague, the priestly redactor inserted a clarification, in God's own words to Moses: "Phinehas . . . the priest turned away my wrath from the Israelites when he zealously acted for my zeal in their midst, and [so] *I did not put an end to the Israelites* through my zeal" (25:11). Offering an interpretation for an event that had already happened, he explained why his genocidal power had remained inoperative.

Placing together the five violent episodes in the priestly sources,[112] we may better grasp the nature of the genocidal threat and the two distinct modes of sovereign action in the priestly theocracy. We already noted the reactive mode involved in the desecration of the holy. It could be instinctive, unmediated (Lev. 10:1–3; Num. 25:9); swift but not immediate (Num. 17:10–11); or swift but provoked by a human plan and action and open to negotiation (Num. 16:16–22, 35). Three of these five violent episodes resulted in targeted killings (Aaron's sons, Datan and Abiram, Korah and his congregation) and two in indiscriminate killings (of the mourning Israelites in front of the Tent of Meeting). In three of the incidents, genocidal threats were explicitly pronounced (Num. 16:21, 17:9) or mentioned after the fact (Num. 25:11). Yet at no moment did God have a plan for replacing his people with another; no scale of accumulated sins had been tipped, no restart was contemplated, and God never says anything about the transgressions to which he reacts. All plans were immediately aborted by human action: Moses's and Aaron's plea to God that succeeded in keeping the scheme of the ordeal intact and forcing the rebels to desecrate the holy (Num. 16:22), thus enabling targeted killing; a purifying ritual (17:11–13); and killing the licentious rebels inside the sanctuary (25:7–9). In all three cases, the genocidal threat was a reactive, instinctive sovereign response; it was articulated and eventually averted within the framework of the established priestly order and practice.

In all its occurrences—in the stories of the flood and of the various rebellions in the wilderness—priestly theocracy relates to the genocidal threat as a contained risk. The holy is essentially a nuclear reactor. Its energy could be fatal—it may even destroy an entire people—but for the priestly regime, the issue was technical and technocratic rather than a question of trust and authority. Even when a "nuclear disaster" did take place, the worst-case scenario was avoided. Not that the rebels did not try to politicize the regime; this is the core of Korah's episode, of the scouts' fiasco, and, more implicitly, of the public prostitution with the Midianite woman. But the ruling power always sought to neutralize the political element of the rebellions, instead presenting resistance itself as a pollution that requires purification. God's instantaneous responses were acts of autoimmunity performed in a closed system. Zealous priests appeared as brave liquidators, and the enormous number of plague casualties after a sacrilegious event was seen as the least of all possible evils. God *could* destroy everything, but this would not happen so long as his priests were in charge, strictly controlling and operating the holy reactor.

The quasi-technical neutralization of the political challenge embedded in the three transgressions share a larger political context. In each case, the quasi-technical response turned into an instituting political act and displayed God's other mode of sovereign action—a proactive use of violence, speech, and miraculous action geared to reform or reestablish the priestly regime. Three such occasions have been noted here. One is a reform within the priestly order (following the killing of Aaron's sons; Lev. 10:4–20); the other reestablishes the hierarchy within it (Phinehas the zealot who killed to purify the sanctuary is granted a "covenant of peace . . . and eternal priesthood"; Num. 25:10–13). The third occasion, the final response to the lingering rebellion of Korah (Num. 17:11–

18:32), reinstitutes the priestly order itself. The analogy between the depth of the political transformation and the means used to achieve it is worth noting. The local reform is associated with a relatively "minor" case of targeted killing and a limited set of laws, the institution of hierarchy—with indiscriminate killing and the granting of the highest authority and the institution of theocratic formation itself—with all aspects of divine action: the use of brute force, teaching and lawgiving, and the performance of miracles. The orchestrated unfolding of all these is worth a closer look.

Once the insulating power of incense was activated by the high priest, the cascading disaster finally came to an end. At that moment, terms for a new ordeal were set, proclaimed by God himself. No violence was involved, and the outcome was a peaceful reinstitution of priestly theocracy. Twelve staves representing the twelve tribes of Israel are brought to the Tent of Meeting. Only one of them would bloom, and the tribe it stood for would be the one chosen by God. The elimination of Korah and his company, together with their claim for equal share in the holy, were already inscribed into the terms of the ordeal, for the staff representing the tribe of Levi was marked by Aaron's name (Num. 17:18).[113] Educational theaters tolerate no surprises. On the next day, only this staff bloomed and produced almonds, establishing at one and the same time Aaron's primacy among the Levites and the Levites' primacy among the Israelites. Here too, the divine decision in the ordeal was postponed until the next day. And here too, priestly authority was asserted in front of all the Israelites, who were there *to see* the proof of the privileged position of Aaron's clan and to signal their acceptance of his verdict by taking back their staves (17:24).

The chosen staff was to be displayed as "a sign for rebels" (17:25), to remind the people of both the divine decision and the fate of those who challenged it. Yahweh thought that this would be the end of it, that "with this there [will] be an end to their murmurings" and that the rebellious spirit that endangered the people would stop (17:25). But the discontent had not been dissipated entirely. The people, still shaken by the rebels' terrible demise, were not reassured. They no longer cared about gaining access to the holy but rather were scared by its very presence in their midst. "Look, we perish, we are lost, all of us are lost. Whoever so much as comes near the Yahweh's Tabernacle will die. Are we done with perishing?" (17:27–28). Only then, finally, did God speak directly to Aaron: "You and your sons and your father's house with you, you shall bear the guilt of the sanctuary, and . . . of your priesthood" (18:1). The quiescence of Israel's dread and grievances came with the positioning of Aaron and his descendants as mediators and lightning rods, absorbing the lethal energy of the holy:

And your brothers, too, the tribe of Levi, your father's tribe, bring forward with you, and they will be levied with you and *serve you* . . . and they will keep your watch, the watch of all the Tent. Only they must not come near the vessels and the altar, so that they do not die, both them and you . . . and you shall keep a watch of the sacred zone (*mishmeret hakodesh*) and the watch of the altar, that there be no more fury (*ketzef*) against the Israelites. (18:2–5)

The order of the holy has been (re)established. The Levites' separation from the rest of Israel is announced clearly and unequivocally, together with the Levites' internal hierarchy, the separation, special duties and privileges of the priests, and the benefits for the other Levites that came with service and risk. They are not allowed to enter the tabernacle but are assigned a clear position in its surroundings, between Israel, on the one hand, and the priests, on the other.[114] Violence continued to hover above the tent. The people once struck by plague feared its return. But the people who turned to Moses in fear of their proximity to Yahweh's dwelling place no longer challenged the theocratic authority or sought access to the holy or a part in the rule based on it; they rather sought its protection (17:27). Political dissent was replaced by a plea for help, and the aid would come from the cultic technocrats serving at the sanctuary and according to their protocol of operations. It is only then, as the priestly order was articulated in detail (Num. 18), that questioning this divinely constructed order was explicitly defined as a crime. Only at this point could the catastrophe be perceived as a response to that crime. The horrifying specter of violence hovering above the Tent did not only help preserve the law but also—and perhaps primarily—preserve the memory of its own, catastrophic eruption. The blooming staff, a "sign for rebels," sealed the series of past catastrophes and, if everything was kept in order, would substitute for the next one. Behind that staff lurked a trembling earth, the smoke of divine fire, the wrath of the plague. The institution of the earthly rule resides in divine judgment, divine judgment is an act of divine rule whose form and laws were now established, and that rule was born from an unprecedented catastrophe. This is the most expansive biblical example of what Benjamin called "lawmaking" or "constitutive" violence and not, as he claimed, the paradigmatic example of its opposition, that is, of "divine violence" as he envisioned it.[115]

SUBSTITUTION AND CONTAINMENT

The redacted Korah episode is a magisterial display of God's sovereignty in priestly theocracy. Its raison d'être and mode of operation is encapsulated in one verse: "As for me, look, I have taken your brothers the Levites from the midst of the Israelites, as a gift to you they are given to Yahweh, to do the work in the Tent of Meeting." (Num. 18:6). Speaking directly to Aaron, God succinctly presented the rationale for the priestly order, which he goes on to describe in detail. This short statement encompasses three moments of God's sovereignty that need to be unpacked: *the choice* of the Levites from among the Israelites, *the possession* of the Levites, and *the gift* to Israel. A decision, a possession, and a gift. Once these three aspects are unpacked, we will be better able to grasp the configuration of rule and violence at stake in Korah's rebellions, that is, Yahweh's lordship, which comprised and aligned mastery and possession, risk and protection.

The Technocracy of the Holy

The choice of the Levites. Let us first note a pattern in biblical genealogies, which recur throughout the Pentateuch and beyond.[116] Since the time of Abraham, firstborn children are repeatedly described as deprived of love and attention and distanced from their inheritance, while the younger brothers are preferred, loved, and sometimes elected and elevated beyond their older male sibling.[117] The prophet Malachi put this in the most straightforward way, giving the literary theme its theological reason:

> I have loved you, said Yahweh, and you said, "How have you loved us?" Is not Esau Jacob's brother? says Yahweh. And I loved Jacob, but Esau I hated, and I made his mountains a desolation and his estate for the desert jackals. (Mal. 1:2–3)

The same pattern applies to Moses, who was favored over his older brother, Aaron, and to Aaron's two eldest sons, Nadav and Abihu, who died in priestly service and were replaced by their younger siblings Elazar and Itamar (Num. 3:4). Perhaps Korah reiterated that tradition—primogeniture was not a factor and may be ignored—when challenging the position of firstborn Aaron, the high priest. If the privileges of the firstborn were not granted and "all the congregation is holy, every one of them," equality among community members must follow.[118] For the same reason, the narrator felt no need to explain why, among all the tribes, the Levites had been chosen and not any of the other tribes. They were preferred as Jacob was preferred over Esau or Benjamin over Reuben, a matter not of principle but of love (or another groundless preference of one over the other, a decision to bring closer or take possession over, which "love" often expresses).[119] For the priestly narrators and redactors, Korah was proven wrong, of course, but this moment of groundless decision will prevail. It is an indispensable aspect of God's sovereignty that persists through all the formations of theocratic reasoning in the Bible.[120]

The Levites are a gift to Aaron. The priestly cultic work was explicitly called a "gift work" (Num. 18:7).[121] Taken from the midst of the Israelites, the Levites, God tells Aaron directly, are "a gift to you," and at the same time "they are given to Yahweh" (18:6). The Levites were "taken" in order to be "given," and while being "a gift" to Aaron they are still "given" to Yahweh. While giving them to another (Aaron), they were still given to God, who had not loosened his grip on them. In their very being, the Levites were in a state of gift. They were given from one to another, but they belonged to both, for while their service was given to Aaron (and to the priests more generally), their life belonged to God. The gift was not only doubled but also split, and it could not be completed (Aaron never received the Levites as his possession; God never gave up his possession of the Levites). At the same time, the gift was completed in the service, because it was given to Aaron and his sons, to help them in their own service to God at the Tent of Meeting, where, as priests, they were responsible "for every matter of the altar and for inside the curtain" (18:7). In other words, the Levites were taken to be, given as, and remained God's servants. The gift was one that Yahweh gave to himself. But the circulation exposed here places us inside an entire economy of exchanges and substitutions that we have to unveil.

The reason for this gift of service, as well as for the division of labor between Levites and priests and for the different access the two groups have to the holy of holies "inside the curtain," is a service that would let the people of Yahweh live while they are his and he dwells in their midst. The Levites were dedicated "to do the work of the Israelites in the Tent of Meeting, to atone for the Israelites, that there would be no scourge against the Israelite" (8:19). Three moments are entangled here: atonement, service, and danger. The verse is part of the section in which the dedication and role of the Levites are introduced and described in detail. We have to read this section with Numbers 18, where the order of the Levites' service is reestablished. First, in Numbers 8, it is established that atonement through cultic work at the altar was a necessary condition for life as God's subjects—"Israel" is mentioned four times in that verse (8:19). Then the Levites' service is described in both sections as necessary for the work at the altar (8:22–26, 18:2–4). Finally, in Numbers 18, following the demise of Korah's rebellion, when the limited and well-controlled access to the altar[122] is presented as necessary for keeping alive both Levites and priests while they work in great proximity to the holiest of holies, the death warning is issued three times: "Only they [the Levites] must not come near the sacred vessels and the altar, so they do not die, both they and you . . . and no stranger shall come near them . . . and the stranger who comes near [the altar, the holy of holies] be put to death" (18:3–7).

The restricted role of the Levites, their peculiar status, and the limited access to the holy they have can all be seen as part of God's—or the narrator's—response to Korah's challenge. The elimination of the rebels was not the end of their rebellion. The closure of the dangerous political opening created by the rebels was achieved only with the careful reconstruction of the basic inequality between the priestly clan, the rest of the Levites, and the rest of Israel. As the cultic order is reconstructed, the text reveals what all Levites, the priests included, share: a highly dangerous workplace. They were chosen to protect the Israelites from God's holy wrath, to stand at the front line to protect the rest. For this role the Levites were remunerated for their services with different portions of the sacrifices, reflecting differences in their access to the holy and the risks they took in enjoying that access. It is not clear, however, what kind of indebtedness *to God* the gift created, for it was God's choice—not Israel's—to bring Israel close to him, thus exposing them to the danger of his holiness. If the gift was made necessary by that originary choice, it actually reflects God's indebtedness to Israel and not vice versa. In a sense, it may not be far from the gift of nourishment and protection that parents owe to their offspring, following another gift—birth giving—that initiated the need of nourishment and protection in the first place.[123]

The possession of the Levites. Hence the gift chain was theocentric: The Levites were a gift to Aaron, and through him to Israel, but only insofar as they were given to Yahweh (*netunim lee*) and dedicated to help in his service.[124] God dedicated the Levites to himself because they were his in the first place, literally "given, given to [him]" (Num. 8:16).[125] This is a crucial piece of the priestly logic and the basis of its economy, which Korah ignored. Its full version appears elsewhere: "And as for me, look, I have *taken* the Levites from the midst of the Israelites *in place of every firstborn* womb-breach of the Israelites, that the Levites be Mine, for Mine is every firstborn. On the day that I struck down every firstborn in the land of Egypt, I consecrated to Me all the firstborn in Israel, from man to beast. Mine they shall be. I am Yahweh" (Num. 3:12–13).[126] In other words, before the Levites could be given, they had to be taken. That the Levites (and not others) were gifted for service (and protection) by God's arbitrary choice, an expression of a preference (or his "love"), needs no justification, but that an act of appropriation was involved does need justification. The appropriation or possession of the Levites was made possible—and justified—by the logic of substitution, which in turn had been put into motion by the supreme act of violence that set the Israelites free from Egyptian bondage, the climax of the Exodus drama. Taking the Levites, God gave them to himself, as he performed a basic act of any ruling power, divine or human—taking hold of what has never been given to him by another, proclaiming his right to possess it, and making this right the basis of a new legal order. He took them in order to substitute for the firstborn Israelites whose lives had been spared when killing the Egyptian firstborns. That right to possess and give the law, the reader surely remembers, was preceded by and predicated on a spectacular display of power, which now, in retrospect, appears as an originary moment of constitutive violence.

There is, however, a principle that is tacitly presupposed in the formula explicated here. In the Levites' case, the act of self-constitution, where God's might creates God's right, presupposes and demonstrates as a given an economy of substitutions and is, hence, not entirely arbitrary. It is a rationale that the priestly texts dealing with the Levites and their role in the realm of the holy seem to follow, rather than establish, drawing the specifics of the relation without ever articulating, let alone grounding, the principle that governs it.[127] The stories of rebellions and murmurs woven together in Numbers 16–17 are clustered between two legal discussions of substitution. The chapter that precedes them consists mainly of a (probably late) supplement to the cultic codes in Leviticus[128] and contains instructions for sacrifices (a burnt offering of a bull and a goat) offered to atone for inadvertent offences, so "it will be forgiven for all the congregation . . . for it was by mistake for all the people" (Num. 15:24–28).[129] The chapter that follows them presents detailed and comprehensive instructions for a system of priestly "share" in "all [the Israelites'] offerings" brought to the sanctuary (18:8–19).[130] The Israelites disown their "prime yield" from their fields and their cattle, of which the "richest of the oil, of the wine and of the grains" and "the flesh" of the sacrificed animals are given to the priests to consume (18:12–13, 17),[131] but "the human firstborn, and the first born of unclean beast," should not be sacrificed but rather redeemed, and their value in silver coins, it is implied, is for the priests to keep (18:15–16). The nonpriestly Levites, for their part, are "given every tithe in Israel as an estate in exchange for their work that they perform, the work of the Tent of Meeting" (18:21). The inadvertent sinners should be redeemed, "for it is an errancy" (15:25); the firstborn—and this is a more radical claim—should be redeemed even though they already belonged with God. The firstborn, like the inadvertent sinner, could have been put to death, but God preferred not to, thereby establishing the order of substitutions that let his subjects and companions live under his rule and in his proximity.

When God took the lives of the Egyptian firstborns, he spared the firstborn Israelites, and so they, together with their offspring and their cattle, came to be at his possession.[132] They were thus close to the core of divine violence, both deposited and exposed in the realm of the holy. Their belonging to God made them extremely vulnerable but never completely abandoned.[133] It was their own error or sin, not their consecration or the violence of others, that put them at risk of dying. Under the aegis of Yahweh, no one was ever abandoned like a Roman *homo sacer*, in the strict sense Agamben gave to abandonment in this context. *Homo sacer* was under a ban insofar as he was considered someone who could be harmed or put to death with impunity and whose death or harm could not be presented as a sacrifice—a human being whose life could always be taken (in the juridical order) and never given (in the cultic order).[134] He was someone who found himself outside the realm of the civic law, on the one hand, and who could not redeem himself as a martyr in service to the gods, on the other. In clear distinction, the consecrated Levites incarnated a realm where a law that governed everyday life and service to God were one and the same thing. Their role was to prevent the abandonment of Israel's firstborns, that is, to avert their full exposure to divine violence, which they did through a series of substitutions.[135] As the liquidators of divine wrath, the Levites diverted the act of killing from God to humans and substituted the humans that were to be killed with animals. It is thus animal blood spilled on the altar, along with sifted flour, incense, silver, and gold added according to a strict protocol that would act as a sufficient substitute for divine violence. Within this economy, substitution went a long way. It relieved the Israelites of many of their sins, protected them from God's holiness, and provided Levites and priests with their subsistence, remunerations for their hard work and for the risks they were taking as permanent residents in the realm of the holy. The cultic system as a whole was an advanced technology of insulation, separating his holiness and the life of his subjects, while allowing them their allocated share of the holy.[136]

While the Levites and priests were separated from the rest of the community, they were not excluded from it. Indeed, they were most vulnerable but never abandoned or forsaken. Their sacred vulnerability was governed by a detailed, transparent, and well-known system of rules. They were deprived of any inheritance and territorial possession (Num. 18:20–23), but all their provisions were taken care of in an orderly manner. Their relation to the law was special, though not because they were excluded from the realm of its applicability[137] but rather because a large portion of the law was delivered to them,[138] dedicated to them, and applied through their practices. Special and exclusive rules were set for the sanctified, and the law branched out and multiplied mainly for them, through a web of rules that, in addition to their service at or around the sanctuary, regulated bodily conditions, space and time, touch and sight, intimate conduct and public behavior.

The difference from Agamben's model of the sacred cannot be clearer, and not only by virtue of the legal status assigned to the "sacred" subjects. The realm of the holy as a whole and the region within it occupied by the Levites were both governed by a biotechnical apparatus. This apparatus controlled the conduct of space and time; human bodies and their functions; animals, their flesh, and many of their distinguishable organs; the fruits of the earth; and numerous artifacts, some of which are described in great detail. This was the map the Israelites and Levites used to navigate their ordinary lives and all its exceptional moments: from birth to grave, in peace and war, and in relations with strangers living in their midst, the foreigner (*ben nekhar*), the slave, the settler (*toshav*), the sojourner (*ger*),[139] and, above all, Yahweh himself. This configuration of biotechnical power was necessary for living under the rule of a God for whom holiness was the form of his subjectivity, hence of his sovereignty.[140]

The Levites and priests, a designated elite of technocrats at the service of the holy, were not simply those whose task was to mediate this holiness to common Israelites and enjoy the benefits of rule and power that came with the service in the biotechnical apparatus. Since this apparatus was based on substitution and they were chosen to substitute for Israel's firstborns and prevent (or rather postpone) their elimination, they were imparted with a larger share of the holy—and hence with more of its risks—than common Israelites, insulating the latter while exposing themselves. They served as a kind of interface that separated the ruling power from and connected it to its ordinary subjects, displacing the economy of substitution from the realm of "international relations" (where Israel's firstborn are equated with Egypt's) to the realm of living beings (where sacrifices of animals and plants substituted for the lives of Israelite offenders). In this they were responsible for forcing the biotechnocratic web of rules well beyond the site of the Tabernacle, marking its hazards and protecting everyone from the deployment of holiness throughout the social space. And this meant that God had to intervene only in cases of serious breaches to the system, mainly when these took place close to its core. The priestly God was a sovereign who suspended his violence, not his law, and could do this so long as the law was not challenged or violated.[141] The goal of an orderly priestly service was to transform the modus operandi of divine violence from an unmediated eruption incidentally triggered by pollution into a pure potency, that is, into a power that acts precisely by not acting. It is for this purpose that the priests and the Levites were called and commanded to put their own lives on the line.

Once again we are following Agamben's reading of Aristotle's notion of impotentiality (*adynamiai*) and his insistence that potentiality is the power or ability "*not to*" as much as it is the power or ability "to"—to act or not to act, to create or not to create, to kill or not to kill, to care or abandon, to enforce the law or suspend it. It is precisely this potentiality that defines sovereign power. Note, however, that in the pre-priestly theocracy we identified this (im)potentiality as an indication of the mode of divine action, and no relation to either holiness or the law was involved.[142] In priestly theocracy, life in the realm of the holy necessitates the law; the law regulates the distribution of holiness so as to enable a proper, reserved deployment of violence throughout the governed space and to make human life within it possible. God became Israel's sovereign by *killing their enemies'* firstborn while *not killing their own* firstborns. Similarly, he acted as their sovereign by killing the rebels and not killing the entire congregation. On this conjunction and this simultaneity rests the entire logic of Exodus—and the priestly order based on it. Divine violence's pure actuality and pure potentiality coincide. Sovereignty, for priestly Yahweh at least, is not merely an either/or situation—to kill or refrain from killing, to forgive or refuse forgiveness—but a conjunction of killing and not killing, an outburst of violence and its restraint, a precise distribution of the power to kill *and* the power to not kill. We have seen how this conjunction operates in the collagist composition of the two ordeals in Numbers 16. In Egypt, the conjunction of the two modes of power operated through the meticulous work of spatial divisions (throughout the plagues and later at the Sea of Reeds) separating the saved from the doomed, the living from the dead.[143] But this logic characterizes priestly writings more generally—for God, acting *and not acting* could take place simultaneously because violence was directed at and correlated with an already divided space.

The distinction of priestly theocracy does not lie in the simultaneity itself but in the form of its execution. Killing and not killing *simultaneously* is how divine violence was displayed and divine sovereignty marked in all the Pentateuch's sources. But there are clear differences between the three theocracies we are reconstructing here. In the pre-priestly accounts of the flood and Sodom and Gomorrah, not killing was proactive and amounted to saving a few selected individuals (Noah and his family, Lot and his daughters), while the killing was indiscriminate. In Deuteronomic theocracy, as we will see in the next chapter, actual violence belongs to a remote past, and potential violence is placed in an indefinite future; the simultaneity of killing and not killing belongs to the present simply because they are remembered and anticipated together by virtue of an intensive work of the imagination. Only in priestly theocracy—perhaps the most conceptually advanced and politically acute among the Pentateuch's sources—and mainly in its intense moments is divine violence truly and actively killing and not killing simultaneously. In this theocracy, God separated and distributed death while targeting distinct groups and individuals among his people *and* their enemies. The simultaneity of the two poles of the conjunction presupposes this work of separation and distribution, which in turn is made possible by the logic of substitution and the technocracy of the holy.

Violent Priests

In the postdiluvian era, (priestly) divine violence never erupted outside the realm of the holy. The priestly version of the flood amended the Jehovist story of the flood by introducing a closure that ensured a planetary catastrophe would never occur again. In the priestly segment of the scouts' scandal, God punished the entire generation of Israelites without hurting anyone. They would die in the desert, but they would die naturally, and their children would be free to inherit everything promised to the freed slaves. At the level of both narrative and law, the priestly corpus had little interest in violence that was not sanctioned by God and could not be articulated in terms of holiness and its protection, that is, the removal of the pollution and the polluting agents.[144] Lethal violence sanctioned by the law was part of the punishment code, and in most cases its execution was left to ordinary Israelites.[145] If *kareth*, the cutting off of the offender's *"nefesh* from the midst of his people," is literally understood as an extension of capital punishment (which includes the offender and his lineage), a few other cases that involve ritual and moral pollution, as well as desecration, should be added to the list of killings sanctioned by priestly law.[146] All these cases are described in the legal layer of the text, taking place in the idealized world it reflects (which is ideal precisely because every offense meets its proper punishment). But there are two outstanding narratives, inserted into the unfolding legal presentation, that record violence in the desert. They both describe an act of stoning (Lev. 24:10–16; Num. 15:32–36) instructed by God after the case was brought to him by Moses. In these cases—a man vilifies God's name; a man gathers wood on the Sabbath day—ordinary Israelites recognized the sin but not the proper punishment. With God's help, they apply a given law to the particular offence. What these episodes demonstrate is not only that there were specific laws for each instance but also a general division of labor between God and ordinary Israelites when it came to executing sanctioned violence. If this was the case, where did the priests and the rest of the Levites fit in this division of labor? They were busy spilling animals' blood, of course. The priestly elite was responsible for the most extensive, routine production of death in priestly theocracy. We will now try to understand the place of large-scale sacrifice within the system of holy power. This requires a short digression into priestly history.

When God won possession over Israel's firstborns through catastrophe, the chain of substitution first came into being. "On the day that I struck all the firstborns in the land of Egypt, I consecrated them to Me" (Num. 8:17). From that moment onward, his absolute authority would appear across the spectrum, spread between eruptions of violence ignited by pollution and dramatic moments of containment achieved through rituals of purification and sacrifice. Disaster was still very much a part of divine rule, but it was limited in scope and taking place in the sanctuary and its immediate vicinity. Detailed protocols of substitutions and purifications in the realm of the holy ensured survival in Israel's dwellings (as they moved through the wilderness and the land they would later inherit). Rebels, sinners who did not follow the protocol of atonement, and inadvertent offenders of the protocol of service at the Tabernacle were targeted as foreign elements; priests and other Levites were at great risk for working as mediators and liquidators; and animals fit for sacrifice along with agricultural products fit for offering on the altar maintained the circulation of substitutions. The priestly vision of this self-sufficient immune system implies that once political disagreements and acts of resistance were uprooted, politics would be replaced by holy technocracy, and divine violence would only erupt to neutralize threats introduced by negligence that generated pollution and desecration[147] or that interrupted the chain of substitutions. The human victims would be solely responsible for their fate, while animals would be randomly chosen from among those fit for sacrifice. Ultimately, inside the system, all those who were struck by divine violence were scapegoats for the entire community.

The violence exercised at the end of the chain preserved order and never established it; it was an effect and an expression of a well-entrenched grid of distinctions—of the pure and the impure, of the times and the locations of action, the types of the deeds and the status of the doers. The violence at the chain's origin—the death of the firstborn Egyptians—initiated a debt that had been circulating ever since, only its space of circulation was long displaced, leaving the dead Egyptians at the systems' threshold and Egypt as its external background. The offering of animals at the other end of the chain was the lesser evil necessary to maintain the system and to stave off, as much as possible, the eruption of divine violence. This system of offerings was meant to defuse the danger of God's presence while also regulating human violence. It was supposed to keep people within the boundaries of the law, acknowledging it even when they had transgressed it. Sacrifices could be offered to atone for accidental deeds (Lev. 4; Num. 15:24–28) as well as for a whole set of immoral acts that offended, betrayed, or harmed another person, including theft, extortion, fraud, and false swearing (Lev. 5:20–26). The guilt offering constituted atonement and generated forgiveness, in efforts, one may assume, to prevent cycles of revenge.[148]

In contrast to the little interest that priestly sources paid to other forms of human violence, the slaughter of animals on the altar is discussed at great length (mainly in Lev. 1–9). As already mentioned, the physiognomy of animals and the mechanics of taking their bodies apart, spilling their blood, and burning their flesh lie at the heart of priestly biotechnocratic knowledge and practice. Beyond the physiognomic details, slaughter is described and charged in terms of impurity and purity, edible and nonedible. Was the slaughter of animals considered a violent act, and could it be placed on par with the killing of humans? As discussed in Chapter 1, "violence" may be an anachronistic term, but both kinds of killing were closely associated:

> Flesh with its lifeblood [benafsho[149] damo] still in it you shall not eat. And just so, your lifeblood I will require, from every beast I will require it, and from humankind [ha-adam], from everyman's brother, I will require human life [nefesh ha-adam] . . . this is the sign of the covenant I set between Me and you and every living creature that is with you, for everlasting generations. (Gen. 9:4–5, 12)[150]

Humans and animals were endowed with nefesh, and even though their killings were subjected to different rules, the way to atone for a prohibited killing is through another killing. When a human killed another human, his "life" (nefesh) was "required" by God and taken by men, for "He who shed human blood by humans his blood shall be shed" (Gen. 9:6). When the Israelites and those who lived among them slaughtered animals and "consume[d] any blood," God "set [His] face against the living person who consume[d] [banefesh ha'okheleth]" (Lev. 17:10). The killing of animals was strictly controlled. That this slaughter was problematic was certainly understood and was justified by its role in the sacrificial cycle: "For the life [nefesh] of the flesh is in the blood. I have given it to you on the altar to ransom your lives [nafshoteikhem], for it is blood that is ransomed in exchange for life [nefesh] (17:11).[151] The cultic, regular practice of killing animals at the system's heart was a technical matter that required care and precision but involved no moral judgment. It naturalized violence against animals; made it a matter of office and duty, a necessity for the preservation and well-being of the (human) living; and precluded the association of the institution of slaughter or any aspect of it with ḥamas. The covenant God made after the flood with Noah and the other survivors, "and every living creature [*nefesh ḥayah*] of all flesh . . . that is on the earth" (Gen. 9:15a, 17b) was not about killing but about extinction—"the waters will no longer become a flood to destroy all flesh" (Gen. 9:15b), and the institutionalized, well-regulated slaughter of certain kinds of living animals (*ḥayoth*) was supposed to help sustain this promise.

At both extremes of the chain of substitutions—on one end, the miraculous, extraordinary killing of the Egyptians' firstborns that initiated the circulation of substitution without becoming part of it and, on the other, the daily, ordinary practice of sacrificial slaughter of animals that was at the heart of the system of substitutions—the taking of life was sanctioned by God and only thus could become acceptable. Divine violence performed the initial killing, creating the condition within which the divine new rule would be instituted; the ordinary slaughter of animals was performed by humans to honor this rule, preempted new eruptions of divine violence, and provided for the subsistence and well-being of the technocratic elite. The latter presented itself as the liquidator of divine violence while being busy with the slaughter.

Throughout all these killings, God himself does not spill blood—neither at the inaugural moment in Egypt nor in later eruptions of his violence. As far as priestly theocracy was concerned, Walter Benjamin was certainly right to describe divine violence as "lethal without spilling blood," a violence that only "expiates" without "bringing guilt and retribution," striking without threatening.[152] We may as well be tempted to associate Benjamin's reading of divine violence with priestly theocracy because his only example of divine violence is the crushing of Korah's rebellion. But as already noted, Benjamin's depiction of divine violence was deeply misleading, a clear case of dis-reading.[153] Benjamin famously stated: "Mythical violence is bloody power over mere life for its own sake, divine violence pure power over all life for the sake of the living. The first demands sacrifice, the second accepts it."[154] He was wrong on both counts. In Egypt, God exercised his violence for his own sake (Ex. 7:3–5),[155] like any other mythical god, and soon afterward, even before the last plague and the liberation of the Hebrew slaves, he demanded sacrifices from each and every household (Ex. 12:1–13). To imagine divine violence à la Benjamin, one should look elsewhere.

Before parting from Benjamin, however, it is worth returning to a key distinction from his iconic essay "Critique of Violence," which lies at the center of his critique of power, namely, the distinction between constitutive "lawmaking" violence and "law-preserving" violence.[156] Killing the Egyptian firstborns to liberate the Hebrews and make them into a nation and the killing of the rebels in the wilderness before priestly law was reinstituted are two clear case of lawmaking violence. The killings of inadvertent offenders (Aaron's sons) and some sinners, like the man who gathered wood on the Sabbath day or the one who vilified God, are clear cases of law-preserving violence. Benjamin knew well, however, that the distinction between the two types of violence was not solid, as shown in his remarks on the death penalty, and especially on the police, where the forms of violence blend "in a kind of spectral mixture."[157] Our priestly source could provide two related episodes of violence performed or orchestrated by the priestly elite to demonstrate the distinction's immanent instability: first, the killing of the Simeonite prince Zimri and his Midianite female partner Cozbi (Num. 25:6–15) and, second, the war against the Midianites, which was followed by the priest's distribution of their immense captured plunder (Num. 31).

In both episodes, Midianites, and especially Midianite women, were among the victims.[158] The first episode was initiated by the zealous priest Phinehas and sanctioned retrospectively by God. Phinehas's retributive killing "turned back" God's wrath, substituting human zealotry for divine zeal (Num. 25:1). The second example (Num. 31) was Moses's last war, a war ordered by God to "wreak the vengeance of the Israelites against the Midianites (Num. 31:1–2).[159] In Numbers 31:2, God demands vengeance from Israel, but in the next verse Moses delivers this message to the people, calling it "Yahweh's vengeance." A late Midrash tries to explain the surprising shift through a story about an argument between Moses and God. Moses says:

> Master of the world, if we had been uncircumcised or practitioners of star worship or had denied [the binding force of] the commandments, they would not have persecuted us. On the contrary, [they have done so precisely] because of the Torah and commandments which You have given. The vengeance, therefore, is Yours.[160]

The point is well taken. It was God who ordered this war of revenge (Num. 31:1), sending the Israelites into a gruesome war. But the rabbis say more. It was his commandments that separated the Israelites from other nations and his segregationist ethos that put them in trouble. Of course, the rabbinic tradition celebrated the Torah and Israel's special status as God's people, but it also recognized the price—living in the proximity and under the aegis of a violent, vengeful God. The Midrashic intervention highlights the fact that Moses did not simply ascribe vengeance to God but returned it to him, thus presenting God's delegation of the use of massive lethal force to Israel as an extension of his own violence. His holiness was bestowed over the entire battlefield, on the camp that prepared for the war and on that which was convened after it (25:6, 19–24). Both stories articulate how human violence could substitute for divine wrath—and how these were governed by two overarching oppositions, holy and profane, pure and impure.

Yet in both stories, violence that first appeared as law preserving ended up as law making. Phinehas's violent zealotry started as an act of policing, seeking to eradicate idolatry from the site of the sanctuary. It ended with "a covenant of peace" and "perpetual priesthood" (Num. 25:12–13), which sealed the primacy of Phinehas's descendants among the Levitical priests. The holy war against the Midianites is less straightforward in this respect, but the oscillation between the two modes of violence is no less dramatic. The holy war began as a mission of "wreaking vengeance" (31:2). There was a debt of punishment to be redeemed. The debt grew out of the outrageous Midianite idolatry in the Tent of Meeting depicted in Numbers 25. The priestly source closed the story with a divine commandment that orders revenge: "Be foes to the Midianites and strike them" (25:17–18). As the story unfolds, new laws emerge in the wake of the battle. Moses was furious at his commanders and captains for not killing all the Midianite women, as they should have done (31:14–17), but when he gave the order to complete the massacre, he made an important exception: The Israelite men could spare the young virgin women and keep them for themselves (31:18). Moses then instructed his captains to cleanse themselves of the defiling effects of the slayings and the plundering and of any contact with the captives and the corpses (31:19–24). Elazar the priest announces "the statute of teaching" with which God charged Moses (31:21). Next, Yahweh, speaking directly to Moses, delivers a long series of detailed instructions regarding the distribution and allocation of the plunder (31:25–54). The plunder is to be divided between the whole community and the men "who bore arms in battle"; a levy taken for God and the Levites, "keepers of the watch of Yahweh's Tabernacle" (31:27–28, 47); and all the gold and "every wrought ornament" taken by Moses and Elazar to the Tent of Meeting (31:51–52, 54).

In the wake of the holy war against the Midianites, with the murder of numerous captives continuing in the background, a new legal order that regulated the handling of captives and booty in a sanctioned war was inscribed. The term ban (*herem*) is not mentioned and the rules differ substantially from the Deuteronomic ban (Deut. 7:1–5, 25–26; 13:13–19). The ban emerges here as what Agamben would call "a zone of indistinction" between law-preserving and law-making violence. This, we must stress again, does not make the priestly ban the original form of the sacred. It is the other way around—the holy was articulated and displayed as a radical ban from the very beginning and throughout the Bible. The ban applied to the war against the Midianites because it was sanctioned as a holy war, which created an opportunity for the swift transition from law-preserving to law-making violence, but it was not the cause of the war. The transition was a result of what seems a contingent ignorance of the ban's rules.

Introducing the notion of divine violence, a fantasy of a violence that annihilates without spilling blood and expiates without generating guilt, Benjamin wished to overcome the circularity between law and violence that generates an excess of violence and preempts the possibility of achieving justice through human law. He chose to illustrate divine violence with the story of Korah. Our study of the priestly writings on violence and law has taught us that the divine violence demonstrated in the Korah story, and in the priestly corpus more generally, rather illustrates the impasse of the relation between law and violence, which Benjamin tried to avoid or bypass through the concept or, better, the figure or even parable of divine violence. Tempted by Benjamin's parable as I have long been, I must insist that the figure of God portrayed in the priestly corpus is not an alternative to sovereignty in a modern state governed by the rule of law. If anything, the priestly God is the state's archetype, not its alternative, combining in one figure the position of the sovereign and the raison d'être and modus operandi of an entire governmental apparatus.[161]

The division of labor in priestly theocracy between divine and human violence should not prevent us from seeing where (priestly) divine rule belongs. When Yahweh acted alone, his violence inaugurated nations and established their law and order; when humans acted alone, their (divinely sanctioned) violence was law preserving; and when humans acted as vehicles and extensions of divine violence, the distinction between preserving the law and instituting it was blurred. Some aspects of the terror associated with the force of law and the institution of the rule of law in the modern state, its self-instituting myth, its claim for absolute sovereignty, and its fantasy of achieving closure and immunity vis-à-vis its "others" were already laid bare in these ancient writings, staged in the wilderness on the way to the promised land. This is not surprising, given the fact that the nation-state had taken God's place in the theopolitical matrix. It is precisely this divine sovereignty that we must be done with. No God, no priestly God, at least, will save us.

5

THE TIME OF THE COVENANT AND THE
TEMPORALIZATION OF VIOLENCE

Among the three theocratic models, the Deuteronomic is the most explicit. The relative explicitness and accessibility of this regime formation may be the effect of—but also the reason for—the fact that, despite its multiple layers, Deuteronomy is both the most coherent book of the Pentateuch and the one whose internal architecture is clearly visible. This visibility is not unrelated to the book's ideological and theopolitical program, which will occupy us here. The book combines a code of law, a historical record of forty years in the desert, descriptions of covenantal ceremonies and directions for future ones, and a sequence of closures, which, by following each other, work to undermine the very idea of closure. The book is a phantasy of things past, but it opens itself onto the future equipped with a new code of law and a new vision of God's rule and of the role of violence within it. Together they make up a text that is the closest to the utopic genre that the Hebrew Bible came.

At the center of Deuteronomy is a code of laws (12–26).[1] "This book of teaching" (*sefer ha-torah haze*; 30:10), as the collection is called, is to be inscribed again in the future, copied or repeated, retaught, *mishne torah* (17:18)—an expression that gave the book its Greek name, *deutero-nomy*. The code is preceded by a prologue describing the lawgiver, the context of lawgiving, and some of its consequences (6–11). It is followed by instructions for writing the laws (27:1–10), a list of blessings awaiting those who abide by them and the curses awaiting those who violate them (28), instructions for a ceremony in which the curses and blessings will be announced to the people's assembly in the promised land (27:11–26), and a detailed description of a covenant ceremony in "the land of Moab" (29–30), east of the Jordan River. It was there, "in the wilderness in the Arabah, opposite Suph between Paran and Topher and Laban and Hazeroth and Di-Zahab," that Moses spoke "all the words (*dvarim*)"[2] of which (most of) this book consists (1:1). From this opening, the staging of Moses's speeches "in the wilderness," through the final acts and speeches that followed the covenantal ceremonies (28–31) and the instructions for their future repetitions after cross-ing the Jordan River (27:1–8), on Mount Gerizim and Mount Ebal (27:11–26), and in an unnamed place of worship yet to be chosen by God (31:10–13), almost every moment in the text is an element of one long drama. The drama is rarely interrupted, but it has a few distinctive acts and is clearly situated in time and place (1:1–3, 34:1).

After the covenantal ceremonies, Moses slowly (and repeatedly) departs from the scene through a series of acts of closure (31–34), written in several different genres—third-person narrative, confession, poetry, and blessing—and usually ascribed to different sources.[3] Moses appoints Joshua as his successor, writes the book of teaching (*torah*) (which had just been spoken) and gives it to Israel's elders and priests, also delivering some last-minute orders and directions. He assembles the people and bids them farewell with a long poem, blesses each tribe, then goes up to a mountain from which God shows him the land he will never reach. He dies and is buried, but "no man has known his burial place to this day" (34:6). The final scene, the very closure of the whole event, declares Moses's superior qualities (7); celebrates him as a prophet like no other, whom Yahweh "knew face to face" (11); and inserts a final flashback from Egypt, where Moses had delivered "all the signs and the portents" from God to "Pharaoh and all his servants . . . and with all the strong hand and with all the great fear that Moses did before the eyes of all Israel" (34:11–12). This almost cinematic piece of literary composition is the stage on which the Deuteronomic model and con-figuration of divine rule is displayed.

The opening chapters (1–11) consist of a careful recapitulation, revision, and abbreviation of the journey through the desert, from the plagues in Egypt to the end of Moses's part in the journey. The revelation in Horeb is revisited several times (4:10–13, 5:2–5, 19–30; 9:21), including its disastrous aftermath and its proper memorization, the act of lawgiving, and the meaning of becoming God's subjects and entering into a covenant with him (4:23–40; 6:12–25). The narrative is woven through with repeated warnings and promises, preparations for entering Canaan, the Deuteronomic version of the Decalogue (5:6–18), and several other statutes concerning the coming encounter with the inhabitants of the promised land (7:1–5, 25–26).

This dense text concerns us at this point not for its rich contents but for the recurring references it makes to the speech act itself and for the repeated reminders it contains of past moments in which Moses and the people were addressees of another speech, one that delivered God's laws and warning.[4] The things spoken—"*ha-dvarim*"—and the acts of speaking them in the past are recalled now. Together they are placed side by side along the things spoken now and the acts of enunciating them. The self-presentation of the enunciation merges with the former act of enunciation, striving to erase the "re" of their re-presentation, to let the things said, then and now, come into full presence.

This emphasis on the present (to which we will return) is amplified by an emphasis put on the speech act's locations, then and now, and by the recurring commands to "remember" and "do not forget" the events depicted and the commandments pronounced.[5] Recollections from the journey in the wilderness are not limited to the opening chapters but inserted throughout. Most of the text is written as it was delivered by Moses, in the first person, on the eve of Israel's crossing of the Jordan River, as they were about to start the conquest and colonization of the promised land. The historical account covers the forty years in the desert, from the time following the revelation in Horeb to Moses's last words to Israel and the third-person account of his death (34). The account includes some of the episodes of rebellion and unrest in the wilderness and the wars Israel fought along the journey. Notoriously, most of the history recorded in Genesis—including the two versions of creation, the earliest catastrophe, and the adventures of the nation's three Fathers[6]—and most of the details from the miraculous events in Egypt are missing. More recent events receive more attention than more distant ones, with the exception of the revelation in Horeb and the scouts' expedition.[7]

The book is coherent despite its multiple layers, which are both oral and written.[8] Later amendments made to earlier sources reflect changing circumstances and an evolution of theopolitical discourse and ideology—but not their transformation. The few chapters or segments that are considered by many as supplements (27–34) or interpolations (most notably, 4:25–31; 11:26–30; 28:36–37, 62–68)[9] are usually integrated into the presumably earlier, established layer of the text without undermining the coherence of the theopolitical discourse with which we are concerned. Notwithstanding the historical implications, the same holds for placing a cursing and blessing ceremony at Mounts Ebal and Gerizim (11:26–30; 27) and the covenant ceremony that links Deuteronomy to the ceremony of cursing and blessing in Joshua 8:30–35 (a link that emphasizes Joshua's role as heir and substitute for Moses; legitimizes Shechem as a site of worship, according to many scholars; and reflects a rivalry between cultic centers at Shechem and Jerusalem).[10] Although we will take some note of these putative editorial interventions, we will mainly follow the effects of the redacted text, assuming and at times showing that later interventions did not alter the theopolitical reasoning that dominated Deuteronomy and in fact sometimes served to crystalize it. Here, too, the effort to reconstruct this theopolitical reasoning is guided by the distribution of violence across the text (on both narrative and legal layers) and its deployment by the various protagonists. The general pattern of said distribution and deployment, as we shall see, is abatement and containment achieved through ingenious rhetorical ruses, a new division of labor, and a bold theopolitical imagination.

THE EXPERIMENTAL SETTING:
RECALLING VIOLENCE AND REGULATING IT

Deuteronomy is patently clear about the relation between divine law and divine violence. God loves his people (7:7–8); this love was the reason and meaning of Israel's election; the elected people were to "become for Him a treasured people (*am segulah*) among all the peoples that are on the face of the earth" (7:6, 14:2). *S'gulah* is not simply a quality of the people but a way to describe their relation to God, that is, their being his "prized possession."[11] He thus became their suzerain and they his preferred vassals. His teachings made them "a wise and understanding people" and a "great nation," but they also made them different and separate from all other nations and closer to their God than other nations to theirs (4:7). But this proximity put them in greater danger, for other nations were not obligated by God's laws and therefore not vulnerable to the consequences of failing to live by them. The threat of divine violence, the forms of which are no less numerous than the laws, is the adverse side of divine election and the given laws.

Being elected, Israel is declared "a holy people to Yahweh. . . . You Yahweh has chosen" (7:6–7). Election and holiness are intimately related. Holiness is a status proclaimed by a sovereign decision, not an immanent quality of the elected. They became holy when they came to be his people, at the moment of their election. Being elected, being set apart, and being holy are three aspects of the people's new state of being. But this new state would last only so long as they kept his laws (*miṣvoth*) (28:9) and cleansed the promised land from its

Canaanite inhabitants, put them under a ban, and sealed no covenant with them, thus bringing separateness to perfection (16:16–18). Separation, which has a clear geopolitical meaning now, is still a major biopolitical principle and must be actively guarded by avoiding abominations (14:1–3), eating only clean animals (14:4–21), and cleansing the entire camp from whatever might defile it (23:10–15). The domain of the holy expanded far beyond its narrow zone in priestly writings, encompassing the entire camp and all spheres of life in it. At the same time, its "democratization" was followed by a reduction of the danger associated with it and a marginalization of the Levites's service. The injunctions to follow purity laws and guard separateness from the nations of Canaan and their idolatry and their abominations, important as they were, were just items on a long list of orders, not the organizing principle of the book of teachings. Failure to respect them did not trigger any inevitable, immediate response.

Deuteronomy's codes of laws (12–26) incorporate ritual practices and dietary rules within a larger legal system that colonizes a large portion of the Israelites' lifeworld. They pertain to spheres of human affairs previously not addressed, including those of ruling and leadership. Like the separate body of priestly writing, that is, the Holiness Code (Lev. 17–25), they addressed the entire people[12] and were primarily concerned with ordinary human affairs. But the difference between them is clear. For the Holiness Code, becoming holy is both a task and mission, the telos of practices motivated by purity and moral injunctions. For Deuteronomy, being holy is these practices' presupposition and raison d'être.

> And Yahweh spoke to Moses, saying: "Speak to all the congregation of the Israelites, and you shall say to them: 'You shall be Holy, for I, Yahweh your God am Holy.'" (Lev. 19:1–2)[13]

> You are the Children to Yahweh your God. You shall not gash yourselves nor shall you make a bald place on the front of your head. For you are a holy people to Yahweh your God. (Deut. 14:1–2)[14]

The proximity to the holy was conceived literally. Whether in the heavens or on earth, God's place is holy. When the Israelites went to war (the ones sanctioned by God), their camp must be kept holy—separate and clean—because in times of war "Yahweh your God walks in the midst of your camp to rescue you and to give your enemies before you" (23:10–15). When he "look[ed] down from [his] holy dwelling place, from the heavens" (26:15), he watched over Israel to see whether they had "rooted out [from their houses] what [was] to be sanctified [ba-kodesh]" and gave it "to the Levites, to the sojourner, to the orphan and to the widow" (26:13). These verses may come from different sources, but they make perfect sense together.[15] The domain of the holy stretched from earth to heaven, encompassing the entire physical and social space, while the law, which governed personal purity as well as interpersonal relations, was coextensive with it. And while God's dwelling was no longer his transposable tent in the midst of the Israelites' camp but somewhere in heaven (26:15), he was still remembered as the God who used his "strong hand and outstretched arm and great terror" (26:8) in Egypt and as a great power who, in times of war at least, may dwell again in Israel's midst and come to their rescue.

The Deuteronomic theocracy does not sever the intimate link between holiness and divine violence, but it does give this link a distinct configuration that differs from the one encountered in priestly writings. God's presence in Israel's camp was not associated with the sanctuary and was limited to the time of the wars he sanctioned (23:15). Neither "Tabernacle" nor "Tent of Meeting" are mentioned in these discussions—God's sanctuary, an unidentified site that "Yahweh your God chooses to make His name dwell there," is a promise and command for the future, "when you come into the land that Yahweh is about to give you (26:2). "The place that Yahweh will choose from all your tribes" recurs with slight variation without being named;[16] it is usually associated with the Jerusalem Temple, and the centralization of cultic practices in that chosen place is considered to be Deuteronomy's "main innovation."[17] For this conception to hold, one has to assume that the text's audience would recognize the unnamed place chosen by God to be Jerusalem and that only obvious "pseudoepigraphic constraints"[18] prevented the authors from naming the sanctuary's location. One should also accept the centralization of cult as a main task for the Deuteronomists. On this account, it was the anachronism of naming Jerusalem in a speech delivered (or referring back to) the time of Horeb that required leaving the place unnamed,[19] making both the undetermined place and the fictive setting nothing but contingent, external rhetorical devices that may be dropped or ignored.[20]

All three auxiliary assumptions may be dropped once one assumes, as I do, that what best gives Deuteronomy its coherence, at least at the layer of the final editing, was not an ideological task but a literary one: to imagine a Yahwist polity without a commitment to Jerusalem and its temple *or to any other existing institutions*. This framing created its own constraints. That the central site for cultic activity remains unnamed is textual evidence that corroborates this assumption. Such evidence is no less important than archaeological remains. Is it not possible that the inclusion of Mount Ebal and Mount Gerizim as cultic centers, which preceded and followed the code of law emphasizing a single place of centralized worship (11:26–30; 27), also meant to emphasize the undecidability of the place? If Deuteronomy was redacted when the Second Temple was in place, couldn't the *effect* (if not the initial meaning) of including Ebal and Gerizim be to free the imagination from the hegemonic domination of Jerusalem? For us, what may be dropped or ignored are the putative initial intentions of the authors and later redactors of these texts. Crucial is the effect of uncertainty about the sanctuary's location and an emphasis on its futurity, which are perfectly in line with the overall structure of the Deuteronomic theocracy and with the conception of the text as a thought experiment of the utopic genre.[21]

To the futurity of the sanctuary, one must add God's own place and temporality. The promised sanctuary would not be a place for God's presence; neither he nor his holiness would dwell there, only his name. The text does not explain what this name-dwelling means, but proximity to something other than God himself is certainly implied. Since God's dwelling place was said to be "in heaven" (26:15), there is no reason to think that the construction of the sanctuary would have changed this. Note that neither God nor his voice, nor even his name, were ever present while Moses delivered his speech in the plains of Moab, only remembered and anticipated. At the same time, the presence of his people, along with the presence of "this book of teaching [*sefer hatorah haze*]," which seems to take his place, played a key role in staging the covenant ceremonies.[22] In the world portrayed in the text, a central place of worship is still and always to be localized and identified. The historical and existential present was located somewhere in the wilderness, and the people listening to Moses were called again and again to reflect on their very presence at that moment, as Moses's words, all those teachings written in that book, assumed their pressing presence. It is reasonable to imagine that neither they, still stuck as they were in the wilderness, nor the readers who could identify with them cared much about the exact location of any sanctuary to be constructed on the other side of the river they were about to cross.

At the time of Moses's speech, the intensity of holiness (and the onus to guard it from defilement and profanation) had no centralized location. Rather, holiness was distributed along the moving boundaries of the Israelites' camp, where Israel's separation from other nations was most vulnerable. A clear spatial demarcation of the holy would be stabilized only in the future, when the people arrived at the promised land and cleansed it from its former inhabitants. Alliances with the peoples of Canaan, exogamy, and idolatry threatened separateness more than any other offense, all of which might bring about God's wrath and swift annihilation (4:25–26, 6:15, 7:2–4, 8:19–20). The swiftness of his response is emphasized in these verses, but it comes only as a warning attached to the injunction in the legal texts, never in the narratives. None of the many other injunctions were associated with a specific, recognizable punishment, although many general warnings recur. At the same time, the blessings and benefits await-ing those who would follow all of God's teachings abound.

The few warnings to destroy (*lehashmid*) or obliterate (*le'abed*) the Israelites for compromising their separateness should be read against the text's narrative filament. God's mighty hand and genocidal propensity is displayed in a series of recollections, first recounting how it was actualized in the desert wars against the peoples residing along Israel's route to Canaan, how it was withheld when Israel went to war on its own, and then, against this background, how, without being actualized, it affected the terrorized people who took part in the revelation in Horeb.[23] "For Yahweh your God is a consuming fire, a jealous God" (4:24), Moses reminds them. "You said . . . why should we die, for this great fire will consume us" (5:21–22). A putatively later Deuteronomic source transposes the terrorizing moment from a past memory to a future possibility: Forthcoming generations who will "make a sculpted image of any sort[24] and do evil in the eyes of Yahweh . . . will surely perish quickly from upon the land into which you are about to cross the Jordan to take hold of it" (4:25–26). The ominous threat of divine violence on the mountain is still hovering, but its potential eruption may still be averted.

Then, as part of this series of recollections, the Deuteronomists offer milder adaptations of stories of rebellion in the desert drawn from pre-priestly sources.[25] We have already examined the Deuteronomic version of the scouts' story in the final section of Chapter 3. Recollections of other episodes—the golden calf, the graves of lust, or the prostitution with foreign women in Baal Peor (where the selective deployment of divine violence is underlined [4:3–4])—are relatively concise and omit details of the catastrophic events themselves. The episodes in which divine violence crushed popular unrest and dissent are framed between God's fury and genocidal threats (9:7–8, 13–24) and Moses's interventions to stop it (9:18–21, 25–29). For the most part, the people were reminded of ca-tastrophes that never occurred and were likewise not reminded of some that, according to other sources, did.[26] The accounts of the rebellions were accom-panied by a description of God's patience and good guidance throughout the journey.[27] Only one of the disasters that took place when God was not appeased is mentioned in detail—the crushing end of Datan and Abiram, when "the earth gaped open and swallowed them their households and their tents and every-thing existing that was under their feet" (11:6). The spectacular effect of this "great deed" is recalled alongside another catastrophe with a similar sharp, vertical aspect: the climax of the Exodus saga, when the sea swallowed Pharaoh and his entire army and God triumphed over Egypt with his "strong hand" and "outstretched arm" (11:2–5). The Deuteronomist, writes Benjamin Sommer, "wants the audience's acceptance always to occur in the present, not in the past."[28] To achieve this, the entire scene blends past and present tenses, as Moses inscribes a vivid, visual memory of all these great deeds in his addressees' minds, as if they saw them "with [their] own eyes" (11:6).[29]

Against the backdrop of the spectacle at Horeb and the horrors of the desert wars, the descriptions of divine violence perpetrated against dissidents and rebels in the wilderness pale in comparison. These descriptions are also remarkably less detailed than the accounts of human violence prescribed by the law. It is not insignificant that the main instance in which human violence was enlisted as law enforcement was idolatry. The victims of this legal violence were those who incited worship of "other gods": false prophets and sorcerers but also ordinary Israelites, who might be friends and relatives, as well as entire towns that were led astray by idolatrous incitement (13).[30] Idolatry was conceived as a treacherous sedition.[31] When a whole town turned to other gods, it was to be crushed "by the edge of the sword," and anything left should be put under the ban and burned to ashes, "so that Yahweh may turn back from His blazing wrath" (13:16–18).[32] This is a clear case not only of law-preserving violence but of violence preventing worse violence, where humans shedding the blood of other humans was supposed to prevent God from exercising his genocidal wrath. This moment reveals the thresholds and gradations for the *future* exercise of divine violence, when the time comes to respond to Israel's sins.

In the idealized state reflected through the code of law, the fate of the idolatrous Israelites was no different from that of the nations of Canaan worshipping other gods (12:2–3; 13). The language used here is harsh: "All the places" where "other gods" are worshipped should be "utterly destroy[ed]"; all the altars "smash[ed]," "shatter[ed]," and "burn[ed]"; and all their idols "chopped down" (12:2–3). If "other gods" were Yahweh's ultimate Others, those who worship them in the promised land became Israel's enemies, whether they were members of foreign nations or Israelites. Note, however, that in both examples of idolatry, the violence that usually accompanied God's wrath was meant to be meted out by devoted Israelites who took a preestablished and significantly limited part in the economy of divine violence. Idolatry was conceived as the main threat to the people's holiness and their very survival under the rule of a holy God and thus replaced impurity as the archetypal violation that incites divine violence. But the elimination of the threat was now given to Israel's hands, not

God's. Their violence was to be regulated by an established political rule guided by priests, Levites, judges, or kings (17: 9, 14). It did not really matter, in this context at least, which human authority substituted for God's. The key point was the displacement of his violence. He still played an important role in the conduct of wars, as echoed in the words ceremonially uttered by the priest on the eve of the battle (20:4),[33] but he is not directly involved in the perpetration and administration of the violence he has sanctioned.

At the same time, the zone in which divine violence was imminent, which in priestly theocracy was limited to the sanctuary and its surroundings, included the entire land. But, in clear distinction from priestly theocracy, in the Deuteronomist theocracy this violence was mediated by the law and was neither instinctive nor spectacular. Nine times in the code of laws, the injunction "you shall root out the evil from your midst" accompanies a death sentence for different violations of the law.[34] Furthermore, the rules of war against peoples living outside the promised land (20:10–15, 19–20), as well as the injunctions to establish towns of asylum for fugitive murderers (19:1–13), demonstrate a consistent effort to reduce the recourse to violence, whether legal or illegal, human or divine.[35] This effort of regulation is amplified by the way violence was distributed over space and time: Spectacular divine violence was recalled as a memory from events long bygone; a violent mission (the conquest of Canaan) lay ahead, and the deployment of God's mighty arm was promised; legal violence was conditioned on transgression of the laws; and, finally, a threat of divine, genocidal violence hovered above the Israelite camp—"if you indeed forget Yahweh your God, and go after other gods . . . you shall surely perish" (8:19). Such a distribution requires obedience and vigilance but leaves the present at peace. Actual violence, either human or divine, had no trace when Moses delivered his words on the plain of Moab and the Israelites reentered their covenant with God. In that moment of intense presence and self-presenting, the major party to the covenant was absent; only his words, laws, and warnings and the unspeakable images of his past violence were reiterated. Was this intense presence an effect of his absence or a way to forge it? It is hard to tell. It is clear, however, that the immediate, abrupt, and catastrophic gushing of divine violence had been relegated to a distant past and to an indefinite future, creating a peaceful lull at the covenant ceremony. Apparently, the Deuteronomists did not believe in the Nietzschean mnemotechnic of pain but rather in a traumatizing discourse and the reasoned justifications of the law.[36]

This temporalization of violence, perhaps the least noted aspect of Deuteronomic theocracy, should be considered as this theocracy's true hallmark. There are other important and familiar aspects to this theocracy, of course. They include a one and only God, a holy people that must crush all forms of idolatry in the holy land it was about to colonize, a loving God that must be loved in return, the failure to abide by the teachings most crucial for maintaining Israel's holiness qua separateness as the trigger for divine violence, and support for the weak and tolerance toward strangers. But all these elements receive a new meaning from the way they are injected with, followed by, or actively postpone a carefully temporalized divine violence. This temporalization of violence is meticulously and magnificently displayed in the four chapters that follow the code (the covenant preparations at Mount Ebal and Mount Gerizim [27] and the account of the covenant in the land of Moab [28–30]), which probably belong to other sources or later layers of the text.

The temporality of violence is somewhat buried in the earlier code of laws (12–26) and may at first seem to be nothing more than the effect of the generalized and conditional language of the legal injunctions. But the later texts did not add a new dimension to an earlier configuration of divine violence; they succeed in foregrounding one of its key aspects, which I have tried to extract. They intensify a certain aspect of treaties with human kings—the conditional language of the contract—to curtail the violence attributed to the sovereign, and they do this precisely at the moment when the human sovereign is replaced by the divine. These chapters bring to the fore a covenantal theopolitics quite popular in the ancient Near East. The debt of the Deuteronomist authors to ancient Near Eastern codes of law and to Vassals and Succession Treaties is well established in these chapters.[37] Much less clear are the theopolitical meanings of this borrowing of imperial conventions by residents of a vassal state or by refugees who find shelter in the empire's capital, and they greatly depend on the alleged dating of the book's composition. If we read Deuteronomy as a thought experiment in theopolitical thinking, a concerted effort to imagine a theocracy in a space free of existing political institutions, the literary freedom the Deuteronomists took vis-à-vis the imperial documents becomes much more important than the literary and legal borrowings. The relatively late Deuteronomic version of covenantal theopolitics[38] is especially mature, elaborate, and nuanced, going well beyond the model(s) from which it drew. Its aim was not only to ensure the submission and collaboration of a reluctant people but to find a way to live under a sovereign even more powerful than the Assyrian or Babylonian king without succumbing to its wrath. The temporalization of violence was the key.

THE COVENANT AND THE CURSES

The code of laws ends at chapter 26:15. Verses 16–19 and the next four chapters (27–30) describe the covenantal ceremonies and the inscription of the code. Coming from different Deuteronomic sources, they are all considered later additions to the code and present different ways to frame it. Common to these texts is the emphatic assertion of the ceremonial moment and place: *this* day, *this* place.[39] Besides referring to the present of the speech situation, Moses directly addresses those present then and there:

> You are stationed here today, all of you before Yahweh your God: your heads, your tribes, your elders, and your overseers, every man of Israel, your little ones, your wives and the sojourner (*ger*) who is in your camp, from the hewer of your wood to the drawer of your water, for you to *pass* into the covenant with Yahweh your God, and into His oath Yahweh your God is to seal [*koreith*][40] with you today. (29:9–12)

Despite the immediacy of the moment, the contract intended to be far-reaching, with the present moment stretched into an indefinite future: "And not with you alone do I seal this covenant and this oath, but with him who is here standing with us this day before Yahweh our God and with him who is not here with us this day" (29:14–15).[41] The covenant obligated all Israelites of future generations not because they were somehow included among the congregation standing on the steppes of Moab (as a late Midrash had it) or somehow represented or implicated by those standing present there (as modern theories of the social contract would have it).[42] Not merely the consent of future generations is implied here but the turning of all descendants of those present at the covenantal ceremony into addressees of the promises and targets of both the curses and blessings. The curses would reach far into the future, bringing a destruction reminiscent of Sodom and Gomorrah (29:22). And when "a later (*aharon*) generation" (29:21), both foreigners and Israelites, witness the calamity and try to make sense of it, they will recognize God's hand and his reasoning: "They [i.e., a future generation] have abandoned the covenant with Yahweh . . . which he sealed with [them] when He brought them out of the land of Egypt" (29:24).[43] They would also recognize that the catastrophic future was nothing but "all the curses written in this book" (29:26). Then another future is imagined, "when all these things come upon you, the blessing and the curse" (30:1), and Israel's heart will turn back to God, while "Yahweh will exult over [them] for the good as He exulted over [their] fathers" (30:9) and at the same time "shall set all these imprecations (*alot*) upon [their] enemies" (30:7).

When the Deuteronomist used an Assyrian formula of question and answer in 29:21–24,[44] he changed the verb tenses and stretched indefinitely the force of the imprecations pronounced. This future orientation, too, has Near Eastern parallels, for example, the Hittite formula "and the curses shall pursue you relentlessly."[45] The Deuteronomist's innovation in this context seems to be an intensification of the future orientation by combining the curse's inexhaustible power to punish future offenders with the interminable obligation of future generations, foreseen from a remote point in the past. In other words, all future generations would be born into the covenant, already obliged through their ancestors' presence at the moment the covenant was sealed and already objects of the interminable impact of God's curses and blessings. The present reader of the text, in any "now" to come, is always already included.

As far as Moses's immediate addressees were concerned, the promise to the fathers is hailed from a distant past (29:12), while the curses and blessings are extended from that moment to a distant future. They might have sounded differently to authors and readers who lived in Babylonian exile or in postexilic Yehud. They certainly sounded differently to anyone who knew Israel's fate ever since. But the fact that *both* exile and return are included here sustains the impression that even if a reference to recent events was included, the future's uncertainty and open horizon remained intact.[46]

The two routes into the future—blessing and cursing—are not symmetrical. There were many more mentions of curses than blessings (and they were also far more detailed).[47] The moment of sealing the covenant itself was a *rite de passage* in which people literally "*pass (l'ovr'kha)* into the covenant with Yahweh your God and into His oath *(alah)*" (29:11), where "oath" should be understood here in the strict sense of imprecation.[48] Pursuing the addressees into the future (28:45), the presence of the law was implicated in their dread and guilt, and the joy of following it was entangled with fear. It is then, at a late moment in the ceremony, that the shadow of a wrathful, jealous God emerges again (29:19–20) and the scope of his violence demarcated in a concise, general way. The paradigmatic catastrophe at Sodom and Gomorrah, when "the whole land [turned] brimstone, salt, and burning" is recalled and serves as the ultimate threat (29:22). But there is an additional threat—that of reversing the promise to the Fathers and the loss of land the actual addressees were about to conquer: "You shall not endure on the soil to which you are about to cross the Jordan" (30:18). And in between a Sodomite annihilation and exile—"every curse that is written in this book" (29:19, 26).

What is "this book"? In the series of closures that run throughout the last chapters of Deuteronomy (first during the covenant ceremonies [28–30] and then as Moses prepares to depart for his death [31]), "this book" and its inscription appear six times. It is a book of teaching (*ha-torah*), whose actual presence as an object is emphasized by the recurrence of the deictic "this" (*ha-ze, ha-zot*), the act of writing (31:24), and its designated place near the ark (31:26). It includes all "the injunctions of this teaching" (28:58, 30:10, 31:24), together with all the curses uttered in the covenantal ceremony (28:61, 29:20). To these, one may add God's injunction to write down "this song" (which Moses delivers in 32) and Moses's compliance to do so (31:19, 22).[49] The song supplements the book of teaching so as to "be a witness against the Israelites" (31:19) for the time he "will surely hide [His] face" (31:18), when his wrath will flare against them. As God already foresaw, when they arrive to their promised land, they will betray him and "go whoring after the alien gods" of that land (31:18).

Whereas the book of "this teaching" carried into the future both the laws to be enforced and the means to enforce them (the imprecations), the written "song" (31:22) fixed the meaning of the calamities, so that when they ultimately arrived the offenders could comprehend their experience precisely as God intended in the wilderness. Both books had to be taught and therefore transmitted through time (31:19, 22; 32:11, 46). The book of teaching was deposited "alongside the ark of the covenant" (31:26) given to the priests, the sons of Levi, who carried the ark (31:9) and were tasked with guarding it and the book. Together, the inscription of the code and its deposition, the curses that follow the Israelites to the future with their meaning fixed in advance, link the present to the future and turn the covenant into a temporalizing apparatus.

The "face hiding" mentioned in 31:18 as the reason for the "many evils and troubles" that would soon befall Israel, as they would go "whoring after alien gods" (31:6), will become the cornerstone of Tannaitic theology and the hallmark of other diasporic theologies. Most modern scholars see here a clear proof for the postexilic dating of many of these passages (including but not limited to those alluding to the fall of Jerusalem and the Babylonian exile) and certainly of these texts' edits. These passages are read as motivated by the crisis and the need to explain God's role in it.[50] But their effect is not limited to the retrospective explanation of the catastrophe—presented as a warning concerning events that have not happened yet. The effort to link the present of the covenant with all generations to come runs throughout the covenant ceremonies in chapters 27–30. Its aim is not only to explain what has happened but to anticipate everything that may happen and guarantee the perpetuity of the subjects' subjection to divine rule. It is not their disobedience that needs to be preempted—in fact, everything in these passages was built around their capacity to disobey—but their release from the contract. The people will always be able to disobey but would never be capable of liberating themselves from the grip of their subjection to God. Equating disobedience with doom, the perpetuity of the covenant has been established together with its curses.

In this, Deuteronomy's future-oriented covenant went far beyond its Near Eastern sources of influence but did not undermine their logic. Rather, it brought into relief the principle that underlies any aspiration for total rule and projected that principle onto God. In this aspiration Yahweh was no different from any other suzerain in the ancient Near East or, for that matter, from any ruling power in postbiblical eras: the Roman Empire before and after its Christianization, the empires in Central and East Asia, the Muslim Caliphate, or the modern state. To reproduce a relation of domination and submission is the first and most fundamental project of any ruling power. In Stathis Gourgouris's succinct words, "No master [not even a god] can command and ensure a successful regime without being dependent on—being *subjected* to—the will of the servant."[51] Even modern democracy has never dared to challenge this principle; it has only replaced submission to a person with submission to the state and the rule of law. No institution of power (to be distinguished from the people who take positions of power within it) would welcome its own termination and let those born into it release themselves from its grip. And even Yahweh, who was attributed with power that surpasses that of any other ruler, needed a device to guarantee such submission. Because of the power the Deuteronomists attributed to God, and also because they sought a ruling based on the interiorization of threats, not on the actual use of force, this submission should have been unconditional and lasted forever. Hence the Deuteronomists devised a binding contract from which no one could escape. Disobedience and resistance could bring an end to the party under divine rule—the threat recurs numerous times—but the rebels would perish precisely because they are still subjects under his rule.

The device that made this possible was a combination of open-ended curses and the written book that links the future to the moment when submission was established and its terms fixed. Note that for the Deuteronomists, submission and its uninterrupted reproduction were not desired for their own sake; they were means to protect the people from their master, which they could forsake or disobey only at the risk of death. In the context of La Boétie's "voluntary servitude" (which is that of Gourgouris's phrase quoted earlier), one may identify the threatening figure of a violent God as a ruse to deny—and betray—a desire for total submission. But if one assumes that these were people for whom a vengeful God was a basic feature of everyday experience, it is no less probable, if not more accurate, to argue that the special attention given to submission and its reproduction secretly expressed the subjects' silent understanding of their active role in securing the rule of their divine master. If desire is at stake here, it is the desire of the master to receive his subjects' unqualified, voluntary servitude.

The temporalization of the contract and the submission it implies operate through a different, more sedentary act of writing, when Moses charges the people to inscribe "all the words of this teaching" not in a book but on "great stones" coated with plaster, in the promised land (27:2–3, 8). A probable blending of two sources doubles the place and time of this writing.[52] It would occur either immediately after the crossing of the Jordan River, on that very day (27:2), hence near the river, or much later, when enough of the land would have been conquered and Israel would have reached Mount Ebal near Shechem (27:4), where an altar would be built and a sacrificial ceremony performed. In that latter place and on the nearby Mount Gerizim, the curses and blessings would be proclaimed (27:12–13). The Levite would then call in a loud voice to the assembly (27:14) twelve prohibitions preceded by the recurring phrase "cursed be the man who," to which the assembly would respond with "Amen" (27:15–26). How the people would be cursed was never specified, and no blessings were mentioned.[53] The list is rather concise and ends with a general warning: "Cursed be he who does not fulfill the words of this teaching to do them" (27:26).

The chapter (27) that describes this scene quite certainly belonged to an independent source, one different from those of the preceding code of law (12–26:15) and the following chapter (28), with its short list of blessings and long list of curses.[54] The stones on which "all the words of this teaching" should be inscribed were not meant to launch the covenant into the future but rather to serve as its background or even its witnesses. A future moment in the promised land is imagined, in which the time when the teaching was given will be a past event, and the writing on the stone will serve to present in a clear way (b'aer heitev; 27:8) what will already be a teaching given in the past. In a present moment that brackets the future ceremony from both sides—"This day the Lord Yahweh charges you" (26:16), "this day you have become a people to Yahweh your God" (27:9)—a future in which the ominous bond sealed in the present will be recalled and resealed is imagined and determined.

What makes the bond ominous, however, is not the curse as a speech act that carries no specific content but the full scope of evils awaiting the offenders. The formula, borrowed from a tradition of Near Eastern treaties, is one in whose elaborate display the Deuteronomist writers indulged. An abundance of lively, sensual descriptions of the sinners' predicaments make up the long twenty-eighth chapter of Deuteronomy, where "every curse that is written in this book" can indeed be found. The curses appear in a long list (28:15–69)[55] that follows the much shorter list of conditional blessings that ensure the obedient people military and political supremacy over their enemies, flourishing agriculture, and economic prosperity (28:1–14). The curses can be divided into different categories: (1) environmental disasters that generate famine and impoverishment; (2) illness and physical harm; (3) mental suffering, anxiety, and depression; (4) social disintegration; (5) military and political blows, siege, defeat, enslavement, and exile; and (6) other nameless plagues, "astounding, great, and relentless" in scope (28:59).[56] Many of them portray a total loss of control over one's life, hard labor that yields nothing but forfeited expectations, severe disorientation, and a destroyed life. In these curses, which Quick identified as "futility curses,"[57] the curse renders inoperative whatever the cursed person works to achieve. Destruction (*shmad*), total loss (*ovdan*), and annihilation[58] hover over many of these curses, in all categories. The ultimate destruction, the total annihilation of "Sodom and Gomorrah, Admah and Zeboiim," is invoked separately, in the following chapter 29, when the audience is reminded how the Lord overturned the cities in "His wrath and in His anger," leaving only "brimstone and salt, all the land a burning, it cannot be sown and it cannot flourish and no grass will grow in it" (29:22).[59]

The striking difference between the display of that emblematic catastrophe in Genesis and its invocation in Deuteronomy is noteworthy. The familiar outburst of wrath accompanied by genocidal threat (e.g., Ex. 32:10; Num. 14:12, 17:10) was incorporated into the covenant and became part of its juridical-political apparatus. Wrath was bracketed, and divine violence was made conditional, as clear terms were set for the operation of God's force, assuming that even he could be made a subject of his own law. This force could take any form (more on this later), and there were no limits on how, when, or where God could exercise his violence.[60] Like the plagues of Egypt, the curses were also serial. Each plague was a separate disaster. It would be meaningless to cast them all at once as punishment for one sin. At the same time, it is hard to imagine a (contemporary, that is, ancient) form of punishment that would not find its place or at least resonance in the long, fifty-two-verse list. The list goes on and on as if to ensure that no known or imaginable evil would be missed. The application of any item on the list was bounded by the people's disobedience (28:15), but the list itself was unbounded in its scope. To leave no room for doubt, it included "every illness and every plague that is not written in this book of teaching" (28:61). Like the absurd taxonomy quoted by Foucault from Borges's passage on "a certain *Chinese Encyclopedia*,"[61] this taxonomy of evils ensures the table's completeness by leaving one of the cells open to accommodate any calamity that did not fall under the other categories. This empty cell was added to "all the imprecations (*aloth*) of the Covenant written in this book of teaching" (29:20), to grant the limited set with an infinite scope.

The list of laws is far less comprehensive than the list of curses. This fact by itself provides humans with a certain space of action free from looming threats of divine violence. Furthermore, the ultimate threat, total destruction, was undermined or radically reframed by the way destruction was distributed across the list. While many scourges ended in destruction, destruction took multiple forms and was still only one among many possible terrible things awaiting those who dared to turn away from God, and it is not necessarily even the worst of these scourges. When all one has—a house, a vineyard, flock, renown, a wife, sons and daughters—is taken away and one is utterly powerless, "only exploited and crushed always . . . crazed by the sight of [his] eyes" (28:32–34), one may feel like Job, who in despair asked God to "annul the day that [he] was born" (Job 3:3). The diminution of the total destruction implied here becomes explicit and radical in the few Deuteronomic curses related to *exile*, which were presented as what *follows* destruction, not vice versa.

> Every illness and every plague that is not written in this book of teaching Yahweh
> will bring down upon you *until you are destroyed. And you will remain* a scant few
> instead of your being like the stars of the heavens in multitude . . . as Yahweh exulted
> over you to do well with you and to multiply you, so will Yahweh exult over you to
> make you perish, to *destroy you*—and you will be torn from the soil to which you are
> coming to take hold of it. (28:61–63)

Those destroyed remained alive but lost their political independence and homeland. The survivors of a catastrophic war, a siege, and a conquest (28:25, 30–34) are described as an exiled remnant in a later interpolation (28:36–37). Exile is the (later) Deuteronomists' translation of the genocidal threat. The introduction of exile changed the meaning of the entire list, as was demonstrated in the case of captivity. Captivity was first described in the context of military defeat, in terms of submission and servitude, hunger, thirst, "nakedness and . . . the lack of all things . . . an iron yoke on your neck until you are destroyed" (28:48). It was described alongside siege, which was portrayed in its full array of horrors (28:49–57), including extreme famine to the point of cannibalism and complete social disintegration. In siege's context, destruction was also one of the horrible consequences, no more horrible than others, perhaps, but definitive: "until you are destroyed . . . until it has made you perish" (28:51). In the putatively supplementary text of 28:68,[62] however, captivity and enslavement were presented as a preferred but unachievable means of survival under the new exilic condition that *followed* destruction: "Yahweh will bring you back to Egypt in ships, on the way that I said to you, 'you shall not see it again,' and will put yourselves for sale there to your enemies as male and female slaves, *and there will be no buyer.*"

In fact, enslavement and exile set the condition for all the other plagues, which would last as long as Israel was driven out of its land. In other words, this small group of curses and threats (28:36–37, 64–68; 29:27), which allegedly were added by a late redactor, continued to reframe and delimit the genocidal threat, not only postponing it to an indefinite future or blurring it with the most terrible imaginable states of living but actually containing it within the political sphere. For the author of these verses and the redactor of this chapter, total destruction and loss (*shmad* and *ovdan*) denoted the obliteration of the political sphere but not of Israel's physical existence, and it suggested also the indefinite prolongation of its plight. The author of the chapter's final verses refused to—or could not—imagine a fate worse than military and political defeat followed by enslavement and exile.

The explicit tethering of divine violence to divine law and the dwindling, then skipping, of genocidal threat go hand in hand with other effects of the list of curses. Together they transform—logically, if not also historically[63]—the two other theocratic configurations reconstructed in the previous chapters. Much scholarship has been occupied with demonstrating (successfully, I believe) that large segments of chapter 28 borrow much of its language from various Vassal and Succession treaties in the ancient world.[64] Less attention has been paid to the fact that the list borrowed, paraphrased, and elaborated on formulae from several different sources in a way that enabled it to exceed them in length, density, variegation, and creative playfulness.[65] By doing this, there was no kind of trouble left uncovered in the text. The Deuteronomists seem to insist on naming evils that still have no name, on recognizing them even before they take their form, and on infusing them well in advance with their theological meaning. Since every kind of evil was anticipated in Deuteronomy's list of curses, it was possible to recognize each disaster as a punishment for some offense and as an expression of God's raging intervention in human affairs. A metanarrative was set within which one would be able to anticipate every downfall and ascribe to it its theopolitical meaning.

The story could be told in two seemingly opposite yet equal directions: forward, from cause to effect (28:15), and backward, from effect to cause (28:45). The curses migrate between places, communities, individuals, and generations and assume multiple forms, but always materializing as a manifestation of divine power. Each catastrophe could serve as a sign: When calamity struck, he had sent it; if no calamity struck, he had averted it. If it struck Israel, they should repent; if it struck their enemies, Israel should rejoice and be reassured that God has not abandoned them. In both cases catastrophe—any catastrophe—is a revelation by other means. God was the only power capable of domesticating catastrophes and putting them in some legible order. He was the God of all catastrophes, those that had already happened, those about to happen, and those that were dormant potentialities. Yet despite this all-encompassing power to destroy, Israel alone was held accountable for its dispersal. The people, as a multitude and as a nation—the ambiguity here is systemic and productive[66]—were placed at a juncture in which they had to choose life and goodness or death and evil, lawfulness and obedience or lawlessness and betrayal (30:15). They were placed there at the moment of reentering the covenant, and they would remain there forever, caught in this system of causation and responsibility that Jews, Christians, and Muslims would later inherit and keep for centuries to come.

For the people standing on the steppes of Moab, in the midst of the covenant ceremony, and throughout its reiterations, multiple moments of presence became free of actual violence. Only virtual violence remained, invoked as a cluster of memory capsules and hovering through a long list of threats, articulated by the formulaic language of the curses.[67] The memory capsule itself duplicates the same structure. The recollection of the revelation at Horeb is a clear example: "And I will let them hear My words, that they may learn to fear Me . . . for Yahweh your God is a consuming fire, a jealous God" (4:10, 24). Even as a memory, divine violence was conceived as the other side of divine law and as a consequence of its breaching. What linked law and violence was not the sovereign but his subjects, who were responsible for the *passage a l'acte*, that is, for the decision to kill or let live.

In order to play a role in the education of his subjects, the memory of past events turned into threats of future calamities, and the recollected events were often narrated as examples for the catch-all offense "you rebelled against the word of Yahweh, your Lord" (1:26, 43; 9:23). This became a general characteristic of the Israelites, who were deemed "rebellious against Yahweh from the day I [Moses] knew you" (9:24). But at that moment in the steppes of Moab, these events were recalled as part of the history of Israel that Moses uses to introduce the code of laws, including injunctions concerning the judges and priests appointed to lead the people as they follow God's will and execute his plans (17:8–18:8, 20:1–9). The people, who must have experienced or heard eye-witnesses' accounts of these events, were told to recall them on par with the curses, which turned the past into a sign and a warning for the future. They were placed in a space opened between memories and threats, and their only two possible options were to keep or not to keep "all this command" (11:22, 30:15–17). They were placed in the present, in one another's presence, listening to all these laws, memories, threats, and promises. Only Yahweh himself was absent, and his violence was "temporalized away."

Based on this temporalization, a new modality of violence became possible. Violence was inscribed in the psychological scars of a traumatic memory, and the virtual, withheld violence was awaiting its right moment. Encased in memory capsules and formulaic imprecations, this withheld violence sought to become a mechanism of *law enforcement*. The construction of memory in Deuteronomy was far more than a collective memory geared toward a quest for transcendent meanings and cultivation of faith in a God who revealed himself in history.[68] In fact, the reading presented here demonstrates the primacy of power and the auxiliary role of collective memory, together with the identity formations it may bring about. But this was not simply a top-down operation of power, for at the same time, the first if not main purpose of *keeping the law* emerged as a device— the best humans have designed—for keeping divine violence at bay. Simply put, the law became a technology for rationalizing and subduing a sovereign who could destroy everything.

The new modality of divine violence made room for theopolitical guidance and regulation of human behavior, which should help in keeping violence dormant for as long as possible and in making sense of it once it is actualized. But this relative protection came at a price. The full weight and responsibility of the moment of decision over life and death was relegated from the sovereign to each subject (30:11–20). "See I have set before you today life and good, and death and evil" (30:15). It is all very plain. The command is not "in the heavens," and "the word is very close to you, in your mouth and in your heart" (30:12, 14). And while the responsibility was on each subject, the sovereign kept for himself all the power needed to respond to the subject's decision. That moment of decision was meant to be recreated at every instance in which action could be articulated in the language of the law, thus carrying into the future the (always uncertain) power to keep deferring the return of the repressed.

THE WEIGHT OF THE PRESENT

The moment of decision was carefully structured. The scene was staged for an exilic time, "when all these things come upon you, the blessing and the curse . . . that your heart shall turn back among all the nations to which Yahweh your God will make you stray. And you shall turn back to Yahweh and heed His voice . . . and He shall turn back and gather you in from all the people" (30:1–3). The return—of the people to God, of God to the people, and of the people to their land—does not preclude the choice nor make it redundant; it only loads it with a new meaning.[69] There were two parties involved in this scene: the individual subject making the decision and the Lord fixing the terms of engagement ("when you heed the voice of Yahweh your God to keep His commandments" [30:10]). There was a choice between two options—"life and good" or "death and evil" (30:15)—and a subject could survive only by choosing the first. God was represented by his voice, and this voice was represented by Moses, who orchestrated the entire scene without taking part in it, for the whole drama was supposed to take place *within* the choosing individual. The voice was meant to be interiorized, affecting one's body, felt in one's mouth and one's heart, splitting the subject's self and bringing him or her to recognize their master's voice as their own: "For this command . . . is not too wondrous to you nor distant. It is not in the heavens . . . and it is not beyond the sea. . . . But the word is very close to you, in your heart and in your mouth to do it" (30:11–14).

According to the text, this scene happened once, at the moment of the covenant's sealing, when Moses acted as the director of the ceremony. But the text multiplies this moment and undermines any attempt to fix it in any imagined chronology. References to the covenant's sealing and the inauguration of its obligatory power first appear in the conclusion to the first narration of the revelation at Horeb (4:39–40), recurring in the short prologue to the Deuteronomic version of the Decalogue (5:1–3) and again in the verses closing the code of law: "This day Yahweh charges you to do these statutes and these laws" (26:16). That moment was referenced again in the next chapter, between instructions for two future ceremonies (one across the Jordan River, on the day of its crossing [27:2–3], and the other sometime after crossing [27:4], on Mount Ebal). Moses, who would be dead by then, nevertheless gave details for both. Once the ceremony was established as a recurring celebration and projected onto the future, it was displayed in the fullness of its theatricality, with the Levites performing the public reading of the blessings and the curses on Mounts Ebal and Gerizim (27:11–14). The ceremony that Moses orchestrated in the wilderness thus turned into a sort of rehearsal for a future performance of the covenant in the promised land.[70] Instead of stabilizing the spatiotemporal coordinates of the ceremony, all indices were doubled: There were two moments to com-memorate—the crossing of the Jordan River and the arrival at the mountains of Samaria; two locations for the inscription (across the Jordan and on Mount Ebal); two locations for the reading of the curses and blessings (at Mounts Ebal and Gerizim, respectively); a ritual where both burnt offerings (*olot*) and com-munion sacrifices (*shlamim*) were offered (27:6–7); and, lastly, two modes of communication, writing in stone and a live performance with a chorus of Levites, echoed by the people in pronouncing "Amen." And in the midst of this doubling, the moment of sealing the covenant once again came into present: "And Moses, and the Levitical priests with him, spoke to all Israel, saying: 'Be still and listen, Israel! This day you have become a people to Yahweh your God'" (27:9). This is, as Laura Quick aptly puts it, "a multi-media experience, enacted ritually, recited orally, and written upon display stones."[71] As she explains, both the oral and the scribal aspects of the ceremony were performative, and both were integrated with the sacrificial ritual.[72] But on the steppes of Moab, the performance of the ritual was an imaginary anticipation of a future moment, hence all the more theatrical. The ceremony inscribed its own presence in the performative speech while detailing and charging the future ceremony. That ceremony would be both inaugural and iterative, both complete and lacking. It would be complete, for the laws would not only be heard but seen, the sacrifices would be offered, and everything would take place in the promised land. It would be lacking because both God and Moses would be absent, and the divine voice would be supple-mented by an oral performance that would substitute for the absent origin and the first act of mediation. That moment of an intensified theatrical presence on the steppes of Moab portrayed a present into which the covenant's future and past collapsed, thus rendering the covenant indefinitely present.

The future times and places for ceremony were precisely marked, which de-manded a certain course of action, human as well as divine—a conquest of colo-nization that would soon be launched. These times and places are goals to be achieved, definitive as human plans can be. Many past events were also clearly located.[73] But geographical locations of the various ceremonies and their point in a fixed timeline remain obscure, for the place of the speech and of Israel entering the covenant and becoming a people were never mentioned again.[74] We may assume that the ceremony was located "in the Arabah, opposite Suph between Paran and Topher and Laban and Hazeroth and Di-Zahab" (1:1), or "in the valley opposite Beth Peor in the land of Sihon" (4:46). These place names could be read as map coordinates coming from at least two different Deutero-nomic sources.[75] But the way these coordinates are given may also be read as purposefully making the location impossible to identify, as Deuteronomy does with Moses's place of burial: "in the glen in the land of Moab, opposite Beth Peor, and no man has known his burial place to this day" (34:6).

The performance's dual tasks were to be rendered as vividly as possible as an event of inauguration while at the same time making room for the individual who listened to a public reading of the text or read it themselves. For the perfor-mance must have taken place anywhere its readers stood, whenever they read alone or recited in public aloud.[76] The readers introduced into the covenant were thus interpellated into its temporality. They must have been able to tem-poralize divine presence with its violent threat and blessed promises, so as to heed their master's voice and feel protected as his subjects. The uncertain future of proclaimed yet postponed curses and blessings awaited them, no matter how they imagined the geography of the promised land and whether they read Ebal and Gerizim literally or metaphorically,

On that day, on the steppes of Moab, when the covenant was sealed, Israel became a people (this decisive claim recurs in three different chapters [26:18, 27:9, 29:12] ascribed to three putative different sources). From Deuteronomy's first verse, where Moses speaks "these words . . . to all the Israelites across the Jordan in the wilderness" (1:1), Moses mostly addresses Israelites with the plural "you." In doing this, he refers to a collective group with a shared past that goes back to God's revelation and possibly even further back to the promises he had made to their forefathers. We have seen how stories from this past were woven throughout Deuteronomy and then summarized again immediately after the last curse was pronounced and "the words of covenant" concluded (28:69–29:8). But only now, upon entering the covenant that made them a people, could they reclaim these stories as representing their shared origin.[77]

The covenant, with its preambles and perorations, also endowed the people with a shared future. This future can be thought of as the opposite of a destiny. It was not predetermined, for it entirely depended on the way the people chose to go. Although the choice to follow God or not was given to each individual (30:10–17, 19b–20), the predicament was collective: "I tell you[78] today that you shall surely perish; you shall not endure" (30:18–19a). The switch to second-person plural makes clear what should have been clear enough by following the accumulation of the curses. Although many of the curses pronounced in chapter 28 depicted extreme existential and often quite intimate situations, they could not be taken out of the collective—environmental and political—contexts in which they would come about. In the putatively earlier layer of this chapter, the curse of "siege" provides a political context and emblematic image for a cluster of collective scourges (28:48–57). In the putatively later insertion, it is the destruction of the polity followed by exile (28:63–68) that characterizes these same threats. Likewise, the blessings: While pronounced in the second-person singular, they were framed collectively as taking part in the collective event of becoming God's "holy people" (28:9–10). One way or another, cursed or blessed, the people assembled on the steppes of Moab would share a future, even after they ceased sharing the same land, once Yahweh scattered them across the earth (28:64).

The Deuteronomists knew that a shared past and shared future were necessary for the formation of a people and their endurance as a political entity. But they were also fully aware, so it seems, of the constructed nature of this durable entity and understood that a durable covenant ("for all time," *ad olam* [12:28]) depended on reiterated performances to keep the shared past as a living, shared memory and to secure a shared future for the assembled community. The time of the performance, when past and future were woven together to emulate the persisting oneness of the people, was the immediate here and now of its present: "You are stationed here today, all of you, before Yahweh your God . . . every man of Israel" (29:9).

They were "stationed before Yahweh," but he was absent. This was a temporary absence, for they knew that he would show up again, for better or worse, only not then, at that moment of presence. To enable the choice between obedience and disobedience, a choice to be reiterated several times a day, all year, he must be absent but still working behind the scenes. Then, at some point in the future, through his subjects' disobedience, his absence may turn into a special state of presence, when, turning his face away from Israel, his supreme mastery and power would be revealed. When God hides his face, calamity strikes.[79] But if they heeded his voice, the people would thrive in every respect, and God's work behind the scenes would be recognized and reflected in the eyes of "all the peoples" who "will *see* that the name [*but not the face*] of Yahweh is called over" Israel (28:10). What separates one form of absence from the other is the subjects' relation to "this book of teaching." The Torah thus mediates between the veiled but efficient divine cause and the phenomenal realm, along with the entire spectrum of human experience. One must assume that this mediation was constantly at work, but what this mediation would bring about was deferred to the future.

The Deuteronomic theocracy was no less keen on keeping divine presence and proximity closely related to holiness and disaster than its priestly rival.[80]

But each term took its precise meaning from the structure of divine rule and the temporal distribution of its forces. Holiness was not spatially bound, and divine violence was not kept away by respecting its boundaries. Rather, both holiness and violence were strictly bound by the law. Time itself separated human life and action from God's presence, sin from punishment. Bestowed on the whole people, holiness bridged a past event—Israel's election (7:6, 14:2)—with a glorious albeit conditional future; if they followed in God's way, blessing would materialize. God's name—a substitute for his presence—would be recognized and feared by "all the people of the earth" (28:9–10). In between past and future, the only two laws in which holiness was invoked reduced holiness to cleanliness (14:1–21, 23:15), a matter of everyday conduct that required no priestly mediation. Like divine violence, human action too fell along the three temporal axes, with past and future collapsed into the present. The past was a living memory, taught and rehearsed; the present was marked by the presence and recognition (or lack thereof) of the law; and a blessed or calamitous future was encased in the blessings and the curses. Humans became free to choose and fully accountable for their choices, while God was relegated to being a reactive force whose action was unpredictable and could be suspended for generations, if not indefinitely.

From that moment on, any earthly authority that claimed to live by Yahweh's teaching could and should position itself in the void left by God's immediate absence. Not directly present, he provided supervision from afar, and thus his response was always delayed, having been declared in advance and deciphered retrospectively. The price paid for gaining this space was not negligible, however. It was later called theodicy—the a priori justification for all catastrophes to come. God's subjects would never be able to demand justice, because everything was justified in advance. They could only seek to understand. They were offered the entire realm of human affairs as a text, replete with signs from heaven, and were invited to interpret it. In other words, it was precisely by starting to withdraw from the realm of human affairs—the first moment of secularization (and the basic meaning in which the term is used here)—that God's "spirit" pervaded and colonized every sphere of human life. When he went on holiday, his actions being relegated to the past and to the future, his rule became more absolute, more colonizing than ever, but at the same time more abstract, more given to human manipulation. For now he could become part of the human experience, including being the sovereign he claimed to be, only through the mediation of human interpretation. He could do this without displaying his power, and anyway, no such display could secure his rule without this interpretive work.

The encompassing list of the vividly described curses and the much shorter list of blessings provide a general matrix for the interpretative work, offering a spectrum of possibilities without committing to a specific reading of any distinct state of affairs. The matrix works, however, only if one assumes that the future was open yet conditioned according to the terms set by God, which in turn cemented his response to human action. What remained unpredictable was exactly when and how God would react. Any activity subjected to the covenant's laws and statutes partook in initiating a divine response that affected others, often the community as a whole, not only the pious person or the offender. The law itself therefore provided a check on the possibility of this kind of collateral damage and listed several injunctions for actions that must be taken to limit dangerous offenses. They instruct the use of human violence to prevent divine violence.

We may return briefly to the policing of idolatry charged in chapter 13, where a harsh violent response is commanded to a variety of idolatrous acts and incitements to worship other gods. Idolaters must be exposed and killed and their towns demolished, yet no specific human authority was charged for any of this. Rather, the burden was shared by the entire community.[81] The shared burden demanded the community to act as an ad hoc police force. Policing the worship of Yahweh, however, was not a pretext or opportunity for creating hierarchy within the community. It was rather a condition for having a rule of law in the first place and hence a way to fend off divine violence. Policing worship was the ultimate way to exercise divine rule without exercising divine violence, materializing Deuteronomic theocracy "before Yahweh" and in his absence. And in the end, this substitution of divine with human violence added no authority between the divine sovereign and the humans who imposed his will. With this we have come full circle to the ideal state of affairs imagined by the book of teaching. It would take place in the promised land and be one where a direct divine rule would be replaced by the rule of (his) law.

But on the steppes of Moab, the ideal state is even less tangible than the promised land, yet to be conquered. The revelation at Horeb, which Moses recalled vividly before he introduced the code of law, has already become a distant memory. It is invoked at the end of the cursing ceremony, almost apologetically, in an ancillary note: "These are the words of the Covenant that the Lord charged Moses to seal with the Israelites in the land of Moab, *besides* the Covenant that *He sealed with them at Horeb*" (28:69).[82] The covenant's present moment has already taken full precedence over both past and future. This is the moment when the people become his and are called to action that would substitute for divine violence. But they are not there yet; their land is only a promise; and he was no longer there, at least for that interval of time when the covenantal ceremony was rehearsed and reiterated. This moment in those spaces and times should be prolonged as much as possible, long enough for the people to become his good subjects, to be interpellated into the new temporality of divine violence. That lull would be then prolonged as long as they remained good subjects.

Recall that this structuring of the present moment would occur again, after crossing the Jordan River. As was demonstrated earlier in this section, the instructions for the time and place of the inaugural ceremony where the law would be written onto plastered stones seem purposefully confusing. This confusion is insignificant because the future ceremony was automatically invoked by the present one, in addressing "he who is here standing with us this day . . . and with him who is not here with us this day" (29:14). The inaugural moment took place not in Canaan but in the wilderness before crossing the Jordan River. The covenant proclaimed there was not the first, and its reiteration after crossing the river would not be the last. In each future event, the phrase "this day you have become a people to Yahweh your God" (27:9) would be commemorated and reiterated, collapsing the past and future (re)entrances into the covenant in the present. And precisely because it is insignificant, the vagueness of the ceremony's instructions are also telling, as they take part in prioritizing the concrete present of the underdetermined future. Perhaps the redactors were not careless after all. Perhaps they understood that the present outweighed the place and time of sealing the covenant. Perhaps they did try to leave details undefined for future flexibility, inside but also outside the promised land.[83]

The blurring of times and places does not stop there. The first covenant, where the entire people witnessed Yahweh's revelation with dread and listened to the proclamation of the Ten Commandments, was located at Horeb, not Mount Sinai, and its story is told in Deuteronomy three times.[84] The name "Horeb" occurs in all three versions, each time sending the reader back to "the mount of God" in the land of Midian (Ex. 3:1), where God first revealed himself to Moses and sent him back to Egypt. The revelation to the people at Horeb may not have been the first, then.[85] If not the first revelation, was it the first covenant that the Deuteronomist recognized? Even this is not clear, for according to two later texts (27:9, 29:11–12), it was only on the steppes of Moab that Israel became a people. And according to the second version of the covenant at Horeb, it was a treaty sealed "not only with our fathers . . . but with us—who are here today" (5:3). The accumulative effect of these inconsistencies—which could be part of the redactor's strategy—is seriality. Entering the covenant followed a series of events, which extended to the past and to the future, and every moment was curated as a moment of an inaugural present. Blurring the specificity of past and future events helped shift the audience's (or readers') attention from the ceremony's origin to the performance's present, which claimed the status of origin while deconstructing the very possibility of an originary moment.

There was more taking place here, however, than the construction of a recurring originary moment. A covenant with multiple, indefinite points of entry was not the only thing at stake. In a world where to curse was conceived as a way to take control,[86] a list of curses that encompassed all domains of human life and activity asserted a claim for total control. Furthermore, the totalizing project of naming all imaginable evils and building a matrix for individual experience and collective historical understanding would leave Yahweh's theodicy intact. The authors and redactors of Deuteronomy's various layers and segments imagined a historical event—Israel on the steppes of Moab—and reimagined the past and future of that historical moment from the point of its passed present. It is quite certain that they all knew something about the destruction and the exile of the kingdom of Israel (724 or 722 BCE). Some of them may have heard (or heard about) testimonies of survivors who had escaped the horrors of the Assyrian siege, defeat, and expulsion. Therefore, it is quite likely that earlier layers of Deuteronomy responded directly to the fall of the northern kingdom, fearing a similar fate for Judah. When it arrived, later, exilic or postexilic Judean authors and redactors (assuming that the compiling and redaction of Deuteronomy lasted for centuries) could remember or imagine the fear of the approaching Babylonian army and the horrors of defeat and exile that followed it (597–586 BCE). Back in Yehud under the Persian Empire, a century or two later, Deuteronomic writers and redactors could never exclude the possibility that another destruction or exile awaited the newly established Judean community. In other words, whenever they were active in the long, uncertain history of the composition of Deuteronomy, these thinkers had concrete, urgent reasons to look for a theopolitical framework that could come to terms with a God who had abandoned his people.

The astonishing thing is that so little of these putative experiences entered the text. Deuteronomy's political theology bears relatively few marks of its authors' concrete historical events, and those that exist are well embedded in the text.[87] Destruction, captivity, and exile are presented as scourges that are still pending, which could have still been prevented at that long-*passed* moment of the covenant in the wilderness. As noted earlier, they were merely a few of the worst in that long list of all *kinds* of scourges. As a whole, the list cannot be limited to lamenting or justifying the loss of Judean sovereignty or the destruction of the

Temple. The effect, if not the intention, of its assemblage is the a priori justification of all disasters, lesser and greater, retroactively and in advance, and making the people—each individual and the nation as a whole—responsible. The formulaic language drawn from contemporary or more ancient Near Eastern political treaties helped the Deuteronomists free their political theology from any debt to the singularity of historical events. But it was probably their own theopolitical imagination that endowed this language with its strong theodicean flavor.

In the postexilic Deuteronomy chapter 30, the prospect of the future was expanded to include the possibility of return—to God and to the land—that would follow exile and destruction: "And it shall be, when all these things come upon you, the blessing and the curse that I have set before you, that your heart shall turn back among the nations to which Yahweh your God will make you stray" (30:1). Such a possibility further postpones divine violence and opens a new dimension onto the present, as this present becomes the time for the labor of "turning back to Yahweh" and then waiting for him to "turn back" his disciples and subjects to their former state (30:2–3).[88] But even here, in what seems like the clearest trace of exilic or postexilic writing, the author's situatedness is immediately blurred, while the situation of the addressees is generically described. The possibility of return was emphatically planted in the present, at the moment of entering the covenant: "See, I have set before you *today* life and good, death and evil" (30:15). At this point, and always, the catastrophes associated with divine violence were future potentialities, and God's subjects were left with the responsibility to avert them. He was declared their ruler forever and ever, and their disobedience meant evil and death, but his violence had been harnessed to a book of laws that gave form to their subjection and opened a relatively safe space for their action.

THE SUBJECTS' TRAP, OR THE PEOPLE'S IRONY

"He is a holy God. He is a jealous God" (Josh. 24:19).[89] The covenant scene that concludes the book of Joshua—an "orphan" text that presents an alternative closure to the book[90] and whose source has been contested and is hard to determine[91]—forcefully asserts the inseparability of God's jealousy and holiness, which characterizes the economy of violence in both Deuteronomic and priestly sources. Holiness remained menacing, and only an exclusive "sincere and truthful" service (*avodah*) of God (24:14) could provide protection from it. The ceremony took place at Shechem, but it is not the one for which Moses wrote the script on the steppes of Moab and to which the book of Joshua alludes elsewhere

(8:30–35).[92] In fact, in some respects it appears very different from the covenant ceremony that concludes Deuteronomy.

The chapter opens with a brief history of the people that has no parallel in Deuteronomy. It begins "beyond the Euphrates," where Abraham's story in Genesis begins, and all three fathers are mentioned by their names (24:2–4), along with a few biographical details. The chapter presents Joshua as a leader and a prophet, underplaying the role of Moses (who is mentioned only once in this chapter [24:5], along with Aaron, as God's messengers to the Israelites in Egypt) and omitting earlier revelations at either Sinai or Horeb.[93] The law consists of nothing but a monolatrous imperative, while all the catastrophes threatened to those who violate the covenant are condensed into one short warning: "He will not forgive your transgressions nor your sins. If you forsake Yahweh and serve alien gods, He will turn and harm you [*heir'a lakhem*; literally—do evil to you] and make an end of you" (24:19–20). None of Israel's rebellious acts or God's wrathful responses are mentioned. After a long exchange between Joshua and the people, who insist that they are determined to serve Yahweh, their God (24:18), Joshua, accepting the people's commitment as sufficient, seals with them a pact (*brith*), establishes "a statute and law," writes "all these things in the book of God's teaching," and sets a big stone under the terebinth in Yahweh's sanctuary to serve as a witness for the pact (24:25–27).

In other respects, however, Joshua 24 does not simply present a different approach to and a different narrative of entering the covenant; on closer inspection, it seems to challenge one of the key elements of the Deuteronomic covenantal theology—the freedom of choice given to God's subjects (Deut. 30:10–20). Holiness was not attributed to Israel and was presented neither as a condition nor a consequence of the covenant but rather as a reason *to avoid* it: "But Joshua said to the people, 'You cannot serve Yahweh, for he is a holy God. He is a jealous God'" (24:19). Joshua invoked God's lethal holiness in response to the people's rejection of his own suggestion that perhaps they "are loath to serve Yahweh" and would rather prefer "to serve the gods . . . of the Amorites in whose land [they] are settled" (24:15), an offer that the people dismiss, immediately and unambiguously (24:16). Speaking about God's holiness is in fact the second time Joshua opens the possibility of not entering the covenant. The people's refusal of the offer became even blunter: "No, for we will serve Yahweh" (24:21). This time, they did not enter the covenant intimidated by a smoking mountain or a list of curses that promised them hell on earth if they rejected him.[94] They were free to "choose this day which [god they] are going to serve" (24:15). The terms of the choice were clearly set, and so they decided. Even at that point, they could withdraw, for when Joshua heard their determination (and to make sure they were committed in earnest), he called them to be "witnesses for [them]selves," of their own choice, which they "have chosen to serve Yahweh" (24:22). "We are witnesses," they responded. "Yahweh we will serve and His voice we will heed" (24:22–24). Only then was Joshua ready to conclude the ceremony, matching the people's witnessing with its recording by that big stone, which could "be a witness *for us*, for it *heard* all the words that Yahweh spoke to us; it shall be a *witness to you*, lest you break faith with your God" (24:27).

Joshua 24 offers its own version of a multimedia covenantal ceremony that included a speech, writing, the setting up of a monument, and a stone that listened and acted as a witness.[95] Through the interplay between the visual and the oral elements, the text presents the stone as a mirror that reflects and preserves the people's own commitment they had just taken. With the book of teaching and the stone that it lay on, the two acts of witnessing, and the three invitations to the people to reject God, the text materializes the people's commitment and amplifies their responsibility. In turn, this diminished in importance God's own choice—the one he made when he took Abraham from beyond the river (24:3). God's original choice was now tested by the people's decision: By risking their lives, they could prove his choice futile. The possibility of interrupting God's lineage of men of bestowed privilege and undermining the project that he himself initiated and had navigated thus far—from sending Abram to Canaan to settling his descendants in the land he promised him—was clearly stated. The colonization project is presented as a fait accompli now, after a successful conquest of "a land for which [they] did not labor and towns which [they] did not build" (24:13). It was his special weapon, "the hornet" he sent to the front lines, and not their swords and bows that drove out the indigenous peoples (24:12). Still, even at this point, it was not unimaginable—for Joshua, at least, and certainly for those who wrote this with some historical hindsight—that the Israelites would turn to serve the gods of the Amorites, the people in whose land they are now settled (24:15). This is not a farfetched idea. After all, most people did worship the gods of the lands where they lived. Ancient "settler colonialism" often brought the invaders into contact with cultures no less developed or attractive than their own, and acculturation was a two-way street.

Deuteronomy presents the people's choice as one that permeates one's life and assumes that the covenant was a condition no Israelite could escape, an event that became an a priori structure of experience, thought, and action. In clear distinction, the pact in Shechem depicted in Joshua 24 radicalized the choice, placing it at the heart of the constitutive event itself while undermining its lasting structural effect. Here, the choice was an experience one must have undergone and a decision one must have undertaken—no line of flight was possible—upon entering the covenant. Joshua himself even gave an example by announcing his own choice (24:15b). But can this choice be taken at face value? How should we, the readers, understand the real options Abraham's descendants had after being Yahweh's subjects all those years, having incurred debt to his salvation in Egypt, throughout the wilderness, as well as through the conquest of Canaan (24:2–13)? Only because they had already been his subjects could they not worship other gods without punishment. Why should the people abandon a providential deity like Yahweh (as they, like Joshua, present him [24:17–18]), only to become doomed to his unforgivable jealousy (24:19)? In light of these questions, we should also consider whether Joshua's questions were addressed to the people or merely rhetorical.[96] Were these questions nothing but performative gestures seeking to induce a dramatic effect that would simulate choice, a choice never real in the first place? Was the whole drama a way to include a subversive voice but also silence it? What are we to do with this seeming recognition of the existence (or the belief in the existence—it does not matter) of other deities and of a freedom of choice to serve or not serve them? Or was it only upon completing their conquest of the promised land that the Israelites realized that they had a real choice?[97] Does asking these questions mean taking the text too seriously, reading everything at face value, and in doing so missing its irony?[98]

Let us look again at the scene in Shechem. It was a carefully orchestrated performance around a choice where no real choice was ever available.[99] If they opted for worshipping other gods, they chose their doom; if they abided by Yahweh's commandments, they were simply reaffirming that they had been following him all along and could not do otherwise without risking everything. It was seemingly straightforward. But strangely enough, this impasse finds no trace in the text. No fear, frustration, or despair was expressed; no recollection of divine violence or the fate of those who had dared to serve other gods or to question his messengers were mentioned; only the destruction and defeat of their enemies were recalled. The people readily acknowledged all the care Yahweh provided to them (24:16–18). They even presented it as the reason for their loyalty:

> Far be it from us that we should forsake the Lord to serve other gods, for [ki] Yahweh our Lord is He who brings our forefathers and us from the land of Egypt. (24:16–17)

This was their straightforward response to the trap Joshua set for them as he ended his speech:

> If it be evil in your eyes to serve Yahweh, *choose today* whom you should serve, whether the gods that your forefathers served across the Euphrates, or whether the gods of the Amorites, in whose land you dwell. (24:15)

The choice Joshua gave them was between two forms of idolatry, the "other gods" outside of Canaan and within it.[100] As if recognizing the irony of his gesture, they did not speak about that choice at all but instead about their existing commitment to God. And then, almost in the same breath, they switched the reason for their loyalty from Yahweh's past actions to their current situation:

> We, too, will serve Yahweh, *because* [*ki*] He *is our* God. (24:18)

Is this a statement of fact or a report of a decision? It is probably both, except that the decision was made long ago and is now implied in the reported fact. We too, the people say to Joshua, not only you, are servants to this God. He is our God; this relation has long been established, long before the new covenant was offered, when he took us and our forefathers out of Egypt, and we have no intention of resisting or refusing it now. If there was ever a real choice here, it was a choice made long ago by God, not by the people (24:3). What was left for them was only the mode of accepting *his* choice, the gesture for announcing their submission to *that* God, a matter of sheer performance. When Joshua insists, "You will not be able to serve Yahweh, for His is a holy God" (24:19), they simply retort by repeating, "No! For we will serve Yahweh" (24:21). The alternative option presented by Joshua, the "line of flight" he proposed, that is, to serve other gods, was an empty gesture for anyone who chose life over death. This was the exact choice offered in Deuteronomy 30:15, except that here it was not just presented by the leader but actually made, first by Joshua and then by the people. Whereas Joshua merely announced the choice he had made, the people performed it, rejecting Joshua's provocations, demonstrating the emptiness of the choice while acknowledging its consequences—loyalty to God. They exposed the lie of the freedom offered to them by Joshua and exhibited the freedom they still enjoyed, *the freedom of performing their submission.* Joshua, who seemed to ignore the subtlety, was fast to grab the people's response and hold them to it: "You are witnesses for yourselves that you have *chosen* Yahweh to serve Him" (24:22).

Joshua turned an admission of submission into a threshold, which one must have crossed in order to enter the covenant (24:24–25). But what was *his* choice? Could Joshua have chosen something other than life over death? The proclamation with which he ended his speech and summoned the people to make their own decision (24:15) should appear now pompous and pathetic, for the leader was no freer to choose his sovereign than the rest of the people. Yet the whole scene—for Joshua and the people—was set up as if the real decision was being made then and there, in Shechem, upon the completion of the colonization project: "choose *today* whom you would serve . . . but I and my household will serve Yahweh" (24:15). The people did not fall into this trap and refused the invitation to perform their choice as if it had to be made at that moment. Instead, they admitted their subjection as given and related to their fate as always at the mercy of Yahweh: "Far be it from us to forsake Yahweh to serve other gods" (24:16). They were what James Martel calls "mis-interpellated subjects," responding to Joshua's interpellation in a way they were not expected to.[101] Yes, they were God's subjects, and no, they had no real choice, and this was not the moment in which the pact between God and them was inaugurated. The justification they proposed for the affirmative response (24:17–18) sounds hollow not only because it echoed and abbreviated Joshua's historical overview of the Israelites (24:2–13) but because it was superfluous. When Joshua retorted with "you cannot serve Yahweh," the simulation of a choice—hence of a new beginning—should have become obvious. They were his subjects and were thus never free to enter or leave the pact (24:25) offered to them. Joshua and the people talked past each other, revealing a *différend* that ran between the two genres of discourse: the inaugural discourse of Joshua (a discourse of origin that sought to establish the covenant and the commitment it entailed as a constitutive moment) and the antioriginary discourse of the people that saw in the ceremony a reiteration of a commitment together with the relation of subjection that had always been in place.

Where Deuteronomy presents a pact with an indefinite number of entry points and no moment of presence to which it was fixed, thereby capable of recruiting any new reader or listener, the people's response to Joshua reveals the true impasse of subjection to divine rule. Since the beginning of their recorded memory, the power that ruled the people had always hovered above, behind, and ahead of them, always present as always already there, with no line of flight available. The juxtaposition between the leader's rhetoric and that of the people is no less revealing: While Joshua reveled in a freedom he never had (short of choosing death), the people conceded and accepted their submission. And while Joshua set up a display of mutual relations between two parties, the people reiterated their unconditional submission—"Yahweh we will serve and His voice we will heed" (24:24)—echoing the people's unconditional acceptance of God's rule in the Sinai revelation: "Everything that Yahweh has spoken we shall do"

(Ex. 19:8). Joshua's threats and the contrast between his professed choice and theirs preclude this text from functioning simply as another iteration of either covenantal ceremony (in Sinai or the steppes of Moab).

Furthermore, in presenting God to Israel, Joshua inverted the common formula for recording the sins of Israel's and Judea's kings: "doing evil in the eyes of Yahweh." According to Joshua, serving Yahweh could be *evil in the eyes of the Israelites* (24:15). This evil was outweighed, however, by the evil things God himself would do to the people (*heir'a lakhem*) if they abandoned him and served other gods (24:20). The evil connoted in the first threat of "*ra*" is easily overtaken by the harm connoted in the second. In both cases, evil was not a sin that yielded punishment but was the punishment itself, which would come about from serving God (24:15) or not (24:20). Joshua provoked the people by insinuating that for them serving God could be considered evil, a claim they readily dismissed. Evil done by God, however, is a loaded expression, especially when placed, as it is in verse 20, between "turn back" (*shav*, which may mean here simply "turn and repeat")[102] and "put an end to you" (*khillah ethkhem*). Joshua's last interjection (24:19–20) betrays what his long opening speech sought to cover. For it is hard to imagine that the author of Joshua 24 was entirely ignorant of the stories of catastrophic harm that the people had experienced since they had left Egypt or of the many threats to annihilate them. Those threats and violence, which pop up here like a slip of the tongue, contradicted Joshua's idyllic account of the people's past and thus supports our interpretation. The people never seriously entertained the option given to them by Joshua. Their response should be associated with a deeply entrenched—and superficially denied—fear of the recurrence of divine violence, which was the real thing that had always interpellated them.

Whether conscious or not, Joshua 24 reflects a deep understanding of how a people came to be under the yoke of a divine ruling power. They found themselves thrown into a world in which God was always *their* god, and they his subjects. Their commitment to serve him was a response to an existential impasse. In the world imagined by the text, there was no way out of worshiping God that did not involve private and collective death. By performing their choice to serve him, they merely displayed an acceptance of a destiny long in place. This, not a threshold or a new beginning, is what the assembly in Shechem presented.

What does all this mean for our reconstruction of the Deuteronomist theocracy? The answer seems to depend on the chronological relationship between Joshua's final chapter and the various layers of Deuteronomy. If we follow the long tradition of modern Bible scholars from Wellhausen to von Rad, Noth, and many of their students who see Joshua 24 as an early source with strong roots in the northern kingdom (which still includes interventions of Deuteronomist or other redactors),[103] we should look for the way the Deuteronomic authors responded to Joshua's earlier, unorthodox version of the covenant. It is against this earlier version that one may read Deuteronomy 30:11–20, where the author vividly describes the choice Moses presented to the people. Here one finds the climax of the entire *mise en scène* of the people's interpellation into the covenant: "I set before you today life and good, and death and evil" (Deut. 30:15). Here, the choice seems real, for otherwise how could one explain the repetition of the two options and Moses's imploration that "you shall choose life so that *you may* live" (Deut. 30:19)? When every invocation of divine violence was distanced to a remote past or indefinite future, when God was absent from the scene and no immediate threat was visible, the choice could seem real indeed. But if every interpellation is basically a scene of call and response, the Deuteronomist never provided his readers with the people's response. The performance of a real choice, which was made available to all future generations, describes the interpellation without ever passing from the one who calls to the one who was supposed to respond. The text left it to later listeners and readers to complete the response. It is they who are actually interpellated by the incomplete interpellation on the plains of Moab.

One may now note that throughout Deuteronomy we have not heard much from the people. A few moments of frustration, mistrust, and dissidence were bracketed as old memories, explaining the reason for the long journey that had now come to its end. Throughout the covenant ceremony on the steppes of Moab, they were addressees who never assumed any agency. Standing at the threshold of the covenant, they are positioned as not yet subjects of divine power, as if they had not been his subjects all those years in the wilderness and as if he would not be their God if they had chosen to reject Moses's imploration. Their response could not have been registered without contradicting the fact that they had been subjected to divine rule at least since they had left Egypt. The insistence on the long history of their subjection—the core of the people's response to Joshua in the book's last chapter—is exactly what could not be said in Deuteronomy 30. This is, in a nutshell, modern state ideology at its best. The state wants its subjects to be always already subjected *but feel free* at the same time, choosing the state into which they had been born and for which they might sacrifice their lives.

A dissenting voice preserved in Joshua 24 helps us see the Deuteronomist theocracy not only as an attempt to create a space and a time devoid of divine violence but also grasp this space as construed through a familiar move: dehistoricization and naturalization of submission to a power that claims to transcend any of its concrete, earthly incarnations and the relentless effort to turn this submission into a transcendental condition by closing off the horizons of imagination to anything that might escape its grip. The relation to anything beyond the jurisdiction of this ruling power becomes almost unimaginable.

Over the last two decades, the scholarly views regarding the provenance of Joshua 24 have shifted. New methods and a better integration of archaeological findings led some scholars to argue, quite convincingly, that the chapter is a late, postexilic, and perhaps even post-Deuteronomist text.[104] If that is true, does that make this whole effort to deconstruct the "choice" obsolete? Since this reading was not determined by the text's dating, we may try to invert the relationship. For this, we need not detract from anything covered thus far. It was the very juxtaposition of Joshua 24 and Deuteronomy 30 that made us understand the incomplete interpellation in Deuteronomy and the subversive nature of Joshua 24. If the latter is indeed a late text, for which Deuteronomy (as a whole, and especially chapters 27–30) was available, this orphan text could be construed as an ironic, sarcastic critique of Deuteronomy's covenantal ideology. By playfully amplifying that moment of choice, splitting it between the people and their leader and giving the people a voice, this text rehistoricizes the people's relationship to God, thus making it impossible to proclaim with the Deuteronomist authors: "*This day* you have become a people to Yahweh, your God" (Deut. 27:9). And once the subversive nature of Joshua's last chapter is grasped, could there be a better introduction to the theocratic anarchy and the recurrent falls into idolatry depicted in the book of Judges?

A MIDIANITE UTOPIA

The biblical corpus, a strictly guarded collection of canonized books, is known for its resistance to closure. No text is truly closed, of course, but many pretend they are or try seriously to achieve closure. Deuteronomy is a perfect example of the latter, as it performs its own closure from its opening verse. This concern for closure is closely related to its view of divine rule, which, as we saw, depended on the notion that all time, all possible evils, and the inability to imagine otherwise were part of a closed system projected backward and forward simultaneously. But Deuteronomy was just one book among many. And by incorporating the voices that challenged its theocracy,[105] the editors of the Pentateuch and of the Hebrew Bible more generally left these challenges intact. The challenges remained outside "this book" but can be read alongside it.

Joshua 24 presents one such challenge. But an even more radical challenge was preserved in another orphan text, whose subversive story was tamed by the Deuteronomist redactor that incorporated its revised version. It appears as one of the first recollections told in Deuteronomy's first chapter (1:9–18). This is the story of the legal reform proposed to Moses by Jethro in Exodus 18, to which we turn now. In Exodus, the story of Jethro interrupts the sequence of events that came before it (Ex. 15–17) and upsets or suspends the buildup for the drama of revelation that follows it (Ex. 19). The peaceful scene described there took place in the wilderness near the "Mount of God" (5).[106] God did not take part in it, and Moses, who shared the stage with his father-in-law, who appeared as a visitor, mostly listened to him and did not say much. This visitor, a "priest of Midian" (1), brought back to Moses his wife and two sons, whom he had left in Midian upon his return to Egypt. Jethro learned from Moses about what had happened since and blessed the Israelites' saving God. The next morning, after watching Moses as he was judging the people, Jethro proposed a theocratic model that would keep the realm of human affairs under divine law without recourse to divine violence.[107] Here one finds the Pentateuch's most secularized theocracy, a model of divine rule devoid of the physical *force* of law, performed through an elaborate hierarchical system and practice of judgment in which the people and their divine sovereign collaborated.

Jethro was an attentive visitor to the Israelites' camp. Impressed by Moses's judicial practice, as he was sitting alone "to judge the people . . . from morning to evening" (13), Jethro was worried that Moses had taken upon himself an impossible task (18). He proposed to decentralize the judicial process without undermining either God's or Moses's position within it. His model also kept in place the relationship between judgment, the practice of justice, and the teaching of the law set by Moses. When the people approached Moses to "inquire of God," they asked him a question about a specific, probably disputed matter (*davar*), and he "judge[d] between a man and his fellow; and [he] ma[de] known God's statutes and His teachings" (16). The law was made known casuistically each time a disputed case was brought before Moses and according to the way it was resolved. It was this burden of settling everyday conflicts that Moses would now share with others, according to Jethro's proposal. In addition to this division of labor, Jethro advised Moses to warn the people about "the statutes and the teachings" and to "make known to them the way in which they must walk"

(20). A general acquaintance with the law would be equally distributed, independent of the law induced from particular cases. The proclamation of the law was not meant to replace the casuistic acquaintance with the law but to widely distribute the labor of justice.

God's absence and the delegation of his authority to Moses were taken for granted and never problematized in Jethro's reform. Assuming both, Jethro's proposed division of labor was distributed among a relatively large group of "valiant,"[108] "God-fearing men, men of truth, haters of bribes" (21), within a well-defined, branched, and hierarchical legal system, with God and Moses at its top. Moses would attend only to the "great matters," while a force of "chiefs of thousands, chiefs of hundreds, chiefs of fifties, and chiefs of tens" (21) would carry out the "small matter[s]" of human affairs (22). The hierarchal structure resembled a martial order, but what lies at stake is the use of judgment, not of force. The knowledge of the law seems to be equally distributed (16, 20), but fear and a sense of justice were not (21), and the hierarchy of the judicial system was built on this innate inequality. Jethro appears to have believed and Moses to have accepted that the only problem in the translation of the general statutes and teachings into judgments in particular cases was finding enough capable, virtuous judges. No further knowledge was required. Hence, it is assumed, a careful selection of a wide cadre of judges would allow Moses to rationalize the system in which he had been, up to now, the sole arbiter in human affairs. In this conception of the rule of law, just laws given by God and proclaimed (once? every so often? it is not clear) by Moses were presupposed as a background, while the procedure of adjudication—and hence of ruling—was foregrounded. For this conception, it would not really matter whether there was a public revelation in which the laws were given to the people or if everything was communicated to Moses in private. At stake was the practice of the law, not its origin or institution.

The law was attributed to God, we may assume. But contrary to Josephus's insistence on Moses's role in attributing the laws to God,[109] the attribution here is silent and contextual, implied only by *Jethro*'s recognition of God's saving deeds in Egypt and the cadre of "god-fearing" judges Moses is advised to assemble. We may cautiously infer from the text's silence that Jethro did not think Moses required further spectacles or rituals of separation (in addition to the ones performed in Egypt and on the way out of it) to establish and sustain the proposed theocratic rule or that any threats, oaths, or further simulations of entering the covenant performed either at Moab or Shechem were necessary. The administration of justice Jethro proposed did not need additional admonitions or threats; it simply needed to be more efficient. This system would be based on a rational division of tasks among its trusted members, offering them a certain level of legal literacy and limited, variegated authority. The warning about "the statutes and the teachings . . . and the way in which they must walk" (20) did not specify any punishment in case of violation. Teaching the law was a necessary component of the (divine) rule of law but not a sufficient condition for its success. In order to be implemented, justice required a proper distribution of the authority to judge and at least a hint of force ("valiant men").

Jethro's proposed rule of law made both law and justice accessible to the people—without necessarily involving a supreme judge or even mentioning violent enforcement. This availability is the most important feature of the new judicial administration. Once the reform was implemented, the narrator tells us, the chiefs "judged the people at all times" (26). It was the law and its practice—not God—that become virtually omnipresent. The dispersions and distribution of the chiefs depended on a population's density, but it was not territorialized. The system of justice was mobile and could be located anywhere in the wilderness, regardless of the trajectory or goal of the journey—after all, Jethro was a nomad, and his theocratic model was diasporic avant la lettre. At the same time, the decentralization of power and the delegation of legal—and hence political—authority to a relatively large group of people formed an expanded political administration. Since its lower rank was that of "chiefs of tens" (21), this administration, taken "from all Israel" (25), would have been fairly disseminated across the entire population and never too remote from the people it ruled. At the same time, a large elite of God-fearing people would not harm Moses's authority or infringe on the conception of God as the supreme ruler. Besides the labor of justice, the administration's main function was to sift through the more challenging cases and bring them to a higher authority, until reaching God (through Moses). This mechanism guaranteed the stability and durability of the system by assisting Moses, but it also kept God's involvement in the rule of (his) law limited to fewer adjudications and always distant from the realm of enforcement.[110] At each level of authority, judgment required a return to a preexisting law, but at each level a revised understanding of the law in light of the particular case was possible. Hence, Moses stood between the law/God and anyone subjected to its/his rule: "Be you for the people over against God, and it shall be you who will bring the matters (*dvarim*) to God" (19).

After Moses followed Jethro's advice and appointed the trustworthy chiefs, his role was described slightly differently. Now, Moses would be the one to whom the chiefs brought "the hard matters [*ha-davar bakashe*]" (26). These are probably the cases he was supposed to bring to God according to v. 19. Moses was therefore a vehicle for delivering hard legal cases to God, but he no longer partook in the making of legal decisions. At the same time, at the top of the legal hierarchy God attended to the adjudication of the difficult cases and was necessarily also limited by Moses's mediation. The application of the law was invoked from the bottom up, not enforced from the top down. It was a judicial system that served the entire population, not the few who practiced and enforced the law. Even before Jethro offered his advice, this was how Moses presented it in a verse previously quoted (16), carefully noting the temporal sequence: (1) "When they have a matter," (2) "it comes to me," (3) "and I judge between a man and his fellow." The reform Jethro proposed ameliorated an existing judicial system. No one was reminded of its violent origin or of the force needed to sustain it. Neither did anyone deny these aspects of the law. The law was a given, its origin was neither asserted nor questioned, and its authority was taken for granted. The question was how to apply it.

The transparency of this system is quite striking. God's words were accessible to Moses while law and justice were available to the people. God's place at the top of the legal hierarchy was expressed in terms of the difficulty of the cases and had no meaning outside the scale of the matters to be adjudicated. Jethro understood God's role bureaucratically; for the Midianite guest, *Elohim*—this is how he is called throughout the section of the chapter dedicated to the reform—was part of the system, and no mystery was associated with his authority. Jethro was a priest, and he recognized God's authority by placing him at the top of the judicial ladder.[111] But he was also careful to keep God at a distance: Moses should "be for the people over against [*mool*, facing] God" (19), and God should be at the heart and mind of the elected god-fearing chiefs (21). God's might together with his threatening/saving proximity were bracketed between the God-fearing, valiant chiefs and Moses's mediation. His active participation in the world of human affairs was reduced to some responses to Moses's legal queries, transmitted in the privacy of their encounters and made public by Moses.

Hence the division of the political-judicial labor was accompanied by a certain separation of powers, at least as far as the practice of the law was concerned. Justice was performed according to the law by a large judicial system; Moses, who appointed the judges, stood (alone) at the top of the executive branch of power (and perhaps also partaking—this point is not clear—in the performance of justice), merely responding as a reactive force to what the people brought before him; and God was left to preside over the legislative branch and, when asked to do so by Moses, to interpret the laws. He too was a reactive force that no longer initiated anything: His reactions were supposedly harnessed by the law, yet no force was exercised. The authority that established the law remained largely external to its application. This may explain the fact that God was not mentioned again when Moses's application of Jethro's advice was briefly described (24–26).

Jethro did not bother to explain or inquire about the communication between Moses and God. As the priest of Midian, he probably knew something about how this worked and took for granted that Moses knew this as well.[112] The crucial point was general recognition of Moses as the supreme and only *human* leader granted with the power and authority to handle such communication. This was Moses's unquestionable position, which Jethro witnessed at work (13) and on which he built his reform. Note, however, that the Midianite priest did not mention the thick cloud, the thunder and lightning, the angel, or any of the other pyrotechnics accompanying God's epiphany at Sinai or Horeb in pre-priestly, priestly, and Deuteronomic writings. The trust (which the next chapter promised and failed to achieve [19:9]) was already there, and the reform assumed that it could be sustained through justice handed to trustworthy people. Jethro emphasized Israel's redemption but mentioned neither Egypt's destruction nor the goal of the journey through the wilderness, that is, the conquest of Canaan.[113] The spectacle of revelation and the rhetoric of violence were replaced by bureaucratic considerations regarding the practice of judgment that were performed by the most trustworthy among the people, who were equipped with a fair knowledge of the rules and an understanding of the judicial process. The legitimacy of this judicial bureaucracy was beyond doubt, it spread far and wide, and it significantly limited God's personal role and responsibility, not only Moses's. In other words, Jethro's modest reform meant a radical break from each of the three theocratic models we have encountered. Without abandoning God's laws or justice, the text offers a withdrawal of his ruling power.

There is a distinctly utopian flavor to this theocracy. A relative, who was also a stranger,[114] a wise and respectful man experienced in public affairs, coming from afar, observed, took notes, and offered some improvements. But what this man saw was already quite extraordinary. In the wilderness, near the Mount of God, a utopic scene was already taking place. Moses, alone, was occupied from morning to evening in his judicial work, proclaiming God's laws and teaching on a case-by-case basis, with the people surrounding him waiting for their turn to present their case (13–15). When such trust in Moses's judgment and acceptance of God's law were in place, along with the patience required from those waiting for justice (which had never been tested), Jethro's proposal did not seem naïve but astute. But utopias, more than any piece of realpolitik, are basically logical constructions. What would ensure that the people would continuously trust the judicial authorities? How are decisions to be forced on those who lose their litigation? Where is the stick that accompanies the law and keeps the numerous functionaries in the positions assigned to them? What is its source of deterrence and enforcement?

We can only speculate. Perhaps the answer lies in the first title of the judges—*anshei ḥayil*, which should be read here as "warriors" or "valiant men ready to fight"—as fitting the military structure of the juridical administration itself (21).[115] Reading the verse with this prevalent meaning of *ḥayil* in mind, we may argue that the practice of the law was not split between judgment and application, deciding a disputed case and enforcing the decision. The separation of powers Jethro had in mind was rather between multiple tribunals authorized to practice the law. For the most part, the practice of the law was distributed among humans. God was called upon to interpret the hardest cases but was not involved in law enforcement. The law, which was already a given, was lived—and, it is safe to assume, would change—in the judicial process, through its casuistic interpretation and application. If the numerous judges, who were both virtuous and valiant, enforced the law as they interpreted it, the force of law could go hand in hand with the prescribed law, creating a relatively smooth and continuous time and space where God's catastrophic reactions to severe transgression would become superfluous.[116]

The law itself, as a complete system that covered all cases, was not known even to Moses, and this was precisely what kept God in the picture. As far as the people were concerned, it was the law, not God, that revealed itself and, even then, only when it was called upon. For as Moses explained, God's laws were made known to the people following a judgment in a disputed matter (16). A plaintiff—not God, Moses, or any of the chiefs—called upon the law to appear when an unsettled dispute "between a man and his fellow" was brought before the judge. The immensity of the task of judgment lay not only in the understanding of the case in light of the law but also in the courage and wisdom of reinterpreting the law in light of a new case. This was at least one aspect of the valiance ascribed to each of the chiefs, and this responsibility would scale up or down according to one's position in the hierarchy. The higher one went, the greater the chances for a case where judgment could not be simply derived from the general rule. At the top of the ladder there may have been no rules at all, only a decision that perfectly fit the singularity of the case. Yahweh, at this point, may be nothing but a name for the way that the singularity of the case was articulated in Moses's judgment.

"And Moses heeded the voice of his father-in-law and did all that he had said" (24). God was not consulted and did not intervene while the theocratic system, including his own role in it, was reshaped. If taken seriously and read according to the canonic order of the chapters, the theocratic utopia that preceded the Sinai revelation and covenant made these redundant. If read logically, it must be understood as describing a later event—the law was already at work—that transformed the relationship between the law and violence implied at Sinai. This is how many rabbinic commentators read it, placing the story of Jethro after that of the revelation, but they mostly ignored the radical transformation it encapsulates.[117] What helps them bypass this mind-boggling utopia was the way it was incorporated into Deuteronomy's first chapter (1:9–18). They accepted the logic of the parallel story and projected it onto the pre-priestly (Elohist?) version in Exodus: The revelation in Horeb had already taken place (Deut. 1:6), God was involved in leading the people through the wilderness (Deut. 1:6–7), Jethro was never mentioned, and Moses was the one who initiated the judicial reform,[118] which the people readily accepted. Moses's fatigue had a reason not mentioned in Exodus—God "multiplied [the people] like the stars of the heavens," and the blessing made Moses's task impossible to carry out alone (Deut. 1:10–11). It was Moses's idea to share the burden with the "wise, intelligent men, renowned within their tribes" (Deut. 1:14–15),[119] and he proposed it to the people, not to God. In Deuteronomy, the selection of the judges was less meritocratic than in Exodus 18 and took into account tribal representation and perhaps even popularity (the judges were "renowned"), and Moses let the people select their chiefs (1:13).[120] The quasi-military structure of the judicial system was maintained, but the chieftains were commanded—not trusted—to "recognize no face in judgment [and to] hear out the small person like the great one. You shall have no terror of any man, for the judgment is God's" (Deut. 1:17).

A shadow of human violence hovered above the site of judgment in the Deuteronomic version, while God appeared not only as the authority at the top of the hierarchy but as the one who had monopoly over judgment. If "judgment is God's," the able chieftains were clerks who officiated justice but did not partake in generating it through their interpretation of the law. The entire episode is woven into the narrative reconstructing the journey in the wilderness, where God is described as a guide who promises and punishes, separates and sanctifies, and the memory of his magnificent revelation and amazing presence in Horeb is vividly recalled. With God very much in the picture and the judicial reform framed between the revelation at Horeb and the expedition of the scouts, the Deuteronomist version appears as nothing more than a practical reorganization.

As Jethro and his nation leave no trace here, the readers are relieved of the embarrassing meddling of a foreign priest in the life of the holy people.

Deuteronomy's position is consistent: Jethro is redundant.[121] The Deuteronomic version of the legal reform is an internal affair that does not undermine the temporality of divine violence and its dissociation from sanctioned human violence, which supplemented it. The law could not be imagined as functioning without the set of divine threats attached to it. Even when it focused on specific cases "between a man and his brother or his sojourner" (Deut. 1:17),[122] the reform was part of the effort to ensure a way of life that would restrain divine violence. The utopian flavor of the Midianite reform was lost. The Deuteronomist's aggressive redaction of the pre-priestly story of Jethro only highlights the daring decision of the (postexilic?) editors of Exodus not only to include it but also to place it between the war against the Amalekites (Ex. 17:8–16) and the revelation at Sinai (Ex. 17:19). Recognizing Yahweh's great deeds and supremacy, Jethro tried to help Moses create a system of rule in which God's teachings were fully internalized by many, and, for all practical purposes, God's actual presence was not much more than an extension of Moses's leadership, granting a kind of halo to a mortal man. The point, however, was not to exalt Moses but to make God's laws accessible to the masses without overwhelming them with memories or expectations of his ominous epiphanies. Exodus 18 turns theocracy into a rule of law, in which the law was thoroughly invested and disseminated among the multitude of God's subjects—a utopia Deuteronomy could not digest.

A hint that the redactor of Exodus was not oblivious to the radical challenge presented by its eighteenth chapter may be found in the abrupt way Jethro disappears, banished from the story at the chapter's last verse, right before the big event at Sinai. The text reads, "And Moses sent off his father-in-law, and he went away to his land" (Ex. 18:27). A clear line had to be drawn between the Midianite vision of practicing the law and the solemn act of inaugurating it. Jethro, who was not deemed fit to receive the Torah, could not stay in the company of the Israelites after they received it, not even if watching from a distance. He had to be sent back to his land, leaving Moses to implement his utopia and the biblical redactors to neutralize its transformative potential.[123]

And yet, Jethro was not altogether eliminated from the canon. The Bible left the door open for a human system of justice, which, as bureaucratic and hierarchized as it was meant to be, rested on multitudes of trustworthy people who could materialize the rule of law without losing its divine compass and without recourse to divine violence. It was a system in which even a charismatic judge and prophet like Moses could not do without the legal literacy and trustworthiness of the many and in which divine rule could not do without the wisdom and generosity of a stranger. This theocracy was thus a threefold system, composed of (1) a deterritorialized, upright cohort of people who practiced judgment according to the law; (2) God's rule of law, free from divine violence whose interpretation and enforcement were entrusted to humans; and (3) a judicial practice gifted by a passing stranger.

Some elements of Jethro's reform were preserved and radicalized in the early rabbinic adaptation of the Pentateuch's legal codes. For the early rabbis, the practice of the law was a human project devoid of hierarchy, based on casuistic, creative interpretation of the law in ever-new contexts and circumstances. Like Jethro's judges, they were virtuous men (or at least this is how they were usually described) who directed their valiancy from warfare to lawfare and used the law as the medium for their colonial enterprise—for soon Tannaitic law would colonize every domain of life of the Jews who lived under it. They cultivated an ideal of impartial judgment subject only to the law and a trust in the divine origin of the law along with a deep mistrust for anyone who claimed to incarnate it. If Jethro blurred—or did not know—the distinction between interpreting the law and judging on a particular case, they incorporated the particular cases into their creative interpretative practices and implemented their judgment not through enforcing the law but through teaching it.[124] If violence was involved in their juridical and hermeneutic practices, it was mainly because it was embedded in the way the study of the law was practiced (men only, from a very young age, etc.), and everyday life was saturated with it. Without commanding authority and physical force to enforce the law outside their familial practices and communal domains, power was radically decentered and disseminated. Nothing of what the three theocratic formations the Pentateuch could offer made any sense in their diasporic condition. The theopolitical thought invested in those formations dissolved in the sea of rabbinic biblical commentaries like salt in water. The elements of an embryonic state formation that this thought contained were abandoned, if not consciously rejected—and lost.

In the Christian adaptation of the Hebrew Bible, these elements were remnants of old, now obsolete forms of relation between humans and God. But the cunning of history is mysterious and full of surprises. Fourteen or fifteen centuries later, the three Pentateuchal theocratic formations were resurrected and molded into the formation of the modern state.

AFTERWORD: THE PENTATEUCHAL STATE, AND OURS

THE SHARED ELEMENT

I have argued that the theocratic formation, that is, a regime based on divine rule, is the proper context for making sense of divine violence in the Hebrew Bible. I have identified three such formations—one that had to be reconstructed from scattered pre-priestly passages and two more fully elaborated and more clearly articulated in priestly writings and the book of Deuteronomy. The three may be given now their proper names: a protopolitical rule of disaster, the rule of the holy, and the rule of law. The unbounded, unruly, and destructive aspects of God's sovereignty appear most clearly when God's rule is imagined and conceived as the rule of disaster; when divine rule becomes the rule of the holy, it assumes the nature of a governmental apparatus that captures life without abandoning the living; and under the rule of law, the people's introduction into the law appears, more than anywhere else in the Bible, as an ideological state apparatus, a mechanism of interpellations that operates the gentlest mode of divine rule—a mode that is supposed to last as long as the people's timid obedience postpones the eruption of divine violence.

As they appear in the Pentateuch, the three formations seem distinct and incommensurable. Beyond their differences, however, the three theocracies share a vision of power and authority attributed to a mostly but not entirely invisible entity. Proper attributions of power and authority to that entity were at stake in many of the documents, in all three theopolitical traditions. Although they envisioned various and quite distinct techniques for performing those attributions and envisaging that power, they shared some of the attributes of the envisioned entity. It was a personified entity,[1] and the one sovereign figure that seemingly embodied the entire ruling formation was ascribed with all its attributes. All the powers seemed to emanate from him, all the authority was granted by him, and most of the commandments and injunctions were issued by him. His was a holistic, self-constituted formation that rested on nothing but itself and was capable of reaching out to each and every one of the subjects under its rule, and to all of them together, harming or protecting, destroying or saving one and all, and, needless to say, doing all this with absolute impunity. And yet, at the same time, the sovereign person embodying that power, however described, was obsessively concerned with an insatiable desire for legitimation and recognition.[2] Like any other ruling power, he needed its ruled subjects and desperately wanted their voluntary servitude.

They seemed well aware of this. He was their creator and was radically different from them, but they knew well that he ruled them not as subservient extensions of his being but rather as unruly subjects. When they did not rebel they sought his favors, sang his praises, killed in his name, and sacrificed their lives for it. Often, lacking the hindsight of later protagonists or narrators who attributed reason to his actions, they could remain ignorant of *why* he had intervened in their lives, harming or protecting them, and sometimes altering the very conditions of their existence as his subjects. The few humans he selected to help him rule were often late to explain this or failed to do so altogether. These mediators, to whom certain authority was delegated, were responsible for some of the ruling, and there was a certain distribution of power between them and the sovereign figure. They coped with real problems of dissidence and unrest, but they could hardly ever solve them on their own. With or without his delegates his rule was neither stable nor peaceful. To be imagined, the Pentateuchal theocracies needed semiutopic conditions—the nonplace of the desert, a space and time empty of human institutions that he had not authorized—but unlike some of the prophets (notably Hosea 2:16–22; Jeremiah 2:2), Pentateuchal authors never imagined the nonplace as a good place. Their narratives, laws, and, above all, the editing of these into a distinct corpus of writing betray an interest in the working of a real system of rule, taking into account the nature, tendencies, and known patterns of behavior of both ruler and the ruled, coping with the expected pitfalls and risks, tasks, and goals of divine dominion.

God and his subjects were separated by an unbridgeable hiatus and knew that their relations of power could never be inverted, and they always related to his figure and person as embodying all the power that ruled them. And yet they were part of—and a party to—a distinct formation of power in which he was the ruler and they the ruled. And precisely in this sense they shared with him, and he with them, a formation of power that *he could not exhaust*. The priestly authors had a glimpse of this shared element when addressing holiness; the realm of the holy functioned as a shared medium whose logic preceded the sovereign's wishes and will and constrained his acts. The Deuteronomists suggested something similar through the idea of "this book of teaching" (*Sefer ha-Torah ha-ze*). Both parties shared it, Yahweh was Israel's sovereign only as long as he too, due to his promises, was constrained by it, and they were made his people only once they entered the covenant and accepted his laws. The pre-priestly authors had a dimmer grasp of that third, shared element. They understood it as a kind of a staged event rather than an institution (the book of teaching) or a dimension of the real (holiness), an event that took place when his epiphany took a public, catastrophic form. The catastrophe was a temporary stage that the ruling power shared with the people he ruled, who were often at one and the same time those who bore the blows of his epiphany and its ultimate witnesses. As victims they became part of the stuff to be remembered: the rebellions, the failed expectations, the spectacular blows, the irredeemable losses; as witnesses they were survivors obliged to keep and transmit the memory of the moment and the gratefulness for being spared. But the pre-priestly authors could not—or did not want to—envisage that shared space beyond the moments of its recurring, violent inaugurations.

Being fully aware that the subjects could give—or not give—recognition, the Pentateuchal authors understood that power was shared, however unequally, and not merely imposed, hence contrary to first impressions, his person and figure as a sovereign never exhausted the formation of power it embodied. He may have been the agent and the self of the self-constituting act; he had inaugurated that formation, having created and shaped it all by himself. But once constituted, he was taking part in the formation of divine rule together with others—those who were its subjects—and in relation to those who were excluded from taking part in it, that is, all other nations. Embodying it more than any other, by far, he was never alone in being responsible for its well-being, limits and limitations, perseverance, internal conflicts and divisions, or status and image in the eyes of others not subjected to his rule. Pentateuchal theocracy was not simply a relation of domination and submission between God and his people; it was a configuration of power in which God and his people took part, being destined (though not always committed) to a third element they shared and from which all others were actively excluded.

THREE THEOCRACIES, ONE URFORM

Everything said so far is drawn from the documents, extracted and abstracted from the close readings presented in the last three chapters; much of it, however, is intentionally articulated from a perspective that, most probably, was not available to the authors of those documents and in a language that they might have found incomprehensible. In this the extraction of the logic of Pentateuchal theocracy is not different from similar reconstructions of other regimes, whether ancient or modern. A certain work of abstraction and conceptual analysis has been necessary for drawing the main lines of each formation and for delineating the more abstract formation, the urform they share. By calling it "urform" I do not mean to suggest an evolutionary model in which a primordial formation is differentiated, simultaneously or consecutively, into three distinct kinds. The point is merely to designate a clear area of overlap and to suggest the logical primacy of this shared form over the distinctive features of each of the three formations (e.g., the recourse to violence and its pattern or the spatialization of the holy, etc.). These distinctive features presuppose the configuration the three theocracies have in common: a self-constituted formation of power shared by both ruler and ruled, in which the ruler is in constant need of affirmation and recognition and the ruled all too often fall or refuse to grant them. The shared formation precedes and exceeds both ruler and ruled and cannot be reduced to either. This urform is the condition of possibility for the other, differentiating features. The juxtaposition of the three formations and the extraction of their shared urform follows the conceptual analysis that accompanied my reading from its outset.[3] If one is ready to accept it or even entertain it as a kind of thought experiment, the outcome is both striking and recognizable, and striking precisely because it is recognizable: The urform of the Pentateuchal theocracies highly resembles the basic matrix of the modern European state.

According to Foucault, the modern state came into being when the slow integration of apparatuses like big armies, centralized taxation, and a legal system under the authority of a single ruling power "began to enter into a reflected practice" and "to be projected, programmed, and developed within this conscious practice," thus becoming "an object of knowledge (*connaissance*) and analysis . . . part of a reflected and concerted strategy."[4] In other words, the state is not simply a collection of ruling apparatuses and governing technologies but the way these are integrated through a discourse that includes the production of knowledge about what needs to be governed and how and the projection of an image of unity, purpose, and rationality on the various practices of ruling and government.

> The state is what must exist at the end of the process of the rationalization of the art of government. What the intervention of *raison d'État* must arrive at is the state's integrity, its completion, consolidation, and its re-establishment if it has been compromised. . . . The state is therefore the principle of intelligibility of *what is*, but equally of *what must be*; one must understand what the state is in order to be more successful in making it exist in reality.[5]

The Pentateuch's authors and editors did not have armies or tax collectors at their command (one may guess that they could have some access to the practice of law and judgment, though). They could learn about these from their neighboring empires throughout the ages, Assyria and Egypt, Babylon and Persia, but they seem more interested in the treaties between the rulers of these empires and their subjects, and in the state-like presumptions of these rulers and their wish to be known as kings of the entire universe.[6]

But Yahweh was never simply a blown-up projection of a Mesopotamian king, and one of the main reasons for this was that his authority had to be repeatedly claimed and the submission of his subjects was always in question and could never be reduced to his superior might alone. When they reflected on the apparatuses of divine rule, the goal they had in mind was not that different from what Foucault proposed as key for the emergence of the modern state: to provide the principle of intelligibility for grasping how one is ruled, governed, and more generally affected by a single, integrative ruling formation. The formation the biblical authors were thinking about could affect and transform any aspect of life of any ruled subject and could not be reduced to (or embodied in) the figure of a living monarch or of any other visible agent of power. At the same time, within the same discursive effort, they were occupied with understanding and articulating how this integrative formation should be maintained and reproduced in its full governing capacities and imaginary oneness.

This intangible oneness, and its importance as a mark of the novelty of the state as a form of rule, was articulated in a different way in the work of Quentin Skinner.[7] The distinction between the oneness of power (royal or republican, dictatorial or constitutional) and the multitude of individuals who are subject to it (a people, a nation, a society, subjects, or citizens) and the right way to sustain this distinction and articulate this difference while stabilizing the relations between the ruler and the ruled have occupied Western political thought since its inception. According to Skinner, the modern state came into being when a third element was added to the dichotomy between rulers and ruled, an element that was conceived as what brings the two together, requires their differentiation, and stabilizes their hierarchy. The most basic, most general principle of the modern state is the appearance—and eventual naturalization—of that medium which the rulers and those subject to their rule share, by which both are encompassed, and which is neither an extension of nor reducible to either. Only when it appears like this—independent of and logically prior to the two poles it brings together, the contribution of each to its very establishment, and the particular type of the ruling power and the people ruled by it—can the state be grasped independently of the various forms it may take, based on the nature of its prevailing regime (royal, republican, populist, tyrannical, and so on).

It might seem counterintuitive, if not utterly wrong, to ascribe this independence of a medium shared by the ruler and the ruled to the Pentateuchal theocracies discussed here. After all, It was God who chose his people, promised them their land, sent them to that no-man's land in the wilderness, appointed their rulers, established most of the institutions, and expected everyone to follow suit. Indeed, in biblical theocracies, even more strictly than in ancient monarchies, the multitude, the demos, or the nation is forced into a scheme of power relations whose space, time, and materiality emanate from the supreme power and depend on it. The inversion was unimaginable; the most radical acts of resistance and rebellion are always directed at Moses, not God. Pentateuchal theocracy could not have come to an end by the people taking over God's power; the only way it could have ended was by a radical separation, when God would withdraw and abandon his people, as the Deuteronomist authors were clearly able to imagine.[8] This separation meant the end of divine rule as the Pentateuchal authors imagined it. Moreover, it may seem utterly false to think about God as being "encompassed" by—and limited to—a formation of power he had created, even if in some sense he shared it with his human subjects.

But from a political perspective, the Pentateuch goes well beyond the unilateral relation between the ancient king and his people, and at the same time, theologically, its figure of God is radically different. The creation of Heaven and Earth and all forms of life had been absolutely spontaneous and unbounded, setting boundaries from a position that is entirely external to the bounded realms. But since his early visitations, this was no longer the case. No matter how destructive God's actions were, even in Genesis they were carried out from within an already established bond between God and humans, where God responded to human failures to live up to his expectations (the flood, Sodom and Gomorrah) and to the unpredictability of their actions (Babel). And in any case, except for the first nineteen chapters in Genesis, the Pentateuchal God was arrested in his relations with Israel and never appeared independently of them. The figure of God as a mighty sovereign and the reception of this figure in postbiblical antiquity tend to overshadow this fact, but when these are bracketed or pushed to the background and the urform is grasped, it becomes clear that for much of the Pentateuch, the theocratic formation is not a projection of the divine figure of the sovereign but the other way around: The establishment of God's sovereignty is a textual matter, an affair of the political imagination, and as such inseparable from the theocratic formation of which it is but one element. In Pentateuchal theocracy as much as in the modern European state, sovereignty was a peculiar embodiment and specific articulation of the power formation, not its progenitor. Even if he founded this formation, God's sovereignty came into being as one of its effects and did not exist outside it, while the foundation narratives were integral to its ideology and had little meaning outside their ideological function.

There is more. The Pentateuchal theocratic models offer more than the urform of the modern European state. They offer three distinct, clear-cut configurations that came into being in the course of its development, crystallization, and rise to unrivaled global hegemony as the supreme legitimate form of political power. The pre-priestly theocracy rested its rule on a politics of disaster, in which a sovereign capable of generating disasters and providing rescue was able to harness disasters and use them as means of governance. It offered an ancient blueprint for a matrix of rule stretched between mass extinction and well-differentiated acts of salvation that has characterized the modern state since the end of the nineteenth century. The priestly theocracy, a mode of spatializing power and governing bodies, offered a blueprint of the modern state's biopolitical apparatus that reaches out to each and every member of the people under their rule, colonizing their entire lifeworlds. The Deuteronomist theocracy presented an ancient sophisticated equivalent to an ideological state apparatus; it based itself on the rule of law and promised a lull in divine violence as long as the rule of law was upheld. The Deuteronomist shaped an early version of the position of an obedient, ever-indebted, ever-suspected subject who would always be willing to serve, always fearing the shortness of his or her response, and forever living under the lingering threat of the multiple forms of violence stored in and suspended by this theocratic formation.

What the modern state enabled but the ancient theocracies were incapable of imagining was a formation of power that could steadily grow, differentiate itself into multiple subformations, and keep integrating ever-new modes of rule and governing. Ever since the sixteenth century in Europe and its colonies, this integration followed in the wake of an image of all-encompassing power, which in principle could extend its rule indefinitely and make everything—bodies, relations, things, texts, techniques, practices, etc.—governable. The three theocratic models recognized this image well but could only articulate separately each of its known modalities, each according to its own logic of rule and governing. Neither the Pentateuch's late editors nor later biblical authors who could read the Five Books as a single literary unit ever made an attempt to imagine dynamic, integrative relations among the three theocracies; in fact, they were careful to keep them apart.[9]

NOT A GENEALOGY:
ISOMORPHISM AND UNEXPECTED REITERATIONS

Several blueprints of the modern European state are found in ancient Hebrew writings. They certainly echo elements from ancient Near Eastern empires but also demonstrate a consistent attempt to think beyond and against these. God was not a mortal living in a palace, and his kingdom offered more than submission, a certain protection from the elements of nature, glorious victories over the king's enemies, and a share of the booty. Although throughout the Hebrew Bible Yahweh was often called a king, in the Pentateuch this happens only three times, in marginal relics of ancient poetry.[10] The Pentateuchal authors clearly tried to think his rulership along different lines. Divine rule offered a way to take part in something to which he too was committed, a shared project—becoming holy by sharing his holiness, becoming good subjects by interiorizing his laws, or, at least, in the dimmest blueprint, bearing witness to a memory of a spectacular salvation. And even when the ruler's words were delivered in direct speech, they could not have been heard or read without the subjects' active mediation.

None of these blueprints, however, is presented here as a moment in the genealogy of the modern European state. Even though the Hebrew Bible became a highly significant source for early modern European political thinkers, it was mainly for the rule of humans, not of God, and the gap between their realm and his was not bridged. In the eighteenth and nineteenth centuries, European and American authors who drew inspiration from the Bible and sought there their model for an ideal state, whether an enlightened monarchy or a functioning democracy, already presupposed the *raison d'état* of their time. It was not an early modern awakening, a new awareness of the Pentateuchal theocracies presented

here, that contributed to the discourse of the early modern state in Europe or
to the emergence of its governmental practices and institutions. If the Hebrew
Bible was involved, it was mainly through the mediation of Josephus Flavius and
his idyllic, Mosaic theocracy or the short-lived moment of unmediated divine
rule in Spinoza's *Tractate*.[11] Except for this very short moment in Spinoza, the
theopolitical thinking unearthed here and the various configurations of violence
with which this thinking was occupied have been mostly buried by the traditions
that transmitted the biblical texts. These traditions had to be removed in the
present reading like layers of dust and recent debris in an archaeological site.

There is probably no family tree, no trail of mutations, no chain of hidden
knots and stray lines leading from the Hebrew Bible to the Castilian nation-state
established in the Iberian Peninsula at the end of the fifteenth century[12] or to
Hobbes's *Leviathan* in the seventeenth century.[13] Even if there is, this book's
final argument does not depend on it. What has been discovered here is neither
a point of origin nor early moments of crystallization of ever-changing configurations in a genealogical tree that reach to the present. Rather, this book has
demonstrated that the urform of the modern state or at least a key aspect of it
had been thought and imagined by ancient Hebrew texts without ever being realized and that that form had been consolidated and later reiterated during several centuries of composition, compilation, and editing of the biblical texts and
then lost and forgotten, buried under layers of later readings of a canonical text
which millions knew by heart. This ancient form of theopolitical discourse and
imagination reemerged many centuries later, under very different conditions,
which made possible, perhaps even motivated, its translation into discursive and
governmental practices. It was a disguised form, however. In the ancient theocracy, God was depicted as the origin and telos of the theocratic formation, and
his figure tended to cover almost its entire scope, leaving, like in a solar eclipse,
only some margins where traces of that third element or the medium he shared
with his subjects could become visible and be carefully reconstructed, albeit
partly and briefly. The modern state form presents an inversion of this image.
It emerged when all the main features of divine rule were completely absorbed
within the state formation and only some margins of deification survived the
eclipse by the modern, secularized state apparatuses.

These margins, however, are undeniable and cannot be explained by the logic
of the secular state's apparatuses. They include:

(1) declaring the unity of the state and consecrating its oneness;

(2) proclaiming any threat to this oneness as the highest form of sacrilege—
treason;

(3) exercising violence with impunity;

(4) having the right of the last word in every conflict;

(5) delegating authority to multiple agents without that authority ever becoming the inalienable property of anyone to whom it is granted—in other words, being transcendent to any authority that claims to represent and work in its name;

(6) being capable of reaching out to, caring for, or harming every one of its subjects while determining the nature of their collectivity, counting it and accounting for it, narrating its past and projecting its future, setting its boundaries, and deciding who belongs to it and who is excluded, who is welcome and how;

(7) ascribing to itself self-constitution, sanctity, lawfulness, and, a few centuries later, the monopoly on administering disasters, that is, the distribution of extreme violence and scarcity along with the means of rescue and protection.

The sovereign who executed these functions, issued edicts and all kinds of injunctions to bring them into effect, declared exceptions, and proclaimed the last word in any dispute he sought to bring to an end was often ascribed with a divine right to rule, a rule he claimed to be absolute. But absolute monarchy did not halt the advance of the modern state; it merely helped disguise how divine rule was absorbed and diffused well beyond the figure of the king, across the entire governed space. Gradually the state took over almost everything that belonged to the king, shrinking his figure and role to nothing (in republics) or to that of the main actor in a symbolic, gradually redundant theater (in constitutional monarchies). As long as absolute monarchies lasted, the king, his figure and position, lent a perfect umbrella to the processes of centralizing the state's government, integrating distinct modes of rule and governmental techniques and, most importantly, creating that aura of transcendence with which the state—the idea, the image, and the phantasmatic construction—was endowed. That aura of transcendence precedes and exceeds any authority or agency that claims to represent it or act in its name, thus assuring the excess of the state formation over any of its actual embodiments.

The strange isomorphism that emerges here, the reiteration, however disguised, of the state's urform about two millennia after its blurry emergence in Pentateuchal texts, should not be conceived as another fundamental structure of the human that governs and explains overt phenomena (like the structure of the psyche, the form of production, or the structure of the savage mind). It is a discovery that cannot be used to explain anything; it rather needs to be explained, a coincidence of human history that owes its existence to contingent historical circumstances. The modern state did not emerge out of biblical thinking; the

Hebrew Bible did not project or herald it in any meaningful way. Most probably, there was no dialectical process that transformed the hidden form while
translating it from a figure of theopolitical imagination to a discursive construct
enabling the growth and development of governmental technologies and modes
of ruling, which was then further developed and naturalized by the effects of
this growth. But the effect of this strange isomorphism on the critical study of
the modern state may be quite significant. Pentateuchal theocracies are offered
here as a prism and inspiration for studying—and eventually deconstructing—the
deification of the modern state.

It might seem that I have come back full circle to my starting point only in
order to accept a "figurative interpretation" of divine violence, whose flat rejection was the launch pad for this project. It might seem that I have only displaced
the figural interpretation from the Bible's violent scenes, on the literal reading
of which I insisted, to the theopolitical formations within which divine violence
is supposed to make sense. These formations, one may argue, are precisely the
recurring figures that assume new manifestations of the same form, and this "notion of the new manifestation, the changing aspect, of the permanent," about
which Eric Auerbach writes in the opening of his seminal essay *Figura*, "runs
through the whole history of the word" and is presupposed by every figurative
interpretation.[14] Furthermore, the figurative reading of the Old Testament was
practiced by Christians since St. Paul and thematized at least since Tertullian foregrounded the temporal distance between the urform and its new manifestations;
this reading understood the former as a "prefiguration" of the latter, in which it
saw the "fulfillment" of the earlier figure.[15] Am I not concluding this project now
by claiming that the Pentateuchal theocracies prefigured the contemporary form
of the state, which is their true fulfillment?

Indeed, the urform of the state in the Pentateuch can be said to be a prefiguration of the modern state. But I would never add that the latter is a "fulfillment" of
the former, not even when the three ancient theocratic formations are shown to
be integrated in the form of the contemporary state. Prefiguration—the promise
for a recurrence of the form—was, from Tertullian onward, ingrained in escha-
tological, teleological temporality, which we have no reason to resurrect. We
have no more reason to expect an inversion of this temporality in the form of a
Nietzschean "eternal return of the same." Committed to the radical contingency
of historical time and the historicity of human institutions, language, discursive
formations, and concepts, we can only speculate about the conditions that, quite
rarely, let similar figures—discursive and imaginary formations, in our case—
resurface and take hold, far away and mostly independently from each other.

THE DEIFICATION OF THE STATE

The state is one. You should not have other states beside your one and only state. You should not try to divide the state or multiply it. The state might hide its face in times of disaster, economic crises, or climate catastrophes, but even when hidden you should never forget it.

Some think that the state *must* hide its face and call upon "the free market" to take responsibility and find the most efficient ways to deal with any crisis and opportunity. But no matter how far and from where the state is forced to withdraw, it is there—at least expected or feared to be there—to guarantee the withdrawal and protect the forces of "the free market" from the vengeance of their victims. Because it may hide its face or appear from nowhere, fully armed and ready to take or to give, the state can be inflated and deflated, but its complete absence is hard to imagine. The presence of the state as the *potential* closure of a governable space within a system of encompassing-colonizing governing apparatuses is the presupposition of all parties to the political game, those who try to inflate the state as well as those who try to deflate it, those who try to help other states maintain their enveloping structures as much as those who try to penetrate them.[16]

The fiction of the sovereign state, which lies at the discursive foundation of the contemporary global order, means that the absolute authority of a state—to welcome or expel, to punish or not to punish, to forgive or take revenge, to kill or let kill with impunity, to abandon people or send them to their doom, to rescue these at the expense of those, to destroy in order to build and build in order to destroy—is always presupposed or wished for. Reports on "human rights violations" are not a means to put limits on this absolute authority but rather sacrificial rituals made by good-willed cosmopolitans as a way to appease the wrath of the rogue state, whose authority they presuppose. The liberation struggles across the globe, the revolutionaries' battle cries on the way to toppling one government and crowning another, even most activists' calls to defund, decolonize, restructure, and repair—all these presuppose that enveloping, totalizing, absolute authority, the authority of the state most rebels and activists seek to reclaim. A liberated, decolonized, restructured state, with a defunded police and a shrunk army, is still a state—one encompassing and ultimate ruling authority.

The state is monotheism's true contemporary figure. Its deification has not ceased since its inception as the ultimate form of political power. It transcends any government that incarnates it, any ruler who claims to speak in its name;

it provides the ultimate reason to resist any government and crush any form of resistance. Fascists and liberals, racists and progressives swear to protect it; oppressing majorities seek to keep it intact; oppressed minorities seek to get one for themselves. Those who believe in other gods—of a modern "free market" or the old church—would be forced to curb their commitments when the clash becomes inevitable; they are less of idolaters than those rebels or traitors who speak in the state's name without being authorized. Those who dare to imagine a world free of the state form are ridiculed as daydreamers, out of touch with reality, dangerously crossing the sacred limits of the possible, which is often presented as morally necessary. It is necessary because the state is the ultimate guarantor of the right to have rights, and if no other reason suffices, the sacredness of this right should be enough to prevent us from doubting the necessity of the state.

The fate of millions of stateless people, the contemporary wretched of the earth, often inhibits or is actively invoked to curb and suppress any radical critique of the state. Such a critique, it is often said, is a luxury those who have lost or fled the states that abandoned or prosecuted them cannot afford. Those who struggle to establish a state of their own in their lost homeland, to take back control of the state that has ruined their lives, or to be welcome into a state of others don't have the luxury of thinking beyond the state. Their statelessness is the root of their suffering and humiliation; a decent state that would grant them their right to have rights is the condition for restoring their dignity and well-being. But this reasoning presupposes—hence cannot validate—the very idea of the state that is questioned here. Statelessness has been an awful malaise only since the globe has been divided into nation-states. Each state defines its own total, closed realm of rule and governance, and together they enclose the earth as a whole. Rebels, terrorists, and refugees, and the atrocities with which these groups are associated, are symptoms of states that have become too strong or too weak. But in fact, without closed borders and people who are willing to kill for the sanctity of their deified states, the impact of a malfunctioning state, one that has become too strong or too weak, would have certainly been much less severe. The realpolitik that seeks to stabilize a global state system as a cure for persecutions, systemic oppression, and genocide keeps producing the nation-state that makes them possible, deifying it as humans' one and only acceptable form of rule, whose authority and power every subject must have always already accepted.

Today a pagan conception of the state is almost inconceivable. Monotheism apparently is not simply a dimension or aspect of the state that can be peeled off at will. It seems that without its monotheism, the institution of the state, the political imagination invested in it, and its conceptual articulation would be so radically transformed that there would no longer be any state to talk about. In the reconstruction of biblical theocracy we have encountered three components of the monotheism of the state: monism, closure, and sanctity. The state-like urform that emerged is a configuration that integrates all three and enables the supreme power to endow its display of force and the materiality of its presence with an aura of transcendence. We may take this as our starting point when try-ing to imagine the possibility of a *pagan state*. Instead of peeling off the three components of monotheism, we may imagine a state that constantly struggles to suppress and contain them wherever they seem to appear. A pagan state is not a state of anarchy. To be a form of rule, the pagan state needs a new concept of ruling in which the ruled people can—occasionally and often enough—reshape the way they are ruled, including the boundaries of their associations and the commitments those imply. A pagan state would be an institution that follows and protects—not enforces and not merely regulates—the changing modes of associations of its members, the multiple bonds in which they are entangled, and their freedom to renew and transform their modes of being together, including their modes of being governed, paying obedience, and taking their liberty. At no point would a pagan state claim a transcendent authority, one whose link to the association of the ruled cannot be demonstrated and challenged at the same time. With no claim to transcendence, the pagan state would be the first element of the common.

In a pagan state, there will be no need to privatize religion or to separate state and church. Religions would multiply—but may also cease to attract—since the right to associate and dissociate would not be subject to a totalizing, quasi-transcendent authority that pretends to be the ultimate, pregiven form of asso-ciation, and no religion would be able to assume a state-like authority or need protection against it. Predatory corporate capitalism will not find support in a pagan state, for it will not be able to rely on a totalizing, quasi-transcendent au-thority to control and curtail the movement of workers and to protect the free movement of goods. In a world made up of a fluctuating mosaic of pagan states, those threatened by the wrath of the gods of others, including the gods of preda-tory capitalism, and by the violence exercised in their names may find protection and refuge wherever predatory capitalism has been curtailed and others' gods have lost their power. In a world made up of pagan states, multiple citizenships will be available and augmented by transnational solidarities. And if it is not too late, such a new global order may be better equipped to cope with the global catastrophes of climate change.

This is but a basic blueprint, and it leaves many questions open.[17] To think through these questions, one must revisit the idea of the state equipped with a better understanding of its repressed theological dimension. My reading of the Hebrew Bible seeks to offer an opening for this investigation.

NOTES

INTRODUCTION

1. Luther (1955–1986, 1:283). This was a very peculiar literal sense, for it required a special "typological reading," a reconstruction of names, places, events, and people mentioned in the Old Testament as types that find their countertypes in the New Testament. The typological reading was supposed to guarantee that the coming of Christ and his message would be the ultimate literal sense of the Hebrew text.

2. I am thinking here with Foucault's (1994 [1970]) notion of discourse.

3. Spinoza (2001, 206–8).

1. STAYING WITH THE VIOLENCE

1. Many tried to absolve God for this responsibility with no support in the text. I am joining Ron Hendel (1991) and Regina Schwartz (1997, 2–3, 82–83), among others, who insist on recognizing God's unexplained bias.

2. I am following Robert Alter's translation (2019) unless otherwise indicated. Cain and Lamech, the other killer, may have been saved, but revenge-taking has never stopped (e.g., Gen. 34), and in one case was made into a commandment (Deut. 25:17–29). The two first killers belong to one of the two lineages listed in Genesis's primordial history. One issues from Cain and the other, cited from "the book of lineage of Adam," comes from his third son, Seth (4:17–26; 5:3–32). Only the second leads to Noah and the rest of humanity; the other ends with the second killer, Lamech. Brett (2000, chap. 1) reminds us that this is a lineage of violence that ends with the flood generation.

3. The Mishna reads this as a proof of God's "patience, for each one of those generations provoked [Him] continually" (*Avot* 5:2). If this was not written with tongue in cheek, the provocation must have been extrapolated to protect God's benevolence and silence, which the rabbis doubt on this matter.

4. He addressed his entourage in a language mirroring that of the city dwellers who "said to each other . . . come let us build a city" (cf. Gen. 11:3–4 and 7). The parallel created here strongly suggests the presence of God's unnamed addressees (Garr 2003, 45–50; Alter 2019, 1:38n3).

5. Paraphrasing Jeremiah 45:4.

6. Here "Bible communities" designates three kinds of communities of speakers whose words and actions are reported in the biblical texts: (1) authors, redactors, scribes, and reciters; (2) the text's audiences at the time of their composition and rendition; and (3) the readers and commentators for whom the Bible has become a sacred or canonical text.

7. A mere favor in this case, unlike that of Noah. Lot and his family were offered refuge because he was Abraham's kin (Gen. 19:29).

8. The same principle of separation recurs in the plagues in Egypt (e.g., Ex. 8:12; 9:7, 26; 12:22–23) and the crossing of the Sea of Reeds (Ex. 14:19–20). Before crossing the sea, the Israelites saw the Egyptians chasing them (14:10); when they looked at them again from the other bank, the latter were already "dead on the shore of the sea" (14:13, 30).

9. Leibowitz (1970, 124–28); Greenstein (1995).

10. "Therefore say to the children of Israel: 'I am the Lord; I will bring you out from under the burdens of the Egyptians, I will rescue you . . . redeem you. . . . Then you shall know that I am Yahweh your God" (Ex. 6:6–7).

11. The presence of this audience will serve Moses again when he pleads for God's mercy (Ex. 32:12).

12. But he might have had an entourage with which to consult (cf. note 4) and occasionally was even willing to negotiate the execution of his destructive plans (with Abraham, Gen. 18:23–32; Lot, Gen. 19:18–22; and Moses, Ex. 4:1–17, 32:3–34; Num. 14:11–24).

13. On the different approaches to the pillars of fire and cloud, see Weinfeld (1992, 201–9).

14. E.g., Ex. 14:19–20; Deut. 5:18–22; Num. 17:7.

15. For God's view, Ex. 32:2; 33:3, 5; Deut. 9:13. For Moses's, Ex. 34:9; Deut. 9:6, 31:27.

16. Perhaps God knew of the sins in Sodom and Gomorrah. But then was the tedious negotiation with Abraham done in good faith? Did he put his disciple up to another test or simply stage a show to impress later readers?

17. Against a long tradition of readers who borrowed such attributes from whatever religious background they came from and projected them onto the Hebrew Bible. For a recent example, see Walzer (2012, 199). For a nuanced attempt to replace omnipotence as a "static" accomplished matter of fact with a dynamic "drama" in which God overcomes "setbacks," see Levenson (1988).

18. On his part in the world of humans, see Kugel (2003); on his multiple materiality, see Sommer (2009).

19. This binary is questioned twice, in the stories about Enoch (Gen. 5:24) and Elijah (2 Kings 2:11).

20. Many mythological gods were immortal but not entirely invincible, and they could also be cheated; he was invincible and uncheatable.

21. This skill was even inserted into one of his names "Wail, for the day of the Lord is at hand! It will come as destruction (*Shod* שֹׁד) from *Shadai* (שַׁדָּי)" (Is. 13:6; see also Josh. 1:15). The prophet tied one of his names, by which he was introduced to Abraham and Jacob—*Shadai*, usually translated as "Almighty"—to robbery and destruction, thus lending it a new meaning. See Botterweck et al. (1974, 412, 418, 441–46); Kohler and Baumgartner (1999, 1420–22).

22. From creation to the Israelite kingship, Martin Buber writes hyperbolically, the Bible is the story of his disappointments (1948, 127–33).

23. Alter's translation, "do justice," is rendered "do right" by the KJV and "do the just thing" in the NRSV. The Hebrew *mishpat* is both compatible with and missed by all three translations. "Judge," *shophet*, is the one who "does" *mishpat*, a ruling based on acts of judgment (in arbitration, conflict, or war).

24. Tannaitic midrash could not accept this logic and tried to explain away the moral scandal. The midrash proposed various "proofs" for his hesitations before executing his judgment and for his attempts to warn the residents of the two cities, offering them ample opportunities to repent. See *Bereishit Rabbah* 39, 49.

25. His sense of justice was questioned by various prophets (e.g., Jer. 2:11, 31:28; Ezek. 18:29), most radically by Job, whose searing questions were ultimately silenced, as he refused to give an account for Job's destitution (Job 38–42). "Where were you when I founded the earth? . . . Did you take in the breath of the earth? Tell, if you know it all. . . . Do you know the laws of the heaven, can you fix their rule on earth? (38:4, 18, 33). It is only when he directly confronted Job and needed to justify his conduct that he resorted to the finitude of man and his own superiority as the origin and lawgiver of heaven and earth. Job, who readily admitted this, remained speechless. "Look, I am worthless. What can I say back to you? . . . I know you can do anything, and no devising is beyond you" (40:4, 42:2). The very inclusion of Job in the canonized text could be read as an effort to show the futility of a debate regarding the shared moral sense, to preempt the questioning of future calamities suffered by a few righteous individuals, and to send to oblivion, in advance, the memory and future of total destructions.

26. Is. 10:22, 13:19; Jer. 49:17, 50:40; Zeph. 2:9.

27. Paul categorically rejected any attempt to question his judgment and in the same context described his wrath and destructive power, along with his patience and mercy (Rom. 9:19–23). As proof, Paul cited (or paraphrased) Isaiah: "Though the number of the children of Israel were like the sand of the sea, only a remnant of them will be saved; for the Lord will execute his sentence on the earth fully and decisively. . . . If the Lord of Hosts had not left us offspring (*sperma*, survivor, a remnant) we would have been like Sodom and become like Gomorrah" (Rom. 9:27–29; Is. 10:22, 1:9). For Paul, just like for Isaiah, the potential of total destruction is the other side of his mercy and justice (cf. Gaventa 2016).

28. The term is used here in a straightforward manner, i.e., the violence ascribed

to God, trying not to load it with the theoretical connotation it owes to Benjamin's "Critique of Violence" (Benjamin 1996).

29. Schwager (1987, 55).

30. Wells (2010, table of contents, 359–67).

31. Fretheim (2004). Presenting divine violence as a response to human evil is a common theme; see Creach (2013, 2016).

32. Dawkins (2006, 51).

33. Seibert (2016) counts seven types of Christian ways to do this in recent scholarship, while Jenkins (2011) proposes a variety of strategies to admit the violence without using its descriptions to replicate it, incriminate God, or denigrate those who still pray to the God of the Old Testament. For a Jewish theological response that finds ways to live with the scandal, see, e.g., Blumenthal (1993) and Levenson (1994).

34. As Jews do every year, on the first night of Passover, when reading the Haggada and thinking about their oppressors and enemies (Ophir 1994).

35. A good example is Yochanan Muffs (2005), who looked at cases of divine violence as expressions of divine rage and interpreted the rage in the context of God's emerging and developing personhood (which, Muffs claims, distinguishes the biblical God from other ancient deities, usually endowed with "thin" or "flat" personalities). Israel played a key role in this development, and the relationship between the two partners, which Muff reads as a literary drama, was the medium for God's "coming of age." God needed interpersonal relations, but the partner he chose could not live up to his expectations and kept failing him. The recurring frustrations are the source of his rage. God does not keep his rage to himself (this could be even more dangerous), but once it finds an outlet, it cools down and is diffused (30–34). Even though he insists on a nonfigurative interpretation of the divine wrath and accepts the anthropomorphic dimension of the figure of God, Muffs says almost nothing about the destruction and violence God inflicts. When he mentions the deluge, for example, it is only in order to say that God confronts the immense human corruption as a "stunned utopist" (94–96).

36. See, for example, *Yerushalmi Taanit* 2,2 (65:2); *Bavli Megillah*, 10b; *Bavli Berakhot*, 7a, 32a; cf. Lorberbaum (2010).

37. Roncace (2012, 80).

38. Philo's reading of the destruction of Sodom and Gomorrah is a good example. He indulges in juicy descriptions of divine violence, stretching his imagination far beyond what the texts provide, only to turn the page to declare that "such is the natural and obvious rendering of the story as suited for the multitude," and then look for "the hidden and inward meaning which appeals to the few who study soul characteristics rather than bodily forms" ("On Abraham," 26–32; quote from 29.147). In "The Life of Moses," where allegory is not used and God's violence is narrated in a realistic manner (again, beyond what the Bible tells), God's use of his powers is rationalized, showing how the means were justified by its ends and, in doing so, never questioning it either (e.g., II.19.113–17).

39. Bates (2015); Lieu (2015).

40. See Maimonides, *Guide for the Perplexed*, esp. part 1.

41. Otto (1929, 78ff.) asserts that "the numinous" supersedes rational understanding and demands the believers' awe and fear. He reads phrases such as "his fury," "his jealousy," "his wrath," or his "consuming fire" as "akin to the 'holiness' of Yahweh [and] ever enclosed in and permeated with the 'awfulness' and the 'majesty,' the 'mystery' and the 'augustness,' of His non-rational divine nature that surpasses human understanding."

42. Lieu (2015, 355). Cf. Römer (2013a, 3–6). For the distinction between "the textual God" (of the Old Testament) and "the real God" (of whom the New Testament is a much better testimony), see Fretheim and Froehlich (1998, chaps. 5–6); Richardson (2014, 47–76); Seibert (2009, 169–73).

43. Römer (2013a, 6–7).

44. Römer (2013a, 92). Since Frankena (1965), this claim was associated with King Josiah's reform, which allegedly took place at a time of Assyrian decline and meant to replace vassalship to the Assyrian kind with submission to Yahweh.

45. E.g., Noort (1998); Kratz and Spiekermann (2008).

46. For example, Zevit (2007) offers a useful synoptic view but does not engage in a close reading; Rees (2015) offers a series of fascinating, close readings of one episode, Num. 25 (esp. 75–86, 100–5, 121–27, 161–63), but not a synoptic view; and Bal's (1998) pathbreaking work offers close readings and a synoptic view of violence, but it is limited to a single book, Judges, and does throw light on divine violence.

47. The scholarly literature on violence in general and extreme violence in particular is vast. In my discussion here, I am indebted to the works of Foucault (1979), Benjamin (1996), Tausig (2003), Chamayou (2015), Gros (2006), and Balibar (2016).

48. Benjamin (1996, 236), emphasis mine. Note, however, that the critique consists in "expounding" violence's relation to something else (i.e., that it is conducted through a phenomenological inquiry). The critical twist is embodied in a descriptive effort, not added to it as an afterthought.

49. Our definition is open to the historicity of terms such as "custom," "law," and "justice," "habitude," "morality," and "legality." All it assumes is a gap between the way things are and how they ought to be according to some generally accepted expectation.

50. From Job's friends to contemporary Evangelical preachers, a pious discourse has tried to attribute that failure to the victims, not to those who caused the harm or could have prevented it. Since Marx and Engels (with various precedents in Spinoza, Rousseau, Bentham, and others), critique sought to counter the pious hermeneutics of suffering with strategies of ascribing harm and injury to ruling powers, law, and justice. Concepts like "structural violence" (Galtung 1969), "slow violence" (Nixon 2011), and my own "order of evils" (Ophir 2005, chap. 7) seek to redeem the violent nature of what passes as bad luck or a "natural disaster." Belated invocation of law and

justice should be distinguished from their suppression or denial. The latter imply a (forbidden) relation to law and justice; hence a violent act is at stake.

51. But Derrida's "Force of Law" (1992) will be on our mind as we go forward.

52. Which discourse? This may vary. Benjamin thought that it must be legal and moral, while his critique led him from the moral to the theological. But the list should be extended to include statistical, economic, technoscientific, and even aesthetic discourse.

53. For a prophetic expression of the idea, see Is. 11:1–10. We may wonder whether the difficulty in recognizing this possibility is epistemic-political (learned ignorance of those actual cases of a nonviolent rule of law that did take place) or ontological (the task is humanly insurmountable). Jewish halachic communities are often cited as an example of a nonviolent rule of law (e.g., Flatto 2020, esp. chaps. 6–8). But is there really no violence involved in introducing male children to the law at an early age and raising them as halachic subjects? Or in excluding women from studying and practicing halachic law?

54. The distinction between law and governmental rules and regulations is neither assumed nor challenged here. The point is rather the recourse to violence, which is (more or less) readily available when authority is exercised.

55. Cf. Benjamin's (1996, 238) insistence that a critique of violence should be accompanied by its inverse form—the critique of the law (and of "order," governance and power, more generally)—and should expound on how both relate back to violence.

56. The economy of violence is part and parcel of a general "order of evils" (where "an evil" means any harm, injury, suffering, or loss), to which I dedicated an extensive study (Ophir 2005) and on which part of this argument is built. On the terror and efficacy of withheld violence, see Azoulay and Ophir (2012, 127–39).

57. The latter is often overshadowed by the former, but the Bible has its own version of systemic violence and chronic disasters, with suffering, destruction, and death placed in relation to justice and law, hence to power and authority.

58. "Original scene," in quotation marks, refers to the scene as experienced by its direct victims, to be distinguished from violence's later representations and incarnations. I assume that the difference between these exists even when it cannot be properly articulated or where it erodes as time goes by. This difference is at the root of my disagreement with Derrida's treatment of violence, from "Violence and Metaphysics" onward (Ophir 2010b).

59. Especially in Foucault (1970, 1971).

60. Foucault (1979).

61. Following Arendt (1958, esp. chaps. 24–28), Rancière (1999), and Balibar (2002, 2014). For a full presentation of the concept of the political employed here, see Ophir (2004, 2020, 2022, 173–234). No act, statement, or event would be considered political without the coexistence of publicness and problematization. Problematiza-

tion may refer to any aspect of power. Power is potentially political because its claims to agency, capacity, and authority—especially the authority to use harmful force—depend on the attribution and recognition of those who come in contact with it and therefore may always be publicly questioned. (The free use of the term "political" I have made so far should be understood in the same way—when one calls power, system, authority, or relations "political," one acknowledges the public problematization of the power at stake.)

62. The political makes its appearance in a conceptual space opened between power and force. But it takes more than the presence of authority and dissent as such—among scholars, in the family, between friends—to turn things political. A debate becomes political when the power at stake is attributed with the capacity and authority to use force. At the limit of a family quarrel, litigation, or scholarly debate there hides a sword or a gun. When one enters such a debate while trusting that no one would use it, it is often because someone else is supposedly ready to use it outside the assembly court, the halls of justice, or the ivory towers, to protect or threaten those inside.

63. For the critique of kingship, see Buber (1967); Lorberboim (2011, chap. 1); Flatto (2020, introduction).

64. Paraphrasing Assmann's notion of the theologization of politics and law (2008, chap. 4).

65. Contra Assmann (2008).

66. Along with moral phenomena come moral facts. On moral facts and against the "is-ought" distinction on which this claim is based, see Ophir (2005, 323–93).

67. "Worlds" here relies on the "world making" power of literary texts (Goodman 1978). In using the term "world" we should bear in mind that it was not available to the Bible's authors and protagonists. The biblical God did not create "the world" but rather "heaven and earth" (Gen. 1:1).

68. Tertullian, *Contre Marcion*, 1, 13–14.

69. For example, asking for less: Gen. 18:25; asking for more: Is. 51:9–10, Jer. 14:8–9; asking for both: Lam. 3:42–65.

70. Most bluntly, Ex. 17:7, and by implication, Gen. 28:16–17; Jud. 6:22, 36–40.

71. Is. 45:7; Ex. 12:35–36; Jonah 3:10; 2 Kings 2:23–25; a partial list. All the examples are taken from Lieu's reconstruction of Marcion's arguments (2015, esp. chaps. 10, 12). Second Temple Jewish sources had a similar concern (*Testament of Abraham* 10).

72. Surprisingly, there is a relatively limited change in God's position as a speaking subject, even though his words may assume new meanings.

73. The first reluctance to depict God's epiphanies and action in a sensual, materialist way is documented in the Bible itself. See e.g., Deut. 4:11–19; 1 Kings 19:11–12.

74. See the section "The Blind Spot," in Chapter 2 of this volume.

75. Zevit (2007, 19).

76. In many translations, from King James to the New Revised Standard Version, most of the term's occurrences are translated as "violence." But the Septuagint rendered *ḥamas* as *adikias*—injustice or inequity. Alter usually prefers "outrage" (e.g., Gen. 6:11, 13; Jer. 6:7; Hab. 1:2, 3) to capture the protest and the invocation of (in)justice often associated with it (but he renders it as "violence" elsewhere, e.g., Jer. 22:3). The author of the entry "Violence in the Old Testament" in the *Oxford Research Encyclopedia of Religion* sees in the word *ḥamas* "a logical starting point" for reconstructing "how ancient Israelites thought about violence and how the subject then affected the overall shape of the Old Testament" (Creach 2016, 2).

77. Jer. 20:8, Hab. 1:2, Job 19:7. The verbs associated with *ḥamas* are cry (*qara*), shout (*ṣa'aq*), or scream (*za'aq*). In all three cases it is addressed to God and left unanswered.

78. Cf. Gen. 27:34, Ex. 3:7, 9; 12:30.

79. A person who "testifies falsely against his brother" is called "a witness of *ḥamas*" (Deut. 19:18, cf. Ex. 23:1; Ps. 27:12, 35:11).

80. Here is a partial list: (*a.n.b*, rape—e.g., Gen. 34:2; 2 Sam. 13:12); *h.r.g* (kill—e.g., Gen. 4:25, Ex. 2:14, Num. 11:15); *r.ṣ.ḥ* (murder—e.g., Ex. 20, Num. 35:27, 1 Kings 21:19); *m.ḥ.h* (wipe out—e.g., Gen. 6:7; 7:4, 23); *k.l.h* (complete, finish, consume—e.g., Ex. 32:10; Num. 16:21); *sh.m.d* (annihilate, destroy, exterminate—e.g., Deut. 2:12; 4:26; 28:24, 48, 63); *sh.ḥ.th* (*shiḥeth*, corrupt; *hishḥit*, destroy, demolish, obliterate—e.g., Gen. 6:10–12, 19:13; Jer. 36:29); *n.t.ṣ* (break into pieces, demolish—e.g., Lev. 14:45; Jer. 1:10, 31:28).

81. Zevit (2007, 19ff.).

82. The zealot must know how to read and interpret the divine will but may sometimes fail, as the comparison between God's response to the acts of Phinehas (Num. 25:6–13) and Elijah (1 Kings 18–19) makes clear. God's critique of Elijah (1 Kings 19:1–18) is subtle, but many have recognized it (e.g., Abarbanel's or Malbim's commentaries on 1 Kings 19:12, https://www.sefaria.org/I_Kings.19.12?lang=bi&with=Commentary&lang2=en).

83. Violence is delegated to the Adversary (the *Satan*), but the permission to experiment with an innocent, righteous man by pushing him to his limits, taking from him "all that he has" but his own person, is given by God (1:12).

84. "Aesthetics" is used here in its literal meaning, as relating to sense perception, the sentient, the perceived, the felt, etc.

2. THEOCRACY: THE PERSISTENCE OF AN ANCIENT LACUNA

1. That this truism has all too often been read metaphorically in ways that stripped God's use of force from its straightforward political contexts is something we must acknowledge but, for the purpose of this study, ignore. Cf. Flusser (2020).

2. We may recall here Plato's basic insight in his *Politea*: The constitution of the souls of rulers and subjects and of the city they share reflects and affects one another.

This Platonic insight that links subjectivity and form of rule has been articulated over time by many political thinkers, in various theoretical idioms. See, for example, Althusser (2014), Balibar (2017), Butler (1997), Brown (2017).

3. Josephus, *Against Apion*, 2.160, 164–67; Barclay (2007, 259, 261–64); emphasis added.

4. Josephus, *Against Apion*, 2.158.

5. Josephus, *Against Apion*, 2.166; Barclay (2007, 263).

6. Attridge (1976); see Pearce (1995a, 1995b, 2006); Spilsbury (2016).

7. See especially *Antiquity*, bk. 3–4. Cf. Barclay (2007, 259n620); Flatto (2020, 82–106).

8. As Flatto (2020, chap. 4) shows convincingly.

9. Josephus mentions by name some ancient Greek legislators (*Against Apion*, 2.154, 2.161).

10. On this distinction, see Barclay (2007, 263n639).

11. Josephus, *Against Apion*, 2.162–63. Note that the Greek "ὑποτίθενται," which Barclay translates as "attribution," retains the tentative, presumptive aspect of the attribution. In this it differs from the sense of attribution emphasized earlier, as well as from the meaning of both verbs mentioned in 2.164, ἐτέρεφαν and ἀναθείς.

12. See Barclay (2007, 260n627).

13. In *Antiquities*, Josephus follows the biblical text quite closely and ascribes to God numerous direct interventions in human affairs. But when it comes to the events that seem truly incredible (e.g., the parting of the Sea of Reeds), he distances himself from the biblical account and leaves open the question of the event's ascription to God (2.16, 347–48).

14. *Against Apion*, 2.169.

15. *Against Apion*, 2.170.

16. *Against Apion*, 2.166–2.171; see also 2.175, 2.178, 2.277–78.

17. *Against Apion*, e.g., 2.218–21.

18. He is not the first one to do this but is rather partaking in a Hellenistic tradition, which he also claims to correct. See Gager (1972).

19. The success of Moses's educational project, its reproducibility, and the harmonious political body it is said to produce seemed miraculous to many. See, e.g., Weiler (1988, chap. 1, esp. 9–12).

20. Assmann (2008, chap. 4; 2018, 236–40).

21. Machiavelli (2019, chap. 6); see Hammill (2012, chap. 2).

22. Machiavelli, who used each name and story as exemplary models in his observation of political life, cared about the lesson of the story, not about its historical truth. I do not want to understate the importance of stories that may be ascribed with historical truth in general, and with truth regarding the historical existence of theocratic regimes in particular, but the story of Moses is not one of them. I am therefore

bracketing here the question of the possibility of historical theocracy in ancient Israel, which Cataldo (2009, 2012, 2018) has impressively surveyed and advanced.

23. Flatto (2020, 103). Flatto goes on to add that this manner "is clear from the wider context; through God's comprehensive laws, as conceived by the legislator Moses," which leaves the mystery unaccounted for.

24. Pollard (2018); Goodman (2019, chap. 2).

25. Nelson (2010, 30, 37–38); Abolafia (2014), Goodman (2019, chap. 3).

26. Abolafia (2014, 299–300).

27. For a full account of Spinoza's critique of Josephus and his reception by the political Hebraists, see Abolafia (2014).

28. Spinoza (2001, 185). The English translator renders these Latin phrases introducing chapter 17 as "The Hebrew State" and the "Theocratic State." The importance of the *Tractate* in the history of Bible studies, on the one hand, and the history of political theology, on the other, is the reason for this short digression.

29. Spinoza (2001, 190).

30. Spinoza (2001, 189).

31. Spinoza (2001, 191–204). Spinoza's mentions of God should be read carefully, bearing in mind that they mean one thing for a general audience taken by the stories and willing to believe them and a very different thing for the philosopher who remembers that God is nature or the totality of being. We are dealing here only with the stories and their impact, of course, and my claim is that Spinoza omits their impact from the story *he* tells.

32. Spinoza (2001, 189–90).

33. See, for example, Cataldo (2009, 125), Weiler (1988, 12–14), and Cancik (1987, 56–77).

34. Flatto (2020, 105) phrases the same idea in a constructive tone: "Josephus successfully propounds a political-theological vision of Judaism that can be sustained even in a dramatically transformed landscape." Seth Schwartz (1990, chap. 5) suggests that Josephus describes the early community of rabbinic sages that emerged in his time, where a voluntary subscription to the rule of Torah replaced the forceful submission to the rule of God. At the same time, Schwartz shows that the rule of God was conceived as being embedded in the law, its study, and its expansion. Cf. Flatto (2020, 102–5).

35. Nelson (2010) and Hammill (2012) portray different, conflicting, and complementary aspects of interest in the Bible by early modern thinkers.

36. Hammill (2012, 32). Hammill is right in his characterization of Machiavelli but, as I will show in what follows, wrong in associating his notion of divine violence with "constitutive violence" in Walter Benjamin's "Critique of Violence" (1996).

37. For the recent surge of interest in Jewish political theory, see Elazar (1997); Hazoni (2012); Walzer et al. (2000–2003).

38. This section may be skipped without losing the thread of the book's main

argument. Its purpose is to illustrate what I find missing in contemporary political readings of the Hebrew Bible.

39. There are certain overlaps, agreements, and acknowledgments among them but no real conversation between them. Schwartz (1997) refers to Walzer's (1985) earlier work on Exodus, and Walzer (2012) later refers to Schwartz (1997). Assmann (2010, 2018) refers to both.

40. Critiquing divine violence was never too far from Jewish hatred and, later, anti-Semitism. The three thinkers discussed here might seem to act as tacitly acknowledging this and do their best to not be associated with anything that would resemble anti-Jewish readings of the Hebrew Bible. From this perspective, the careful navigation between violent fathers and their violent God (Schwarz), human zealots and divine wrath (Assmann), and the blunt separation of politics from religion (Walzer) seem like three ways of fencing a study of the Hebrew Bible on a slippery slope. To be clear, this is not an attempt to guess what these authors think but to describe how they write, but even as such, this impression is misleading. The three authors discussed here do not hesitate to read the Bible critically, pointing out its myogenic, chauvinist, proto-nationalist, or exclusivist themes while underlining its plurality of conflicting voices and the traditions that kept it alive. Assmann is different from the other two, however. He seems more troubled by the danger of anti-Judaism and anti-Semitism, probably because he was often blamed, wrongly, for his alleged anti-Jewish positions and because as a German intellectual, he has assumed full responsibility for the history he inherits (e.g., Assmann 2010, Introduction).

41. Schwartz (1997).

42. Walzer (1985, 2012).

43. Assmann (2008, 2010, 2018).

44. All page references to *The Curse of Cain* in this section are in parentheses.

45. It is important to note that Schwartz's view of the Bible does not replicate a model of scarcity and is far from being monolithic. She does offer an alternative model of identity formation, one that originates in plenitude, not scarcity, and characterizes several biblical stories. She endorses this alternative model not only for its own sake but also as a critique of the dominant one. My attention here is limited to identity formation based on scarcity, for this is where most of the violence, and certainly divine violence, lies.

46. I am using here "servant" instead of "subject" or "worshipper" to better capture the Hebrew term *oved*, literally "laborer," the one who labors for God.

47. Freud (1939).

48. Schwartz (1998). In the "Noah Complex" the phallus is circumcised, not castrated, to mark the covenant and to display its imminent bloodshed (21–32), which Schwartz traces in the blood of the cut animals (Gen. 15:9–10) and those sacrificed on the altar (Ex. 24:5–7), "the blood of the covenant" (Ex. 24:8), and the blood of the circumcised son of Moses (Ex. 4:25).

49. Freud too committed the original sin, for example when he "imagined one breast," emphasized "emotional ambivalence," and understood "piety as excessive solicitude" (116). But this is an imagined, constructed scarcity, and it must have come into being (unconsciously, of course) as a solution to a problem. If there was no patriarchy before the invention of this scarcity, we are left guessing what problem catalyzed its invention. But, let me add, even if left unsolved, the question of the origin's origin does not undermine Schwartz's original readings or affect the beauty of how she weaves them into the texture of her argument.

50. Schwartz refers here to the enigmatic passage in Genesis 6:2–3.

51. This is an abbreviated quotation, but the full quotation is not much longer. Besides Jesus's suffering on the cross, it does not include other biblical stories.

52. E.g., Sodom (107), or the fate of the Egyptians when they hosted Abram, his half sister, and wife Sarai (93): ". . . well, plagues for instance," referring to Genesis 12:10–20.

53. Schwartz's reading of the plagues in Egypt is echoed (without being acknowledged) in Jan Assmann's work on Exodus (2018, 138–54).

54. See the struggle between Jacob and the angel (Gen. 32:22–32) and possibly the enigmatic encounter between Yahweh and Moses on the way back to Egypt (Ex. 4:24–26).

55. Even monotheism could have been imagined otherwise, as a monotheism of plenitude (33–34).

56. The golden calf (Ex. 32:1) and Israel's rebellion against Rehoboam, son of Solomon (1 Kings 12:1–4, 16) are but two examples.

57. Note that we are not committed here to the existence of any particular "One" (i.e., Self, Father, Sovereign, Law, God, etc.), only to an image of a singular authority.

58. Walzer (1985). Unmarked numbers in this and the following four paragraphs refer to page numbers in this text.

59. Barthes (1989, 141–48).

60. Walzer let the interpreters dispute the question of who ordered the killing, Moses or God.

61. Walzer (2012). In the rest of this section, unmarked numbers in parentheses refer to page numbers in this book.

62. And he is less interested in revolutionary politics and emancipatory struggles, although the bitter polemic with Edward Said about the conquest of Canaan (Said 1986; Walzer and Said 1986) may still loom at the background and is implicitly revisited in Chapter 3.

63. E.g., 35, 48, 64, 100–8. Walzer sounds here like Spinoza in the *Theological-Political Treatise*: "Knowledge of all these things—that is of almost all the contents of Scripture—must be sought from Scripture alone" (2001, 87). But in fact, he is much more open to take into consideration the claims of the philologists, historians, and archaeologists.

64. Walzer (2012, 29, 96), where he qualifies this omnipotence by recalling God's anger and frustration and his suffering from the ignorance and wickedness of the humans he created.

65. The problem with this reasoning is not only the a priori exclusion of God from the political but, as I will try to show, looking for God's political nature through the prism provided by kingship.

66. Both terms have no equivalences in biblical Hebrew.

67. This statement comes with a caveat: "but he certainly did decree an ethics."

68. Buber (1967).

69. Buber (1949, 135ff.).

70. Buber (1967, 63–64).

71. Buber (1967, 63–64).

72. Weber (1952 [1921]).

73. Buber (1967, 64–65). Theopolitics is, accordingly, "action of a public nature from the point of view of the tendency toward the actualization of divine rulership" (57).

74. Weber's *Ancient Judaism* (1952) accompanies Walzer throughout his book, and many of his references to Weber imply or include the reiteration of the division between the two spheres.

75. Against Weber (1952, 112) and Weinfeld (1992, 167), Walzer insists that the religious origin of the genocidal ban cannot serve as an excuse, and the ban should be censored even as a religious fantasy (46).

76. Most eloquently and sympathetically by Flatto (2014).

77. Assmann (1997, chap. 2, 151–55, 167–69).

78. In two important aspects, Assmann's theory of collective memory and its history brings him close to Schwartz (1997). He sees the work of Freud, particularly *Moses and Monotheism* (1939), as an object of both inspiration and critique, and he interprets the conscious biblical effort to control the construction of memory as a practice of identity formation.

79. On the "Mosaic distinction," see Assmann (1997, 1–8; 2008, 84–89; 2010, 10–15).

80. The violence recorded at the origins of these two distinct and historically unrelated monotheistic revolutions was read against the background of the extreme violence of the twentieth and twenty-first centuries. "It is impossible to speak of religion, especially with a focus on violence without thinking or referring to the Holocaust and/or the events of 9/11" (Assmann 2008, 5).

81. Assmann (1990; 2008, chap. 4; 2010, 52–56; 2018, 236–40).

82. Assmann (2008, 84; cf. 86–88).

83. Assmann (2008, 84–85, 88). Assmann tacitly reworks here his two concepts of religion and two types of theology, which he proposed when working on the sphere of the divine in polytheistic Egypt (2001).

84. Assmann (1997, 3ff.). Monotheism is conceived as a counter-religion through-out Assmann's work.

85. Assmann (2010, 8–9, 108).

86. Assmann (1997, 1).

87. There were also groundless, vicious accusations of anti-Semitism; e.g., Wolin (2013).

88. Assmann (2008, 127–28; 2018, 79–90). He still insists on the true-false division as crucial for Second Isaiah, Jeremiah, and other late or postexilic prophets (2014b).

89. Assmann (2008, 127–28).

90. These two types of "religious violence" are two of five forms of violence in a typology, which Assmann (2008, 142–45) briefly explains in an ad hoc manner.

91. Assmann (2008, 111–20). For the popularity of internecine violence, Assmann draws on Schwager (1987, 47), who counts "over six hundred passages that explicitly talk about nations, kings, or individuals attacking, destroying, and killing others."

92. All quotations in this paragraph are from Assmann (2008, 118, 116); emphasis mine.

93. Instead of coping with the rhetoric of "anti-Semitism" itself, as a dubious discursive strategy, Assmann opted to prove himself innocent, further expanding the blind spot in his work and amplifying the silence on the recent anti-anti-Semitism discourse.

94. E.g., the inevitably exclusive aspect of monotheism, which could still be "hu-manized," or the distinction between "phases" of monotheism, or between slaughter and sacrifice (Deut. 12:13–19) as a pretext for the massacre in Shitim (Num. 25: 1–11). Assmann (2008, 114, 116).

95. Assmann (2008, 2).

96. The distinction between true and false religion cannot be found in the "Exodus tradition" (Assmann 2018, 79). In the rest of this section, all references in parentheses are to this book.

97. Assmann assigns each of these articulations to a different part of the book, according to the development of the narrative, but in fact, their actual distribution across the book does not follow this rule. At most, it's a matter of predominance.

98. See Ex. 19:12–13, 16, 18, 21–24; 20:15–18; 24:5–8.

99. For more on the "voluntary" entrance to the covenant, see Chapter 3 and the fourth section of Chapter 5.

100. To be distinguished from the covenants God entered with individuals—Noah, Abraham, Jacob, and David.

101. Assmann (2014a, 117); emphases mine.

102. Assmann (2014a, chap. 7).

103. Schmitt (1985, 36).

104. Assmann (2014, 119). When he first proposed the "Mosaic Distinction" (1997, 1–2), Assmann claimed that the opposition between true and false religion could

not be reduced to the friend/enemy distinction. But as he extended his reading of the Bible and qualified his early insights, the Schmittian paradigm surfaced with less reservation. Only the possibility of an inverse transposition (theologization versus secularization) was added. Assmann (2000, 29ff.; 2014a, 113–19; 2018, 232) and Steinmetz-Jenkins (2011).

105. Assmann (2008, 109; cf. 7–8).

106. "The ever present possibility of combat" (Schmitt 1976, 32), echoing Hobbes's *Leviathan* (1996, 88 [62]).

107. Assmann (2014a, 117). There was, of course, human violence before entering the covenant, besides the Egyptian oppression (Ex. 2:11–14, 17; 17:8–16), which Assmann leaves unaccounted.

108. Assmann (2014a, 118).

109. The parenthetical pagination in these pages refers to Assmann (2018).

110. These included first the "Deuteronomic tradition" and later the book of Exodus and "the Exodus tradition."

111. Assmann disregards here a common view of the scene as a combination of two different sources. See Chapter 4.

112. Assmann thinks that the friend/foe distinction applies to political violence but not to the political as such, as well as to religious violence but not to religion as such. He finds two different parallels to Schmitt's moment and logic of the exception, the Deuteronomic conception of breaching the covenant, and the anticipation of a coming apocalypse, which was heralded in the Hebrew Bible.

113. The imaginary element is crucial for this understanding of *shilton*, and it comes close to the notion of the "presumptive state" proposed by Richardson (2012, 2017) in the context of Mesopotamian polities. Also echoed here is Hansen and Stepputat's (2005) definition of sovereignty as the right to exercise violence with impunity and to Graeber and Sahlins (2017, 73), who cite them. Speaking about *shilton*, not sovereignty, I am bracketing the marks of "indivisibility, self-reference, and transcendence," which Hansen and Stepputat (2005, 8), following a long European tradition, attribute to sovereign power. But their insistence that sovereignty is an effect of previous actions that need to be performed repeatedly in order to be maintained applies to *shilton* as well. Like Graeber and Sahlins, I will focus not only on the performance of the agent to whom sovereign power is attributed but also on that of those who recognize the ruling figure and attribute to it power and authority.

114. The capacity to channel force between harm and protection, destruction and construction (in which God excels; see, e.g., Jer. 31:27) is crucial for the efficiency and superiority of a ruling power, but it already assumes the authority to use force.

115. Note that attribution and recognition do not mean legitimization.

116. The ruling power's dependence on attribution means that for power's sake, attribution should be regulated and the authority to attribute limited. This is one of the ruling power's main concerns and roles, for at stake are the boundaries and

composition of the political association itself. Struggles over the right to attribute and the right to be counted are two sides of the same coin. A proper account of both lies beyond the scope of this study.

117. Josephus, *Against Apion*, 2.167.

118. Josephus, *Against Apion*, 2.160.

119. Josephus, *Against Apion*, 2.169–83.

120. Josephus, *Against Apion*, 2.184–85.

121. See Flatto (2011).

122. The omission is not limited to the rule of God. Rather, it is a chronic problem in political and legal theory and in political discourse more generally. See most recently Frazer and Hutchings (2020).

123. This does not mean to exclude the possibility that both the authors and their audience "truly believe" in their attributions but rather to free us from attributing such beliefs to them. We are interested in their attributions—the performative speech acts that relate attributes to an agent—not in their beliefs.

124. For the covenant with mankind, see Gen. 9:9–17; with his elected disciples, e.g., Gen. 15; with Israel, e.g., Ex. 19, 24, 34; Lev. 26; Num. 25:12–13; Deut. 4–5, 7, 28:69–30:20.

125. Knohl (2018); Brettler (2020).

126. E.g., Is. 40:11; Jer. 2:2, 32; Ezek. 16; Hos. 1:9–2:6, 2:18–19.

127. E.g., Lorberbaum (2011, chap. 1); Oeming and Sláma (2015); Halbertal and Holmes (2017).

128. Alter (2013, 276).

129. Cf. Jud. 8:33–9:21; 1 Sam. 2:12–36; Halbertal and Holmes (2017, Introduction).

130. Jud. 9; 1 Sam. 2:27–36, 4.

131. Buber (1967, 62–65).

132. Jud. 17:6, 18:1, 19:1, 21:25; and the reference to Jud. 17–18 in Hosea 3:4–5.

133. On God's "self-effacing" withdrawal from yet ongoing involvement in the realm of human affairs after the establishment of the kingship, see Halbertal and Holmes (2017, 164ff.).

134. For God's politics of disaster in these two cases, see Ophir (2013, 169–81).

135. Those prophets scolded sinful kings and rival priests and harnessed the elements to punish the people or to relieve them from drought and famine. Elijah also fought vehemently against the cults of other gods, magically killed one hundred soldiers of Ahaziah, king of Israel (2 Kings 1:9–14), and orchestrated a mob massacre of 850 prophets of Baal and Asherah (1 Kings 18); Elisha participated in power struggles, helped in bringing an end to Akhav's rule (2 Kings 9:1–13), and changed the course of wars (e.g., 2 Kings 3:10–25); he also brought about the killing of forty-two young lads because they jeered at him (2 Kings 2:23–24). Once the prophets' lethal power is attributed to God, a distinct figure of divine violence emerges (Ophir 2013, 161–69).

136. The passage is usually read alongside the story of Josiah's cultic reform and centralization (2 Kings 22–23). The incentive for the reform, a book of teaching (Torah) found in the temple (22:8–11), is read as referring to "a copy of this teaching" (*mishneh hatorah*), which the king is supposed to read according to Deuteronomy (17:18–20). This reading was crucial for the attempts to date the composition of Deuteronomy.

137. In fact, the injunctions concerning kingship interrupts the rules concerning the Levitical priests that resumes in the next verse (Deut. 17:1–13, 18:1–8).

138. Besides the people's request for a king (Deut. 17:14), the Pentateuchal law regulates two other situations that are considered optional: the nazirite vow (Num. 6:2) and meat eating (Deut. 12:20).

139. Note that the prohibition on a non-Israelite king is phrased as if God is not the one who makes the choice and anoints the king, as was stated in the same verse (17:15), a difficulty that did not escape traditional commentators. See *Bamidbar Rabbah* 9:7 (https://www.sefaria.org/Deuteronomy.17.15?lang=en&with=Bamidbar%20 Rabbah&lang2=en) and Ramban's commentary on this verse (https://www.sefaria.org /Deuteronomy.17.15?lang=en&with=Ramban&lang2=en).

140. Flatto (2020, 12–14) reads this as a moment of a clear separation of powers avant la lettre.

141. As was discussed, Gideon refused the request of "the men of Israel" to establish hereditary rule, insisting that only "God will rule over you" (Jud. 8:23), which Buber (1967, 64) calls "direct theocracy." I assume that indirect theocracy, as it is implied, would complement Buber's term: the rule of God incarnated in and mediated by human institutions (cf. Cataldo 2009, chap. 4). This distinction only partially overlaps with Assmann's, who describes direct theocracy in ancient Egypt as a rule by God's will, which was announced by the oracular proclamations that "directed not only the acts of government but also the conduct of everyday life" (2002, 203) and manifested in the unfolding of historical events (2002, 243). For him, the opposite of direct theocracy is "representative theocracy," where "by virtue of their symbolic power [to represent the gods], state, cult, temples, rites, statues, and images make present the divine and establish an irremediably indirect contact with the gods" (2002, 185).

142. This is how Levinson (2006) presents it, limiting his reading to the legal code: "A historical-critical reading of Deuteronomy presents a utopian model of community governance that anticipates the modern conception of a 'constitution' in two interesting respects: the separation of powers among distinct branches of government; and the rule of law over all political actors—including the monarch" (1857).

143. In Collins's (2018, 37) words, the Deuteronomic code "was rather a utopian vision of an ideal Israel, proposed in stark contrast to the royal ideology of Judah." And earlier, Levinson (1997, 149–50) made a similar point, as he presented Deuteronomy as a radically new vision projected on a fictional time and place from the nation's past.

144. Quoting Bell (1997, 145–50) and Bibb (2009, 57, 59), Hundley (2011, 5–6) comes close to this idea but limits its scope and ignores its political significance: "To communicate the authority of the system, the authors purposefully distance their system from the compositional and redactional present. They set their story in the timeless past to establish the timeless preeminence of YHWH and his system, and the preeminence of the priestly authority."

145. One institution, the elders of Israel, which is never formalized, appears throughout Exodus–Deuteronomy as a relic from a pretheocratic time. The elders join Moses on numerous occasions (e.g., Ex. 3:16, 12, 18; 24:1, 9; Num. 11:16–30, Deut. 27:1, 29:9) but are never bestowed with an authority of their own. Their agency is neutralized. Cf. Walzer (2012, chap. 11).

146. Despite their differences, the sources considered J and E share the same theocratic formation, as we shall see in the next chapter.

147. One can hardly speak about a literary integration of narrative and law in J and E beyond Ex. 19–24, but the two elements coexist.

148. Ex. 5:19–21; 14:11–14; 15:22–26; 17:1–7; 32–33; Num. 11, 12; 13:17–24, 27–31, 33; 14:11–25; 39–45; 21:4–8; 25:1–5. On the J fragments in Num. 16, see Chapter 4.

149. Pre-priestly sources include sources identified as Jehovist and Elohist (to the extent that these are distinguishable). Alleged interpolations by a Holiness Code (H) editor mostly fall within the priestly formation, while its main body (Lev. 17–26) is a variation of P that incorporates significant Deuteronomic elements. My close reading of Joshua will be limited to a single, exceptional chapter, 24.

150. Here are some examples from Genesis: 8:20–21; 14; 18:1, 4–8; 21:21, 22–34; 23:3–20; 24:11–14; 25:27–34; 27:1–4; 34; 38; 39:6–20. In the first two chapters of Exodus, God appears once, quite obliquely, as an object of the midwives' fear, and perhaps as he who "made houses for them" (1:21), but the entire scene is dominated by Pharaoh's rule and is therefore quite realistic, with abundant details describing objects, materials, landscape, cattle, violence, and all sorts of activities.

151. "Abram dwelled in the land of Canaan and Lot dwelled in the cities of the [Jordan] plain" (Gen. 15:11b–12a). This is made clear just before another off-script (Jehovist) note reminds the reader of the coming catastrophe: "and he [Lot] set up his tent near Sodom. The people of Sodom were very evil offenders against Yahweh" (15:13). For these verses' provenance, see Friedman (2003, 52) and Baden (2012, 70, 179).

152. With the exception of the colorful description of the Gibonites' visit to Joshua's camp in Gilgal (Josh. 9:4–5, 12–13). But this vivid realistic moment is not unrelated to the fact that the Israelites who made a pact with the Gibonites "did not inquire of Yahweh" (9:14). The colonization campaign was orchestrated by God and led by Joshua, Moses's servant whom God appointed to replace Moses (Num. 27:18–23; Deut. 31:14). Joshua encountered "the commander of Yahweh's army" (Josh.

5:13–15) and acted like the field marshal of the conquest campaign reporting to a re
mote chief of staff. He also reenacted the covenant envisioned in Deuteronomy (Josh.
8:30–35; Deut. 27; and in different versions, in Josh. 23 and 24.). This affinity of
Joshua to the Pentateuch could give support to the idea that Joshua was originally part
of a six-book unit, the Hexateuch, and was removed from this corpus in a later stage
of the editing, an idea popular in the nineteenth century. The idea has been rejected
by many, as part of the critiques and revisions of the documentary hypothesis, but has
not lost its appeal entirely (e.g., Carr 2011).

153. Richardson (2012, 3–9). Cf. Richardson 2014, 2017. Unfortunately, I came too
late across this important work to properly integrate it in my reading.

154. On the architectonic of Plato's *Politea*, see Ophir (1991).

155. Since the mid–twentieth century, the consensus on the composition's dating
has been fractured, but one thing seems indisputable—some of the texts, or the oral
traditions that preceded them, go back at least to the eighth century BCE, and the
final editing was not over before the end of the fourth century BCE. See Collins (2017,
21–61), Römer (2007, chaps. 5–6 and the works cited there), Bin Nun (2016), Hendel
and Joosten (2018).

156. Here are a few examples: Römer (2007, 104–33, 178–83; 2008 and the works
cited there); Albertz (2011); Olyan (2011); Collins (2017, 39–43; 2018, 63–68); Knohl
(2011); Nicholson (2014).

157. Friedman (1981b); Albertz (2003); Römer (2007, 111–33); Otto (2013); Collins (2017, 41–42).

158. The same conditions that brought about the transition from monolatrism to
monotheism could have created the climate for the thought experiments I am proposing here, even though none of the theocratic formations described here implies or
presupposes a monotheistic God. Hence Cataldo's (2009, 2018) compelling argument
for dating the emergence of monotheism to the Persian period supports my assumption. Note, however, that even if the dating of the formative editing is pushed back to
the seventh century BCE, between Josiah's reign and the fall of Jerusalem, one may
still ascribe the Pentateuch's editors with a similar motivation in response to the fall of
Samaria and the growing pressure on Judah by the Assyrian and Babylonian empires.
Other historical motivations may be considered as well. A pre-exilic priestly source
might have presented the Tabernacle and the entire domain of the holy as a critical
parable or an idealized mirror of the still-existing Temple in Jerusalem. The Deuteronomic Code could have been a seventh-century BCE "programme for reorganization
of the Judean state" (Römer 2007, 81) or "a utopian vision of an ideal Israel, proposed
in stark contrast to the royal ideology of Judah" in the time of Jehoiakim and Zedekiah
(Collins 2017, 37, referring to Albertz 2005).

159. But see note 155 in this chapter and some difficult cases in what follows:
Chapter 3, notes 116 and 119, and Chapter 5, note 3.

160. Doublets and contradictions are marks of edited passages where different

sources were integrated and are warning signs that distinct formations might have been mixed there, but they do not necessarily trace these formations.

161. At the same time, the fact that the theopolitical formations are consistent with a large body of research concerning the identification of D, P, and, to a large extent, the pre-priestly sources may add some force to the defense of a contemporary version of the document hypothesis, as practiced, for example, by Schwartz (2011a, 2011b) and Baden (2009, 2012).

162. This meaning should not be ascribed to the authors' intention; it belongs to the rules of the language games of the narratives, speeches, and legal documents, as far as we can reconstruct them.

163. My main guide here is Baden (2009, 2012).

164. Baden (2012, esp. chap. 1 and the conclusion).

165. Baden (2012, 247–48).

166. Baden (2012, 249). Baden does not exclude the possibility that the literary reconstruction of the sources and the work of the compiler would frame the historical questions he bracketed to allow his reading. I state this option explicitly: Once a theopolitical formation is reconstructed, one may start looking for the historical conditions that made it possible and the authors, editors, and listeners/readers who took part in articulating, developing, replicating, and preserving it.

3. THE RULE OF DISASTER: EXTINCTION, GENOCIDES, AND OTHER CALAMITIES

1. Throughout the Bible (and beyond it), judgment was considered one of the king's foremost tasks, where his rule is demonstrated and evaluated. See, e.g., Exodus 18; 2 Samuel 8, 15–18; 1 Kings 3, 9, 11–13, 28. Cf. Flatto (2020, 4–18). This conception of the divine and kingly judge should be clearly distinguished from the divinely appointed saviors of Israel, also called judges. The latter were leaders with no assigned or acquired territory whose role was to conduct wars against the oppressors of Israel or some of its tribes. The judge's rulership could last for decades, but the Book of Judges gives very few hints about the way it was conducted.

2. When the story of a post-Edenic, human world begins, the question of immortality seemed to be settled. No humans in the biblical corpus struggle to achieve immortality or even lament its denial, loss, or unattainability. There are two exceptions, two men who crossed the line: Enoch, a man "who walked with God and . . . was no more, for God took him" (Gen. 5:24), and Elijah. whom God took "up to heaven in a whirlwind" (2 Kings 2:1, 11). In both cases, however, the responsibility for the transfiguration rests with God; no human desire for immortality is mentioned. Only once, in an archaic fragment that lacks a context or any later echo in the Bible, long human life is hinted as a problem (Gen 6:1–4).

3. In Arendt's sense of the term, as described in her *Human Condition* (1958, part 5).

4. These include Noah and his family and Lot and his daughters. We do not know whether the people of Babel knew why they were scattered, having lost their common language and the world they had shared.

5. The instrument is Pharaoh's heart, which God hardened as he pleased, as the text cares to explain repeatedly (Ex. 4:21; 7:3, 13–14, 22–23; 8:11, 15, 28; 9:12, 35; 10:1, 20, 27; 11:10; 14:4, 8, 17).

6. Assmann (2008, 21; 2018, 82–90) expresses a common view when he says that as an overlord and legislator, God does not appear before Egypt, i.e., in Genesis, and that the "semantic of loyalty"—and the violence it entails—"was alien to it" (2018, 231). Here and in what follows I am trying to contest this claim.

7. He responds to Cain by multiplying the threat of vengeance against anyone who would dare hurt the nomad (Gen. 4:15), but this, just like the curse that preceded it, sounds more like a prophecy than a commitment to kill or an act of ruling.

8. The priestly version of the Noah story makes this explicit (Gen. 9:5–7). More generally, the covenant with Noah described by the priestly source (9:8–17) places the entire story in a political context, where God enters—unilaterally—into a contract with humans and animals. This interpolation finds a single resonance in the Bible, in Isaiah 54:9–10.

9. Money, nature, desire or beauty, jealousy and competition, fear, and faith may motivate people for action and exert small or great control over the way they manage their affairs. But without being thematized, recognized, and problematized as such in public, none of these motives would ever become political.

10. For a reading of Moses's interpellation at the burning bush, see Ophir (2015, 72–75).

11. See, e.g., Ex. 7:15–18, 8:5–7, 9:13–21, 10:1–2.

12. That a relatively short time passes is only implied in the Jehovist source, especially since only a handful of events is briefly mentioned after the end of Cain's episode, including the obscure affair between "the sons of God" and "the daughters of men" (Gen. 6:1–4). This episode too is placed in the very beginning, "as humankind began to multiply (5:1). J mentions seven generations but stops before reaching Noah (Gen. 17–26). When Noah first appears in the J source (6:8), his father is not mentioned. J's genealogy includes Lamech, however, Adam's descendent in the seventh generation, and the same name is mentioned as Noah's father (5:28–29) in the parallel genealogy, cited from "the book of the lineage of Adam" (*sefer toldom Adam*, Gen. 5), an independent source that was probably added by a later redactor (Gertz 2012).

13. Considine (1969, 85–159); Kratz and Spiekermann (2008); Chen (2013). Cf. Sloterdijk (2010, chap. 2).

14. Noort (1998).

15. Mesopotamian myths of the deluge do not mention human guilt; they referred instead to human overpopulation and the noise they made when conducting their

affairs. See the comprehensive comparative work of Ed Noort and the scholarly literature cited in his essay (Noort 1998).

16. Frymer-Kensky (1988, 121–24).

17. The Epic of Gilgamesh, standard version, tablet XI, iv (Dalley 2008, 109–15).

18. Alter's translation (2019, 26) seems to capture some of the richness of the Hebrew expression, which combines "heart," "thinking" (*makhshavot*), and "form" or "formation" (*yetzer*). *Yetzer* is derived from *y.tz.r* (י.צ.ר), the root of *tzura* (form) and *yatzar* (created, also formed).

19. See Müller (1985, 296ff.); Noort (1998, 33–36). Noort suggests that the moral justification was added to allow the incorporation of the myth into the biblical corpus, because a destruction of the magnitude of the flood could not be told without a reason.

20. This notion of evil as a substance whose accumulation might trigger a disastrous reaction will find echoes in the priestly conception of the sacred that undergirds priestly theocracy.

21. See Hendel (1991); Muffs (2005, 89–95); Lorberbaum (2009, 2010).

22. Sloterdijk (2010). His study of theological and psychological aspects of rage refers to the Bible in passing only.

23. E.g., pent-up aggression, loathing, vengeance, competitiveness, honor, passion for the affirmation of the self. Other moods characteristic of divine rage—fury, wrath, jealousy, and a sense of vulnerability and offense that are expressed by God and some of his emissaries—reverberate in Sloterdijk's analysis as well.

24. Lorberbaum (2009, n6). Lorberbaum points out important differences between the parallel moments of regret, promise, and restraint in the two sources.

25. Various holistic expressions appear eighteen times in the four chapters devoted to the flood. Seven of them appear in the Jehovist version of the text: "from human to cattle to crawling thing to the fowl of the heavens," "all the earth," "all existing things," "all the high mountains under all the skies," "all that had quickening breath of life in its nostrils," "all living things." The priestly expressions are "all flesh" and "every living creature." The priestly source uses a similar and quite detailed language of totalization for the living beings saved in the ark (Gen. 7:14, 16; 8:1, 17–19), assuring the replication of creation after the flood.

26. The same insistence on the totalizing scope of his rule is articulated in the covenant he established with his people: "for all the earth is Mine" (Ex. 19:15).

27. The priestly reason for the first decision is not very different from the Jehovist one—"all flesh had corrupted its way on the earth" (Gen. 6:11–13)—but it misses the parallel with the reason for the second regret.

28. While all living beings are included in the covenant, humans' superiority is reaffirmed, and the eating of animals' flesh is permitted, with certain restrictions (Gen. 9:1–5).

29. Lorberbaum (2009).

30. For an older summary, see Romanoff (1932). For a more recent account see Van Seter (1992).

31. From here to the chapter's final section, I am following only Jehovist and Elohist sources.

32. Here and in what follows I am following Agamben's interpretation of Aristotle's concept of potentiality and his insistence that potentiality is the power or ability "not to" as much as it is the power or ability "to"—to act or not to act, to kill or not to kill, to care or abandon, to enforce the law or suspend it—and that it is precisely this potentiality that defines sovereign power. Agamben (1998, 39–48; 1999, chap. 11).

33. Selective punishment, also used as a warning, was not unimaginable, as demonstrated by Amos, an early prophet: "I would send rain on one city, and send no rain on another city; one field would be rained upon, and the field on which it did not rain withered" (4:7).

34. Each version of the flood story has a different timeline.

35. Imperial rulers in the ancient Near East often boasted how they turned their rebellious cities into ruins and their ruins into a perpetual wasteland by sowing them with brimstone and salt (Wiendfeld 1992, 109–14).

36. In Gen. 11:1–9, placed midway between Gen. 6:5 and Gen. 18:17. If it was not a punishment for hubris, perhaps it was a way to force the first commandment ("be fruitful and multiply and fill the earth and conquer it"; Gen. 1:28), which building the unilingual city contradicted (Brett 2000, 46–48).

37. See, most conspicuously, the ambiguous reference to *bnei ha-elohim* ("the sons of the gods/the sons of the god") in Gen. 6:2, 4; the appeal in the plural to some anonymous others in Gen. 11:7—"Let *us* go down and baffle their language"; and the use of the first-person plural in Gen. 1:26: "let us make man in *our* image and *our* likeness."

38. See Garr (2003, 45–50).

39. At least not in the JE sources. In Deuteronomy 28:21–23, Sodom and Gomorrah serve as an emblem of total destruction and an ultimate incentive to abide by God's teaching, but this is part of a wholly different theocratic model, which I will discuss in Chapter 5. In JE there are only some hints in that in Abraham's time God was recognized; explicitly by his two wives, Sarai and Hagar (Gen. 16:5, 13), and implicitly by kings with whom Abraham was associated (Melchizedek, "a priest of El the Highest" [14:18–20], and Abimelech, king of Gerar, who was warned by God in a night dream [20:3–6]).

40. He saved Sarah and Rebecca from becoming concubines to the local king or one of his subjects without hurting the king, who mistook the women for their husbands' sisters (20:1–7; 26:6–11). He saved Hagar when she ran away from her mistress (16:6–14) and, again, with her son, after she was "sent away" and left alone in the desert (21:12–21). He scolded Abraham for Sarah's mistrust, but did not punish the doubtful wife (18:13–15).

41. This is made clear by comparing the Jehovist version of the promise (Gen. 15:18–21) with the priestly insertion (15:13–16), which presents the colonization and eradication as a punishment for the yet-to-be-accomplished crimes of the colonized nations.

42. The implicit threat was spelled out in the alternative, Deuteronomic version of the inaugural moment (Deut. 5:4–5) and was recognized as genocidal in the Babylonian Talmud: "This teaches that the Holy One, blessed be He, overturned the mountain upon them like an [inverted] cask, and said to them, 'If ye accept the Torah, 'tis well; if not, there shall be your place of burial." R. Abdimi b. Hama b. Hasa, *Babylonian Talmud*, Shabbath 88a, 16, http://www.come-and-hear.com/shabbath /shabbath_88.html.

43. This may be an injection from an E source (Baden 2012, 117–18). The motif recurs in the Deuteronomic version (Deut. 5:5). Baden contrasts the E and J sources on account of the people's fear of God: in E they "fear of hearing or approaching Yahweh" whereas in J they "are so fearless that they need to be restrained from rushing to the mountain." Despite their sharp thematic diversions, God's violence is looming and activated in both sources. This is one of the clear examples demonstrating the shared theocratic formation of the two pre-priestly sources.

44. The language of Sodom and Gomorrah cannot be missed here. Compare Gen. 19:28 and Ex. 19:18.

45. Even though Moses's disappearance triggers the transgression (Ex. 32:1), the golden calf has been interpreted as a figure of God or of Moses, whom the people also viewed as a deity. See Propp (1998, 550–53, 580–83); Knohl (2008, chap. 9).

46. The different sources use three verbs to convey the sense of total extinction of the targeted group: *m.kh.h* (wipe out—Gen. 6:7; 7:4, 23; Ex. 17:14; Deut. 9:14; 29:19); *k.l.h* (complete, finish, consume—Ex. 32:10; Lev. 26:38; Num. 16:21, 17:10; Deut. 28:21); *sh.m.d* (annihilate, destroy, exterminate—Deut. 2:12; 4:26; 7:23; 9:8, 14, 19, 20, 25; 28:24, 48, 63). The last term, however, is often qualified to mean "scattering" and implies the persistence of a remnant (e.g., Deut. 28:63–64).

47. Ex. 32:7–14 and the recollection of the scene in Deut. 9:7–29; Num. 14:11–25.

48. As we will see, the Deuteronomists turned the genocidal threat outward, shifting it from Israel to the nations of Canaan, whom Israel is ordered to eliminate. Deut. 6:10–19; 7:1–7; 20:10–18. The genocidal imagination in the Later Prophets and the book of Esther, and its amazing, chilling articulation in the apocryphal text *Third Maccabees*, lie beyond the scope of this study. On the later texts, see Rosen Zvi and Ophir (2020).

49. Taubes (2004, 28–38).

50. On regime-made disasters, see Azoulay (2019, 51–54, 359–66).

51. The motif of the wake should resonate here; see its compelling elaboration in Sharpe (2016).

52. For a systematic, comprehensive study of genocides that places the annihilation

of Jews during the Second World War as one in an ongoing series of modern geno cides, see Levene (2005, 2013). See also Ophir (2005, chap. 9).

53. Separation is a prominent priestly theme (see, e.g., Milgrom 2004) but is not exclusive to the priestly documents, as the following makes clear (cf. Greenstein 2001). Priestly authors did not invent this theme but rather highlighted and developed an existing discursive matrix. The different sources offer different versions and principles of separation but share the basic discursive formation of a generative separation: No matter which separation is thought as originary, others followed from and in relation to it.

54. For it was not God who spilled the blood, but his role in igniting Cain's envy cannot be ignored either. Cf. Schwartz (1997, 1–4). On Schwartz's reading of the politics of selection, see Chapter 2.

55. The quintessential *havdalah* that culminates creation in the priestly source, the separation of the seventh day from the rest of the week, presents the exact opposite: a day of rest and regeneration, in which all work ceases. But as we will see, the priestly source too had its way to link separation with the disastrous nature of divine violence.

56. The differences between the two versions of the story (usually considered J and E, respectively) are quite significant (Baden 2012, 56–57, 220) but have little bearing on my argument. There is no lasting damage in E, but the disaster looms large.

57. A priestly redactor understood the logic of linking separation and violence and supplemented the traumatic experience with a vision of a remote future in which the link is thematized and dissolved at the same time: The promise would only be fulfilled after four centuries of suffering and after judgment is served to the people's oppressors (Gen 15:13–14). See Friedman (2003, 54).

58. Schwartz (1997, 31).

59. Noah and his descendants were separated before the covenant, by the flood.

60. Human blood was spilled once during the coronation of Joash (2 Kings 11) when the priest Jehoiada "made a *bĕrît* between Yahweh and the king and the people to be a people of Yahweh, and between the king and the people" (11:17).

61. Cf. Schwarz (1997, 21–25) and her Girardian interpretation of the violence in the covenant ceremony. But Schwartz also relates the animals' blood near God's mountain (Ex. 24:4–11) to the bloodshed after the sin of the golden calf (Ex. 32:26–28), where the two events are separated not by four hundred years but by forty days.

62. I am referring of course to the chapter from the *Phenomenology of Spirit*, "Independence and Dependence of Self-Consciousness: Lordship and Bondage," along with its Lacanian adaptation.

63. The epithet is reiterated three times in the context of the golden calf scandal (Ex. 32:9, 33:3, 5; 34:9) and then recalled by the Deuteronomist in the same context (Deut. 9:6, 13; 31:27).

64. We have no evidence, however, that the separation involved prohibitions on mixed marriage and other forms of interactions between the two groups. The opposite may be true, as suggested by the fact that the man chosen to lead the people out of Egypt was a stepson of an Egyptian princess (Ex. 2:10) who later married the wife of a Midianite priest (2:16–21), and by the "mixed crowd" that joined the Israelites as they left Egypt (12:38).

65. I am following here the narrative of the redacted chapter, in which the Jehovist, Elohist, and priestly sources are neatly woven together. J, E, and P sources seem to be complete, distinct versions here, and they differ in the playful ways the separation between the saved Israelites and the drowning Egyptians is displayed (Friedman 2003, 142; Gertz 2014). But these are all stories of separation, of the two parties and of the elements—land, water, and air—sharing the same logic, and the effect of the redaction is to amplify its impact. However, the intimate link between separation and disaster is characteristic only of the pre-priestly writings.

66. "Motley throng" is Alter's translation for *Erev Rav*; King James rendered it "mixed multitude."

67. They will meet other people as enemies in the battlefields, and once in idolatrous, sexual exchange that ends in catastrophe (Num. 25). One foreigner, Moses's father-in-law, will come for a short visit (Ex. 18). We will study these episodes in Chapters 4 and 5.

68. And note the totalizing claim, "Mine is all the Earth" (19:5), that underscores the people's exceptional status. On "treasure" (*s'gulah*), see Weinfeld (1992, 226), Greenberg (1995), and Chapter 5. On "holy," see Chapter 4.

69. Carmichael (2012, esp. chaps. 2, 5–6) captures some aspects of this inversion when he reads the Book of Numbers as a critique of Genesis and specifically the figure of Joseph as an enlightened ruler in Egypt, the land of plenty.

70. Or four hundred years (Gen. 15:13), or four hundred thirty years (Ex. 12:40–41).

71. Baden (2012, 77).

72. For the dubious origin of this formula, see the differing views of Weinfeld (1992, 335, 337); Propp (1998, 375); Friedman (2003, 146); and Baden (2012, 76–77).

73. Such acts of withdrawal characterize both E and J sources (but see Baden 2012, 117–19). These acts bear some echoes to the more famous scene of withdrawal, as when God agrees to the people's request for a king, which he interprets as his own rejection. 1 Sam. 8:4–22; cf. Halbertal and Holmes (2017, 1–16).

74. See Muffs (1992, 14–15).

75. As if to save his honor, God still calls the Israelites "your [i.e., Moses's] people," even after granting the forgiveness Moses requested and reiterating the terms of covenant (34:10). Chapters 32–33 are usually considered E, and 34 is presumably J, but clearly 34:1–10 does not make sense without the two earlier chapters (*pace* Baden 2012, 77–78), and it is only there that Moses's worries and his requests are answered.

Verse 10 may already belong to the Jehovist version of the book of covenant that follows (10 or 12 to 28; Alter 2019, 1:349n10).

76. This whole chapter is considered a JE (Levine 1993, 72–74) or E (Friedman 2003, 258–60) source. Baden (2012, 82–102) proposes a compilation of two independent stories, the story of the quails (J) and the story of the Elders (E). The differentiation of the sources has little bearing on my reading here; the same type of divine rule is found elsewhere in sources considered J and E alike.

77. Lack of trust on a different occasion was the sin due to which Moses and Aaron did not live to reach the promised land (Num. 20:7–12). But here, like in another episode of mistrust (Gen. 18:10–15), a short sarcastic response substitutes for any further punitive reaction.

78. Baden (2012, 88–90); Frankel (2002, 22–26). Like Baden, Frankel distinguishes here two distinct non-priestly narratives.

79. Even when he is not mentioned in the people's appeal, God tends to feel blamed and rejected. Cf. 1 Sam. 8:1–8. His narcissism, which goes far beyond these two episodes, is well documented throughout the Bible, from the desire to create man "in our image" (Gen. 1:24) to the blasting speeches to Job, when he sees himself in any living creature and in any created being, including heaven and earth, light and darkness, death and time (38–41).

80. Carmichael (2012, 60) attributes the sin in this episode to the request to go to Egypt. But this would apply to the whole camp, not to those executed while hoarding and eating quails. They in particular sparked God's rage and their sin—lust (*taava*)—gave the site of this episode its name, "graves of lust" (Num. 11:34). But where in the laws already given was this kind of lust forbidden?

81. On the psychological dynamic of denied recognition, see Sloterdijk (2010, 22–25).

82. Cf. Num. 14:18; Joel 2:13; Jonah 4:2; Nahum 1:3; Ps. 86:15, 103:8, 145:8; Neh. 9:17.

83. Benjamin (1996, 298); cf. Derrida (1992, 51–54); Martel (2017, chaps. 4–5).

84. In both Exodus and Numbers, the non-priestly stories include J, E, and other independent textual sources. See Frankel (2002, 73–81) for further textual breakdown of the nonpriestly additions in these books. Note that in the version of the manna story in Ex. 16, which is generally accepted as a priestly text (with very few nonpriestly insertions: 4–5, 35b), complaints, contentions, disobedience, and rebellious spirits are not answered with violence. If Baden (2012, 82–102) is right and the story of the Elders (Num. 11:11–12, 14–17, 24–30) is neatly separated and identified as an E source, violence would be limited here to the Jehovist source alone.

85. The putative E (angel) and J (cloud) sources are combined into one verse; the two, the angel and the cloud, play the same role.

86. E.g., Ex. 13:21; 33:9–10; Num. 34–36.

87. Agamben (1998, 27).

88. Assmann (2018, 236–40).

89. Jethro's elaborate proposal for a judicial system was presented (Ex. 18) but not implemented. See the fifth section of Chapter 5.

90. A similar appeal to God's mercy appears in the priestly story of Korah, but there Moses and Aaron address God as a universal deity "of the spirits for all flesh" and appeal to his sense of justice in a way that was never invoked in the desert stories: "Should one man offend and against all the community You rage?" (Num. 16:22).

91. On God's sense of self, cf. Muffs (1992, 45).

92. Benjamin (1996) famously distinguished between lawmaking and law-preserving violence and presented divine violence as a third category that neither institutes the law nor preserves it but rather destroys it (249). Assmann (2018, esp. chaps. 8–9) greatly emphasizes the revolutionary aspect of Exodus, but when he comes to describe the revolutionary spirit of the Sinai revelation, he has to borrow the theme of destruction of foreign law from Deuteronomy.

93. For the source of the elder's story see Baden 2012, 117–18, 126. Cf. Num. 11:24–29, 14:24, 27:18.

94. Divine violence is a signifier that must be consumed together with its signified.

95. "Less possible and also less urgent for humankind, however, is to decide when unalloyed violence has been realized in particular cases" (Benjamin 1996, 252).

96. Scholem (1999).

97. Scholem seems to read "return" as repentance, but this reading holds even when, accepting Lambert's compelling argument (2016, 27, chap. 4), one insists on a nonmetaphorical interpretation of *tshuva*.

98. Schmitt (1985); Agamben (1998).

99. Agamben (1998, 26–38, 63–67).

100. "Although he [the sovereign] stands outside the normally valid legal system, he nevertheless belongs to it" (Schmitt 1985, 7; cited by Agamben 1998, 15).

101. But if this is the case, the crucial decision is displaced from God to his subjects—it is the decision to attribute—or to not attribute—to him the irruption of violence or its suspension.

102. The source is identified as E and finds a partial echo in the other E passage cited earlier (Ex. 32:34, 33:2–3). Whether these passages refer to the same messenger (e.g., Reiterer 2007) or not (Hundley 2016), the role of the two is rather different. The protective role of the first messenger is underlined, and its introduction is accompanied with a general warning to heed the angel's voice, (Ex. 23:22–23). The introduction of the second (Ex. 32:34–33:3) is already integrated in the deferral of judgment and is part of God's handling of the golden calf crisis, his withdrawal from Israel's camp, and his negotiation with Moses.

103. Cf. Derrida (1981). Divine presence was materialized in his column of cloud and fire and in his ark. When led by the ark and the cloud they are protected (Num.

10:33–35); when they go to war without the ark, they are defeated (Num. 14:44–45).
But when God materializes in the appearance of His "glory" (*kavod*) things may turn
either way (Ex. 16:10; Num. 14:10, 14).

104. Benjamin (1996, 248).

105. "If mythical violence brings at once guilt and retribution, divine power only
expiates; if the former threatens, the latter strikes; if the former is bloody, the latter is
lethal without spilling blood. . . . The first demands sacrifice, the second accepts it."
Benjamin (1996, 249–50).

106. Agamben (2005, 62).

107. In the course of their journey near the eastern borders of the Amorite and
Moab territories, the people reach a well of water. The water is ascribed to God, but
a poem celebrating it ascribes the digging of the well to anonymous captains and
nobles. The source may be "the book of the battles of Yahweh" (Num. 21:14; Levine
2000, 72–73). To this one should add an E text describing a rare moment of trust and
intimacy in the company of God, when Israel's seventy elders joined Moses, Aaron,
and his two sons to conclude the covenant, "saw the God of Israel," and the "sap-
phire pavement . . . beneath His feet . . . and they beheld God and ate and drank" (Ex.
24:10–11). Both poetic episodes convey a moment of thanksgiving to a protecting
warrior God and seem to belong to more ancient layers or to a different strain among
the pre-priestly sources. The Song of the Sea (Ex. 15:1–19) and the Song of Miriam
(15:20–21) are generally considered an earlier, independent source (which, Propp
argues, was already included as such in JE; 1998, 482–83; 2006, app. A).

108. The pre-priestly source is indicated below as J. I am following Friedman's
(2003, 262–66) identification of J and P verses: J = 13:17–24, 27–31, 33; 14:4, 11–
25, 39–45; P = 13:1–16, 25–26, 32; 14:1–3, 5–10, 26–38.

109. Levine (1993, 348) and Friedman (2003, 263) ascribe the first verse (32) to a
priestly source and the second (33) to a Jehovist one.

110. Caleb's dissenting voice in 13:30 is identified as J; the clash with Caleb and
Joshua in 14:6–10 is ascribed to P. Rebellious moments are mentioned in all three versions: Num. 14:4 [J], 14:1–3, 10 [P]; Deut. 1:26 [D]. Friedman's identification of Num.
14:4 as J is controversial (e.g., Levine 1993, 348). The rebels' preference of Egypt or
the desert over Canaan is a priestly theme and does not appear in the other sources,
but it echoes the pre-priestly expression of the same sentiment (Num. 11:4–6); the
refusal to go forward recurs in all three versions.

111. Amalekites and Canaanites in J (Num. 14:43); Amorites in D (Deut. 1:44).

112. Much of the philological debates centers on Num. 14:4: "Let us put up a
head and return to Egypt." Frankel (2002, chap. 3) surveys a range of views about
the story's exact composition and offers a much more complex composition with a
significant late, "post editorial" layer that integrates J sources. Frankel suggests that
this story is a patchwork of original priestly and nonpriestly text, with later priestly
additions comprising the final story (121), meaning there were two separate events

of priestly writing. But even this reading does not undermine the coherence of the Jehovist version and its theopolitical distinction: A rebellious reaction to Moses's command is answered by a genocidal threat.

113. I accept Baden's methodological rule (2012, esp. chap. 6) as the place where one should begin. If a composition of sources is assumed, one should look first for formerly coherent independent stories, which are encountered as scattered fragments in the edited text.

114. Frankel (2002, 121–22) believes that later priestly additions to the story were actively omitting portions of the original story and revising some of its elements, such as Canaan being described as inhospitable (P) or fertile (JE). He claims that some of these revisions demonstrate an awareness of the pre-priestly sources and are relatively late.

115. For the Deuteronomists' knowledge of the pre-priestly version, see Baden (2012, 134). For the differences between J and P sources that were kept in Num. 13–14, one should look for the redactor, not to any of the sources, and for his decision not to blur them. The redactor was careful to keep the two modes of divine intervention separate, even as he tried to present a single coherent story. This is still true even if Frankel is right and the scene was a late addition, as the separateness of the genocidal episode is maintained. In the story of the flood, we have already encountered a priestly version of a pre-priestly theocratic model in which the priestly intervention includes an assurance that catastrophe will not recur, adding a covenant and a mechanism of self-restraint (the rainbow) to the promise of the earlier source. Accordingly, if Num. 14:11–25 is considered a late Jehovist-style interpolation added to a priestly story, one could still expect that the genocidal act would be acknowledged and revoked.

116. Knohl (1994, 98–99); Levine (2000, 503–7). But see Carr (2011, 74n29) and the convincing evidence he amasses to refute Baden's attempt to establish Num. 32:7–15 as P (2009, 143). Cf. Frankel (2002, 177–78). In fact, our analysis of the different patterns of divine violence's deployment in the scouts' story may strengthen the evidence for a nonpriestly source.

117. Whether that violence erupted or not we do not know, for at this point in the narrative the redactor cut the priestly source and inserted a Jehovist text (14:11 may be read as the continuation of 13:33, the last preceding verse from J). It may well be, however, that P echoes a story about a violent revolt that did take place.

118. In his attempt to renew the document hypothesis, Baden (2012) foregrounds cases in which the sources tell different but related stories, and those are stitched together by a single compiler. In our case, the three sources are telling the story of the same traumatic event, and the redactor's most significant act in Numbers 13–14 is to weave J and P together while leaving intact the traces of divine violence and Moses's plea in J without creating or adding its echo in P.

4. HOLY POWER: STATES OF EXCEPTION, TARGETED KILLINGS, AND THE LOGIC OF SUBSTITUTION

1. "Priestly" will be used here in the wide sense to include any source that is neither pre-priestly nor Deuteronomic. Distinctions between priestly Torah and texts associated with the Holiness School or the earlier corpus and later redactions will be made occasionally and tentatively. Many of the episodes read closely in this chapter were identified by Knohl (1995) as HS (for a summary, see 104–6), but this identification is contested (Milgrom 2001, 1337–44; Nihan 2007, 559–75; Blum 2009, 31–44). I mostly bypass this debate here, for I've found the major elements relating to the divine violence and other aspects of the theocratic formation carefully displayed at the level of the edited texts (more so than in pre-priestly and Deuteronomic sources; see esp. the second section of this chapter, on Num. 16–18).

2. Knohl (1995, 149–50, 205–6; 2003, esp. chap. 1) claims that the priestly school reached a peak of abstract thinking that would not be reachieved until the Jewish philosophy of the Middle Ages. Cf. Kaufmann (1960, 60ff.), and the systematic account of Hundley (2011).

3. The conceptual grid and the entire symbolic system associated with the concept of the holy were studied widely. I relied extensively on Milgrom (1991, esp. 595–612); Schwartz (1999; 2000, 251–66); Olyan (2000, chaps. 2–3); and Klawans (2006, chaps. 1–2). But I could not find there or elsewhere in the vast scholarly corpus on priestly holiness much attention to or interest in the rule of God, certainly not in his use of force as it was imagined through and embedded in this conceptual grid and symbolic system.

4. Alter's translation of *hol* is not entirely accurate here, for *hol* means both the negation of the holy but also its own domain, the "common," as NRSV has it. In the cited verse that proclaims the general injunction defining the opposition, the two connotations, profane and common, cannot be separated (as is the case in Ezek. 22:26, 44:23, where the violation of the separation is lamented). As a domain, *hol* should be translated as "common"; as a quality, it may often be rendered "profane."

5. The first verse is usually identified as a priestly text (P), and the second is taken from the Holiness Code (H). Identifying H sources outside Lev. 17–26 is highly debated, but as far as I can tell both sources share the same discourse, including the basic conceptual grid organized around the two pairs of oppositions, activated by a priestly elite that serves a holy God who bestowed holiness and demands sanctification through moral and ritual purification. The differences between the two bodies of texts, to the extent they can be determined, are played out within a shared discursive configuration I will describe in what follows, but they are not pertinent for what concerns us here. I will consider only those few that seem relevant.

6. The two oppositions are comprehensive and exclusive (all members of the

group to which they apply are *either* one *or* the other). Cf. Olyan (2000, 124n6). The profane should be carefully distinguished from the impure (*tamē*). The point has been long debated. I accept Olyan's view of the formal distinction (2000, 130–31n12) and his critique of Milgrom (1991, 731–32) but follow the latter's emphasis on the critical, lethal antagonism between the holy and the impure, which Olyan (2000, 130) acknowledges but does not elaborate on.

7. At least half of the occurrences of the term *kadosh* and its cognates in the entire Hebrew Bible, and the vast majority of its occurrences in the Pentateuch, are in priestly sources (including the Holiness Code).

8. For the human act of hallowing, see, e.g., Ex. 40:9–15, Lev. 8:10, 15, 30; Num. 7:1.

9. Ezek. 24:21 is a rare example of God's acts of desecration.

10. B. Schwartz (1999, 264–65, and the sources cited in note 68); Olyan (2000, chap. 2).

11. Greenstein (1984, 90–95).

12. Among which skin diseases, especially *ṣara'at*, were prominent. *Ṣara'at* was translated as "leprosy" in older translations, "scaling" or "skin blanch" in more recent ones, but no agreed modern clinical equivalent has been established.

13. When Olyan (2000) insists that the Levites "have been separated but are not holy" (at least according to Num. 16), he refers only to holiness as a quality; whereas when he speaks about their "privileged status" and the "intermediate position" they occupy "between the priests and the rest of the congregation," he speaks about their place in the realm of the holy (29).

14. Olyan (2000, 17).

15. Many of Knohl's (1994, chap. 4) observations regarding differences between P and H may be understood as effects of this generative aspect of a shared priestly discourse.

16. Addressing this issue extensively in a different context, Klawans (2006, chaps. 1–2) argues that the reasons to consider purity rituals, dietary laws, and sacrificial practices as belonging to different historical layers and systems of meaning in the priestly corpus are flawed on both textual and theoretical grounds.

17. Olyan (2000, 17).

18. E.g., Lev. 11:44–45, 19:2, 20:26. Ascription of holiness to God in human speech (which is ubiquitous in Isaiah and Psalms and may be found elsewhere in the Bible) never appears in the priestly Pentateuchal corpus.

19. All terms related to holiness come from the same root, *k.d.sh*. Hebrew does not allow for a simple rendering of the semantic differentiation made possible in English and other European languages by the difference between "holy" and "sacred" and their equivalents and derivatives.

20. Following Klawans's (2000, 21–42; 2006, 53–56) distinction between ritual and moral defilement. Ritual defilements coming from ordinary bodily functions

and excretions or accidental mistakes from the performance of rituals require ritual
purification and sacrificial expiation. Some moral offenses can be expiated through
sacrifice; others are beyond repair.

21. On gradation of proximity, see, e.g., Milgrom (1991, 1–16, 721–26); Olyan
(2000, 28–35, 38–40, 50–54, 121–22). Both follow Douglas (1996, 1999).

22. *Vatokhal*, literally "eat" or "ate" (Lev. 9:24).

23. The theme is expressed more clearly in J and D sources with respect to the ark
(e.g., Num. 10:33, 14:44; Josh. 3:9–17; 1 Sam. 5–6; 2 Sam. 6:1–13).

24. Everything that was part of the booty became hallowed through the ban
(*herem*), which required the confiscation of everything taken from the enemy, objects,
animals, and people alike, and its dedication to God. See Niditch (1993, chap. 1);
Greenberg (2007, 10–13); Stern (2020).

25. This nomadic theater certainly fits the framework of the metanarrative, the
forty-year journey from the Nile to the Jordan River. A nomadic conception of the holy
could have been just as well suited to address the theopolitical concern of people
who had just been traumatized by exile and migration. On dating the composition and
redaction of P, see, e.g., Knohl (1994, chap. 5); Römer (2007, 178–83); against, e.g.,
Weindfel (2004), Pitkänen (2018).

26. In Deut. 26:15 and in Solomon's prayer upon consecrating the Temple in Jerusalem: I Kings 8:12, 23, 27, 30, 39, 43. See Breuggman (2000, 107–13).

27. See Ophir and Rosen-Zvi (2018, 27–31). Other foreigners (stranger [*ben
neikhar*], settler [*toshav*], and hired worker [*sakhir*]) are explicitly mentioned just to
be excluded.

28. In this respect (and only in his respect), the priestly holy is the domain of
indistinction between facts and norms, precisely as Agamben (1998, 17–18) proposes
to understand the Roman notion of *sacer*.

29. The reconstruction of the basic grid underlying this biopolitical system is
indebted to Mary Douglas's influential work (1984, 1993, 1999).

30. Knohl (1994, 189–98).

31. For P, see, e.g., Ex. 12:19, 43–49; for H, Lev. 17:8–15, 19:33–36. See Milgrom
(1991, 1–16, 689, 725, 1411–12, 1762). Cf. Knohl (1994, 197–98).

32. The imperative to separate themselves from the rest of the nations is necessitated by the nations' impurity and "abominations," i.e., their indifference to Israel's
rules of purity and practices of separation. The injunction to separate from them
stems from their modes of life, not their intrinsic nature (hence the exceptional status
of the *ger*). The ethnic or national (Lev. 20:24, 26) separation plays a double role: It is
a constitutive divine act that sets the condition for the human performance of separation, and at the same time, as far as Israel is concerned, it is only one element in a
comprehensive system of divisions and certainly not its organizing principle.

33. Milgrom (1991, 689, 725, 1761). The idea has its roots in the midrash (Sifra
Kedoshim, 1). Note, however, that *imitatio dei* is not limited to issues involving

separation and does not include all aspects of separation. See also Milgrom (2004, 219–20).

34. Schwartz (2000, 56–57) cites several commandments in which the analogy clearly does not hold, such as the command to honor parents and the laws of sacrifice. But his overly literal reading seems to miss what I take as the crucial point of the analogy.

35. Klawans (2006, 62–65) insists on a thematic understanding of the principle but does so in one limited context (in the care and selection of the animal to be sacrificed).

36. With the exception of the Nazarite vow (Num. 6). Cf. Ophir and Rosen-Zvi (2018, 50n86).

37. See Gen. 15:1, 12–21; 1 Sam. 3:3–10; Ex. 3:1–6, 33:17–23, respectively. Schwartz (2000, Torah, 257) justly states that understanding the holiness of God as his separateness is not limited to the Holiness Code.

38. Olyan (2000, 17).

39. There are a few passages of priestly origin in which God's holiness appears as an event and a task, not only a fact, and seems to have a dynamic nature (Lev. 22:32; Num. 27:14; repeated with some variations in Deut. 32:51; Isa. 5:16; Ezek. 20:41; 28:22, 25; 39:27). But what is actually at stake there is not a process that God's holiness undergoes but the event of its revelation to human eyes, its public display, even an audience of nations, as Ezekiel has it. In the same vein, desecration affects God's name, not his holiness (Lev. 22:32).

40. With a dim anticipation in Job 5:9. The conception of God's holiness presented here appears in passages that Knohl (1995, 104–6) identifies as P and H alike.

41. Milgrom (1991, 615–17, 689, 732); Schwartz (1999, 254–55). When judgment is given in a human tribunal and it fails to respond and to execute the offender, this human tribunal is ignored by God. "I Myself shall turn my face against the man and his clan, and I shall cut Him off . . ." (Lev. 20:2–5).

42. E.g., eating sacrificial meat after its holiness time has expired desecrates God's "hallowed offering" (Lev. 19:8) or name (Lev. 22:32) without defiling anything.

43. Priestly capital punishment is not limited to offenses against God's holiness (e.g., the one who vilifies his father, his mother, or God—Lev 20:9, 24:16).

44. For the dual nature of the Tent, see Hundley (2015). On the use of ritual to delimit sovereign power see, for example, Graeber and Shalins (2017, chaps. 1, 7).

45. Haran (1978, 175–88); Greenstein (1989, 48–49). Jenson (1992, 89–114); Hendel (2008), and the systematic reconstruction of gradation of proximity to holiness, risks, and means of protection in Hundley (2011, chaps. 6–7).

46. This includes lepers, men or women who have discharge from their body, birth-giving women, and people who have killed an animal or touched dead bodies. The detailed instructions take six chapters in Leviticus (12–17). These peoples' obligatory offerings serve the purpose of cleansing, not atonement (cf. Milgrom 1991, 742–68).

47. Greenstein (1989, 48).

48. The analogy between defilement and death and cleanliness and life is underlined in Milgrom's (1991) translation and interpretation of Leviticus. For holiness as the signifier of life, see Greenstein (1984, 91–93). In what follows, I try to further extend the analogy.

49. This is even more so in the case of sanctification, according to the texts identified as H, where it is understood as a state of constant becoming (Knohl 1994, 179–86; Olyan 2000, 174), against Milgrom (1991, 686–87), who understands the injunction to sanctify as a condition: If you follow the rules of sanctification, you would be holy.

50. See Ophir and Rosen Zvi (2018, 39–45).

51. Note the clear difference between this reading of God's intolerance, zealotry, and frequent reliance on violence with the one proposed by Jan Assmann (2008, 2010, 2018) and the interpretation presented earlier.

52. Hendel (unpublished, 12).

53. Klawans (2006, 71). The theme recurs in Lev. 26:30–33, but for the most part this chapter belongs to a different theocratic formation and will be addressed separately in our next chapter. On God's withdrawal from his desecrated dwelling place and its far-reaching ramifications, see Olyan (2000, 39–40). The idea that God departed or expelled the inhabitants of the land only after their evils and inequities accumulated and crossed a certain unarticulated threshold, which is implied in these passages, is more explicit in the scene of "the great abominations" in Ezek. 8–9. Elsewhere Ezekiel suggests that the priestly doctrine of punishment for desecrating God's name or temple may be initiated by God himself (24:21) but could be revoked through human atonement or divine reform (Ezek. 33:10–20, 36:22–32).

54. As Hundley (2011, 39) puts it, "God dwelling in the tabernacle is both the cause and the result of the tabernacle's construction, dedication, and inauguration." He associates the movement of divine presence with its permanence.

55. Hundley (2011, 39) describes God's "semi permanence" in the tabernacle as an "intrusion of heaven into earth" (49). Given that "heaven" (*shamayim*) is mentioned in priestly writings only in the context of creation and never appears in Leviticus or Numbers, this phrase seems to me an unwarranted description of God's externality. I propose to speak here of excess but not of transcendence or height. The distinction should be underlined. Unlike Hundley and the entire tradition he relies on, I do not assume that "divine presence, like divinity itself is difficult to explain, much less envision, as one must describe in human terms what by definition transcends them. Such a quest remains an effort to grasp the ungraspable." This statement, which frames Hundley's otherwise astute reading of divine presence (2011, chap. 2), seems to me anachronistic and misleading. The difficulty appears only when the "ungraspable" (like "heaven") is read into the text. God's "fire" and "cloud," for example, are not indications of a difficulty but of a majestic imagination, which through the use of a

graspable image carries the listeners and readers beyond the visible *without invoking the problem* of grasping the unseen. The externality of God in P is not a problem; it is a fact.

56. The term appears in numerous priestly episodes, e.g., Ex. 16:7, 10; 24:16–17; Lev. 9:6; Num. 14:10, 21.

57. For the appearance of the glory in the cloud, see, e.g., Ex. 16:10, 24:16, 40:34–35. The cloud often marks his epiphany without mentioning his glory (e.g., Ex. 19:9, 33:9–10, 40:36–38; Lev. 16:2, 13). A text ascribed to a priestly redactor (Num. 9:15–23) summarizes the choreography of God's presence and movement, omitting the fire and using the cloud as its main marker. Cf. Num. 10:11–12, 17:7. On the difference between the use of "the column of fire and cloud" as a marker of divine presence in JE and the cloud and the fire in P sources, see Hundley (2011, 43–49).

58. Knohl (1995, 105), who identifies these verses as P, forgets them when he writes (2003, 9) that the priestly Torah avoids "the attribution of any physical dimensions to God . . . save the act of commanding." While he is right about the abstract tendency of the priestly conception of God, he typically disregards the violence still attributed to him.

59. E.g., Ex. 26:31–33; Lev. 10:12–20, 15:31–33, 16.

60. Onkelos translates "stranger" (*zar*) as secular or profane (*hilonet*). "Shall be put to death" (*yumat*) is more ambiguous, but since killings associated with transgressions at the Tabernacle were ascribed to divine executions and no instructions were given for human execution (who, where, how, etc.), this phrase was read by Tannaitic rabbis and latter rabbinic authorities to mean a warning announcing slaughter "by Heaven's hands" (Bavli, Sanhedrin 84a, Rashi's commentary on the verse in Numbers, among others). Slightly different versions of the same warnings, with or without the death threat, repeat elsewhere (Num. 17:5, 18:3–4). The exception—Num. 25:5–9—is discussed in what follows.

61. Douglas (1984, 52–55).

62. Hendel (unpublished).

63. Otto (1924); Douglas (1999). For a precise, abstract model of holiness in Douglas and its thorough critique, see Kunin (2004, chap. 2, esp. 51–66, 83–98).

64. They certainly did in the story of creation (Gen. 1), the priestly version of the flood in Gen. 6–9, and the list of pure and impure animals (Lev. 11), and perhaps also when introducing the Sabbath of the land (Lev. 25:1–13).

65. "On Mount Sinai" (Ex. 31:18; Lev. 25:1, 27:34), "from the Tent of Meeting" (Lev. 1:1), in the Tent of Meeting (Num. 1:1), or in an unnamed place, but always in the wilderness.

66. The identification of much of the Korah episode in Num. 16 and of Phinehas's Zealotry in Num. 25 as priestly has been questioned by Knohl (1994, 73–85, 96–98), who attributes these passages to the Holiness Code. One of his reasons is that "a direct punishment by God is foreign to the conception of the Priestly school" (96).

67. I read these chapters as demonstrative of divine rule in priestly sources, not as its exception (cf. Baden 2012, 163). The reinstitution included the priests' own birthright and supremacy (Num. 17:16–25), the rules governing their privileged access to the Tabernacle, the benefits accompanying their sacrificial practice (18:1–19), and the Levites' duties and privileges (18:20–32).

68. Unless otherwise indicated, all references in this section are to the Book of Numbers.

69. For reasons explained later, I prefer to translate *'eidah* as congregation and *qahal* as assembly.

70. The man named On is only mentioned in 16:1, but his name may be a trace of a story about a third group of rebels.

71. Korah and his congregation—v. 5; Dathan and Abiram—vv. 12, 25, 27b; two hundred and fifty men—v. 35. The deconstruction and reconstruction of the fragments of which our story consists, and the precise role and method of their redactor(s), were subjects of great scholarly attention and produced a variety of mosaic-like compositions out of what is clearly a multilayered text. Modern scholars largely agree in identifying the pre-priestly source that tells the story of Dathan and Abiram: 12–14, 25–26, 27b–32a, 33–34, according to Friedman (2003, 268–70), to which Levine (1993, 405, 411–17) adds 1–2, 27a, and 32b. They mostly disagree about the composition of the priestly fragments, and especially on the chronological and thematic place of Korah. Knohl (1995, 73–78) identifies two stories stitched together through several redactions, to which the story of Korah (identified as H) was added to bridge their differences. Friedman's and Baden's reconstructions of two coherent stories (which I generally follow here) group Korah with the chieftains and separate Korah's congregation (*edah*) from Dathan and Abiram (Friedman 2003, 268–70; Baden 2012, 149–68). Frankel (2002, 255–58) notes how different verses associate Korah with each of the two other groups. Taking all this into account, my attention below will be focused, as usual, on the theopolitical contours of the various scenes stitched together.

72. See Walzer (1985, 110–12). Knohl (1995, 76–77) attributes the claim "all the congregation is holy" to the chieftains and sees Korah as a later addition. If this is accepted, "*eddah*" refers to all of Israel, "a kingdom of priests and a holy nation," in line with his insistence on the conception of "inclusive sacredness that characterized the holiness school" (180–86). Others insist on the text's priestly affiliation and read "*eddah*" as referring to the Levites only. See Olyan (2000, 136n63); Baden (2012, 153).

73. See the warning to "the sons of Kohath," Korah's clan, "do not touch the holy" (Num. 4:15, 17–20). The warning may concern their specific task of dealing with the ark's cover and other vessels at the heart of the service practice (5–14). Cf. Baden (2012, 161–63).

74. Walzer (1985, 111).

75. Baden reads this phrase as a straightforward refusal to adhere to Moses's call ("and Moses sent to call . . ." [Num. 16:12]), a response that forces Moses to go to

their place (16:25). But the use of the verb *naale* ("come" or "go up"; Num. 16:13, 13:31) and the reference to the "land of milk and honey" (Num. 16:13; 13:31), clearly echoes the twelve scouts episode.

76. I am using the term "inoperativity" in the sense given by Agamben (2015, 247–48)—"restoring [the] potentiality" of an actual existence or a conventional form of acting—and demonstrated earlier in his essay on Bartleby (1999, 243–72) and his reading of Paul's first letter to the Corinthians (7:29–31; 2005, 19–29).

77. Frankel (2002, 228–29), who rightly insists that both fragments challenge Moses's and Aaron's leadership, fails to notice this difference. Nonpriestly sources (probably E) mention two other episodes in which Moses's authority was at stake, beyond and without any specific complaints (Num. 11:26–29; 12:2–8), and both involve the order of prophecy.

78. Moses's response echoes Samuel's response to Israel's demand for a king (1 Sam. 8:6). In both cases the pressure is put on a prophet, God's direct delegate. Moses's humility is asserted hyperbolically by another nonpriestly (E) fragment (Num. 12:3).

79. For Dathan and Abiram: 16:15, 28–30; for Korah and his congregations: 16:5–7, 16–19 (cf. Baden 2012, 158–60).

80. 16:1b; cf. note 71. Note that no defilement was involved here, only a challenge to the priestly order, hence suspension of God's verdict was possible.

81. *Vayov'du*, lost, wiped out.

82. Sawyer (2018, 116–17) thinks that Korah is "fully aware" of the risks he is taking, and what he is proposing makes no sense without his knowledge of the high stakes involved. The threat is also implied, he believes, in Moses's response to Korah (Num. 16:8–9). But the fact that no coercion was needed to bring Korah and his band with their fire pans to God's service on the next morning may indicate that they truly believed in their right and underestimated the risks involved in claiming it.

83. Holiness plays here the same role that freedom plays in a Greek polis. Equal distribution could be claimed by slaves or women but was more likely to come from nonaristocratic free males.

84. The Korah episode is a perfect example of Rancière's concept of the political (Rancière 1999, chaps. 1–2). I am borrowing the form of Rancière's argument without endorsing the claim that this form of resurgence is the only form a political event may take (see Chapter 1 and Ophir 2020, 169ff.). If the political is understood as an act that embeds a public problematization of relations of power (Ophir 2022, "The Political"), both rebellions in Num. 16 (not only Korah's) are exemplary political acts.

85. Moses kept his harsh language limited to his appeal to God (Num. 16:26); cf. Greenstein (1974, 123–24).

86. The priestly narrator later supports Moses's interpretation of Korah's grievance by describing his arrival to the test with a phrase taken almost verbatim from the cere-

mony of Aaron's investiture: "assemble[d] all the congregation by the entrance of the Tent of Meeting" (Num. 16:19; Lev. 8:3). Cf. Baden (2012, 155).

87. Moses plays with the ambiguity of the holy and the proximity to it—a *pharmakon* that may equally heal or kill; those who sought to prove their closeness to the holy would soon find themselves consumed by it.

88. Clearly, for the author of the story, it was much more important to prove Korah's wrongdoing through divine intervention in the political *mésentente* than to present Moses's putative reasoning or Korah's true motivation (a quest for equality or for material and political benefits).

89. Unlike other ordeals in which the identity of the true God is decided—e.g., in Egypt, confronting the Egyptian magicians (Ex. 7:8–13); and on Mount Carmel, confronting prophets of Baal (1 Kings 18)—here what lies at stake is the status of the worshippers and their political standing.

90. In fact, the two ordeals of Num. 16 have no parallel in the entire biblical corpus. Abraham's ordeal (Gen. 22) was set by God; in the ordeal set by Elijah (1 Kings 18:20–40), God provides the proof, but the violence is ordered by his prophet and executed by "all the people" (18:39–40).

91. In other words, Yahweh is not a Schmittian sovereign whose self-constituting authority is limited to declaring or proclaiming the exceptionality of a case with respect to an existing *juridical order*, for his power over the exception applies to the entire order of Being.

92. Badiou (1988, 95–115).

93. Agamben (1998, 25).

94. See Chapter 3, "The Sovereign's Moment."

95. Agamben (1998, 85). The boundaries are cancelled the moment God brings Korah and his congregation close to him (16:5) and consumes them in his fire (16:35). Note that they are "brought close to (*hikriv el*) him," not sacrificed to (*hikriv le-*) him.

96. Agamben (1998, 82).

97. Using JSP translation, not Alter's. Note that the priestly writings do not tell the story of this election and do not use the term. But the entire priestly corpus cannot be read without the Sinai revelation and the Ten Commandments (Ex. 19–20); the institution of Israel as "a kingdom of priest, and a holy nation" (19:6); and Israel's status as an exceptional nation by virtue of its relation to God. Throughout the priestly corpus, the realm of the holy applies only to Israel.

98. As if to compensate for this, God acts on his own soon after, when the next occasion occurs (Num. 17:6–15).

99. On the exception in pre-priestly theocracy, see Chapter 3. The meticulously staged performance of divine violence in Num. 16 appears from this perspective as a corrective to Lev. 10:1–7, where God reacts "automatically" to the desecration of the holy (1–2), while the priests' performance is limited to cleaning the mess (4–7).

100. This is true for Korah's rebellion, whether one reads the two rebellions separately, together, or follows the redactor and understands Num. 16–18 as a single literary unit.

101. Agamben (1998, 84).

102. Agamben (1998, 84). "Political" is used here in Agamben's (Schmittian) sense that reduces it to the sovereign's instance.

103. Agamben (1998, 84).

104. For the anachronistic term "religious," one should instead read here "worship" and all aspects of human activity, including labor, war, and government, that concern things, places, and times on which the holy has been bestowed. In priestly theocracy, the juridical order centered on the regulation of worship. The Holiness Code (Lev. 17–26) should be considered a part of (or a corpus closely related to) priestly writings in this respect, and hence the entire sphere of social relations where holiness rules apply to every Israelite (i.e., non-Levites) should be added. These rules too are still governed by the overarching command "be holy" (e.g., 19:2, 20:26); cf. Knohl (1995, chap. 4).

105. There is a consensus among scholars that the phrase "the dwelling of Korah, Dathan, and Abiram" (Num. 16:24, 27) is a result of a redactor intervention. Some believe that Korah's name was inserted into a JE fragment (e.g., Levine 1993, 415–16), while others assume that Dathan and Abiram were added to the priestly version (e.g., Frankel 2002, 212–13; Friedman 2003, 270; Baden 2012, 154–56). The "entire congregation" is assembled by Korah (Num. 16:19), and the phrase echoes the assembly of the people on the occasion of the investiture of Aaron and his sons (Lev. 8:3).

106. Alter (2019, 1:536n34).

107. In the third episode discussed in what follows, the priestly narrator of the story of Israel's prostitution at the Tent of Meeting names the victims of the slaughter only after the episode is concluded (Num. 25:14–15).

108. The two verses differ in one word: "*separate* yourself" (*hybadlu*, which Alter translates as "divide"), in the first case, and "*lift* yourself" (*harimu*) in the second.

109. For the identification of Num. 25:1–5 as a J text, see Levine (2000, 294); Friedman (2003, 287).

110. The singular appearance of *kuba*, a Semitic word designating a curved structure (from which "cupola" and "cup" are derived) including a shack or a tent, may signal an attempt to create a distance between the place as a holy site where Yahweh communicates to his people and the desecrated site of promiscuity.

111. No reason for the "weeping" is mentioned; it is implied by the artful stitching of the two fragments.

112. Lev. 10:1–3; Num. 16, 17:6–15, 25:6–18.

113. "For one staff there is for the name of their father's house" (Num. 17:18). That Aaron's name, not Moses's, was written on the Levite's staff is yet additional

evidence that the priestly redactor was more interested in closeness and access to the holy (hence in Aaron's status) than in Moses's authority. See Knohl (1994, 76–77).

114. Olyan (2000, 28–35) shows that the Levites' place in the hierarchy is expressed in a range of precepts that organize the service at the tabernacle and even distinguishes the high priest from the rest of the priests.

115. Benjamin (1996). Benjamin refers to an isolated moment from the Korah episode (probably Num. 16:31–34) to exemplify, erroneously, I think, his own idiosyncratic concept of divine violence. More on this in this chapter's last section.

116. No genealogy appears in Deuteronomy, but the election of the Levites and their status is clearly stated (18:1–8).

117. Yitzhak over Ishmael; Jacob over Esau; Joseph over all his brothers; Ephraim over Menashe; the Levites over all the tribes and, with the coronation of Saul, the smallest tribe, Benjamin, over all the others; David and Solomon over their many brothers. Primogeniture is respected in two earlier genealogies (Gen. 5, 11).

118. This may explain why Korah could ascribe the division of labor and hierarchy among the Levites to Moses and Aaron but not to God.

119. Love as a groundless preference, a reason for taking possession, and a basis for inheritance is a central Deuteronomic theme.

120. Job dared to challenge it only in order to end up with a grand reassertion of the arbitrary nature of divine rule—or of the shortcoming of human understanding, which is virtually the same: There may be a reason, but humans will never grasp it, yet their obedience is demanded nevertheless.

121. Cf. Olyan (2000, 27).

122. The same hierarchy is described differently in Ezek. 40–48 and 1 Chron. 23:13. Cf. Olyan (2000, 27–33).

123. Biblical authors were not oblivious to this logic, as the stories of Hagar and her son Ishmael (Gen. 21:15–16) or Jochebed and her son Moses (Ex. 2: 1–6) reveal.

124. The same phrase, *netunim li*, appears several times in the description of the priestly order, and not always in relation to God. In Num. 3:8–9, the Levites are "given to Aaron and to his sons . . . given, given to him." The emphatic gift indicates service and subordination—this is what Levites are (given) for, to be dedicated to the service of Aaron and the other priests in the latter's service of God.

125. Alter translates the emphatic doubling of the Hebrew *netunim* as "wholly given."

126. The phrase is repeated with some variations in vv. 41, 45.

127. These texts belong to the Levite Treatise, which Knohl (1995, 80–81) considers a Holiness School source.

128. See, among others, Levine (1993, 385–86).

129. For parallels and variations, see Lev. 4–5.

130. "To you [Aaron] I have given them as a share [*l'moshhah* לְמָשְׁחָה] and to your

sons as a perpetual statute. This will be yours from the most holy things from the fire, all their offerings . . . and all their guilt offerings that they give back to me" (18:8–9). For reading לְמָשְׁחָה as "share," see Levine (1993, 442–43).

131. On sacrificial offerings as a gift that implies ownership and disowning, see Klawans (2006, 84–85) and the two sources on which he relies: Milgrom (1991, 441; 2000, 1875–76); Barr and Kennedy (1963, 871).

132. Note that the Israelites' firstborns were spared twice, in fact, first from their enemies and then from their God. It did not take much for the sovereign to switch sides, from the external enemy to the internal one, to kill his subjects (or purpose-fully let them be killed) and not kill their enemies, or to kill them as if they were his enemies: "And it will come about that as I had thought to do to them [the peoples of Canaan, Israel's enemies] I shall do to you" (Num. 33:56). In the two episodes discussed earlier, God treated Israelites as if they were his enemies (Num. 17:6–15, 25:9). "Not killing the enemy" is exemplified in the war against the Amalekites and the Canaanites, mentioned in a J fragment that the priestly redactor chose to incorporate to conclude the story of the scouts (Num. 14:40–45). The stories about the impact of the Holy Ark that accompanies the Israelites in their wars in Canaan follow the same logic (e.g., Jud. 20:26–28; 1 Sam. 4:1–11).

133. In the parallel E source, all of Israel's firstborns belong to God and need to be consecrated "to Him." Those whom God let live should be redeemed (i.e., substituted), but all Israelites, not just the Levites, are charged with their redemption (Ex. 13:1, 11–16). A different conception of belonging, also rooted in Egypt, is found in the Holiness Code: "For Mine are the Israelites as slaves, they are My slaves whom I brought out of the land of Egypt: I am Yahweh your God" (Num. 25:55). Here the Israelites do not need to be redeemed in order to be protected from the threat of divine violence. Rather, the opposite is true. It is because they belong to God that they are protected from human violence.

134. Agamben (1998, 8ff.). In a holy war, the ban (*herem*) implies strict rules re-garding taking or sparing life and property. Outside of this context, no abandonment is commanded. Per Agamben (1998, 96–100), Hagar and Joseph should be considered as abandoned and saved by direct or indirect divine intervention, while Jephthah's daughter is sacrificed after a period of suspension, in which she becomes the biblical example for the status of a devotee who has survived the sacrificial oath. However, the vow that led to her sacrifice and the decision to respect it was Jephthah's, not God's. God granted Jephthah his spirit (Jud. 11:29) so he could win the war but granted not the voice that could have annulled his vow.

135. Following Levine (1974, 22–27; 1968, 79–80), Anderson (1987, 91–126), and others, Jonathan Klawans (2006, 71–72) argues that the main role of sacrifice is to generate and ensure God's proximity. "Sacrifice attracts and maintains Divine Presence; moral defilement resulting from grave sin repels the divine presence." More specifically, the purpose of the daily sacrifice is "to provide regular and pleasing odors

to the Lord." It is "completely devoid of any concern with expiation" and does "not undo the damage done by grave transgression. Quite the contrary, grave transgression undoes what the daily sacrifice produces." Some passages support this reading, of course. The emphasis on divine presence at the sanctuary is evident; moral sins defile the sanctuary and the entire land and might bring divine presence to an end. Even God's pleasure at the scents coming from the altar is mentioned. For this interpretation to hold, however, one must do much more than ignore the explicit rationale for the Levites' service (e.g., Num. 8:19) and the sacrifices specifically meant to atone for misdeeds. One must also understate the immense danger in God's proximity and the terror associated with the sanctuary (Lev. 8:35; Num. 8:19, 17:27–28) and conceive his violent eruptions and their larger political contexts as irrelevant. In doing so, one relegates them to a different, unrelated layer of the text or, at best, recognizes them as marginal exceptions or corrections to a system whose rationale is drawn from human interests. To interpret the interest in sacrifice as humans' attempts to manipulate and extort God means to give up on God's role, plans, and interests in the sacrificial drama.

136. In Propp's words (2006, 492): "For the Priestly Source, the whole goal of religion, in all its facets, is to maximize and prolong contact between Yahweh and Israel." Hendel (unpublished, 27), who quotes Propp, emphasizes that this includes the rules concerning transgressions in the realm of the holy.

137. As Agamben (1998, part 1, chaps. 1–2; part 2, chaps. 1–3) has it with respect to the figure of *homo sacer* in ancient Roman law.

138. Directly, when God spoke to Aaron and Moses together (e.g., Lev. 11:1, 13:1), or indirectly, through Moses (Lev. 6:2, 18; 17:1; 21:1; 22:2).

139. For non-Israelites, see Ex. 12:43–49; Lev. 25:6, 10; Num. 15:15–16. Cf. Ophir and Rosen Zvi (2018, 25–39).

140. The general scheme of this biotechnocratic web remained more or less intact when the Deuteronomic school made Israel a holy nation and applied the imperative "sanctify" to every one of its members. See Weinfeld (1992, 225–32).

141. An important difference between the Priestly Torah and the Holiness Code with respect to violence should be noted here. Priestly laws that concern cultic life can be read as drawing fences around the dangerous core of the holy, anticipating its immanent violence and trying to preempt it. But the Holiness Code extends the participation in ritual practices to the entire people, charges "all the community of the Israelites" to sanctify (Lev. 19:1), reads larger spheres of life in terms of purity and impurity, and adds important sections that regulate social and economic relations (19:9–18, 33–37; 25) so as to limit oppression and dispossession (and do this in a way we would recognize today as driven by a moral interest). These laws are explicitly related to future divine violence that would take revenge of the offenders (Lev. 26:14–43). The description of this future violence displays many clear resemblances with and affinities to Deut. 28. Since the next chapter will play a key role in reconstructing

the Deuteronomic theocratic formation (see the second section of Chapter 5), I will skip dealing with it here. I leave unanswered the historical and philological questions concerning the relation between these two distinct conceptions of divine violence in priestly writings.

142. See the end of the second section in Chapter 3.

143. Exodus 14, which tells the story, mixes pre-priestly and priestly sources, but one of the clearest moments of separation—"and the waters were split apart. And . . . the water were as a wall to them" (14:21b–22)—is considered priestly (Friedman 2003, 143) and confers its logic on the entire scene. The verb *pasaḥ*, from which the holiday's name—Passover—comes, used to designate the separation, meant "save" (e.g., Is. 31:5) before it meant "pass over" (Ex. 12:23).

144. There is only one moment where a threat of such violence is mentioned. After the return of the scouts, when the entire congregation "meant to pelt [Joshua and Caleb] in stones" for insisting on carrying out God's plan, "the Glory of Yahweh appeared in the Tent of Meeting," and the threat immediately dissipated or at least eluded mention (Num. 14:10–11).

145. Gen. 17:14; Ex. 12:15, 19, 31:14; Lev. 24:16–17, 20, 27:29; Num. 15:32–36, 35:17–19, 31. *Nefesh*, the living, animated element, is translated by Alter in these verses as "person." The killing of a murderer is the duty of the blood avenger; the idolater (Lev. 20:1–4, 27), the man who vilifies God or his parents, and the one who desecrates the Sabbath should be stoned by the entire community. There are no rules for killing those guilty of sexual transgressions (Lev. 20) or captives who fall under the law of the ban (Lev. 17: 29). Nothing is said about the need to establish the fact of the matter first.

146. *Kareth* is the punishment for eating "what is leavened" on Passover (Ex. 12:19), for not bringing one's sacrifice to the sanctuary (Lev. 17:9–10), or for consuming blood when eating animal flesh (Lev. 17:11–15). According to a sweeping injunction in Num. 15:30, any purposeful transgression of God's laws ("with a high hand") is considered a blasphemy and requires execution of *kareth*.

147. Best exemplified by the recurring cases of inadvertent touching of the moving ark (1 Sam. 6:19–21, 2 Sam. 6:6–8).

148. The idea that sacrifice may avert revenge, redistribute violence, bring it under control, and make its patterns somewhat more predictable was advocated by Rene Girard, in a number of influential and controversial works (e.g., Girard 1979, 1986; Williams 1996). The person or animal to be sacrificed is a scapegoat is picked arbitrarily, by fate or lottery; his, her, or its sacrifice appeases victims of previous violence and is accepted as a repair by the rival parties caught in a cycle of violence. Often an animal substitutes for the human victim of a future revenge, reducing further the irredeemable cost of sacrifice. The sacrificial violence thus interrupts a chain of revengeful acts and prevents the circulation of more violence, and it does this without assuming, promoting, or sustaining a centralized, hierarchized, asymmetric structure of power

relations. If the sacrificial act and the scapegoating of a random victim succeeds in stopping the chain of revenge, it will be repeated only when the next incidental act of violence would trigger it.

As far as I can see, Girard's ideas about the origin of sacrifice and its evolution, compelling as they are, cannot be used in interpreting priestly sacrifice and substitutions. In fact, the analysis here shows that the priestly sacrificial practice and ideology present an economy of violence that consistently contradicts the one proposed by Girard. Sacrificial practice takes place at the heart of a system of power that is structured, hierarchical, and asymmetric; sacrifice does not only substitute for violent actions (thus mitigating violence) but is also a site and occasion for new eruptions of violence; the determination of who and what is sacrificable may appear arbitrary, but once established, there is nothing arbitrary about the execution of the recurring violent act; only a small portion of the sacrificial activity aims to mitigate human violence and is rarely a direct response to it, and most of it is part of an ongoing exchange relation with the divine ruling power.

149. "In its *nefesh*." *Nefesh* in this context is literally "life" or a "living [creature]." Throughout these passages, "life" or "living" is always rendered in the Hebrew *nefesh*.

150. Gen. 9:1–17 is a priestly source, echoed in Lev. 17:10–16.

151. It is not unlikely that pre-exilic priestly authors were familiar with laws related to animal suffering in E and D sources (Ex. 23:4–5, 12, 19; Lev. 25:28; Deut. 22:6–7, 10, 25:4), and it is quite certain that these passages were known to exilic and post-exilic authors and redactors. Cf. Rosenblum (2016, chap. 1); Stone (2018, chap. 4).

152. Benjamin (1996, 249–50).

153. "Dis-reading" should be clearly distinguished from "misreading." Benjamin's enigmatic essay has become a fetish text in recent critical theory, but most of those who have used the wealth of its insights have been oblivious to this dis-reading. Sawyer (2020, 113–19) is a clear exception.

154. Benjamin (1999, 249–50).

155. God explains that he is going to "harden Pharaoh's heart" so he can "multiply [His] strikes to let Egypt . . . know that I am Yahweh." The passage is usually recognized as a priestly source (Knohl 1995, 61; Propp 1998, 262).

156. Benjamin (1999, 240ff.).

157. Benjamin (1999, 241ff.). Cf. Derrida's (1992, 38–48) emphasis on the deconstruction of distinction in the process of its articulation and how the "spectrality" of police violence emblematizes this "internal" deconstruction.

158. In the first case (discussed briefly earlier), a Midianite woman was killed because she had sex with an Israelite at God's sanctuary as part of a rite for an alien god. In the later text, Moses, reproaching the Israelites for "let[ting] every [Medianite] female live," reminded them of the Midianite women's part in the betrayal of "Yahweh's trust in the affair of [Baal] Peor" (Num. 31:16). He drew from that sacrilege the injunction to kill all captive Midianite women except for the virgins. They alone

among the captives were allowed to live, and only they among the plunder were handed as property for Israel's use (31:17–18, 26–28). This is a strange exception, for not only does it deviate from the law of the ban (perhaps representing a separate version of it; Frevel [2013]; Rees [2015, 86]), but also approves sexual relations with the Midianite women, who were just presented as this war's *casus belli*. For the bitter enmity toward the Midianites in priestly writings, see Dozeman (2008, 277–81).

159. The priestly redactor of the passage replaced the Moabites in the J fragment (preserved in Num. 25:1–4) with Midianites. Knohl (1995, 96–98) attributes both passages to the Holiness School.

160. Midrash *Tanhuma Bamidbar* (S. Buber Recension, edited and supplemented by R. Francis Nata), Matot 3, trans. Townsend 1989.

161. Michael Sawyer (2018, 105–19) is right in juxtaposing the Korah episode to Rousseau's social contract in order to argue that Korah's punishment demonstrates the lethal coercion necessary for the exercise of the general will. Sawyer's juxtaposition implies the affinity I am trying to expose here between biblical theocracy and the modern state, with the impunity of their respective sovereigns and the precarity of their unwanted subjects.

5. THE TIME OF THE COVENANT
AND THE TEMPORALIZATION OF VIOLENCE

1. Unless otherwise indicated, all chapter and verse locations in this chapter refer to Deuteronomy.

2. *Dvarim* is the second word in the opening phrase that gave the book its Hebrew name. It could mean "things spoken," "*logoi*" (speech, enunciations), but also "issues," "things of concern." The seemingly clear location is in the "land," "wilderness," or "steppes" of Moab (1:5; 28:69; and 32:49, 2:8, 34:1, respectively). The different names may reflect different sources.

3. It is generally agreed that the "Song of Moses" in Deut. 32 is an independent source. There is no agreement about the rest. Friedman, for example (2003, 358–68nn.), identifies Deut. 31:14–15, 23, and 34:5–7 as pre-priestly sources; 34:8–9 as priestly; and 31:28–30 as late Deuteronomist. Baden (2012) considers chapter 31 in its entirety as D (138–39) while "taking over" and incorporating some E stories (147); Moses's poem in chapter 32 is "an independent piece . . . taken up by the D author and framed accordingly" (139) and God's words to Moses that conclude the chapter (31:48–52) as Deuteronomic adaptation of a P source; Moses's blessings in chapter 33 is a "J poem" on par with Jacob's deathbed speech in Gen. 49 (147); and chapter 34 consists of a compilation of the depiction of Moses's death by the three non-Deuteronomist sources (J, E, and P) (148). Neither Baden nor Sonnet (1997), who generally pays closer attention to the literary effect of the editorial work in Deuteronomy, considers the effect of the series of closures.

4. Deut. 1:1, 5; 4:1; 5:1; 6:6, 7:7, 8:1, 12; 11:26. "A wheel within a wheel (Ezek.

1:14) . . . an act of communication within an act of communication," writes Jean-Pierre Sonnet (1997, 1) in his fine reading of Deuteronomy (cf. 258). This is Sonnet's organizing theme and his interpretive compass, but he is interested mainly in one direction of this contraction of time, the one bridging Moses's address, "in the represented world . . . and the book's address to its reader" (1). I am interested first in the other direction, the one bridging, in the represented world, the *dvarim* spoken then, in the story's past, and now, in the presence of Moses's addressees. This point is made by Römer (1992, 74) and is explicitly rejected by Sonnet (1997, 11); it is not a clue for deciphering "the poetic parameters" that should guide the reading for it would contradict the Pentateuch's most basic assumption: "its claim to tell history." We, however, have placed this assumption between brackets and under a different logic once we started reading Deuteronomy as a thought experiment in utopic thinking.

5. Past events are described at length in 9:7–29, 11:2–6, 29:1–8, and mentioned in 30, 34:12, and in the numerous commandments to remember: 4:9, 16; 5:14; 7:18; 8:2, 18; 9:7; 15:15; 16:12; 24:9, 18, 22; 25:17, 19. More generally, the theme of memory runs throughout Deuteronomy (see, e.g., Brueggemann 2001; Sacks 2019).

6. With a few exceptions: an explicit reference to God as creator of man (4:32), a more elliptic reference to all earthly creatures and heavenly bodies (4:16–19), a quick reminder of Sodom and Gomorrah (29:22), and two brief allusions to "your fathers" (10:22) and "my father . . . an Aramean about to perish" (26:5) who descended to Egypt. Assuming that the Deuteronomic authors were familiar with a least some of the Fathers' stories from Genesis (cf. Baden 2012, chap. 4), the complete silence with respect to the events that preceded the migration to Egypt is quite brutal and may reflect a deliberate decision to pave a radically new theopolitical path. "Fathers" are mentioned almost fifty times in Deuteronomy, often as bearers of the promise made by God regarding the fate of their descendants, and with a few exceptions (e.g., 9:5, 27; 29:12; 30:20), they remain nameless. Römer (1990, 2000a) ascribes the few exceptions to a late redactor and understands the nameless fathers as a designation for the Israelites' ancestors that came out of Egypt. Hwang (2012) argues, more convincingly, I believe, that "your fathers" does not refer to any single generation; it may signify ancestors who first entered the covenant.

7. On the Deuteronomic version of the scouts' affair, see the last section in Chapter 3. The differences between Exodus's and Deuteronomy's accounts of the Sinai/Horeb revelation have been widely noted. For us, two are of special importance. The first is the Deuteronomist's emphasis on the public reading of the laws, which is absent in Exodus (cf. Frankel 2011, 80–82). The second is the Deuteronomist emphasis on the prohibition of visual representation not only of God but of the memory of his revelation (4:15). This has been interpreted as an indication for the transition from monolatrism to monotheism (Römer 2007, 173; cf. Sommer 2015, 64–74).

8. See Baden (2012, chap. 4).

9. For the alleged supplements, see Lundbom (2013, 799–805, 827–32). The ear-

lier view of Haran (1978, 46–51), which identifies only the first ten verses of chapter 30 as possible, hypothetical late redactions of the curses and blessings, is mostly rejected. Friedman identifies Deuteronomy 27:63–68; 29:21–26; and 30:1–10, 15–20 as late redactions. On the dating of Deuteronomy, see Friedman (1981a, 34–37; 1981b, on the putative attribution of the later layer to the exile in Egypt; 2003, 317, 353–54); Römer (2007, 67–81, 167–82); Otto (2013); Nicholson (2014); Schubert (2018).

10. See Na'aman (2000), Römer (2007, 181). For similar parallels between Deut. 30:15–20 and Josh. 24:14–24, see further in this chapter.

11. For *S'gulah*, see Weinfeld (1992, 226), Greenberg (1995, 173–78), Lundbom (2013, 336).

12. That the people are (or should become) holy does not mean that each member took equal share in holiness (as Weinfeld 1992, 228, proposes with respect to Deuteronomy). What may seem a logical consequence of the holiness of the entire people does not find an echo in Deuteronomy, whose authors chose to ignore—or may never have heard—Korah's story but were fully conscious of Datan's and Abiram's rebellion (11:6).

13. Cf. Lev. 11:44, 20:7, where holiness is a telos of an orientation, and intentionality is even more explicit: "and you shall sanctify yourselves and become holy."

14. Deut. 14:1–2 extends the prohibitions on self-mutilation, which in P and H applies to priests, to the people as a whole (cf. Deut. 26:19).

15. Dwelling in heaven does not by itself preclude earthly visitations and a prolonged presence. The different images of God's presence (26:15 vs. 23:15) are contradictory only when an anachronistic concept of transcendence is projected on these texts and 26:15 is read metaphorically.

16. Deut. 12:5, 11, 21; 14:23, 24; 16:6, 11; 26:2. The "Tent of Meeting" is mentioned once (31:14–15), in a passage that is commonly considered a priestly insertion.

17. Na'aman (2000, 147), reflecting a widespread consensus. Levinson (1997, 23) presents the argument and rejects some of the dissenting voices.

18. Na'aman (2000, 158).

19. Na'aman (2000, 143–44); cf. the critique of Schorch 2011, 29.

20. These three questionable assumptions are built on further tacit assumptions: that the relevant parts of the code of laws were pre-exilic; that the putative, implied reference to the temple that no longer existed would not have bothered the putative exilic redactors, and, that later, the postexilic redactors, who were active at a time of competition with the cultic center in Samaria, would not have used the occasion to clarify that Jerusalem was meant to be the place of the sanctuary. Römer (2007, 57, 61–63), echoing others, stresses an exilic reinterpretation of centralization and suggests that omitting the name of "the place" is part of an effort to dissociate divine presence from the temple and associate God's dwelling place with the land as a whole. The dating of the entire code of laws to the time of Josiah or one of his

successors (mid– or late seventh century BCE; Collins 2017, 29–35) has been challenged (Pakkala 2009; Collins 2017, 36). The other assumptions are questionable even
without a new historical insight.

21. The accommodation of an ancient tradition (e.g., Rofé 1985; Weinfeld 1988),
the effort to revive it (Na'aman 2000), or the possibility of inventing such a tradition
to legitimize a gesture toward an existing northern rival (e.g., Schorch, 2011; Schubert
2018, 74–87) would all be absorbed in the final stage of editing with similar effects.

22. "This book" is another phrase that recurs several times, sometimes with,
sometimes without "teaching." Römer (2000b) shows an eloquent transition from the
temple to the book of laws in King Solomon's prayer (1 Kings 8:12–53), a Deuteronomistic text in which God's dwelling place and the sanctuary where his name dwells
are clearly at stake.

23. 2:18–27; 3:2–11; 9:1–4 for the wars; 1:41–45; 4:10–12, 23; 5:4–5, 18–22 for
Horeb.

24. The text repeatedly denies the visual experience at Horeb while emphasizing at
the same time what the people saw with their own eyes in catastrophic episodes along
the journey in the wilderness (e.g., 1:30–31, 4:3, against 5:3–4, 20–21).

25. The Deuteronomists consistently omit stories from P sources. See Baden
(2012, 133ff.), Römer (2007, 125).

26. The Deuteronomists omit from the story of the golden calf both the Levites'
massacre (Ex. 32:26–28) and God's plague (32:35). When mentioning Baal Peor,
divine violence is mentioned and human violence (Num. 25:4–8) omitted.

27. Especially so in 1:31–34; 2; 3:1–23.

28. Sommer (2015, 195).

29. Even though most of the generation of those who came out of Egypt must have
died by this point. Note that when speaking about this visual experience (10:21, 11:7),
Moses explicitly addresses those who witnessed the "great and fearsome things" God
did in Egypt (10:21), not their children "who did not know and did not see" (11:2).

30. Scholars have long associated the strong emphasis on idolatry and the centralization of worship in chapters 12–13 with Hezekiah's and Josiah's reforms and
iconoclastic purge (2 Kings 18:4–6; 22–23; cf. Lundbom 2013, 6–7, 11–13, 442–
47; Collins 2017, 27–38). Of special attention was the relation of chapter 13 to the
language, content, and style of Vassal Treaties of Esarhaddon, a hotly contested issue
(cf. Crouch 2014, 78–92, 117–23, 138–45; Collins 2017, 33–35). The link to historical events, whose dates are well established, played a crucial role in the attempts to
determine the putative date of Deuteronomy's urtext (without settling the debate,
however). What is crucial from our perspective is that *explicit* traces of historical
events were carefully erased here, as elsewhere throughout the legal code.

31. Cf. Weinfeld (1992, 91–92).

32. Cf. (Deut 17:1–5; 18:20; 20:16–18).

33. The ceremony is part of the laws of war (20). The reiteration of the stories about God's mighty hand in sanctioned wars means that his providential violence was not sealed in the distant past; rather, it is projected onto a near future.

34. The expression is unique to Deuteronomy: 13:6; 17:7, 12; 19:19; 21:21; 22:21, 22, 24; 24:7.

35. Asylum for inadvertent killers is mentioned briefly in Exodus (21:13–14) and presented at length in Numbers (35:9–34). For the relationship and differences among these three legislations of asylum, see Stackert (2007, chap. 2).

36. "If something is to stay in memory it must be burned in: 'only that which never ceases to hurt stays in memory. . . . Man could never do without blood, torture, and sacrifices when he felt the need to create a memory for himself. . . . Pain is the most powerful aid to mnemonics" (Nietzsche 1989, 60–61). For the explanatory character of the Deuteronomic law that took the form of "an intensive preaching activity," see von Rad (2005 [1965], 221–26).

37. "The defining characteristic of Deuteronomy is appropriation and reinterpretation of earlier compositions and forms" (Knafl 2020, 1). The debt is clear, but to whom exactly, how it was incurred, and how freely and imaginatively the borrowed material was used is not.

38. Late because it probably comes from a relatively late layer of the Bible (with the presumed exception of Chapter 27), and certainly late with respect to similar covenants of suzerains and their people in the ancient Near East.

39. See Deut 27:1, 9, 11; 28:1, 14–15; 29:4, 6, 9–14; 30:11, 15, 18–19. Cf. Sommer (2015, chap. 5).

40. The Hebrew designating the sealing of the covenant, *koreth*, is always in the present. "Is sealing" could better capture the intensity of the present.

41. In the Deuteronomist version of the first covenant at Horeb, future generations were not mentioned (not even implied, as Sommer [2015, 91–93] claims), only the people present at the event, "us—we who *are* here today, all of us *alive*" (5:3). What the two moments have in common, however, is a radical extension of the covenant— from the time of the Fathers to the present in Horeb (5:3) from the present to an indefinite future in the plains of Moab (29:13).

42. The rabbinic tradition addressed the problem of obligating those who could not refuse and had to take an oath to commit themselves in various ways. A late Midrash (*Tanchuma*, Yitro, 11) suggests that all the souls of future Israelites were present at the ceremony: "'*Not standing here with us this day*' is not written in this verse but rather '*Is not here with us this day*.' This alludes to the souls who were to be created in the future, since *standing here* could not be said of them. They were included in the general statement." Later rabbinic commentators claim that the verse meant to obligate those present to educate their offspring and bring them into the covenant (Or, *Ha-Chaim*). And others made sure to include all the converts to come (Ralbag, *Biur Hamilot*).

43. This is said explicitly by "all the gentiles" (29:23) but is also implied by "the later generation" and "the stranger coming from afar" (29:21–22). Cf. Weinfeld (1992, 115); Alter (2019, 1:719n21).

44. The formula appears in the Annals of Ashurbanipal, where a similar question and answer are presented—*in the past tense*—by "the inhabitant of Arabia" after suffering Ashurbanipal's vengeful wrath. Rassam Cylinder IX, 68–74, Pritchard (1969, 300), quoted in Lundbom (2013, 812).

45. Weinfeld (1992, 108).

46. The text places its future readers in a quite unusual situation: They are invited to keep in mind simultaneously the time of the speech situation represented in the text, the time of the text's composition indicated in text, and their own time as it is anticipated by the text.

47. The full list in chapter 28 includes fourteen verses of blessing (1–14) against fifty-four verses of curses (15–68).

48. Note that *alah* is sometimes translated as "oath" (29:11, 13, 18, 20) and sometimes as "imprecation" (30:7). English translators mostly follow KJV and prefer "oath," but the word cannot be understood here in the general sense of a solemn promise. It should be understood only in its narrow connotation as "imprecation," as is made clear by its use throughout these chapters.

49. I am consciously ignoring the assumptions and speculations about the different sources combined here and the different books that may be implied in each (and illuminated by Sonnet 1997, chaps. 3–4), paying attention only to the accumulative effect of the edited text.

50. E.g., Friedman (1981a, 1981b), Nicholson (2014).

51. Gourgouris (2019, 38). The context is a discussion of La Boétie's *Discours de la servitude volontaire* (2002 (1573]).

52. Weinfeld (1992, 146–49).

53. The Misnah (*Sotah* 7:5) tried to supplement what was missing and imagined the blessings as straightforward negations of the curses: "blessed be anyone who does not make a graven molten image . . ."

54. Chapter 27 is often identified as an ancient "Elohist Shechem tradition" (Weinfeld 1992, 165) that interrupts the transition from chapter 26 to chapter 28, or calls one to reconsider its dating (Schorch 2011). See Lundbom (2013, 737–38).

55. Of these fifty-five verses, fifty-two detail about twice as many curses.

56. It is tempting to dwell on the abundance of evils: blight, panic, disaster, plague, consumption, fever, inflammation, burning, desiccation, emaciation, jaundice, bronze from heaven and iron from the earth, rain that turns into dust, defeat on the battlefield, unburied carcasses that become food for the birds, burning rash, hemorrhoids, boils and scabs, madness, blindness and confounding of the heart, exploitation and robbery, a betrothed bedded by another man, a house built and not lived in, a planted vineyard that does not yield fruit, cattle stolen and slaughtered by one's foe, sons and

daughters given to another nation, powerlessness, mental and emotional harm to those witnessing the unfolding disaster ("And you will be crazed by the sight of your eyes" [28:34]), evil burning on the knees and on the thighs, incurable diseases, exile, derision ("you will become a derision, a byword, and an adage among all the peoples where the Lord will drive you" [28:37]), locusts and worms that destroy the seed of the field, dropping away of olive trees, sons and daughters who go off in captivity, grasshoppers who despoil the crop, and sojourners who rise high and push the citizens down far below.

57. See Deut. 28:30, 31, 38–41. Quick (2018, chaps. 3–4) finds this formula of curses in several old Aramaic inscriptions and across the Bible. Quick's finding is crucial for understanding the diversity of sources available to the Deuteronomist authors and their ingenious editorial and interpretative work in borrowing and transforming them, a claim that expands and radicalizes Levinson's previous contribution (1998, 2001), which was limited to the New Assyrian context (cf. Quick 2020, 5–6). For our purposes, it is important to note that the inclusion of these curses and their sheer number amplify the general sense of a total collapse of the cursed person's lifeworld and the total control of the one who curses.

58. The two words *shmad* and *ovdan* are used here as synonyms and recur throughout the text. *Shmad*: 28:20, 21, 22, 24, 45, 48, 51, 61, 63; *ovdan*: 28:20, 22, 63. Annihilation is implied in the phrase "until he wipes you out" (*ad khaloto otcha*, 28:21).

59. The prospect of total destruction is a distinctive Deuteronomic feature that none of the other treaties in the region could have. God threatened like every other contemporary sovereign but acted like no other, surpassing all others, and calling upon no other for help.

60. Violence may always be postponed; the offenders may be spared and their innocent descendants stricken in some future generation.

61. Foucault (1994, xv–xxiv). The "Chinese Encyclopaedia" divides animals into: "(a) belonging to the Emperor, (b) embalmed, (c) tame, (d) sucking pigs, (e) sirens, (f) fabulous, (g) stray dogs, (h) included in the present classification, (i) frenzied, (j) innumerable, (k) drawn with a very fine camelhair brush, (l) et cetera, (m) having just broken the water pitcher, (n) that from a long way off look like flies."

62. On the late, postexilic interpolations, see the introduction to this chapter and note 9.

63. Baden (2012, chap. 4) shows that the Deuteronomist authors of chapters 1–32 knew and incorporated multiple elements from pre-priestly sources, in both narrative and legal segments of the text, and that no such explicit links exist to P. This absence of P traces in Deuteronomy do not necessarily mean ignorance, as Baden argues; it is still possible that this absence was a consistent strategy of the Deuteronomists in a situation of intellectual rivalry.

64. There is a solid agreement among Bible scholars that much of the chapters

dedicated to the covenant in the steppes of Moab belongs to this genre of loyalty oaths prevalent in the ancient Near East in the second and first millennium BCE. Mendenhall (1954) offered evidence of parallel passages in Hittite state treaties; Frankena (1965) and Weinfeld (1965) showed clear parallels in the Neo-Assyrian Succession of Esarhaddon (written in Akkadian); and since then, the debate on the political sources and contexts, on the language and forms of transmission, on literacy and translation that made transmission possible, and on the ways that these sources were revised, elaborated, and subverted has shifted grounds but never been settled. The many similarities that have been pointed out include the covenant's formal pattern and the expressions characteristic to it, the language of the preamble, justifications for subordination and the demand for the subject's absolute loyalty and love to the ruler, and the formulaic phrasing of many of the curses (e.g., Weinfeld 1972, chap. 2; Weeks 2004, chaps. 5–6; Berman 2008, 29–49; Quick 2018). For overviews, see Quick (2020), Knafl (2020); for some examples of the different positions, see Weinfeld (1992), Levinson (1998, 2001), Lewis (1996), Crouch (2014), Quick (2018), Russel (2020).

65. Cf. Quick (2018, chaps. 5–6). Quick also emphasizes the Deuteronomist elaborated play with the oral and graphic dimension of the curses.

66. Frequent shifts from second singular to second plural forms of the verb (and vice versa) occur throughout Deuteronomy. Cf. Lundbom (2013, 9, 21).

67. The metaphor "memory capsules" does not deflate the importance of memory, which many have noted, but rather tries to capture its rhetorical form and function. The expression is a paraphrase from Yerushalmi's (1996, 12) "history capsule."

68. Yerushalmi (1996, 13, 15).

69. As noted earlier, chapter 30 is commonly recognized as an exilic or postexilic text. Friedman (2003, 357) thinks that vv. 11–14 belong to an earlier layer, but this should not affect our reading, for the passage must have been inserted to complete and intensify the effect of staging the decision in v. 15.

70. A Deuteronomist redactor of the book of Joshua was careful to add that the ceremonies at Mounts Ebal and Gerizim were performed under Joshua's leadership, "just as Moses, the servant of Yahweh, had commanded the Israelites" (Josh. 8:30). Citing or paraphrasing the parallel passages in Deuteronomy, the narrator describes how Joshua followed Moses's entire choreography of the event, including the construction of the altar, the sacrificial ritual, the writing "on the stones a copy of the law of Moses, which he had written" (Josh. 8:32), and the reading of "all the words of the law, the blessing and the curse . . . before all the assembly of Israel, and the women, and the little ones, and the strangers who walked among them" (8:34–35).

71. Quick (2018, 169). Quick, who rightly adds ritual to the oral and written performance, ignores the significance of the multiple locations and temporal ambiguity, hence also the active temporalization of the ceremony at play. For a different account of the Deuteronomic emphasis on the present, see Levinson (1997, 151–52).

72. Quick (2018, 169–72). On the basis of allusions to other biblical texts and significant archeological evidence, Quick also argues that the multidimensional aspect of covenant sealing, that is, the integration of inscribing and oral performances with sacrificial acts, can be found in less official contemporary contexts in the region.

73. See esp. Deut. 1–3, 9:22–23, 10:6–7.

74. Note that in the historical parts of the text, memory capsules usually include consistent place names.

75. This may be a literary effect of the blending of several sources (Baden 2012, 136–37). On place names in Deuteronomy, see Johnstone (1997); on locations in Deut. 34, see Baden (2012, 148–49).

76. As shown in detail by Sonnet (1997).

77. On the foundational aspect of the Deuteronomist's covenant in the steppes of Moab overtaking the earlier covenant in Sinai/Horeb and its impact on the composition of the book as a whole, see Levinson (1997); Frankel (2011, 78–92). What both miss, however, is how the multiplication of the inaugural event transformed the relation to the law and its force; that is, the new code came with a structure that temporalized the distance separating the proclamation of the law from the application of its force.

78. "*Lakhem*." The second-person plural is used here and in the next two occurrences of "you."

79. The hiding of God's face is mostly associated in the Bible with a flare of divine violence (e.g., Deut. 31:17; Is. 54:8; Jer. 33:5; Ezek. 39:23–24, 29). But the epiphany of God's face could be just as destructive (e.g., Ezek. 14:8, 15:7). This understanding of God's hidden face can be considered a first step in the process of God's withdrawal from the realm of human affairs. The phrase and the idea it expresses, which appears in this more general connotation in Micah 3:4, has been noted, studied, and discussed widely (e.g., Balentine 1983; Friedman 1995; Römer 2013b, 154–57).

80. Beyond the purely conceptual level, this rivalry unfolded in the history of the Bible's reception. Its role in the history of the Bible's composition cannot be answered, but its possibility should be left open.

81. In the case of a relative (13:7), the sanctioned killing and destruction was charged first to that person's kin and then to the entire community (13:10–12). From this one may infer that every member of the community may be charged with killing idolaters.

82. In the short historical description that immediately follows (29:1–8), spanning the events from Egypt to that present moment of the steppes of Moab's covenant ("this day" and "this place"), the covenant at Horeb was not even mentioned.

83. Just as they left open the identity of the "fathers" who carried God's promise and to whom the one who entered the covenant related, as Hwang (2012) shows convincingly. It is worth noting that the undefined locations of the promises and the covenants with the fathers are not mentioned at all in the covenants' chapters.

84. The replacement of Sinai with Horeb is part of the larger Deuteronomist project to replace the covenant code in Exodus with the Deuteronomic code (Levinson 1997). Each version of the commandment at Horeb foregrounded a different aspect of the event: revelation and God's nonrepresentability (4:10–24), the Decalogue and the great fear (5:2–30), and the scene (and sin) of the molten calf (9:8–22).

85. This was also the place where Aaron met Moses upon his return to Egypt (Ex. 4:27), where Jethro met Moses after he led the Israelites out of Egypt (Ex. 18:5), and where the Israelites "stripped themselves of their jewelry," as God's rage flared after the sin of the golden calf (Ex. 33:6). All four occurrences are usually identified as Elohist. Neither these specific details nor the name "Mount of God" is mentioned in Deuteronomy; only the name Horeb remained. But two of the stories are incorporated (Deut. 1:9–18, 9:11–21), and a Deuteronomist text in 1 Kings 19 makes the link explicit. Elijah walked in the wilderness for "forty days and forty nights, to Horeb, the mount of God" (19:8), where a dramatic revelation took place, echoing Deut. 4:11–12: "Now there was a great wind, so strong that it was splitting mountains and breaking rocks in pieces before Yahweh, but Yahweh was not in the wind; and after the wind an earthquake, but Yahweh was not in the earthquake; and after the earthquake a fire, but Yahweh was not in the fire; and after the fire a sound of sheer silence. . . . Then there came a voice to him that said, 'What are you doing here, Elijah?'" (11–13).

86. Cf. Anderson (1998).

87. Most notably 28:62–68, 29:21–28, 30:1–11.

88. A new conception of human action is implied here, in which divine response to offenses is further suspended by the space open for the "turning back" or "return" (*veshavta*). Humans' responsibility for humans' fate grows accordingly, and God is further distanced, but all the more present in his absence, and a whole new *psycheagogy* is ready to emerge from the position he has just evacuated. But as Lambert (2016) has shown convincingly, the biblical turning is not yet an inner psychological experience but a practical return to a law-abiding practice. In later versions of this theopolitics, repentance and redemption replace the double return, of humans and God, and were developed into a central axis in the relations between Jews and Christians and their God, and the biblical language of return was read anachronistically to fit the new paradigm.

89. Henceforth, all references in this section are to the Book of Joshua unless otherwise indicated.

90. The book's last two chapters (23, 24) present Joshua's final words, but these words are different, including a very different account of the conquest of Canaan. For chapter 24, the mission was accomplished with all the people of Canaan expelled (11–13, 18); for 23, the mission was ongoing, and abstaining from any contact with those "nations that remain alongside you" was at the center of Joshua's warning and legacy (4–13).

91. The chapter has been attributed to every possible school of biblical authors,

and the controversy has been intense. Koopmans (1990) described the debate and claimed that the chapter relied on the J and E sources and affected D ones. Anbar (1999, 3–13) lists over fifty positions on the issue ranging from the beginning of modern Bible studies in the seventeenth century to the end of the twentieth century. According to Knohl (2008), regardless of the chapter's late date of editing, it contains a much earlier, ancient tradition, which he ascribes to migrants from Haran who had mixed with indigenous Samaritans. In his bold thesis on the history of the Deuteronomistic school and the composition of the Pentateuch, Römer (2007, 178–83) suggests that the chapter was written by a group of postexilic dissidents, a "Deuteronomist-priestly Hexateuch coalition" who insisted on including Joshua (and the conquest story) in the "book of the law of God" (*sefer torath haelohim*; Josh. 24:25; Neh. 8:18) and opposed the formation of the Pentateuch as "the book of Moses." The analysis that follows, which demonstrates a clear sense of rivalry and dissidence, could support Römer's thesis on independent textual grounds.

92. For a thorough comparison of the two, see Na'aman (2000, 153–55).

93. Weinfeld (1992, 152–56) contends that the contractual nature of the Sinai covenant, which parallels those of the ancient world, is not found in the Shechem covenant. Anbar (1999, chap. 5) believes that the text does not silence the revelation at Sinai simply because it predates the composition (or distribution?) of its account.

94. This has been often noted. See von Rad (2005, 122–23). The most radical opinion on this matter is that of the nineteenth-century Hebrew thinker and author Micha Josef Berdyczewski (1962), who views the Shechem covenant as the first contract between God and Israel. Knohl (2008, chap. 11) accepts his claim as is.

95. This led von Rad to view the first part of the chapter as one of the most ancient summaries of the people's history, and he ties it to a yearly ritual of covenant renewal that took place in Shechem (von Rad 1966, 36–39; 2005, 16–17, 122–23).

96. See, for example, McConville and Williams's (2010, 90) theologically oriented reading: "These are best taken as sharp rhetorical devices. . . . They might equally be taken as prophetic, since Joshua speaks here with the voice of a prophet."

97. As argued, for example, by Koopmans (1990, 346–47) and Anbar (1999, 118).

98. On ironic writing in the Bible and a reading attuned to it, see Sharp (2009).

99. Unless one includes the choice of risking collective death for not serving Yahweh. To die free and not serve a foreign rule was a real alternative for Judean rebels in their war against the Roman Empire (ideologically, at least, if not historically), but it seems quite anachronistic to invoke this option in any biblical context.

100. Anbar (1999, 118) underlines this point and notes that Joshua recognized the people's choice only after they declared their commitment to Yahweh.

101. Martel (2017).

102. Since the actual good preceded the potential bad in Joshua's account, "*shav*" probably means turning from the good to the bad.

103. Koopmans (1990, chaps 1–2, conclusion); Knohl (2008, chap. 11). The text was associated with a northern tradition because the event took place in Shechem, and no other covenant was mentioned.

104. E.g., Na'aman (2000); Römer (2007, 178–82); Popović (2009); Schmid (2018, 24–29).

105. The challenge is logical, conceptual, and ideological, not necessarily historical.

106. All subsequent references in this section are to Exodus 18 and will include the verse number only. Neither Sinai nor Horeb are mentioned, but, as mentioned earlier, "Mount of God" is mostly associated with Horeb.

107. In what follows, the two episodes, the meeting and the reform, will be read as one textual unit. Exodus 18 was first identified as an E source, but some scholars believe it consists of an earlier E source (describing the encounter between Jethro and Moses and Jethro's departure [vv. 1–11, 27]) and a later priestly or postexilic source (13–26) (describing Jethro's legal reform) (Schwartz 2009; Jeon 2017). Even if true, the elegant, simple stitching of the two parts (connected by two Hebrew words, *vay'hi mimaharat*, "and it happened on the next day" [13]) creates a coherent story with no overlap or contradiction. At the conceptual, theopolitical level, the second part, with which we are mostly concerned here, bears no trace of a priestly discourse. Some scholars associated it with accounts of other legal reforms in the Bible, the one administered by the Judean king Jehoshafat (2 Chron. 19:4–11; Knierim 1961) or the instructions that the Persian king Artaxerxes gave to Ezra to appoint judges who knew Mosaic law (Ezra 7:12–26; Russel 2015). In both cases, the text is read as coming from royal circles, an assumption that is not supported by my analysis.

108. I am diverging from Alter's translation here. See note 115.

109. See Chapter 2, first and third section.

110. Ex. 18:23 emphasizes God's role in a somewhat ambiguous way. Friedman (2003, 151) translates it literally: "If you will do this thing, *and* Yahweh will command you, then you will be able to stand, and also this entire people will come to its place in peace." The "and" connecting Jethro's advice and Yahweh's command makes sure that the Midianite priest would not be considered the last authority to sanction the reform or the efficient cause behind it; the acceptance of Jethro's advice is still pending on God—not on Moses (as v. 24 implies). That Jethro's reform had to be sealed by a divine decree is clear, but why did God need Jethro's advice?

111. In the putatively pre-priestly source (vv. 1–11, 27), Jethro, who calls God Yahweh, recognizes his supremacy and pays him his due in blessings and offerings (8–12).

112. A few cases of uncertainty regarding the application of the law followed by divine response and instruction are recorded in four P and H sources (Lev. 24:10–16; Num. 9:6–13, 15:32–36, 27:1–11). In three of these cases, Yahweh responded to an

explicit query; in the other (Num. 15:32–36) the query was implied. In the latter case, God intervened after a man who collected wood on the Sabbath was left under watch "because it has not been determined what should done to him" (Num. 15:34).

113. When Moses spoke of "all that Yahweh had done to Pharaoh and to the Egyptians for Israel's sake" (8), Jethro rejoiced only in "all the bounty that Yahweh had done for Israel" (9).

114. A fierce war against Midian is described twice in priestly writings (Num. 25:6–19, 31:1–16; cf. the third section of Chapter 3) and again in the story of Gideon in Judges (6–7). For these authors Jethro was not merely a stranger but a leader of an enemy nation. If the reform is indeed a postexilic addition, this could only add to the utopic flavor of this text.

115. The Hebrew *ḥayil* could mean strength or force (most clearly Zech. 4:6), skill, or success, but the expression *anshei ḥayil* is used numerous times in the Bible in military contexts. But from King James to Robert Alter, this connotation has been often lost in translation, as both translators and interpreters preferred to call the appointed chiefs "able," "capable," "leaders," or spiritually strong men.

116. The text is silent about the possibility of such transgressions, and also does not seem to foresee delays that could take place when cases are relegated to higher chiefs, all the way up to Moses and God.

117. E.g., Rashi's commentary on Ex. 18:13, 15. But some, like Nachmanides, disagreed. He argued that the section was in the right place and took place before the giving of the Torah, explaining it by arguing that Ex. 18:8–10 does not refer to the covenant at Sinai but rather to the liberation from Egypt and the journey through the desert. Propp (1998, 627–28) accepts this position in his commentary to Exodus.

118. Rashi was bothered by the way Moses took credit for the reform. His solution was to read "saying" (*l'emor*, that is to say) in Ex. 18:9 like this: "What is the meaning of saying? Moses said to them, 'Not by my own accord do I speak to you [and tell you that I cannot carry you alone] but by the command of the Holy One, blessed is He.'"

119. My own translation, which follows the understanding of "*y'du'im l'shivtei-khem* by most medieval commentators. Modern translators often render *y'du'im* (from the root y.d.a' [ידע], to know) as "knowledgeable" or "experienced," following the Septuagint translation: συνετούς (intelligent). But this reading separates *y'du'im* from *l'shivteikhem* (literally, "to your tribes"). Together the two words could easily mean "known within (or to) their tribes."

120. Walzer (2012, 193), who also follows the medieval commentators in reading Deut. 1:13.

121. Yitro m'yootar. The Hebrew name is inscribed like a conjugation of the root y.t.r. The root could be conjugated to mean "more," "add," "surplus," or "superfluous."

122. This echoes the parallel verse in Exodus and develops the idea it expresses (Ex. 18:16).

123. This account of Jethro's departure stands in sharp contrast to the first pre-

priestly (Jehovist?) narrative episode in the Book of Numbers, where "Hobab son of Reuel, the Midianite, Moses' father-in-law," is invited to join the Israelite in their journey "to the place of which Yahweh said to us" (Num. 10:29–32; for the incongruity of the names, see Alter 2019, 1:511n29). Hobab refuses Moses's first plea ("I shall not go, but to my land and to my birthplace I shall go") and leaves unanswered the second ("pray, do not leave us . . . you will serve us as eyes . . . we shall be good to you"). The stories from Exodus and Numbers clearly come from different traditions; it is the way they are kept apart by the redactors that is significant. The abrupt ending of the passage in Numbers and the fact that it finds no echo in the Exodus story may betray a sense of discomfort concerning Jethro's abrupt departure in Ex. 18:27. A midrashic interpretation of this verse is fully aware of the need for an explanation for Jethro's departure, which is also an excuse for the way Moses let him go: "'And he went away to his land': to convert the members of his family" (Mekhilta de-Rabbi Ishmael, Jethro, Amalek 2; quoted by Rashi in his commentary on Ex. 18:27).

124. Rosen-Zvi (2019, 113–14) counts no more than five instances in the Tannaitic Mishna where mechanisms of law enforcement were mentioned.

AFTERWORD: THE PENTATEUCHAL STATE, AND OURS

1. In various degrees: The most pronounced personification belongs to the pre-priestly formation and the least pronounced to the priestly formation.

2. As we saw throughout, the need for recognition was not simply an autonomous psychological drive; both the demand for recognition and the failure to provide it worked in the service of ruling.

3. Some readers might find the analytical gaze presented here as foreign to the texts they have come to know and cherish. But is its foreignness greater than that introduced by the philologist's razor and scissors? And can one separate the way one is at home within a discipline, or a mode of reading and thinking, and the foreignness of the text one reads? A work of translation is always at stake, great care should be taken not to introduce foreign elements into the interpreted texts without looking for relatively safe bridges that carry one from the ancient text to the present reading, and certain failures are unavoidable.

4. Foucault (2007, 247, 287).

5. Foucault (2007, 287). Emphases added.

6. Cf. Richardson (2014, 2017). Here is one example: At the beginning of the eighth century BCE, the Neo-Assyrian king Adad Nirari III proclaimed himself as "great king, mighty king, king of the universe, king of Assyria, son of Šamši-Adad, mighty king, king of the universe, king of Assyria, son of Shalmaneser, king of the four quarters" (Hallo et al. 2003, 2.114a; qtd. in Cataldo 2018, 28).

7. E.g., Skinner (1997). Cf. Ophir (2010, 67–69).

8. Outside the Pentateuchal corpus, the most radical thought in this respect was that such a unilateral abandonment could have its benefits: Believing that he had

abandoned them, the people of Jerusalem felt free to worship other gods (Ezek. 8:71–72).

9. New questions pose themselves at this point. Are there resonances of the three theocracies elsewhere in the biblical corpus and beyond? Are there any examples of crossing over among the divine rule of law, the rule of the holy, and the rule of disaster among the late prophets or in postbiblical literature? Do these formations have traces in halakhic or aggadic midrash of late antiquity or in medieval Kabbalistic writings? These questions call for a new research project. Prima facie, such traces and resonances may be far and between. After all, halakhic discourse kept God outside the realm of the rule of law, whose reproduction and proliferation were controlled by all-too-human authorities, while the kabbalists used parables, myths, mystery, and magic to imagine God's separate realm. In both cases, God was no longer a partner to earthly, human politics. But traces of alternative traditions, anecdotal and rudimentary as they might be, are certainly scattered in this vast corpus and are worthy of further investigation.

10. Ex. 15:10; Num. 23:21; Deut. 33:5. Cf. Knohl (2018); Brettlet (2020).

11. Cf. the brief reference to these moments in the first section of Chapter 2.

12. Accepting Mahmood Mamdani's (2020) claim that "the history of the prevailing state system begins in 1492, with the Reconquista, whereby the Castilian monarchy took over regions of Iberia that had been for centuries under Moorish rule" (5).

13. Certain genealogies are definitely welcome. E.g., a genealogy of the sanctity of secular political institutions; of the law-abiding, ever-guilty, ever-threatened subject; of a secularized politics of disaster. I tried to offer a sketch for the latter in Ophir (2013).

14. Auerbach (1984, 12).

15. Auerbach (1984, 50–56).

16. For the claim sketched here, see Ophir (2007).

17. Can the pagan state function without keeping itself apart from each and all other institutions? Can its fabricated transcendence be entirely eliminated without undermining its capacity to govern? In giving up its authority to limit associations and to command killing and being killed in its name and for its sake, how will it protect, enable, and regulate other vital institutions or curtail those that compete with it or threaten to undermine it and harm its citizens? And how to imagine the relations among multiple pagan states that cross one another's territories and share parts of one another's populations? Can a pagan state exist at all without becoming the new global order, replacing the global order of nation-states? In other words, does the idea of a pagan state find the limits of its toleration, fluidity, and flexibility when it encounters the monotheist nation-state?

WORKS CITED

Abolafia, Jacob. 2014. "Spinoza, Josephism, and the Critique of the Hebrew Republic." *History of Political Thought* 35(2): 295–316.

Agamben, Giorgio. 1998. *Homo Sacer: Sovereign Power and Bare Life*. Stanford, CA: Stanford University Press.

———. 1999. *Potentiality: Collected Essays in Philosophy*. Stanford, CA: Stanford University Press.

———. 2005. *State of Exception*. Trans. Kevin Attell. Chicago: University of Chicago Press.

———. 2009. "What Is an Apparatus?" In *What Is an Apparatus? and Other Essays*. Stanford, CA: Stanford University Press.

———. 2015. *The Use of Bodies*. Stanford, CA: Stanford University Press.

Albertz, Rainer. 2003. *Israel in Exile: The History and Literature of the Sixth Century BCE*. Atlanta: Society of Biblical Literature.

———. 2005. "Why a Reform Like Josiah's Must Have Happened." In *Good Kings and Bad Kings*, ed. L. L. Grabbe, 27–46. London: T&T Clark.

———. 2011. "The Late Exilic Book of Exodus (Exodus 1–34*)." In *The Pentateuch: International Perspectives on Current Research*, ed. T. B. Dozeman, K. Schmid, and B. J. Schwartz, 243–56. Tübingen: Mohr Siebeck.

Alter, Robert. 2019. *The Hebrew Bible: A Translation with Commentary*. Vols. 1–3. New York: Norton.

Althusser, Louis. 2014. *On the Reproduction of Capitalism: Ideology and Ideological State Apparatuses*. London: Verso.

Anbar, Moshe. 1999. *Joshua and the Shechem Covenant* [Hebrew]. Jerusalem: Bialik Institute.

Anderson, Gary. 1987. *Sacrifices and Offerings in Ancient Israel: Studies in Their Social and Political Importance*. Atlanta: Scholars.

Anderson, Jeff S. 1998. "The Social Function of Curses in the Hebrew Bible." *Zeitschrift für die alttestamentliche Wissenschaft* 110:223–27.

Arendt, Hannah. 1998 [1958]. *The Human Condition*. Chicago: University of Chicago Press.

Assmann, Jan. 1990. "Guilt and Remembrance: On the Theologization of History in the Ancient Near East." *History and Memory* 2(1): 5–33.

———. 1997. *Moses the Egyptian: The Memory of Egypt in Western Monotheism.* Cambridge, MA: Harvard University Press.

———. 2000. *Herrschaft und Heil: Politische Theologie in Altägypten, Israel und Europa.* München: Fischer Verlag.

———. 2001. *The Search for God in Ancient Egypt.* Trans. David Lorton. Ithaca, NY: Cornell University Press.

———. 2002. *The Mind of Egypt.* New York: Metropolitan.

———. 2008. *Of God and Gods: Egypt, Israel, and the Rise of Monotheism.* Madison: University of Wisconsin Press.

———. 2010. *The Price of Monotheism.* Stanford, CA: Stanford University Press.

———. 2014a. *From Akhenaten to Moses: Ancient Egypt and Religious Change.* Cairo: American University in Cairo Press.

———. 2014b. "Autour de l'Exode: monothéisme, différence et violence." *Revue de l'Histoire des Religions* 231(1): 5–26.

———. 2018. *The Invention of Religion: Faith and Covenant in the Book of Exodus.* Princeton, NJ: Princeton University Press.

Attridge, Harold W. 1976. *The Interpretation of Biblical History in the Antiquitates Judaicae of Flavius Josephus.* Harvard Dissertations in Religion. Cambridge, MA: Scholars Press for Harvard Theological Review.

Auerbach, Eric. 1984. "*Figura.*" In *Scenes from the Drama of European Literature.* Minneapolis: University of Minnesota Press

Azoulay, Ariella Aïsha. 2019. *Potential History: Unlearning Imperialism.* London: Verso.

Azoulay, Ariella, and Adi Ophir. 2012. *The One-State Condition: Occupation and Democracy in Israel/Palestine.* Stanford, CA: Stanford University Press.

Baden, Joel S. 2009. *J. E. and the Redaction of the Pentateuch.* FAT 68. Tübingen: Mohr Siebeck.

———. 2012. *The Composition of the Pentateuch: Renewing the Documentary Hypothesis.* New Haven, CT: Yale University Press.

———. Undated. "What Was the Sin of the Golden Calf?" TheTorah.com. https://www.thetorah.com/article/what-was-the-sin-of-the-golden-calf.

Badiou, Alain. 1988. *L'être et l'événement.* Paris: Seuil.

Bal, Mieke. 1998. *Death and Dissymmetry: The Politics of Coherence in the Book of Judges.* Chicago: University of Chicago Press.

Balentine, Samuel E. 1983. *The Hidden God: The Hiding of the Face of God in the Old Testament.* Oxford: Oxford University Press.

Balibar, Étienne. 2002. "Three Conceptions of Politics." In *Politics and the Other Scene,* trans. Christine Jones, James Swenson, and Chris Turner. London: Verso.

———. 2014. "Hannah Arendt, the Right to Have Rights, and Civic Disobedience." In *Equaliberty*, trans. James Ingram. Durham, NC: Duke University Press.

———. 2016. *Violence and Civility: On the Limits of Political Philosophy*. New York: Columbia University Press.

———. 2017. *Citizen Subject: Foundations for Philosophical Anthropology*. New York: Fordham University Press.

Barclay, John M. G. 2007. *Josephus Flavius, Against Apion: Translation and Commentary*. Leiden: Brill.

Barr, James, and A. R. S. Kennedy. 1963. "Sacrifice and Offering." In *Dictionary of the Bible*, ed. James Hastings, 868–76. New York: Scribner's.

Barthes, Roland. 1989. "The Reality Effect." In *The Rustle of Language*, trans. R. Howard, 141–48. Berkeley: University of California Press.

Bates, Matthew W. 2015. *The Birth of the Trinity: Jesus, God, and Spirit in New Testament and Early Christian Interpretations of the Old Testament*. Oxford: Oxford University Press.

Bell, Catherine. 1997. *Rituals: Perspectives and Dimensions*. Oxford: Oxford University Press.

Benjamin, Walter. 1996. "Critique of Violence." In *Selected Writings*, vol. 1: *1913–1926*, trans. Edmund Jephcott, ed. Michael W. Jennings, 236–52. Cambridge, MA: Harvard University Press.

———. 1999. "The Destructive Character." In *Selected Writings*, vol. 2: *1927–1934*, trans. Edmund Jephcott, ed. Michael W. Jennings, 541–42. Cambridge, MA: Harvard University Press.

Berdyczewski, Micha Josef. 1962. *Sinai and Gerizim: Bible and Research* [Hebrew]. Holon: Moreshet Mikhah Yosef.

Berman, Joshua A. 2008. *Created Equal: How the Bible Broke with Ancient Political Thought*. Oxford: Oxford University Press.

Bernat, David A., and Jonathan Klawans, eds. 2007. *Religion and Violence: The Biblical Heritage*. Sheffield: Sheffield Phoenix.

Bibb, Bryan. 2009. *Ritual Words and Narrative Worlds in the Book of Leviticus*. LHBOTS 480. London: T&T Clark.

Bin Nun, Igal. 2016. *A Short History of Yahweh* [Hebrew]. Tel Aviv: Resling.

Bloom, Harold, and David Rosenberg. 1990. *The Book of J*. New York: Grove Wiedenfield.

Blum, Erhard. 2009. "Issues and Problems in the Contemporary Debate regarding the Priestly Writings." In *The Strata of the Priestly Writings: Contemporary Debate and Future Directions*, AThANT 9, ed. S. Sechtman and J. S. Baden. Zürich: Theologischer Verlag Zürich.

Blumenthal, David R. 1993. *Facing the Abusing God: A Theology of Protest*. Louisville: Westminster/John Knox.

Botterweck, Gerhard Johannes, Helmer Ringgren, and Heinz-Zosef Fabri, eds. 1974. *Theological Dictionary of the Old Testament*. Trans. Douglas W. Scott. Grand Rapids, MI: Eerdmans.

Brett, Mark G. 2000. *Genesis: Procreation and the Politics of Identity*. London: Routledge.

———. 2009. *Decolonizing God: The Bible in the Tides of Empire*. Sheffield: Sheffield Phoenix.

———. 2019. *The Locations of God: Political Theology in the Hebrew Bible*. Oxford: Oxford University Press.

Brettler, Marc Zvi. 2020. "God's Coronation on Rosh Hashanah." December 29. TheTorah.com. https://www.thetorah.com/author/marc-zvi-brettler.

Brown, Francis, S. R. Driver, and Charles A. Briggs. 1977. *Enhanced Brown-Driver-Briggs Hebrew and English Lexicon*. Oxford: Clarendon.

Brown, Wendy. 2017. *Undoing the Demos: Neoliberalism's Stealth Revolution*. New York: Zone.

Brueggemann, Walter. 2001. *Deuteronomy: Abingdon Old Testament Commentaries*. Nashville, TN: Abingdon.

Buber, Martin. 1948. *Israel and the World: Essays in a Time of Crisis*. New York: Schocken.

———. 1949. *The Prophetic Faith*. New York: Macmillan.

———. 1967. *Kingship of God*. Trans. Richard Sheimann. New York: Harper and Row.

Butler, Judith. 1997. *The Psychic Life of Power: Theories of Subjection*. Stanford, CA: Stanford University Press.

Cancik, Hubert. 1987. "Theokratie und Priesterherrschaft: Die mosaische Verfassung be Flavius Josephus, c. Apionem 2, 157–198." In *Theokratie*, ed. Jacob Taubes, 65–77. Munich: Fink/F Schöningh.

Carasik, Michael. 2000. "The Limits of Omniscience." *Journal of Biblical Literature* 119 (2): 221–32.

Carmichael, Calum. 2012. *The Book of Numbers: A Critique of Genesis*. New Haven, CT: Yale University Press.

Carr, David M. 2011. "Scribal Processes of Coordination/Harmonization and the Formation of the First Hexateuch(s)." In *The Pentateuch: International Perspectives on Current Research*, ed. T. B. Dozeman, K. Schmid, and B. J. Schwartz. Tübingen: Mohr Siebeck.

Cataldo, Jeremiah W. 2009. *A Theocratic Yehud? Issues of Government in Yehud*. Library of Hebrew Bible/Old Testament Studies. London: T&T Clark.

———. 2012. *Breaking Monotheism: Yehud and the Material Formation of Monotheistic Identity*. Sydney: Bloomsbury.

———. 2018. *A Social-Political History of Monotheism: From Judah to the Byzantines*. London: Routledge.

Chamayou, Gregoire. 2015. *A Theory of the Drone*. New York: The New Press.

Chen, Yi Samuel. 2013. *The Primeval Flood Catastrophe and Early Development in Mesopotamian Traditions*. Oxford Oriental Monographs. Oxford: Oxford University Press.

Collins, John J. 2017. *The Invention of Judaism: Torah and Jewish Identity from Deuteronomy to Paul*. Oakland: California University Press.

———. 2018. *Introduction to the Hebrew Bible and Deutero-Canonical Books*. 3rd ed. Minneapolis, MN: Fortress.

Considine, Patrick. 1969. "The Theme of Divine Wrath in Ancient East Mediterranean Literature." In *Studi Micenei*, ed. Egeo-Anatolici, no. 8, 85–159. Rome: Edizione dell'Ateneo & Bizzari.

Creach, Jerome F. D. 2013. *Violence in Scripture: Interpretation: Resources for the Use of Scripture in the Church*. Louisville, KY: John Knox.

———. 2016. "Violence in the Old Testament." In *The Oxford Research Encyclopedia of Religion*. Oxford: Oxford University Press. http://oxfordre.com/religion.

Cross, Frank. 1961. "The Priestly Tabernacle." In *Biblical Archaeologist Reader I*, ed. G. E. Wright and D. N. Freedman, 201–28. Garden City, NY: Doubleday/Anchor.

Crouch, Carly L. 2014. *Israel and the Assyrians: Deuteronomy, the Succession Treaty of Esarhaddon, and the Nature of Subversion*. ANEM 8. Atlanta: Society of Biblical Literature.

Dalley, Stephanie. 2008. *Myths from Mesopotamia: Creation, the Flood, Gilgamesh, and Others: A New Translation*. Oxford: Oxford University Press.

Dawkins, Richard. 2006. *The God Delusion*. London: Bantam.

Derrida, Jacques. 1981. "Plato's Pharmacy." In *Dissemination*, trans. B. Johnson, 61–171. Chicago: University of Chicago Press.

———. 1992. "Force of Law: The 'Mystical Foundation of Authority.'" In *Deconstruction and the Possibility of Justice*, ed. D. Cornell, M. Rosenfeld, and D. G. Carlson, 3–67. New York: Routledge.

Douglas, Mary. 1984. *Purity and Danger: An Analysis of Concepts of Pollution and Taboo*. London: Routledge.

———. 1993. *In the Wilderness: The Doctrine of Defilement in the Book of Numbers*. Supplement Series 158. Sheffield: JSOT.

———. 1999. *Leviticus as Literature*. Oxford: Oxford University Press.

Dozeman, Thomas B. 2008. "The Midianites in the Formation of the Book of Numbers." In *The Books of Leviticus and Numbers*, ed. Thomas Römer. Leuven: Peeters.

Elazar, Daniel J. 1997. *Kingship and Consent: The Jewish Political Tradition and its Contemporary Uses*. New Brunswick, NJ: Transaction.

Fertheim, Terence E. 2004. "God and Violence in the Old Testament." *Word and World* 24(1): 18–28.

Flatto, David C. 2011. "Theocracy and the Rule of Law: A Novel Josephan Doctrine and Its Modern Misconceptions." *Dine Israel* 28:5–30.

———. 2014. "*In God's Shadow: Politics in the Hebrew Bible* by Michael Walzer." *AJR Review* 38(1): 161–67.

———. 2020. *The Crown and the Courts: Separation of Powers in the Early Jewish Imagination*. Cambridge, MA: Harvard University Press.

Fleming, Daniel. 2002. "Emar: On the Road from Harran to Hebron." In *Mesopotamia and the Bible: Comparative Explorations*, ed. M. W. Chavalas and K. Lawson Younger Jr., 222–50. Grand Rapids, MI: Baker Academic.

Flusser, David. 1993. "The Dead of Masada in the Eyes of their Contemporaries" [Hebrew]. In *Jews and Judaism in the Second Temple, Mishna and Talmud Period: Studies in Honor of Shmuel Safrai*, ed. I. Gafni, A. Oppenheimer, and M. Stern, 116–46. Jerusalem: Yad Izhak Ben-Zvi.

Foucault, Michel. 1979. *Discipline and Punish: The Birth of the Prison*. Trans. Alan Sheridan. New York: Random House.

———. 1980. "The Confession of the Flesh." In *Power/Knowledge: Selected Interviews and Other Writings 1972–1977*, ed. C. Gordon, trans. C. Gordon et al., 194–228. New York: Pantheon.

———. 1994 [1970]. *The Order of Things: An Archaeology of the Human Sciences*. New York: Vintage.

———. 2007. *Security, Territory, Population: Lectures at the Collége de France 1977–1978*. Ed. M. Senellart. Trans. G. Burchell. New York: Palgrave Macmillan.

Frankel, David. 2002. *The Murmuring Stories of the Priestly School: A Retrieval of Ancient Sacerdotal Lore*. Boston: Brill.

———. 2011. *The Land of Canaan and the Destiny of Israel: Theologies of Territory in the Hebrew Bible*. Winona Lake, IN: Eisenbrauns.

Frankena, Rintje. 1965. *The Vassal-Treaties of Esarhaddon and the Dating of Deuteronomy*. Leiden: Brill.

Frazer, Elizabeth, and Kimberly Hutchings. 2020. *Violence and Political Theory*. Cambridge: Polity.

Fretheim, Terrence E. 2004. "God and Violence in the Old Testament." *Word and World* 24:18–28.

Fretheim, Terence E., and Karlfried Froehlich. 1998. *The Bible as Word of God: In a Postmodern Age*. Minneapolis, MN: Fortress.

Freud, Sigmund. 1939. *Moses and Monotheism*. New York: Alfred A. Knopf.

Frevel, Christian. 2013. "The Book of Numbers—Formation, Composition, and Interpretation of a Late Part of the Torah: Some Introductory Remarks." In *Torah and the Book of Numbers*, ed. C. Frevel, T. Pola, and A. Schart, FAT II/62, 1–37. Tübingen: Mohr Siebeck.

Friedman, Richard Elliott. 1981a. "From Egypt to Egypt: Dtr^1 and Dtr^2." In *Traditions in Transformation: Turning Points in Biblical Faith*, ed. J. D. Levenson and B. Halpern, 167–92. Winona Lake, IN: Eisenbrauns.

——. 1981b. *The Exile and Biblical Narrative: The Formation of the Deuteronomistic and Priestly Works*. Harvard Semitic Monographs 22. Chico, CA: Scholars.

——. 1995. *The Disappearance of God: A Divine Mystery*. Boston: Little, Brown.

——. 2003. *The Bible, with Sources Revealed: A New View into the Five Books of Moses*. New York: Harper Collins.

Frymer-Kensky, Tikva. 1988. "The Theology of the Disaster: The Question of Historical Justice" [Hebrew]. *Beer-Sheva: Studies by the Department of Bible and Ancient Near East* 3:121–24.

Gager, John. 1972. *Moses in Greco-Roman Paganism*. Nashville, TN: Abingdon.

Galtung, Johan. 1969. "Violence, Peace, and Peace Research." *Journal of Peace Research* 6(3): 167–91.

Garr, W. Randall. 2003. *In His Own Image and Likeness: Humanity, Divinity, and Monotheism*. Leiden: Brill.

Gaventa, Beverly Roberts. 2016. "Thinking from Christ to Israel: Romans 9–11 in Apocalyptic Context." In *Paul and the Apocalyptic Imagination*, ed. B. C. Blackwell, J. K. Goodrich, and J. Mason. Minneapolis, MN: Fortress.

Gertz, Jan Christian. 2012. "The Formation of the Primeval History." In *The Books of Genesis: Composition, Reception, and Interpretation*, ed. C. A. Evans, J. N. Lohr, and D. L. Petersen, 107–35. Leiden: Brill.

——. 2014. "The Miracle at the Sea: Remarks on the Recent Discussion about Origin and Composition of the Exodus Narrative." In *The Book of Exodus: Composition, Reception, and Interpretation*, Supplements to Vetus Testamentum 164, 91–120. Leiden: Brill.

Girard, René. 1977. *Violence and the Sacred*. Baltimore, MD: Johns Hopkins University Press.

——. 1986. *The Scapegoat*. Baltimore, MD: Johns Hopkins University Press.

Goodman, Martin. 2019. *Josephus's The Jewish War: A Biography*. Princeton, NJ: Princeton University Press.

Goodman, Nelson. 1978. *Ways of Worldmaking*. Indianapolis, IN: Hackett.

Graeber, David, and Marshall Sahlins. 2017. *On Kings*. Chicago: HAU Books.

Greenberg, Moshe. 1995. "Hebrew segulla: Akkadian sikiltu." In *Studies in the Bible and Jewish Thought*, 273–78. Philadelphia: The Jewish Publication Society.

——. 2007. "Herem." In *Encyclopaedia Judaica*, 2nd ed., 9:10–13. Detroit: Thomson Gale.

Greenstein, Edward. 1982. "An Equivocal Reading of the Sale of Joseph." In *Literary Interpretations of Biblical Narratives*, ed. Kenneth R. R. Gros Louis et al., 2:114–25. Nashville, TN: Abingdon.

——. 1984. "Biblical Law." In *Back to the Sources: Reading the Classical Jewish Texts*, ed. Barry W. Holtz, 83–103. New York: Simon and Schuster.

——. 1989. *Essays on Biblical Methods and Translation*. Atlanta: Scholars.

———. 2001. "Presenting Genesis 1, Constructively and Deconstructively." *Prooftext* 21(1): 1–22.

Gros, Frédéric. 2006. *États de violence: essai sur la fin de la guerre*. Paris: Gallimard.

Grougouris, Stathis. 2019. *The Perils of One*. New York: Columbia University Press.

Halbertal, Moshe, and Stephen Holmes. 2017. *The Beginning of Politics: Power in the Biblical Book of Samuel*. Princeton, NJ: Princeton University Press.

Hallo, W. W., K. L. Younger, and William Hallo, eds. 2003. *The Context of Scripture*. Vol. 2: *Monumental Inscriptions from the Biblical World*. Leiden: Brill.

Hammill, Graham. 2012. *The Mosaic Constitution: Political Theology and Imagination from Machiavelli to Milton*. Chicago: University of Chicago Press.

Hansen, Thomas Bloom, and Finn Stepputat. 2005. *Sovereign Bodies: Citizens, Migrants, and States in the Postcolonial World*. Princeton, NJ: Princeton University Press.

Haran, Menahem. 1978. *Temples and Temple-Service in Ancient Israel: An Inquiry into the Character of Cult Phenomena and the Historical Setting of the Priestly School*. Oxford: Clarendon.

Hazony, Yoram. 2012. *The Philosophy of the Hebrew Scripture*. Cambridge: Cambridge University Press.

Hendel, Ronald. 1991. "When God Acts Immorally: Is the Bible a Good Book?" *Bible Review* 7(3): 35–50.

———. 2009. "Mary Douglas and Anthropological Modernism." In *Perspectives on Hebrew Scriptures V, Journal of Hebrew Scriptures, Vol. 8*, ed. Ehud Ben Zvi. Gorgias.

Hendel, Roland, and Jan Joosten. 2018. *How Old Is the Hebrew Bible? A Linguistic, Textual, and Historical Study*. New Haven, CT: Yale University Press.

Hobbes, Thomas. 1991. *Hobbes: Leviathan*. Ed. Richard Tuck. Cambridge: Cambridge University Press.

Hundley, Michael B. 2011. *Keeping Heaven on Earth: Safeguarding the Divine Presence in the Priestly Tabernacle*. Tübingen: Mohr Siebeck.

———. 2015. "Tabernacle or Tent of Meeting? The Dual Nature of the Sacred Tent in the Priestly Writings." In *Current Issues in Priestly and Related Literature: The Legacy of Jacob Milgrom and Beyond*, ed. R. E. Gane and A. Taggar-Cohen, 3–18. Atlanta: SBL.

Hwang, Jerry. 2012. *The Rhetoric of Remembrance: An Investigation of the "Fathers" in Deuteronomy*. Winona Lake, IN: Eisenbrauns.

Jenkins, Philips. 2011. *Laying Down the Sword: Why We Can't Ignore the Bible's Violent Verses*. New York: HarperOne.

Jenson, Philip Peter. 1992. *Graded Holiness: A Key to the Priestly Conception of the World*. Journal for the Study of the Old Testament Supplement Series 106. Sheffield: Sheffield Academic Press; JSOT Press.

Jeon, Jaeyoung. 2017. "The Visit of Jethro (Exodus 18): Its Composition and Levitical Reworking." *Journal of Biblical Literature* 136(2): 289–306.

Johnstone, William. 1997. "From the Mountain to Kadesh with Special Reference to Exodus 32:30–34:29." In *Deuteronomy and Deuteronomic Literature*, ed. M. Vervenne and J. Lust. Leuven: Leuven University Press, Uitgeverij Peeters.

Kaufmann, Yehezkel. 1960. *The Religion of Israel, from Its Beginning to the Babylonian Exile* [Hebrew]. Chicago: University of Chicago Press.

Klawans, Jonathan. 2000. *Impurity and Sin in Ancient Judaism*. New York: Oxford University Press.

———. 2006. *Purity, Sacrifice, and the Temple: Symbolism and Supersessionism in the Study of Ancient Judaism*. Oxford: Oxford University Press.

Knafl, Anne K. 2020. "Deuteronomy: Code or Covenant?" In *The Oxford Handbook of Deuteronomy*, ed. Don C. Benjamin. New York: Oxford University Press.

Knierim, Rolf. 1961. "Exodus 18 und die Neuordnung der mosaischen Gerichtsbarkeit." *Zeitschrift für die alttestamentliche Wissenschaft* 73(2): 146–71.

Knohl, Israel. 1994. *The Sanctuary of Silence: The Priestly Torah and the Holiness School*. Minneapolis, MN: Fortress.

———. 2008. *From Where Did We Come?* [Hebrew]. Tel Aviv: Kinneret, Zmora, Dvir.

———. 2011. "Who Edited the Pentateuch?" In *The Pentateuch: International Perspectives on Current Research*, ed. T. B. Dozeman, K. Schmid, and B. J. Schwartz, 359–68. Tübingen: Mohr Siebeck.

———. 2018. "Rosh Hashanah: Why the Torah Suppresses God's Kingship." TheTorah .com, September 6. https://www.thetorah.com/article/rosh-hashanah-why-the -torah-suppresses-gods-kingship.

Kohler, Ludwig, and Walter Baumgartner. 1999. *The Hebrew-Aramaic Lexicon of the Old Testament*. Leiden: Brill.

Koopmans, William T. 1990. *Joshua 24 as Poetic Narrative*. Sheffield: JSOT.

Kratz, Reinhard G., and Herman Spieckermann, eds. 2008. *Wrath and Divine Mercy in the World of Antiquity*, Forschungen zum Alten Testament Series 2[33]. Tübingen: Mohr Siebeck.

Kugel, James. 2003. *The God of Old*. New York: Free Press.

Kunin, Seth D. 2004. *We Think What We Eat: New Structuralist Analysis of the Israelites' Food Rules and Other Cultural and Textual Practices*. London: T&T Clark International.

La Boétie, Estienne de. 2002 [1576]. *Discours de la servitude volontaire*. Paris: Vrin.

Lambert, David A. 2016. *How Repentance Became Biblical: Judaism, Christianity, and the Interpretation of Scripture*. Oxford: Oxford University Press.

Leibowitz, Nehama. 1970. *Studies in Genesis, Following our Early and Later Commentators* [Hebrew]. Jerusalem: World Zionist Organization.

Levene, Mark. 2005. *Genocide in the Age of the Nation State*. 2 vols. London: I. B. Tauris.

———. 2013. *The Crisis of Genocide*. 2 vols. Oxford: Oxford University Press.

Levenson, Jon D. 1994. *Creation and the Persistence of Evil: The Jewish Drama of Divine Omnipotence*. Princeton, NJ: Princeton University Press.

Levine, Baruch. 1968. "On the Presence of God in Biblical Religion." In *Religions in Antiquity: Essays in Memory of Erwin Ramdell Goodenough*, ed. J. Neusner, 71–87. Leiden: Brill.

———. 1974. *In the Presence of the Lord: A Study of Cult and Some Cultic Terms in Ancient Israel*. Leiden: Brill.

———. 1993. *Numbers 1–20: A New Translation with Introduction and Commentary*. The Anchor Bible. New York: Doubleday.

———. 2000. *Numbers 21–36: A New Translation with Introduction and Commentary*. The Anchor Bible. New York: Doubleday.

Levinson, Bernard M. 1997. *Deuteronomy and the Hermeneutics of Legal Innovation*. Oxford: Oxford University Press.

———. 2001. "Textual Criticism, Assyriology, and the History of the Interpretation of Deuteronomy 13:7a as a Test Case in Method." *Journal of Biblical Literature* 120:211–43.

———. 2006. "The First Constitution: Rethinking the Origins of Rule of Law and Separation of Powers in Light of Deuteronomy." *Cardozo Law Review* 27(4): 1853–88.

Lewis, Theodore J. 1996. "The Identity and Function of El/Baal Berith." *Journal of Biblical Literature* 115(3): 401–23.

Lieu, Judith, M. 2015. *Marcion and the Making of a Heretic: God and Scripture in the Second Century*. New York: Cambridge University Press.

Lorberbaum, Yair. 2009. "The Rainbow in the Cloud: An Anger-Management Device." *Journal of Religion* 89(4): 498–540.

———. 2010. "And the Rainbow Was Seen in His Time" [Hebrew]. *Reshit* 2:5–22. http://reshit.hartman.org.il/Article_View_Heb.asp?Article_Id=29.

———. 2011. *Disempowered King: Monarchy in Classical Jewish Literature*. London: Continuum.

Lundbom, Jack R. 2013. *Deuteronomy: A Commentary*. Grand Rapids, MI: Eerdmans.

Luther, Martin. 1955–1986. *Luther's Works*. St. Louis, MO: Concordia.

Luzzatto, Smhuelle David (Shadal). 1861. *Shadal on Exodus* [Hebrew]. https://www.sefaria.org/person/Shadal.

Machiavelli, Niccolo. 2019: *The Prince*. Trans. Russell Price. Cambridge: Cambridge University Press.

Mamdani, Mahmood. 2020. *Neither Settler nor Native: The Making and Unmaking of Permanent Minorities*. Cambridge, MA: Harvard University Press.

Martel, James R. 2017. *The Misinterpellated Subject*. Durham, NC: Duke University Press.

Mason, Steve. 2000. *Judean Antiquities 1–4*. Ed. and trans. Louis H. Feldman. Leiden: Brill.

McConville, J. G., and Stephen N. Williams. 2010. *Joshua*. Grand Rapids, MI: Eerdmans.

Mendenhall, George E. 1954. "Covenant Forms in Israelite Tradition." *Biblical Archaeology* 17:49–76.

Mettinger, Tryggve N. D. 1982. *The Dethronement of Sabaoth: Studies in the Shem and Kabod Theologies*. Coniectanea Biblica, Old Testament Series 18. Lund: CWK Glreetup.

Milgrom, Jacob. 1991. *Leviticus 1–16: A New Translation with an Introduction and Commentary*. New York: Doubleday.

———. 2000. *Leviticus 17–22: A New Translation with an Introduction and Commentary*. New York: Doubleday.

———. 2004. *Leviticus, a Book of Rituals and Ethics: A Continental Commentary*. Minneapolis, MN: Fortress.

Muffs, Yochanan. 1992. *Love and Joy: Law, Language, and Religion in Ancient Israel*. New York: Jewish Theological Seminary of America.

———. 2005. *The Personhood of God: Biblical Theology, Human Faith, and the Divine Image*. Woodstock, NY: Jewish Lights.

Müller, H. P. 1985. "Das Motive für die sinflut: Die hermeneuticsche Function des Mythos und seiner Analyze." *Zeitschrift für die alttestamentliche Wissenschaft* 97:295–316.

Na'aman, Nadav. 2000. "The Law of the Altar in Deuteronomy and the Cultic Site Near Shechem." In *Rethinking the Foundations: Historiography in the Ancient World and in the Bible. Essays in Honour of John Van Seters*, ed. S. L. McKenzie and T. Römer in collaboration with H. H. Schmid Berlin, 141–62. New York: Walter de Gruyter.

Nancy, Jean-Luc. 2000. *Being Singular Plural*. Stanford, CA: Stanford University Press.

Nelson, Eric. 2010. *The Hebrew Republic: Jewish Sources and the Transformation of European Political Thought*. Cambridge, MA: Harvard University Press.

Nicholson, Ernest. 2014. *Deuteronomy and the Judaean Diaspora*. Oxford: Oxford University Press.

Niditch, Susan. 1993. *War in the Hebrew Bible: A Study in the Ethics of Violence*. Oxford: Oxford University Press.

Nietzsche, Friedrich. 1989. *On the Genealogy of Morals*. Trans. W. Kaufmann and R. J. Hollingdale. New York: Vintage.

Nihan, Christophe. 2007. *From Priestly Torah to Pentateuch: A Study in the Composition of the Book of Leviticus*. FAT II/25. Tübingen: Mohr Siebeck.

Nixon, Rob. 2011. *Slow Violence and the Environmentalism of the Poor*. Cambridge, MA: Harvard University Press.

Noort, Ed. 1998. "The Stories of the Great Flood: Notes on Gen 6:5–9:17 in Its Context of the Ancient Near East." In *Interpretations of the Flood*, F. G. Martinez and G. P. Luttikhuizen, 1–38. Leiden: Brill.

Oeming, Manferd, and Peter Sláma. 2015. *A King Like All the Nations? Kingdoms of Israel and Judah in the Bible and History*. Zürich: Lit.

Olyan, Saul M. 2000. *Rites and Rank: Hierarchy in Biblical Representations of Cult*. Princeton, NJ: Princeton University Press.

———. 2011. "An Eternal Covenant with Circumcision as Its Sign: How Useful a Criterion for Dating and Source Analysis?" In *The Pentateuch: International Perspectives on Current Research*, ed. T. B. Dozeman, K. Schmid, and B. J. Schwartz, 347–58. Tübingen: Mohr Siebeck.

Ophir, Adi. 1991. *Plato's Invisible Cities: Discourse and Power in Plato's Republic*. London: Routledge.

———. 1994. "From Pharaoh to Saddam Hussein: Deconstruction of the Passover Haggadah." In *The Other in Jewish Thought and History*, ed. L. Silberstein and R. Cohn, 139–57. New York: New York University Press.

———. 2004. "Understanding the Political in the Work of Hannah Arendt." In *Hannah Arendt: Half a Century of Polemics*, ed. I. Zertal and M. Zuckermann, 171–98. Tel Aviv: Hakkibutz Hameuchad.

———. 2005. *The Order of Evils: Toward an Ontology of Morals*. New York: Zone.

———. 2007. "The Two States Solution: Catastrophe and Providence." *Theoretical Inquiries in Law* 8, no. 1: 117–60.

———. 2010a. "State" [Hebrew]. *Mafte'akh: Lexical Review for Political Theory* 1:35–60. https://mafteakh.org/wp-content/uploads/2019/09/1-2010-03.pdf.

———. 2010b. "Metaphysics and Violence: Derrida Reads Levinas." *Iyyun* 59, October.

———. 2015. "On Linking Machinery and Show." *Differences* 26(3): 54–80.

———. 2020. "The Political." In *Thinking with Balibar: A Lexicon of Conceptual Practice*, ed. A. L. Stoler, S. Gourgouris, and J. Lezra, 158–82. New York: Fordham University Press.

———. 2022. *On Ruling Power* [Hebrew]. Tel Aviv: Resling.

Ophir, Adi, and Ishay Rosen Zvi. 2018. *Goy: Israel's Multiple Others and the Birth of the Gentile*. Oxford: Oxford University Press.

———. 2020. "Separatism, Judeophobia, and the Birth of the Goy: On Chickens and Eggs" [Hebrew]. *Zion* 85 (1–4): 151–76.

Otto, Eckart. 2013. "The History of the Legal-Religious Hermeneutics of the Book of Deuteronomy from the Assyrian to the Hellenistic Period." In *Law and Religion in the Eastern Mediterranean*, ed. A. C. Hagedorn and R. G. Kratz, 211–50. Oxford: Oxford University Press.

Otto, Rudolf. 1929. *The Idea of the Holy: An Inquiry into the Non-Rational Factor in the Idea of the Divine and Its Relation to the Rational*. Trans. John W. Harvey. 5th imp., rev. with additions. London: Oxford University Press.

Pakkala, Juha. 2009. "The Date of the Oldest Edition of Deuteronomy." *Zeitschrift für die alttestamentliche Wissenschaft* 121:388–401.

Pearce, Sarah J. K. 1995a. "Flavius Josephus as Interpreter of Biblical Law: The Council of Seven and the Levitical Servants in Jewish Antiquities 4.214." *Heythrop Journal* 36(4): 477–92.

———. 1995b. "Josephus as Interpreter of Biblical Law: The Representation of the High Court of Deut. 17:8–12 according to Jewish Antiquities 4.218." *Journal of Jewish Studies* 46 (1–2): 30–42.

———. 2006. "Speaking with the Voice of God: The High Court According to Greek Deuteronomy 17:8–13." In *Biblical Traditions in Transmission: Essays in Honour of Michael A. Knibb*, ed. C. Hempel and J. M. Lieu, 237–48. Leiden: Brill.

Philo. 1937. "On the Special Laws." In *Philo*, vol. 7, ed. F. H. Colson, Loeb Classical Library 320. Cambridge, MA: Harvard University Press.

Pitkänen, Pekka. 2018. "Reconstructing the Social Contexts of the Priestly and Deuteronomic Materials in a Non-Wellhausenian Setting." In *Beihefte zur Zeitschrift für Altorientalische und Biblische Rechtsgeschichte*, ed. E. Otto and D. Markl, 323–38. Wiesbaden: Harrassowitz.

Pollard, Richard Matthew. 2018. "Flavius Josephus: The Most Influential Classical Historian of the Early Middle Ages." In *Writing the Early Medieval West*, ed. E. Screen and C. West, 15–32. Cambridge: Cambridge University Press.

Popović, Mladen. 2009. "Conquest of the Land, Loss of the Land: Where Does Joshua 24 Belong?" In *The Land of Israel in Bible, History, and Theology: Studies in Honour of Ed Noort*, ed. J. van Ruiten and J. Cornelis de Vos, 87–98. Leiden: Brill.

Pritchard, James B., ed. 1969. *Ancient Near Eastern Texts Relating to the Old Testament with Supplement*. Princeton, NJ: Princeton University Press.

Propp, William H. 1998. *Exodus 1–18: A New Translation with Introduction and Commentary*. The Anchor Bible 2. Garden City, NY: Doubleday.

———. 2006. *Exodus 19–40: A New Translation with Introduction and Commentary*. New York: Anchor Bible.

Quick, Laura. 2018. *Deuteronomy 28 and the Aramaic Curse Tradition*. Oxford: Oxford University Press.

———. 2020. "Blessings and Curses in Deuteronomy." In *Oxford Handbook of Deuteronomy*, ed. Don C. Benjamin. Oxford: Oxford University Press.

Rajak, Tessa. 1998. "The 'Against Apion' and the Continuities in Josephus's Political Thought." In *Understanding Josephus: Seven Perspectives*, ed. S. Mason, 222–46. Sheffield: Sheffield Academic Press.

———. 2000. "Josephus." In *The Cambridge History of Greek and Roman Political Thought*, ed. C. Rowe and M. Schofield, 585–96. New York: Cambridge University Press.

Rancière, Jacques. 1999. *Dis-agreement: Politics and Philosophy*. Trans. J. Rose. Minneapolis: University of Minnesota Press.

Rees, Anthony. 2015. *[Re]Reading Again: A Mosaic Reading of Numbers 25*. London: Bloomsbury T&T Clark.

Richardson, Neil. 2014. *Who on Earth Is God? Making Sense of God in the Bible*. London: Bloomsbury.

Rofé, Alexander. 1985. "The Covenant in the Land of Moab (Dtn 28:69–30:20)" [Hebrew]. *Beer-Sheva* 2.

Romanoff, Paul. 1932. "A Third Version of the Flood Narrative." *Journal of Biblical Literature* 50 (4): 304–7.

Römer, Thomas C. 1990a. *Israels Väter: Untersuchungen zur Väterthematik im Deuteronomium und in der deuteronomistischen Tradition.* OBO 99. Freiburg: Universitätsverlag/Göttingen: Van-denhoeck & Ruprecht.

———. 1992. "Le Deutéronome at la quête des origins." In *Le Pentateuque: débats et recherches*, ed. P. Haudebert, 56–98. Paris: Cref.

———. 2000a. "Deuteronomy in Search of Origins." In *Reconsidering Israel and Judah: Recent Studies on the Deuteronomistic History*, ed. G. N. Knoppers and J. G. McConville, SBTS 8, 112–38. Winona Lake, IN: Eisenbrauns.

———. 2000b. "Du Temple au Livre: L'idéologie de la centralisation dans l'historiographie deutéronomiste." In *Rethinking the Foundations: Historiography in the Ancient World and in the Bible. Essays in Honour of John Van Seters*, ed. S. L. McKenzie and T. Römer in collaboration with H. H. Schmid Berlin, 207–26. New York: Walter de Gruyter.

———. 2007. *The So-Called Deuteronomistic History: A Sociological, Historical, and Literary Introduction.* London: T&T Clark.

———. 2008. "Les livres du Lévitique et des nombres dans le débat actuel sur le Pentateuque." In *The Books of Leviticus and Numbers*, ed. Thomas Römer, 3–34. Leuven: Peeters.

———. 2013a. *Dark God: Cruelty, Sex, and Violence in the Old Testament.* Mahwah, NJ: Paulist.

———. 2013b. "Conflicting Models of Identity and the Publication of the Torah in the Persian Period." In *Between Cooperation and Hostility: Multiple Identities in Judaism and the Interaction with Foreign Powers*, ed. R. Albertz and J. Wöhrle, JAJ Sup. 11, 31–51. Göttingen: Vandenhoeck & Ruprecht.

———. 2014. *The Invention of God.* Trans. Raymond Geuss. Cambridge, MA: Harvard University Press.

Roncace, Mark. 2012. *Raw Revelation: The Bible They Never Tell You About.* North Charleston, SC: CreateSpace.

Rosen-Zvi, Ishai. 2019. *Between Mishnah and Midrash: The Birth of Rabbinic Literature* [Hebrew]. Raanana, Israel: Open University.

Rosenblum, Jordan D. 2016. *The Jewish Dietary Laws in the Ancient World.* Cambridge: Cambridge University Press.

Russel, Stephen C. 2015. "The Structure of Legal Administration in the Moses Story." In *Israel's Exodus in Transdisciplinary Perspective: Text, Archaeology, Culture, and Geoscience*, ed. T. E. Levy, T. Schneider, and W. H. C. Propp, Quantitative Methods in the Humanities and Social Sciences, 317–30. Switzerland: Springer.

——. 2020. "Near Eastern Practice of Law in Deuteronomy." In *The Oxford Handbook of Deuteronomy*. Oxford: Oxford University Press.

Sacks, Jonathan. 2019. "Deuteronomy: Covenant Society." *Tradition* 51(3): 4–17.

Said, Edward W. 1986. "Michael Walzer's 'Exodus and Revolution': A Canaanite Reading." *Grand Street* 5(2): 86–106.

Sawyer, Michael, 2018. *An Africana Philosophy of Temporality: Homo Liminalis*. Cham, Switzerland: Palgrave Macmillan.

Schmid, Konrad. 2011. "Has European Scholarship Abandoned the Documentary Hypothesis? Some Reminders on Its History and Remarks on Its Current Status." In *The Pentateuch: International Perspectives on Current Research*, ed. T. B. Dozeman, K. Schmid, and B. J. Schwartz, 17–30. Tübingen: Mohr Siebeck.

——. 2018. "Overcoming the Sub-Deuteronomism and Sub-Chronicism of Historiography in Biblical Studies: The Case of the Samaritans." In *The Bible, Qumran, and the Samaritans*, ed. M. Kartveit and G. N. Knoppers, Studia Samaritana 10, 17–30. Berlin: De Gruyter.

Schmitt, Carl. 1976 [1932]. *The Concept of the Political*. Trans. George Schwab. New Brunswick, NJ: Rutgers University Press.

——. 1985 [1922]. *Political Theology: Four Chapters on the Concepts of Sovereignty*. Trans. George Schwab. Chicago: University of Chicago Press.

Scholem, Gershom. 1999. "On Jonah and the Concept of Justice." *Critical Inquiry* 25(2): 353–61.

Schorch, Stefan. 2011. "The Samaritan Version of Deuteronomy and the Origin of Deuteronomy." In *Samaria, Samarians, Samaritans: Studies on Bible, History, and Linguistics*, ed. Zsengellér, József, Studia Samaritana 6, 23–37. Berlin: De Gruyter.

Schubert, Joseph. 2018. *Dating Deuteronomy: The Wellhausen Fallacy*. Eugene, OR.: Wipf & Stock.

Schwager, Raymund. 1987 [1978]. *Must There Be Scapegoats? Violence and Redemption in the Bible*. Trans. Maria L. Assad. San Francisco: Harper & Row.

Schwartz, Baruch J. 1996. "The Priestly Account of the Theophany and Lawgiving at Sinai." In *Texts, Temples, and Traditions: A Tribute to Menahem Haran*, ed. M. V. Fox et al., 103–34. Winona Lake, IN: Eisenbrauns.

——. 1999. *The Holiness Legislation: Studies in the Priestly Code in the Pentateuch* [Hebrew]. Jerusalem: Magnes.

——. 2000. "Israel's Holiness: The Torah Traditions." In *Purity and Holiness: The Heritage of Leviticus*, ed. J. J. Schwartz and M. J. H. M. Poorthuis, 47–59. Leiden: Brill.

——. 2009. "The Visit of Jethro: A Case of Chronological Displacement? The Source-Critical Solution." In *Mishneh Todah: Studies in Deuteronomy and Its Cultural Environment in Honor of Jeffrey H. Tigay*, ed. N. S. Fox, D. A. Glatt-Gilad, and M. J. Williams, 29–48. Winona Lake, IN: Eisenbrauns.

——. 2011a. "Pentateuch: The Five Books and the Four Documents" [Hebrew]. *Bible Literature: Introductions and Studies* 1:161–226.

——. 2011b. "Does Recent Scholarship's Critique of the Documentary Hypothesis Constitute Rounds for Its Rejection?" In *The Pentateuch: International Perspectives on Current Research*, ed. T. B. Dozeman, K. Schmid, and B. J. Schwartz, 3–16. Tübingen: Mohr Siebeck.

Schwartz, Regina M. 1997. *The Curse of Cain: The Violent Legacy of Monotheism.* Chicago: The University of Chicago Press.

——. 1998. "Freud's God." In *Post-Secular Philosophy: Between Philosophy and Theology*, ed. Phillip Blond, 281–304. London, New York: Routledge.

Schwartz, Seth. 1990. *Josephus and Judaean Politics.* Leiden: Brill.

——. 2001. *Imperialism and Jewish Society: 200 B.C.E. to 640 C.E.* Princeton: Princeton University Press.

——. 2008. *Sacramental Poetics at the Dawn of Secularism: When God Left the World.* Stanford, CA: Stanford University Press.

Seibert, Eric A. 2016. "Recent Research on Divine Violence in the Old Testament (with Special Attention to Christian Theological Perspective." *Currents in Biblical Research* 15(1): 8–40.

Seth, Richardson. 2012. "Early Mesopotamia: The Presumptive State." *Past and Present* No. 215 (May 2012): 3–49.

——. 2017. "Before Thing Worked: A 'Low Power' Model of Ancient Mesopotamia." In *Ancient States and Infrastructural Power*, ed. Clifford Ando and Seth Richardson, 17–62. Philadelphia: University of Pennsylvania Press.

Sharp, Carolyn J. 2009. *Irony and Meaning in the Hebrew Bible.* Bloomington: Indiana University Press.

Sharpe, Christina. 2016. *In the Wake: On Blackness and Being.* Durham, NC: Duke University Press.

Skinner, Quentin. 1997. "The State." In *Contemporary Political Philosophy*, ed. R. E. Goodin and P. Pettit, 55–76. Oxford: Blackwell.

Sloterdijk, Peter. 2010. *Rage and Time: A Psychopolitical Investigation.* New York: Columbia University Press.

Sommer, Benjamin D. 2009. *The Bodies of God and the World of Ancient Israel.* Cambridge: Cambridge University Press.

——. 2015. *Revelation and Authority: Sinai in Jewish Scripture and Tradition.* New Haven, CT: Yale University Press.

Sonnet, Jean-Pierre. 1997. *The Book within the Book: Writing in Deuteronomy.* Leiden: Brill.

Spilsbury, Paul. 2016. "Josephus and the Bible." In *A Companion to Josephus*, ed. H. Howell Chapman and Z. Rodgers, 123–34. Malden: Wiley Blackwell.

Spinoza, Baruch. 2001. *Theological-Political Treatise.* Trans. Samuel Shirley. Indianapolis, IN: Hackett.

Stackert, Jeffery. 2007, *Rewriting the Torah*. Tübingen: Mohr Sicbcck.

Steinmetz-Jenkins, Daniel. 2011. "Jan Assmann and the Theologization of the Political." *Political Theology* 12(4): 511–30.

Stern, Philip D. 2020. *The Biblical Herem: A Window in Israel's Religious Experience*. Brown Judaic Studies 211. Atlanta: Scholars.

Stone, Ken. 2018. *Reading the Hebrew Bible with Animal Studies*. Stanford, CA: Stanford University Press.

Strauss, Leo. 1997. "On the Interpretation of Genesis." In *Jewish Philosophy and the Crisis of Modernity: Essays and Lectures in Modern Jewish Thought*, ed. K. H. Green, 359–76. New York: SUNY Press.

Taubes, Jacob. 2004. *The Political Theology of Paul*. Trans. Dana Hollander. Stanford, CA: Stanford University Press.

Tausig, Michael. 2003. *Law in a Lawless Land: Diary of a Limpieza in Colombia*. Chicago: University of Chicago Press.

Townsend, John T. 1989. *Midrash Tanhuma*. Translated into English with Indexes and Brief Notes. (S. Buber Recension.) Ed. and trans. R. Francis Nataf. Hoboken, NJ: Natav.

Turtillian. 1991. *Contre Marcion. Vol. 1. Introduction* [French]. Ed. and trans. René Braun. Paris: Éditions du Cref.

Van Seter, John. 1992. "The Story of the Flood." In *Prologue to History: The Yahwist as Historian in Genesis*, 160–73. Louisville, KY: Westminster/John Knox.

von Rad, Gerhard. 1966. *The Problem of the Hexateuch and Other Essays*. Trans. E. W. Trueman Dicken. Edinburgh: Oliver & Boyd.

———. 2005 [1965]. *Old Testament Theology*. Vols. 1–2. Trans. D. M. G. Stalker. Louisville, KY: Westminster/John Knox.

Walzer, Michael. 1985. *Exodus and Revolution*. New York: Basic Books.

———. 2012. *In God's Shadow: Politics in the Hebrew Bible*. New Haven, CT: Yale University Press.

Walzer, Michael, Menachem Lorberbaum, and Noam J. Zohar, eds. 2000–2003. *The Jewish Political Tradition*. 3 vols. New Haven, CT: Yale University Press.

Walzer, Michael, and Edward Said. 1986. "An Exchange: 'Exodus and Revolution.'" *Grand Street* 5(4): 246–59.

Weber, Max. 1952 [1921]. *Ancient Judaism*. Trans. Hans H. Gerth and Don Martundale. Glencoe, IL: Free Press.

Weeks, Noel. 2004. *Admonition and Curse: The Ancient Near Eastern Treaty/Covenant Form as a Problem in Inter-Cultural Relationships*. London: T&T Clark.

Weiler, Gershom, 1988. *Jewish Theocracy*. Leiden: Brill.

Weinfeld, Moshe. 1988. "Historical Facts behind Israelite Settlement Patterns." *Vetus Testamentum* 38(3): 324–32.

———. 1992. *Deuteronomy and the Deuteronomic School*. Winona Lake, IN: Eisenbrauns.

———. 2004. *The Place of the Law in the Religion of Ancient Israel*. Vetus Testamentum, Supplements. Leiden: Brill.

Wells, Steve. 2010. *Drunk with Blood: God's Killings in the Bible*. Moscow, ID: SAB
Books.

Williams, James G., ed. 1996. *The Girard Reader*. New York: Crossroad.

Wolin, Richard. 2013. "Biblical Blame Shift." *Chronicle of Higher Education*, April 15.
https://www.chronicle.com/article/biblical-blame-shift/.

Yerushalmi, Yosef Hayim. 1996. *Zakhor: Jewish and Jewish Memory*. Seattle: University of Washington Press.

Zevit, Ziony. 2007. "The Search for Violence in Israelite Culture and in the Bible." In
Religion and Violence: The Biblical Heritage, ed. D. A. Bernat and J. Klawans,
16–37. Sheffield: Sheffield Phoenix.

Zwei, Tamar. 2007. *Parenthesis in Biblical Hebrew*. Studies in Biblical Languages and
Linguistics 50. Leiden: Brill.

INDEX

Adi M. Ophir is a Visiting Professor at the Cogut Institute for the Humanities at Brown University and Professor Emeritus at Tel Aviv University. Among his works are *Goy: Israel's Multiple Others and the Birth of the Gentile*, co-authored with Ishay Rosen-Zvi (Oxford University Press, 2018); *Divine Violence: Two Essays on God and Disaster* (The Van Leer Institute, 2013); *The One-State Condition*, co-authored with Ariella Azoulay (Stanford University Press, 2012); and *The Order of Evils: Toward an Ontology of Morals* (Zone, 2005).

CPSIA information can be obtained
at www.ICGtesting.com
Printed in the USA
JSHW012045031222
34283JS00001BA/2